Scholarship on Fire

Scholarship on Fire

A History of the "Chair of Fire" and Southern Baptist
Evangelism in Theological Education

BEAU K. BREWER

Foreword by Matt Queen

WIPF & STOCK · Eugene, Oregon

SCHOLARSHIP ON FIRE
A History of the "Chair of Fire" and Southern Baptist Evangelism
in Theological Education

Wipf & Stock
An Imprint of Wipf and Stock Publishers
199 W. 8th Ave., Suite 3
Eugene, OR 97401

www.wipfandstock.com

PAPERBACK ISBN: 978-1-6667-1057-1
HARDCOVER ISBN: 978-1-6667-1058-8
EBOOK ISBN: 978-1-6667-1059-5

| October 29, 2021

To Christa,
The greatest wife, partner in ministry and my best friend.
I love you, most.
And my treasured son, Jacob.
You are my blessing and heritage from the Lord.

Contents

FOREWORD

THE CREATIVE GENIUS OF Benajah Harvey (B. H.) Carroll introduced evangelism as a course of study at Southwestern Baptist Theological Seminary. He enlisted Lee Rutland (L. R.) Scarborough as the seminary's first occupant of its first endowed chair—the "Chair of Fire." As the "Chair of Fire," Scarborough became the world's first evangelism professor and introduced evangelism into the theological curriculum of Southern Baptist, as well as Evangelical, seminaries, divinity schools and colleges.

In *Scholarship on Fire: A History of the "Chair of Fire" and Southern Baptist Evangelism in Theological Education*, Beau Brewer investigates the history of Southwestern Baptist Theological Seminary's "Chair of Fire," and traces its contributions to the academic discipline of evangelism, specifically in the six Southern Baptist seminaries. Brewer extends well beyond the classic, historic narratives on the "Chair of Fire" by W. L. Muncy Jr. (*A History of Evangelism in the United States*, 1945), Robert A. Baker (*Tell the Generations Following: A History of Southwestern Baptist Theological Seminary 1908–1983*, 1983), and Charles S. Kelley Jr. (*How Did They Do It?: The Story of Southern Baptist Evangelism*, 1993). *Scholarship on Fire* joins an emerging academic interest on the "Chair of Fire" in the twenty-first century. This monograph expands upon the recent contributions to "Chair of Fire" research by Brandon Kiesling (*"An Investigation of Benajah Harvey Carroll's Contribution to Evangelism within the Southern Baptist Convention,"* 2017) and Daniel Dickard (*"A Man between the Times: A Critical Evaluation of Roy J. Fish and His Contributions to the Evangelistic Spirit of Southwestern Baptist Theological Seminary,"* 2017).

Brewer's singular focus on the chair's history and influence solidifies this volume as the current, authoritative treatise on the "Chair of Fire."

Matt Queen
Professor and L. R. Scarborough Chair of Evangelism ("Chair of Fire")
Associate Dean of the Roy J. Fish School of Evangelism and Missions
Southwestern Baptist Theological Seminary, Fort Worth, Texas

PREFACE

THE STORY OF B. H. CARROLL'S "Chair of Fire" is worth telling. The establishment of evangelism as an equal and integral part of curricula within theological education was a paradigm shift that proved to be the great assembly line for the training of men and women in preparation for the front lines of ministry within the Southern Baptist Convention. A celebrated evangelist, L. R. Scarborough, as the first occupant of the Chair and professor of evangelism, would generate lectures and assignments to enhance the theological education of all seminarians through required course work in evangelism. The curricula for said courses were carefully studied and eventually crafted into textbook publications and assignments designed to spread a working knowledge of personal, mass, and revival preaching and historical evangelism throughout the seminary students of Southwestern Baptist Theological Seminary and eventually into the Domestic Mission Board and pulpits of local Southern Baptist churches.

This historical study of B. H. Carroll, L. R. Scarborough, and the "Chair of Fire" and the subsequent occupants at Southwestern Baptist Theological Seminary is meaningful to one's Southern Baptist heritage. First, Carroll and Scarborough were Texas Baptist men who loved Jesus, believed the inerrancy of the Bible, and regularly practiced soul-winning among the sick and perishing. Scarborough, reared as a cowboy on the Texas frontier, became a well-educated gospel preacher, evangelist, and teacher because of his parents' sacrificial generosity. George and Martha Scarborough were active in his spiritual and formal education. His father, George, was a preacher-rancher on the West Texas frontier and planted many churches. His name is listed on many cornerstones of the Baptist churches in West Texas.

Few people have contributed more to Southern Baptists than L. R. Scarborough, who poured his life into educating and equipping young men and women to be soul-winners and calling Southern Baptist men and women to give their lives to the Gospel ministry. Carroll and Scarborough fought hard to make evangelism in theological education a standard discipline of study. God has used this "Chair of Fire" to impact Southern Baptist evangelism through theological education. Researching the "Chair of Fire" and its occupants provides an even greater context for the value of evangelism in theological education as well as encouragement to further strengthen the demand for evangelism within theological education.

This monograph goes further than the hallowed halls of Seminary Hill in Fort Worth. This is the first time significant evidence of the "spreading fires" of Southern Baptist evangelism in theological education to the other five seminaries has been provided, introducing the reader to the great evangelists whose names live on through endowed chairs of evangelism established in their honor and/or memory. Biographical sketches have been compiled of each of the professors of evangelism who have occupied these academic chairs and reinforced the frontlines of the North American and international mission fields through theological education at their respective places of service. These men have fanned the flames of Southern Baptist evangelism.

The history book you hold in your hand also contains several oral histories from men and women who have shaped the Southern Baptist Convention through their personal involvement in the formation and contributions to evangelism in theological education. The appendices are mostly oral histories transcribed by the author from dedicated hours of interviewing and collecting these treasured stories told by the men and women who have specifically given their lives to serving Jesus Christ and these academic chairs of evangelism by furthering the Lord's kingdom through Southern Baptist evangelism. The "Chair of Fire" and the subsequent chairs of evangelism are not just endowed academic ideology, but the result of a God-sized dream to fulfill the Great Commission through Southern Baptists.

ACKNOWLEDGMENTS

As with any work of this magnitude, many people deserve thanks. Matt Queen consistently stoked my interests in L. R. Scarborough and evangelism throughout my theological studies at Southwestern Baptist Theological Seminary, in particular this history of the "Chair of Fire," and the untold histories of the advancement of evangelism in theological education. And certainly, evangelism and church historian Roy J. Fish had his own influence upon me as he taught me to truly love and seek after the lost.

My friends Brandon Kiesling and Daniel Dickard both explored different aspects of the "Chair of Fire," and paved the way for this 112-year-old history on the chair's formation and contributions to evangelism in theological education. Each of us share a profound love for our Seminary and its founder as well as the spirit of evangelism produced by the tenets of the first endowed chair of evangelism, the "Chair of Fire." Kiesling's dissertation was most instrumental for his research of B. H. Carroll's blueprint for the creation of departments of evangelism at both the Domestic Mission Board and the newly established Southwestern Baptist Theological Seminary first located in Waco, Texas, and later moved to Fort Worth, Texas. My research begins where Kiesling's research ends, by exploring the content and instruction of coursework taught at the first department of evangelism at a theological seminary and develops the spreading flame of evangelism in theological education throughout the other five Southern Baptist seminaries.

And then there is my PhD band of brothers: David Norman, Anthony Svajda, Daniel Dickard, and Sean Wegener, nicknamed "Baa-Baa

Black Sheep" after a Breakfast Café we frequented while teaching together in Penang, Malaysia, where we sat and encouraged one another and discussed theological issues. I have received a great deal of encouragement and prayers from these men of God.

Countless others can be mentioned and thanked, but no one alive deserves more credit for this book than my bride, Christa, and son, Jacob. They are my greatest cheerleaders. I am blessed to have a family that sacrifices time and prays specifically for me, and I thank God for the many prayers said by my son asking Jesus to help me finish this book. I want to thank my wonderful mother Jeanne, and J. O., and my in-laws Dana and Larry for their incredible support, prayers, and love. My father, Keith, and grandparents, Fred and Josephine Nayfa, have already returned home to be with the Lord Jesus, but I know that they would be delighted with the success of this work. I look forward to being reunited again one day in heaven. "Worthy is the Lamb that was slain to receive power and riches and wisdom and might and honor and glory and blessing" (Rev 5:12 NASB).

1

INTRODUCTION

W. L. MUNCY JR. was a professor of Evangelism and Missions at Central
Baptist Theological Seminary whose work, *A History of Evangelism in the
United States*, provides a survey of the great movements in evangelism in
the United States of America from 1607–1944.[1] Within this work, Muncy
documents the work of Southern Baptist leaders involved in the creation
of the first Department of Evangelism and the first chair of evangelism
at Southwestern Baptist Theological Seminary. Specifically, Muncy notes
that Benajah Harvey (B. H.) Carroll, the architect behind this new paradigm in theological education, hand-selected Lee Rutland (L. R.) Scarborough to be inaugurated as the first occupant of this "Chair of Fire."[2]
This initiative was a first in theological education. Soon, other seminaries
would follow the example and leadership of Southwestern Baptist Theological Seminary. Muncy writes, "Since the establishment of 'the Chair
of Fire' in the Southwestern Baptist Theological Seminary in 1908, other
seminaries throughout the country have added courses in evangelism to
their curricula."[3] This book seeks to test Muncy's assertation, and therefore investigates the extent of B. H. Carroll and L. R. Scarborough's roles
in the formation and work of the "Chair of Fire" in Southern Baptist
evangelism training, while tracing the chair's continuing contributions to

---

1. Muncy, *History of Evangelism*, vii.
2. Muncy, *History of Evangelism*, 159.
3. Muncy, *History of Evangelism*, 163.

evangelism as an academic discipline within Southern Baptist seminaries from 1908 to 2020.

First, the book surveys the formation of the "Chair of Fire," specifically eight of its nine occupants and their contributions to evangelism.[4] Second, it examines the "Chair of Fire's" contributions to evangelism in theological education and fulfilling the program of evangelism within the Southern Baptist Convention (SBC). Third, the work investigates the spreading fire of evangelism to the other five Southern Baptist seminaries as they included and implemented evangelism within their regular curricula. Finally, this book gives an assessment of the "Chair of Fire's" overall effectiveness upon Southern Baptist evangelism through theological education.

The L. R. Scarborough Chair of Evangelism has been acknowledged in writings, however, very few works mention the historical establishment or contributions of the "Chair of Fire" to the advancement of evangelism in theological education within the six Southern Baptist seminaries.[5] This book's purpose is to investigate the history of Southwestern Baptist Theological Seminary's "Chair of Fire" and assess its contributions to the academic discipline of evangelism. The study argues that Southwestern Baptist Theological Seminary's "Chair of Fire" contributed to the inclusion and subsequent implementation of evangelism as an academic discipline within the Southern Baptist seminaries from 1908 to 2020.

In the early months of 1906 and acting quickly on the triumph of the decisions made during the 1905 Southern Baptist Convention (SBC) to establish a Department of Evangelism at the Board for Domestic Missions (later renamed the Home Mission Board [HMB], then renamed again the North American Mission Board [NAMB]), B. H. Carroll sent a letter to L. R. Scarborough, the young evangelistic pastor of the First Baptist Church of Abilene, Texas.[6] In the letter, Carroll extended an invitation for Scarborough to join the faculty of a new seminary to be created in Texas for the purposes of ministry training and educating men and women for gospel ministry. "Dr. Carroll was a pioneer and a prophet in his thinking

---

4. Matt Queen, the ninth occupant of the "Chair of Fire," is currently serving on faculty in this role. His tenure will not be examined.

5. See Benefield, "Scarborough and His Preaching," 52–61; Carson, "Architect of a New Denominationalism," 44–47; Hawley, "Concept of Evangelism," 39–40, 44–48; Lefever, "Life and Work," 158–59, 170–71; Queen, "A Theological Assessment," 110–24; Kiesling, "Investigation," 164–92; and Dickard, "Man between the Times," 29–72.

6. Carroll, Initial Letter of Invitation to Scarborough, 1906.

of the place of evangelism in theological education."[7] Carroll, a Southern Baptist statesman, recognized the Convention's need for trained and educated evangelists to fulfill its founding purposes "for the propagation of the gospel," set forth by the initial constitution and by-laws of the SBC in 1845.[8] This initial letter began an in-depth exchange of written discourse between the two men and outlined a vision for a new seminary and a newly-created position in theological education: a "chair of evangelism." In 1908, after two years of correspondence, Scarborough agreed to join the faculty of the newly-created Southwestern Baptist Theological Seminary, then in Waco, Texas, as professor of evangelism and field secretary. Scarborough would lead the charge, at Carroll's instruction, to negotiate, secure funding and land, and relocate the fledgling new seminary to its permanent location in Fort Worth, Texas.

From the inception of the seminary, Carroll had a dream to build an evangelistic seminary that would educate men and women in soul-winning and prepare them for the frontlines of gospel ministry. Carroll called for the messengers of the Baptist General Convention of Texas in 1906 to raise capital funds for the creation of a "chair of evangelism," stating, "There is great need to create and endow a chair of evangelism."[9] However, on July 2, 1908, in a follow-up address to the Baptist General Convention of Texas titled "A Chair of Fire," Carroll states, "The Southwestern Baptist Theological Seminary takes the lead in establishing a chair of evangelism. For years the mind of its president has been impressed that 'the Evangelist' is a distinct New Testament office."[10] The "Chair of Fire," by its design and purpose, was intended to expand Southern Baptist evangelism throughout the Convention through the training of men and women in evangelism. The occupant of this chair would carry out Carroll's fiery goal of gospel expansion through evangelism in theological education in the seminary.

Lee Rutland Scarborough was born July 4, 1870, and died April 10, 1945. During his lifetime, he served in several capacities within the SBC: pastor, teacher, evangelist, denominational leader, and author. His most significant roles were those of inaugural occupant of the chair of Evangelism, nicknamed by Carroll "The Chair of Fire," and his position

---

7. Muncy, *History of Evangelism*, 159.

8. SBC, *Proceedings* (1845), 3.

9. Carroll, "Report on Baylor," 45.

10. Carroll, "Chair of Fire" address.

as second president of Southwestern Baptist Theological Seminary. Scarborough authored seventeen books primarily dealing with topics of evangelism, evangelistic sermons, Southwestern Baptist Theological Seminary history, and his various travels, all of which contributed to the widespread inclusion and subsequent implementation of evangelism in the academic setting.[11] As a result of his efforts, Southwestern Baptist Theological Seminary offered the world's first complete evangelism curriculum in a higher education institution through its Department of Evangelism, which was headed by the occupant of the "Chair of Fire."[12]

The study of the "Chair of Fire" and its contributions to theological education within the Southern Baptist seminaries provides relevance and context to the field of evangelism, discipleship, church growth, and SBC history. Charles Kelley, former president of the New Orleans Baptist Theological Seminary, published a book on the lessons learned from the history of evangelism in the SBC titled *Fuel the Fire: Lessons from the History of Southern Baptist Evangelism*, which traces the trends and history of evangelism methods from 1845 to 2019 within the SBC. According to Kelley's research, "The effectiveness of Southern Baptists in evangelism cannot be separated from their decision to include specific instruction in evangelism in the theological training of ministerial students."[13] Kelley's research provides evidence that a strong correlation exists between evangelism in theological education and the effectiveness of evangelism throughout the SBC.

This study is a detailed analysis of Southwestern Baptist Theological Seminary's contributions to Southern Baptist evangelistic training and utilization. Existing dissertations examine L. R. Scarborough's concept of evangelism and his leadership within the SBC, but none have made a thorough study of the academic chair he occupied first and the work of the chair's subsequent occupants to the academic discipline of evangelism inside the Southern Baptist seminaries. Likewise, the L. R. Scarborough

---

11. Scarborough books in publication order: *Recruits for World Conquests* (1914); *With Christ after the Lost* (1919); *Marvels of Divine Leadership* (1920); *Endued to Win* (1922); *Gospel Messages* (1922); *Prepare to Meet God* (1922); *The Tears of Jesus* (1922); *Holy Places and Precious Promises* (1924); *Christ's Militant Kingdom* (1924); *A Search for Souls* (1925); *How Jesus Won Men* (1926); *Ten Spiritual Ships* (1927); *Products of Pentecost* (1934); *My Conception of the Gospel Ministry* (1935); *A Blaze of Evangelism across the Equator* (1937); *A Modern School of the Prophets* (1939); *After the Resurrection—What?* (1942).

12. Muncy, *History of Evangelism*, 159.

13. Kelley, *Fuel the Fire*, 73.

Chair of Evangelism, the "Chair of Fire," has not been investigated. B. H. Carroll had a vision for Southern Baptist evangelism that would be fulfilled through the work of the newly-formed Texas seminary and its pioneering chair of evangelism, known as the "Chair of Fire." This study will expand the field of research on the "Chair of Fire," demonstrating its significance and explaining the correlation between SBC evangelism and theological education.

To date, the primary documentation concerning the L. R. Scarborough Chair of Evangelism, the "Chair of Fire," are directly from B. H. Carroll. The founding principles of the chair draw attention to his life, work, and theology. Carroll's most commonly used address, titled "The Chair of Fire," has been published in many sources and is the primary piece disclosing the inner workings and fundamental functions of this newly-created academic chair in print.

> Now the object of the seminary Chair of Evangelism is manifold: First of all, there is need to teach connectedly the New Testament doctrines of the office as distinguished from the apostolic and pastoral office. This teaching will bring out clearly the importance and perpetuity of the office and illustrate vividly by showing what particular New Testament evangelists accomplished . . . In the second place, it will be the office of this chair to expound the biblical idea of the kingdom as set forth by Old Testament prophets, by our Lord, and by his apostles, showing clearly not one kingdom visible and another invisible, not one in time and another in eternity . . . Third, it will fall to this chair to expound the principles and methods of gospel propagandism, and to compare these with the principles and methods of propagandism adopted by heathen religions, illustrating by historical facts, and not only heathen religions, but ancient Judaism in its way of proselyting as shown in biblical, interbiblical, and post-apostolic history.[14]

L. R. Scarborough wrote the first history of Southwestern Baptist Theological Seminary in 1939, *A Modern School of the Prophets*, which records the birth of the Southwestern Baptist Theological Seminary and the historic "Chair of Fire."[15] Scarborough compiled letters, clippings, newspapers, periodicals, and personal memories of Carroll's role in the establishment of the seminary and the inauguration of the chair of

---

14. Carroll, "Chair of Fire" address.

15. Scarborough, *Modern School*.

Evangelism, called by Carroll the "Chair of Fire," and the creation of the first Department of Evangelism within theological education in the world. This book is a primary resource to the establishment of Southwestern Baptist Theological Seminary and the first Department of Evangelism in a higher education institute.

Muncy contributed to the documentation of the "Chair of Fire's" significance in theological education. Muncy's work, *A History of Evangelism in the United States,* published in 1945, concisely recognized the pioneering thought of the "Chair of Fire" and recorded Carroll's ideas, dreams, and deep desire for a chair of evangelism at his seminary.[16] He noted, "This training offered to all students would lead to a better understanding of the function of the evangelist and a better co-ordination of his work with the work of other church and kingdom leaders."[17]

In 1983, Robert Baker, professor of church history at Southwestern Baptist Theological Seminary, published *Tell the Generations Following: A History of Southwestern Baptist Theological Seminary 1908–1983,* a continued historical account of the seminary.[18] Baker provides detailed correspondence between Carroll and Scarborough about the professorship in evangelism and the chair which Scarborough would occupy at the new seminary. This history also provides an account of Carroll's Convention involvement surrounding the creation of a Department of Evangelism at Southwestern Baptist Theological Seminary.

Finally, in 1993, Charles Kelley wrote a modified version of his ThD dissertation on the history of Southern Baptist evangelism.[19] This treatise establishes the prominence of the "Chair of Fire" in theological education. Kelley states, "Theological education has been another source of emphasis on personal evangelism in Southern Baptist life."[20] Most recently, Kelley published *Fuel the Fire: Lessons from the History of Southern Baptist Evangelism,* an update to his 1993 monograph, *How Did They Do It?*[21] It echoes the historical overview of the value and contributions of the "Chair of Fire" to theological education in evangelism situated within the history of Southern Baptist evangelism.

16. Muncy, *History of Evangelism,* 158–63.
17. Muncy, *History of Evangelism,* 159.
18. Baker, *Tell the Generations.*
19. Kelley, *How Did They Do It?.*
20. Kelley, *How Did They Do It?,* 72.
21. Kelley, *Fuel the Fire.*

In the second part of this assessment a necessity arises to familiarize oneself with research pertaining to the founder and occupants of the "Chair of Fire," and consider those occupants' personal contributions to the chair and to the academic discipline of evangelism in theological education. Recently, Brandon Kiesling published a dissertation on Benajah Harvey Carroll's contribution to evangelism.[22] This research gives historical background to Carroll's role in the formation of the Evangelism Department at the Home Mission Board. Kiesling's work also includes introductory material into Carroll's creation of the Department of Evangelism at Southwestern Baptist Theological Seminary and also provides brief biographical sketches of eight of the nine "Chair of Fire" occupants. From Kiesling's dissertation a call for further research is given to the necessity "on the 'Chair of Fire' and its influence on theological education at other Southern Baptist seminaries," which is the basis of this book.[23]

A biographical work on Scarborough was published in 1996 by Glenn Thomas Carson titled *Calling Out the Called: The Life and Work of Lee Rutland Scarborough.*[24] Carson completed a doctoral dissertation at Southwestern Baptist Theological Seminary and adapted this 1996 work from his research.[25] The book opens with similar biographical information on Scarborough's life and times on the West Texas frontier and selected events from his Christian home that formed his character and theology. Carson's research meticulously paints his subject as an SBC denominational leader. Carson also provides a fair critique of Scarborough's work for the seminary, his new ideas for the Convention, and the controversies that ensued his ministry. This biography also provides an account of Carroll's conception of the first evangelism chair and his appointment of Scarborough, who occupied the "Chair of Fire" and filled the role of Southwestern Baptist Theological Seminary's field secretary.

Carson's dissertation is the most extensive research conducted on the statesmanship of Scarborough. The dissertation, published in 1992, was written in fulfillment of the Doctor of Philosophy degree at Southwestern Baptist Theological Seminary. This research critiqued Scarborough's work as a Southern Baptist statesman and his inception of New

---

22. Kiesling, "Investigation."
23. Kiesling, "Investigation," 200.
24. Carson, *Calling Out the Called.*
25. Carson, "Architect of a New Denominationalism."

Denominationalism.[26] Carson's work provided a fair critique of Scarborough's contribution to Southern Baptist evangelism.

L. R. Scarborough's calling and denominationalism were one in the same. His life exemplified Southern Baptist conviction, doctrines, and evangelistic practice. Like Carroll, he too stood firm in the face of many challenges during his ministry. Only Carson's dissertation has explored the significance of these challenges. The Seventy-Five Million Campaign, the J. Frank Norris controversy, and the ownership and control of the seminary are the most known and notable challenges.[27]

In the same year, at New Orleans Baptist Theological Seminary, Michael Hawley also produced another dissertation that examined Scarborough's concept of evangelism. The research critically probes Scarborough's concept of evangelism by investigating his biographical factors, theory of evangelism, and practical application of evangelism.[28] This dissertation provides in-depth study into the evangelism of Scarborough.

A third dissertation was published in 1992 at New Orleans Baptist Theological Seminary by David Leavell on the "Chair of Fire's" third occupant, Cassius Elijah Autrey.[29] Leavell delivers information about Autrey's concepts of evangelism and also provides an overview of denominational service. Autrey served as Southwestern Baptist Theological Seminary's first full-time professor of evangelism and "taught evangelism to over 5500 students."[30]

---

26. Carson, "Architect of a New Denominationalism."

27. Between 1919 and 1925, the last five years of Scarborough's first decade as president of Southwestern Seminary, Scarborough would use the seminary as a platform to promote the cooperation of the Southern Baptist Convention. It developed from observing other successful financial campaigns during World War I, which brought millions of dollars to wartime benevolences. The Seventy-Five Million Campaign was unsuccessful due to the Great Depression following the war. The second challenge came from a controversy with J. Frank Norris, senior pastor of the First Baptist Church of Fort Worth, Texas, who sought to bring Southwestern Seminary to an end. Norris and Scarborough disagreed on the direction of the seminary's control and argued bitterly over ecclesiology and denominationalism. And the final challenge was transferring the ownership and control of Southwestern Seminary from the Baptist General Convention of Texas to the Southern Baptist Convention, which took place in 1925. The seminary became property of the SBC. See Carson, "Architect of a New Denominationalism," 58–135.

28. Hawley, "Concept of Evangelism," 1.

29. Leavell, "Cassius Elijah Autrey."

30. Leavell, "Cassius Elijah Autrey," 65. See also Autrey, Personal Biographical Notes. These personal notes are held by the family of C. E. Autrey and were used by

In 2017 Daniel Dickard published his dissertation on Roy Fish's contribution to the evangelistic spirit of Southwestern Baptist Theological Seminary through Fish's preaching ministry.[31] Dickard also provides brief sketches into the gospel content of the work of the "Chair of Fire" occupants, further supporting the idea that the "concomitant threads of preaching and evangelism are deeply interwoven into the historical tapestry of the seminary."[32] Dickard's dissertation focuses on the evangelistic preaching of the "Chair of Fire's" longest occupant and is the first major work on Fish.

Finally, Timothy Trillet of Southeastern Baptist Theological Seminary completed his Doctorate of Education dissertation, titled *The Educational Philosophy of Leighton Paige Patterson,* in 2012.[33] The research provides sketches of the men who molded Patterson and then critically examines the teaching and educational methods of Patterson. Trillet's use of firsthand oral interviews with the subject provides intimate details into Patterson's biblical convictions and leadership styles which have influenced the administration of three Southern Baptist institutions.

In order to investigate the extent of the "Chair of Fire's" contribution to the inclusion and subsequent implementation of evangelism as an academic discipline within the Southern Baptist seminaries, this book uses primarily a historical research methodology. Chapter 2 investigates the formation of the "Chair of Fire" and the guiding principles set by the seminary founder, primarily looking at the writings of Carroll and Scarborough. Chapter 3 includes historical details of selected works of the chair's occupants regarding the development of evangelism courses and training within theological education and investigates the evangelistic outreach of the "Chair of Fire" throughout the SBC from 1908 to 2020. Chapter 4 examines selected works regarding the inclusion of evangelism in theological education to the other five Southern Baptist seminaries and investigates the implementation of evangelism as an academic discipline influencing the creation of other chairs of evangelism at these Southern Baptist seminaries from 1908 to 2020. The research concludes with an assessment of the practice of evangelism within the Southern Baptist seminaries in order to identify the current state of Southern

personal permission by Leavell for dissertation research.

31. Dickard, "Man between the Times."

32 Dickard, "Man between the Times," v–vi.

33. Trillet, "Leighton Paige Patterson."

Baptist evangelism in theological education and encourage a revival of the "Chair of Fire" prominence and contribution to theological education in evangelism and the work of the evangelist.

AN ACADEMIC CHAIR PRECEDING THE "CHAIR OF FIRE"

Forty-two years before the inception of the Southwestern Baptist Theological Seminary in Fort Worth, Texas, and its "Chair of Fire," Alexander Duff of Scotland "proposed the erection of a chair of evangelistic theology" in June 1866 at the General Assembly of the Free Church of Scotland.[34] Andrew Walls, a British historian and a pioneer in the academic study of world Christianity at the University of Edinburgh, in his chapter contribution to *Missiological Education for the 21st Century: The Book, the Circle and the Sandals,* states, "This chair of missiology (as it would probably be called today) was only the first stage of Duff's scheme. Associated with the chair would be a 'missionary institute,' which would address the questions arising from the encounter with other cultures."[35] This academic chair of evangelistic theology was officially established in 1867.[36]

Walls acknowledges that much of the gathered information about this first chair of missiology founded in Scotland is "chronicled by the venerable apostle of cooperative missions studies, Professor Olav Guttorm Myklebust of Oslo."[37] Myklebust, in his unprecedented work *The Study of Missions in Theological Education: An Historical Inquiry into the Place of World Evangelization in Western Protestant Ministerial Training with Particular Reference to Alexander Duff's Chair of Evangelistic Theology,* recognizes Gustav Warneck as "the founder of the scholarly study of the Christian mission," but concedes the "decisive contribution to our subject" of Duff and others from Scotland, Europe, and the United States of America were making in scholarship.[38]

The Alexander Duff Chair of Evangelistic Theology existed from 1867 to 1909. "In 1909, on the eve of the Edinburgh Missionary Conference, what had once been the chair of evangelistic theology came to an

---

34. Walls, "Missiological Education," 12.

35. Walls, "Missiological Education," 13.

36. Myklebust, *Study of Missions,* 25.

37. Walls, "Missiological Education," 12.

38. Myklebust, *Study of Missions,* 24.

end."[39] While the writings about this first chair of missions in theological education seemingly cross between foreign and domestic missions studies, the chair of evangelistic theology was predominantly focused on missiology, not the functionality and practice of evangelism as seen in the precepts set forth by Carroll's "Chair of Fire."

History of the "Chair of Fire"

In order to lay the foundation for the history and formation of the "Chair of Fire," this historical account focuses predominantly on the primary sources that are available. Most of the published and unpublished works of Carroll and Scarborough are available through special collections found in the J. T. and Zelma Luther Rare Books and Archives in A. Webb Roberts Library on the campus of Southwestern Baptist Theological Seminary, including compilations of letters, newspaper articles, books, and other writings. The seminary's first written history, *A Modern School of the Prophets: A History of the Southwestern Baptist Theological Seminary, a Product of Prayer and Faith, Its First Thirty Years, 1907–1937*, contains priceless primary sources of the creation of the seminary and of the chair that distinguishes her cause and mission to the world.[40] An examination of historical events, such as Carroll's reaction to the Whitsitt controversy, links the establishment of the "Chair of Fire" with a call for evangelism education across the SBC.

Some unpublished works of Carroll and Scarborough furnish the correspondence between these two definitive leaders of Southwestern Baptist Theological Seminary and provide details pertaining to Carroll's selection process of Scarborough to hold this prestigious chair of evangelism at the seminary. Through Carroll's and Scarborough's notes, the researcher can reconstruct how their thoughts and understanding developed regarding the importance of evangelism in theological education and shaped and set the standard of work in evangelism for the occupants of this "Chair of Fire."

Carroll's contribution to evangelism, as researched by Kiesling in 2017, develops his thoughts on evangelism in theological education within the seminary and the local church and his activities as a statesman

---

39. Myklebust, *Study of Missions*, 240.
40. Scarborough, *Modern School*, 130–33.

within the SBC.[41] The interaction between these two men established the first chair of evangelism and department of evangelism in a higher educational institution, thrusting Southern Baptist evangelism to the forefront in the twentieth century.

The Subsequent Occupants

Biographical information of the eight subsequent occupants of the chair provides context for this historical methodology. The subsequent occupants of the chair were E. D. Head (1942 to 1950), C. E. Autrey (1955 to 1960), Kenneth Chafin (1960 to 1965), Roy Fish (1965 to 2006), James Eaves (1973 to 1990), Malcolm McDow (1982 to 2005), L. Paige Patterson (2007 to 2014), and Matt Queen (2014–).[42] In this section, research traces each occupant's contributions to evangelism in theological education and clarifies how the principles and ideals of the "Chair of Fire" set by Carroll have impacted Southern Baptist evangelism and the other seminaries.

Contributions of Evangelism to Theological Education

This section of research examines Carroll's conviction of the New Testament "Office of the Evangelist," as seen and interpreted in Ephesians 4:11–12. Careful historical research discloses the historical context of events in 1906 with which Carroll determined that a Southern Baptist seminary should include evangelism as an independent academic discipline. The use of the B. H. Carroll Collection in A. Webb Roberts Library at Southwestern Baptist Theological Seminary provides many unpublished letters and writings by Carroll on the thoughts, practice, and office of the evangelist, all of which he used to formulate his conviction concerning the need for a chair of evangelism. Brandon Kiesling's dissertation provides an account of Carroll's dream of establishing the first chair of evangelism and a department of evangelism.[43] Plainly, Carroll was determined to give evangelism equal standing with all other courses of study within theological education.

A paralleled connection exists between the Department of Evangelism at the Home Mission Board, now the North American Mission

41. Kiesling, "Investigation," 167–72.
42. Kiesling, "Investigation," 172–92.
43. Kiesling, "Investigation," 170.

Board, and the Department of Evangelism at Southwestern Baptist Theological Seminary, headed by the "Chair of Fire." Carroll understood that the SBC's formation and organization in 1845 to spread the gospel message through both domestic and foreign missionary work meant that Southern Baptists would need education in evangelism in order that this work could be achieved. From its conception, the "Chair of Fire" has maintained the highest standards in theological education and pedagogy for the training and mobilization of Southern Baptist evangelism. Charles Kelley credits evangelism in theological education as an essential element in Southern Baptist life.[44]

L. R. Scarborough's book published in 1919, *With Christ after the Lost*, gives evidence of the third essential function of the "Chair of Fire" as outlined by Carroll.[45] This textbook provides extensive scriptural teachings on the propagation of other faiths or evangelism education for sharing Christ with other world religions. Carroll states, "It will fall to this chair to expound the principles and methods of gospel propagandism, and to compare these with the principles and methods of propagandism adopted by heathen religions, illustrating by historical facts, and not only heathen religions, but ancient Judaism in its way of proselyting as shown in biblical, interbiblical, and post-apostolic history."[46] Carroll encouraged Scarborough to develop educational lectures on the "History of Evangelism in the various Christian denominations and the elements of power in the propagandism of other religions to be delivered only when you have prepared yourself to your own satisfaction for a lecture."[47] These lectures were given to assist in teaching Southern Baptist evangelism while on the field and to make the "Chair of Fire" known.

Textbooks have assisted with the spread of evangelism as an academic discipline throughout the Southern Baptist seminaries. Scarborough published books primarily on evangelism, evangelistic preaching, Southern Baptist history, Southwestern Baptist Theological Seminary, and his various travels. Carroll requests in a letter to Scarborough

> that while traveling and doing field work you carefully study book by book and prepare one by one the lectures that will make your fame, taking full time in preparation of each lecture,

---

44. Kelley, *How Did They Do It?*, 72–73.

45. Scarborough, *With Christ*.

46. Carroll, "Chair of Fire" address.

47. Carroll, Initial Letter of Invitation to Scarborough, 1906.

making each one a masterpiece individually, and so prepared as
to fit into a series for publication as a text book.[48]

This call to publish literature in evangelism has been carried through
today by all of the chair's occupants. In most recent days, the current
occupant of the "Chair of Fire" has published three works on personal
and local church evangelism.[49] These works have been distributed Convention-wide and are also used as supplemental textbooks in evangelism
courses. The methods promoted in these resources are easily adopted as
personal and local church models of evangelism.

The Spreading Fire

In the fifth chapter of this book, the researcher draws connections between the torchbearers at each Southern Baptist seminary. The spreading
fire of evangelism in theological education has presently reached each
of the remaining five Southern Baptist seminaries with full listings of
courses in evangelism being taught throughout these institutions. Kelley
states, "The effectiveness of Southern Baptists in evangelism cannot be
separated from their decision to include specific instruction in evangelism in the theological training of ministerial students."[50]

This research establishes a causal link between the expansion of
evangelism as an academic discipline and expansion of the doctrine of
evangelism within the SBC. Carroll undergirded the "Chair of Fire" with
his theological persuasion that the evangelist, too, was an office in the
New Testament church, and that "this teaching will bring out clearly the
importance and perpetuity of the office."[51] With this doctrine expounded
in the classrooms of theological institutions, the SBC experienced the
spreading fire of an expansion in evangelism.

This book finds significance in forging fresh historical research and
inquiry concerning the chairs and departments of evangelism in seminaries other than Southwestern Baptist Theological Seminary. Delineations
made introduce the histories of the Roland Q. Leavell Chair of Evangelism at New Orleans Baptist Theological Seminary; the Billy Graham

48. Carroll, Letter Offering Chair of Evangelism, 1908.

49. Queen, *Everyday Evangelism*. See also Queen, *Mobilize to Evangelize: The Pastor
and Effective Congregational Evangelism*, and Queen, *And You Will Be My Witnesses*.

50. Kelley, *How Did They Do It?*, 74.

51. Carroll, "Chair of Fire" address.

Chair of Evangelism at The Southern Baptist Theological Seminary; the E. Hermond Westmoreland Chair of Evangelism at Gateway Seminary; the Bailey Smith Chair of Evangelism at Southeastern Baptist Theological Seminary; and the Gary Taylor Chair of Missions and Evangelism at Midwestern Baptist Theological Seminary. A compilation of the historical account of each chair's creation, namesake, and brief biographical sketch of each chair's occupants provides context for the contributions of each to Southern Baptist evangelism.

2

The Formation of the L. R. Scarborough Chair of Evangelism, the "Chair of Fire," and The Founding Occupant

Few men in Southern Baptist history stand out amidst struggles to establish a culture of evangelism throughout the Convention like that of Benajah Harvey (B. H.) Carroll. He possessed a prophetic voice for the work of the gospel. Carroll, a strikingly handsome, tall man, towering over six feet and two inches, spoke with a booming voice. His notable legacy is his commitment to theological education and establishing a seminary as a means for men and women in the southwest to become fully equipped for gospel ministry throughout the frontiers of North America and the world. This chapter investigates the formation of the Department of Evangelism and the "Chair of Fire" at Southwestern Baptist Theological Seminary, the guiding principles set by the seminary founder, primarily looking at the writings of B. H. Carroll and L. R. Scarborough, and provides an overview of the roles and responsibilities of subsequent occupants of the Chair.

First, Carroll's concept of the evangelist will be assessed through his theology, writings, and sermons. This chapter explores the Whitsitt controversy at The Southern Baptist Theological Seminary and how the controversy shaped Carroll's designs for a new seminary and a chair of evangelism. Second, this chapter provides an overview of the creation the Southwestern Baptist Theological Seminary and the world's first academic chair of evangelism, called "The Chair of Fire" by its creator, B. H. Carroll, and in October of 1982 renamed the "L. R. Scarborough Chair of Evangelism" ("Chair of Fire") by the seminary's Board of Trustees. Third, research draws from the background, education, theology, writings, and sermons of L. R. Scarborough in order to document the initial principles and contributions of the first occupant of the "Chair of Fire."

B. H. CARROLL: BEFORE SOUTHWESTERN SEMINARY AND ITS "CHAIR OF FIRE"

Benajah Harvey Carroll was born December 27, 1843, near Carrollton in Carroll County, Mississippi, to parents Benajah and Mary Eliza. He was the seventh of thirteen children, named after his father. His father, Benajah, was a bi-vocational preacher and farmer. The Carrolls moved from their home in Mississippi to Drew County, Arkansas. B. H. Carroll attended grade school there. At sixteen, young Carroll began his education at Baylor University in Independence, Texas. Carroll's education was interrupted by the Civil War. "Carroll debated persuasively against secession, but eventually his Southern loyalty caused him to enlist."[1]

Upon his return from his Confederate service, he attended a Methodist camp meeting at his mother's insistence, where he surrendered his life to Jesus Christ.

> Though he had vowed never again to enter church, that autumn his mother persuaded him to attend a Methodist camp meeting. The sermon left Carroll cold, but the closing appeal burned through his soul. The minister's exhortation "to make a practical, experiential test" of Christianity and his unique translation of John 7:17 opened Harvey's eyes: "The knowledge as to whether doctrine was of God depended not upon external action and not upon exact conformity with God's will, but upon the internal disposition—'whosoever willeth or wishes to do God's will.'"[2]

Carroll "was known as an influential denominational leader . . . He gave particular emphasis to evangelism, prohibition, Christian education, and the work of home missions."[3] He himself gave wholeheartedly to the

---

1. Spivey, "Benajah Harvey Carroll," 164.

2. Spivey, "Benajah Harvey Carroll," 165, as cited originally in Carroll, *Sermons and Life Sketch*, 21.

3. Cox, "B. H. Carroll," 233.

promotion of the gospel and to evangelism within the Southern Baptist Convention (SBC). Carroll often led the Convention through speeches and sermons with arousing zeal to the expansion of the kingdom of God through evangelism. His lasting legacy would be the founding of the second Southern Baptist seminary. "Carroll's greatest contribution to Baptist life, as well as to American Christianity, was the founding of Southwestern Baptist Theological Seminary."[4] The seminary was founded on March 14, 1908, in Waco, Texas, and later moved to "Seminary Hill" in Fort Worth in 1910.

B. H. Carroll's Concept of the Evangelist

Jeff D. Ray, both a professor of homiletics and rural sociology at South-western Baptist Theological Seminary and a biographer of B. H. Carroll, states,

> I suppose no man ever lived who believed more thoroughly in evangelism, who contended more stoutly for the evangelis-tic functions, or who recognized more fully the incomparable value of the evangelist. And yet, when revival meetings were to be held in his own church, his rule was to hold them himself. I am safe in saying that in twenty-nine years he did not send out a half-dozen times to get help for a revival meeting.[5]

During his long pastorate at the First Baptist Church of Waco, Texas, Carroll placed high emphasis on the work of evangelism. "Carroll was known as an expository or biblical preacher. His sermons, with few exceptions, were based upon texts from the Bible. He chose a text and re-peated it and referred to it many times in the sermon. He would consider his preaching a failure if he had not employed a text."[6]

Carroll's concept of the evangelist drew directly from his interpreta-tion of English biblical references found in Acts, Timothy, and specifically in Ephesians 4. He believed that each office given to the church listed in this Scripture was a specific gift of the Holy Spirit to the local church, and that while some evangelists were pastors, the office of the evangelist was a unique and separate office from the pastorate. "The evangelists, 'who labor in the kingdom at large,' along with the pastors and teachers

4. Lefever, *Fighting the Good Fight*, 181.

5. Ray, *B. H. Carroll*, 88.

6. Segler, "B. H. Carroll," 9.

'were illumined to understand and expound these limits.'"[7] Evangelists do not act separately from the local church, but have a broader field of service to the kingdom of God outside of the local church. The evangelist considered his ministry as inter-church, meaning that they work between the local churches for kingdom expansion, gospel sowing, and disciple-making. "He held to the New Testament teaching that the first function of the evangelist was 'the perfecting of the saints.' He believed that this was to be accomplished through an inter-church ministry of preaching, teaching, and challenge to larger cooperative undertakings."[8]

In one of the volumes of Carroll's Bible commentary, *An Interpretation of the English Bible, Vol. 12: The Acts,* he conveys that the work of the evangelist is general in nature, not confined to one local flock, but rather a work unto the kingdom. Like Philip, who was confirmed to the office of deacon in Jerusalem,

> he became an evangelist, and boldly carried the gospel to the Samaritans, as our Lord himself had done (John 4), and under Spirit-guidance, went into the desert near Gaza, and led the Ethiopian treasurer, a Jewish proselyte, to Christ through which convert, according to history and tradition, Ethiopia was evangelized.[9]

The apostles in Jerusalem oversaw the evangelistic work of Philip, the evangelist, among the Samaritans. "Superintendence of the apostles continued, Peter following up the work of Philip on the Mediterranean coast. Peter leading, the door of the kingdom opened to the gentiles at Caesarea, and their baptism in the Holy Spirit—Acts 10."[10]

Carroll further exemplifies that the work of the evangelist is in concert with, and not working separately from, the local church. An important detail is that Philip's work as an evangelist was a part of the disciple-making process of the local church. This disciple-making process is seen in Acts 8, when Philip joins the Ethiopian in his chariot, explains the meaning of Isaiah 53 to him, leads the Ethiopian to saving faith in Jesus, and then baptizes him by immersion. Philip was an agent to the broader field, but acted by the endorsed authority of the local church in Jerusalem, with complete support and knowledge of the apostles.

7. Crisp, "Pastoral Theology of B. H. Carroll," 124.

8. Muncy, *History of Evangelism,* 159.

9. Carroll, *Interpretation, Vol. 12: Acts,* 164.

10. Carroll, *Interpretation, Vol. 12: Acts,* 174.

Carroll viewed the work of evangelism as the main work for all
who profess Christ as their Lord and Savior. Carroll would often preach
on the Great Commission of the Lord Jesus Christ from the Gospel of
Matthew 28:16–20. In one of Carroll's sermons, he states, "It constitutes
the 'marching orders' issued by the great Captain of our salvation. It
is his final order to the church militant. There will be no other. It is an
order—not an admonition. It is mandatory—not optional."[11] This view
is consistent with the Scriptures, specifically the Great Commission of
our Lord Jesus Christ, and with Carroll's views of the work of the local
church. A differentiation is needed and necessary between the work of
the evangelist and the work of evangelism. All Christians are called to
regularly practice evangelism, while the Holy Spirit calls some to the office of *evangelist* in the local church. In a sermon preached to a group of
baptism candidates, Carroll states,

> The apostles themselves, prophets, teachers, healers, pastors,
> and evangelists were all "set in the church" (1 Cor 12:28; Ep.
> 4:11–16). Officers, whether special or ordinary, passed away, but
> the church was an abiding institution (Matt 16:18) and to be
> forever "the pillar and ground of the truth" (1 Tim 3:15); with
> power to fill offices when vacated by unworthiness or death
> (Acts 1:15–26; 6:1–6; 2 Tim 2:2; 1 Tim. 3:1–16; Titus 1:5–9),
> that the ministry of the word might be perpetuated.[12]

Carroll preached that, from the beginning of "new birth" among
new believers, God could call them to special offices within the local
church. The very nature of God's church was to fill office vacancies "that
the ministry of the word might be perpetuated."[13]

Carroll established himself among Southern Baptists as a statesman,
preaching and speaking on Baptist causes at the Baptist General Convention of Texas and at associational meetings across the state. Carroll
made his lasting mark on the SBC at the Annual Meeting of the Southern
Baptist Convention of 1906. During the Convention, Carroll raised many
persuasive questions of how the Home Mission Board (HMB) would
send forth evangelists into the domestic fields. In 1906, after a careful
study by the Convention, the board was instructed to create a department
of evangelism. In his paramount address to the SBC in Chattanooga,

11. Carroll, *Christ's Marching Orders*, 15.

12. Carroll, *Sermons and Life Sketch*, 296.

13. Carroll, *Sermons and Life Sketch*, 296.

Tennessee, entitled "Evangelism," Carroll expounds on his interpretation of the Ephesians passage, stating, "Apostles and prophets have fulfilled their mission, but evangelists, pastors, and teachers remain."[14] "This was not achieved before a tense and critical battle on the floor of the Southern Baptist Convention. In the midst of the struggle, B. H. Carroll of Texas turned the tide in an eloquent address."[15]

Carroll called for the Convention to send him men and women with the evangelist heart and soul. The Convention, which was struggling with doctrinal mistrust due to the ongoing Whitsitt controversy, refused to send their young people to The Southern Baptist Theological Seminary, where they assumed they would receive instruction that conflicted with their beliefs. Carroll further committed to giving aid to the SBC by training men and women for evangelistic ministry. He was already training young ministers at Baylor University. He desired to use evangelistic men and women to achieve the HMB's goal of reaching North America with the gospel. Carroll saw a need for the proper role of evangelists within the local churches.

Evidence from modern accounts indicates that by the time Carroll addressed the Convention in 1906, his unspoken plan to create a new second seminary in Texas with a department of evangelism was already conceived. Carroll's vision was to create a world-class Southern Baptist seminary with a "Chair of Fire" and a department of evangelism. "When he founded Southwestern, shortly after that denominational battle, he decided that evangelism needed to be included in the regular course of theological studies."[16] Carroll envisioned that many of these trained evangelists from his new seminary in Texas would answer the call to serve the Convention at the HMB.

Trouble at Southern Seminary: The Whitsitt Controversy

The Whitsitt controversy began as a result of a senior professor and the chair of church history at the Southern Baptist Theological Seminary, William H. Whitsitt. Carroll was a member of the Board of Trustees for the seminary when he became involved with the controversy. "In the summer of 1880, Whitsitt spent several months in the libraries of

14. Carroll, "Address on Evangelism."
15. Baker, *Southern Baptist Convention*, 292.
16. Kelley, *How Did They Do It?*, 73.

Great Britain and concluded from his study that Baptists in England and America had baptized by sprinkling or pouring before 1641, when they adopted immersion."[17] He also uncovered a history of English Baptists pedobaptism.

> William H Whitsett [*sic*] was president of Southern Baptist Theological Seminary and refuted the Landmark Baptist doctrine of unbroken Baptist succession from Jesus to the present day. Whitsett [*sic*] believed instead that, while Baptist doctrine originated in the New Testament, those identifiable as Baptists did not appear until the seventeenth century. Texas Baptists contributed the involvement of B. H. Carroll attempting to refute Whitsett's teaching.[18]

Whitsitt's views, formed by his research in England, clashed with the Landmark views of Carroll. Brandon Kiesling states in his dissertation, "Throughout the controversy, Carroll attempted to moderate both sides in order to unify the SBC."[19] Carroll's theology held that all Baptists found their succession from John the Baptist at the time of Christ. "From a later perspective, it appears that a conflict between the older method of 'historical assumption' and the newer method of 'exact documentation' was inevitable at some point."[20]

The view of Baptist Church successionism was also held by Carroll's brother, J. M. Carroll, who authored a book titled *The Trail of Blood: The History of Baptist Churches from the time of Christ, Their Founder, to the Present Day.*[21] His small book traces a continued presence of Baptists (succession) throughout history from the time of Christ and John the Baptist and further refutes Whitsitt's controversial conclusions on English Baptists. "[B. H.] Carroll's views resembled Landmarkism: he emphasized the local church and disregarded its universal nature."[22] Nevertheless, his views encouraged more cooperation with other local churches and associations. "Although the Southern Baptist Convention never officially

---

17. Baker, *Tell the Generations*, 88.
18. Ledbetter, *Texas Convention*, 15.
19. Kiesling, "Investigation," 152.
20 Baker, *Tell the Generations*, 88.
21. Carroll, *Trail of Blood*.
22. Garrett, *Legacy of Southwestern*, 8.

endorsed the Landmark teachings of J. R. Graves, many local Baptist churches, particularly in the Southwest, did accept Landmarkism."[23]

Carroll struggled with Whitsitt's conclusions on Baptist succession for their attack on many longstanding Landmark leanings and convictions, but this was a minor issue in comparison to Whitsitt's views on a major Baptist doctrine of baptism by immersion. During the heat of the controversy, Whitsitt had published his findings in *Johnson's Universal Encyclopedia* in 1886 on the English Baptist's practices of pedobaptism.[24] Pedobaptism is the practice of baptizing infants into the faith and membership of the local church, before the child understands the gospel. Whitsitt's teachings were contrary to the scriptural teachings of "believer's baptism," which was defined as an act of public obedience to Christ that follows a person's conversion and salvation through personal saving knowledge in Jesus Christ. At the same time, Whitsitt endorsed the practice of pedobaptism by giving his blessing to his sister, born into a Southern Baptist family, to marry and follow her husband into a Presbyterian church, which practiced pedobaptism.

The Whitsitt controversy became an unavoidable fight for Carroll to avoid and he acted with others to work to resolve the issues on behalf of the Board of Trustees and the Convention. Robert Baker, professor of church history at Southwestern Baptist Theological Seminary, records in his book *The Southern Baptist Convention and Its People*, "This controversy, aimed as it was at a central tenet of Landmarkism (Baptist church succession), infuriated the disciples of Graves (who had died in 1893)."[25] Carroll fought for the Southern Baptist distinctive tenet of believer's baptism by immersion. "He helped shape reports on foreign and home missions, on the work of seminary education, and in resolving controversy, such as the Whitsitt controversy in 1897."[26] This controversy had sparked much controversy and discord among the SBC. "Texas Baptists fell into several categories, practically all opposing Whitsitt. Some wanted to withdraw all support from the seminary; some wanted the entire faculty to resign; some wanted to support the seminary only after Whitsitt had resigned."[27] The Convention was on the brink of a schism when Whitsitt

---

23. Lefever, *Fighting the Good Fight*, 85.

24. Cox, "Whitsitt Controversy," 1496.

25. Baker, *Southern Baptist Convention*, 281.

26. Segler, *Model for Ministers*, 17. As originally cited in Carroll, *Colossus*, 96.

27. Baker, *Tell the Generations*, 90–91.

resigned from the Southern Baptist Theological Seminary on July 13, 1898.

> The Whitsitt controversy revealed a deepening rift within the denomination. Although tensions between Landmarkers and non-Landmarkers set the controversy in motion, this rift was of a different character. It was a rift between traditional orthodoxy and the new progressive evangelicalism of many seminary graduates. Many were "evangelical liberals" who demanded freedom from denominational and creedal constraints. Whitsitt became the accidental martyr to their cause. The controversy set the trajectory of twentieth-century theology at the seminary in a progressive direction.[28]

The trustees at Southern Baptist Theological Seminary were left in despairing prospects as they found division among themselves with regard to the decision regarding Whitsitt's successor. In an effort to avoid any further controversy, the trustees created two main criteria, first the new president could not be a Landmarker and secondly, the president needed to be one not involved in any way with the Whitsitt controversy.[29]

Edgar Y. Mullins was not a Landmarker. He agreed privately with Whitsitt, but managed to stay clear of the acidic fray of the controversy. "His relationship with B. H. Carroll was similarly strained at times. They engaged in an extensive correspondence discussing their major disagreement over a minor point related to baptism."[30] So naturally, his election to the presidency of Southern Baptist Theological Seminary was opposed by Carroll. "Mullins's election also represented a new kind of academic freedom at the seminary, at least in principle."[31] Mullins's treatment of the Abstract of Principles were broad strokes, and once in the office of the presidency he declared to a prospective faculty member, Charles Gardner, "We are progressive as well as conservative."[32]

The Whitsitt controversy played a pivotal part in Carroll's mental arrangement of the Board of Trustees he would form at Southwestern Baptist Theological Seminary. Carroll's experience in the ongoing debate gave him an awareness of the organizational importance in strong trustee

28. Wills, *Southern Baptist Seminary*, 228–29.

29. Wills, *Southern Baptist Seminary*, 229.

30. Wills, *Southern Baptist Seminary*, 236.

31. Wills, *Southern Baptist Seminary*, 237.

32. Wills, *Southern Baptist Seminary*, 237. As initially cited from Mullins, "Edgar Y. Mullins to Charles S. Gardner," 342.

control and denomination oversight over the Baptist doctrines and theo-logical educators at a Southern Baptist institution.[33] Southwestern Baptist Theological Seminary's original Charter of 1908 states, "Said corporation shall be under the patronage and general direction of the Baptist De-nomination in the State of Texas as represented by the Baptist General Convention of Texas, which Convention shall ordain and establish the Articles of Faith and permanent laws for the operation, management and control of said Seminary."[34] When the time came for the organization of a new seminary, Carroll then placed directly into the blueprint designs of his new seminary certain checks and balances granting powers to the Board of Trustees in an effort to ensure the solvency of his new theo-logical seminary and make certain that this kind of doctrinal controversy would not happen again within the life of a Southern Baptist educational entity.

A New Seminary; A New Chair

The history of the "Chair of Fire" is inextricably tied to the formation of Southwestern Baptist Theological Seminary. The seminary, by design, formed a hearty evangelistic foundation for the chair of evangelism. Car-roll's concept of theology and evangelism informed every decision about the curriculum and education offered at his Baptist seminary founded on the frontiers of the Southwest. "Dr. Carroll was a pioneer and a prophet in his thinking of the place of evangelism in theological education."[35]

As a pastor, Carroll's burden was to train the nearly three thousand Baptist preachers of Texas in sound Baptist theology. Southern Baptist Theological Seminary of Louisville, Kentucky, was the only location for Southern Baptists at this time to receive ministerial, seminary training. Carroll argued that Southern Baptist Theological Seminary did not have the faculty to handle such a large student increase. He believed that the South needed a second seminary. "The creation of a seminary in Texas seemed a natural step to many Southern Baptists in 1901, including some Baptists on the East Coast."[36]

33. Lefever, *Fighting the Good Fight,* 110. As originally cited from Carroll, "Article Three," 1. Also cited in Scarborough, *Modern School,* 169.

34. Lefever, *Fighting the Good Fight,* 488.

35. Muncy, *History of Evangelism,* 159.

36. Lefever, *Fighting the Good Fight,* 153.

S. P. Brooks, president of Baylor University, did not agree with Carroll's viewpoint on the Whitsitt controversy. In an attempt not to appear as though the university was producing a rivalry with Southern Baptist Theological Seminary and to maintain public neutrality on the Whitsitt controversy, Brooks hindered the enlargement of the Department of Theology at Baylor. "Baylor had long been uncomfortable with defining its role in the theological education of young ministers."[37]

In 1905, Carroll, who was the president of the board of trustees of Baylor University, made two motions that would create and fund a seminary in Texas. He did so without the knowledge or approval of the university president. "Not only was Carroll president of the trustees of Baylor (and could thus institute action without the sanction of the university's president), but S. P. Brooks happened to be in Europe during the summer and had not yet returned to Waco."[38] These approved motions by Carroll separated the Department of Theology from Baylor and instituted the Baylor Theological Seminary. Carroll was named the dean of the new seminary.

Early in Carroll's thoughts and plans was the creation of the "Chair of Fire." A handwritten letter dated November 1, 1906, to Lee Rutland Scarborough serves as primary evidence to this fact.[39] The letter came to Scarborough on the heels of Carroll's eloquent Convention address on the need for work of evangelists in the Home Mission Board (HMB) in the SBC.

Carroll proposed that Scarborough should prayerfully consider leaving his pastorate of the moment, First Baptist Church of Abilene, Texas, which Scarborough had held since 1901, and join the teaching faculty and become the field secretary of the newly instituted Baylor Theological Seminary, then housed on the campus of Baylor University. In Carroll's mind, L. R. Scarborough was the qualified evangelist for the post of first professor of evangelism and field secretary: "You I prefer above all men."[40] This he stated in his 1906 letter to Scarborough. "The offer thrust upon Dr. Scarborough a long struggle and a difficult decision."[41] Carroll admitted that he had two men in mind for this prestigious opportunity,

37. Lefever, *Fighting the Good Fight*, 152.
38. Lefever, *Fighting the Good Fight*, 121.
39. Carroll, Letter from Carroll Discussing Work, 1906.
40. Carroll, Letter from Carroll Discussing Work, 1906.
41. Dana, *Scarborough*, 80.

but that Scarborough was his first and best choice. The other candidate is not named in Carroll's writings.

Scarborough initially turned down the invitation, but the discourse and invitation remained a topic of conversation until 1908, by which time Carroll had successfully established Southwestern Baptist Theological Seminary. H. E. Dana described how Scarborough's calling to join the faculty at the seminary came while he was preaching in a revival meeting at the First Baptist Church of Pine Bluff, Arkansas: "Right there in that pulpit, as he poured out his heart to a subdued and tendered audience, the preacher's own soul became prostrate before the altar of divine appointment . . . Clearly, unmistakably now the Spirit of the living God was speaking to his heart—'Go to the Seminary!'"[42] In a letter dated February 24, 1908, from Scarborough to Carroll, Scarborough writes, "My decision was final. God clearly leads me to give my word to this great Seminary Movement."[43] In his letter he accepted the president's offer to join the faculty as professor of evangelism and field secretary, but conveys the heartache to the congregants of the First Baptist Church of Abilene in learning of their beloved pastor's resignation. Scarborough would become the inaugural occupant of the "Chair of Fire." Carroll said, "No man among Baptists was better qualified to make it a 'chair of fire' than was Lee Rutland Scarborough."[44]

The "Chair of Fire"

Carroll articulated his concept of the evangelist in the announcement address about the chair of evangelism published in the *Texas Baptist Standard* on July 2, 1908. He named the first endowed chair of evangelism "*a Chair of Fire.*" In 1945, W. L. Muncy recorded in his historical account of the history of evangelism in the United States that "the first American theological seminary to establish a department of evangelism was the Southwestern Baptist Theological Seminary of Fort Worth, Texas."[45] In Charles Kelley's book, *How Did They Do It?: The Story of Southern Baptist Evangelism*, he confirms Muncy's assumptions: "Evangelism was not included in normal theological education until B. H. Carroll established

---

42. Dana, *Scarborough*, 84.

43. Scarborough, Letter to Carroll, 1908.

44. Dana, *Scarborough*, 80.

45. Muncy, *History of Evangelism*, 159.

Southwestern Baptist Theological Seminary."[46] Carroll then gives suc-
cinctly the defining attributes from his own scriptural interpretation why
this academic chair is necessary for Southwestern Baptist Theological
Seminary's success in theological training.

> The Southwestern Baptist Theological Seminary takes the lead
> in establishing a chair of evangelism. For years the mind of its
> president has been impressed that "the Evangelist" is a distinct
> New Testament office. That while the evangelist, as other offi-
> cers, is "set in the church," and each evangelist is responsible to
> the church of his membership for character, doctrine and con-
> tinuance in office, yet his field, unlike the pastor's, is the king-
> dom instead of a particular church. That the ends of his ministry
> are kingdom ends rather than congregational.[47]

The article continues by defining four main objectives for the seminary's chair of evangelism. These objectives are based on Carroll's scriptural explanation for the "Chair of Fire."

> First of all there is a need to teach connectedly the New Testa-
> ment doctrines of the office as distinguished from the apostolic
> and pastoral office . . . In the second place it will be the office
> of this chair to expound the Biblical idea of the kingdom as set
> forth by Old Testament prophets by our Lord and his apostles,
> showing clearly not one kingdom visible and another invisible,
> not one in time and another in eternity, but one kingdom in its
> various features, prophetic, visible, invisible, in time and eter-
> nity . . . Third, it will fall to this chair to expound the principles
> and methods of Gospel propagandism, and to compare these
> with the principles and methods of propagandism adopted by
> heathen religions, illustrating by historical facts . . . Last of all,
> to show from both Testaments that revivals of religion are the
> hope of the world.[48]

Carroll saw that the first duty of the "Chair of Fire" was to train
men and women for the office of evangelist in order to serve the local
church, associations, and state and national mission boards. The local
church was lacking properly trained evangelists. Carroll desired evangelistic men who could expound the biblical truths of the gospel on the
home front and carry the gospel abroad with boldness. Southwestern

---

46. Kelley, *How Did They Do It?*, 72.

47. Carroll, "Chair of Fire" address.

48. Carroll, "Chair of Fire" address.

Baptist Theological Seminary's Department of Evangelism envisioned the treatment of the office of *evangelist* and its own uniqueness of calling just as the Department of Theology prepared the training of pastors. "This teaching will bring out clearly the importance and perpetuity of the office and illustrate vividly by showing what particular New Testament evangelists accomplished."[49] Carroll's concept of evangelist, as noted in his writings on Philip and Paul, further demonstrated his conviction that the Southern Baptist Convention in fact needed evangelists to see healthy growth throughout local churches.[50]

The second emphasis of the "Chair of Fire" was to equip men and women with the necessary tools and evangelistic strategies needed to do the work of the evangelist between local churches for kingdom expansion. These evangelism students were to be equipped to train churches in programs of evangelism, through evangelistic preaching and teaching. Carroll's chair of evangelism occupant was to demonstrate the work of an evangelist to the Southwestern Baptist Theological Seminary students.

The "Chair of Fire" was to teach and train students with biblical foundations how "to expound the principles and methods of gospel propagandism, and to compare these with the principles and methods of propagandism adopted by heathen religions, illustrating by historical facts, and not only heathen religions, but ancient Judaism in its way of proselyting as shown in biblical, interbiblical, and post-apostolic history."[51] Carroll believed that every evangelist must be trained, prepared, and ready to interact apologetically with lost people holding other beliefs. The importance of studying comparative religions is to become familiar with the false teachings of other world religions and unorthodox Christian faiths, such as Mormonism and Christian Science, in order to better witness to them and deal fairly with their belief systems.

He determined that the "Chair of Fire" would personally demonstrate the art of preaching revivals and to stir the hearts of young evangelists to do likewise throughout the local churches. "That all the work of this chair may not be mere theory and historical delay, the occupant of this chair must himself be a practical field evangelist all the time illustrating, between lecture series, the power of his office in great revival

---

49. Scarborough, *Modern School*, 131–32.

50. Carroll, *Interpretation, Vol. 15: Colossians, Ephesians, and Hebrews*, 147.

51. Carroll, *Interpretation, Vol. 15: Colossians, Ephesians, and Hebrews*, 132.

meetings."[52] Revival preaching is the most visible aspect of the "Chair of Fire" and a regular evangelistic methodology employed by its occupants.

Lee Rutland Scarborough: The Founding Occupant

Lee Rutland Scarborough, the son of George and Mary Elizabeth Scarborough, a West Texas frontier pastor and his wife, was born July 4, 1870, in Colfax, Louisiana.[53] Scarborough was reared as a cowboy on the open range and ever with the gospel message before him. Lee Scarborough was the eighth of nine children, but only five would live to see their adulthood. Both parents prayed, sensed, and guided his call to ministry during his early years. Glenn Carson, biographer of Scarborough, noted in *Calling Out the Called*, "One cannot underestimate the sway of Scarborough's parents in relation to his conversion and decision to enter the ministry."[54]

Scarborough heard the gospel of Jesus from both his father and mother at an early age. It appears that his mother played a prominent part in his conversion.

> "Son, I want to see you." I sat on a stool, on which she had been resting her feet, at her knee and listened to the story, the sweetest of all the ages, how Christ was born of the Virgin Mary, was baptized of John in the Jordan, lived, taught, healed, preached, and wrought and was crucified on Calvary, buried in Joseph's tomb, and rose again for the salvation and justification of a lost world. Mother's voice was mellow and tender and her speech was interupted [*sic*] by tears and sobs as she told me that story. I pillowed my head on her loving lap and wept the first bitter tears of conviction.[55]

A few years later, at age seventeen, Scarborough would attend a revival meeting and fall under conviction of sin, have an argument with his mother, and the following day surrender his life to Jesus Christ as Lord and Savior.[56]

After Scarborough had completed degrees at Baylor University and Yale, he returned home to Texas. Having surrendered to ministry during

---

52. Carroll, *Interpretation, Vol. 15: Colossians, Ephesians, and Hebrews*, 133.

53. Scarborough, "Evolution."

54. Carson, *Calling Out*, 6.

55. Scarborough, "Evolution."

56. Dana, *Scarborough*, 54–55.

his time at Yale, he began pastoring First Baptist Church of Cameron in 1896. In 1901, Scarborough was called as the pastor of the First Baptist Church of Abilene, Texas. "The growth experienced at the Cameron church was duplicated in Abilene. In addition to increasing membership threefold from four hundred to well over one thousand, Scarborough led in establishing two mission churches of First Baptist."[57] Both pastorates were outstanding displays of God's hand upon Scarborough, and each church grew under his tenure.

The Inaugural Occupant of the "Chair of Fire"

"The Southwestern Baptist Theological Seminary takes the lead in establishing a Chair of Evangelism," read the opening of an article announcing the upcoming inauguration of the chair by Carroll in *The Baptist Standard*, dated July 2, 1908.[58] The article lists four main objectives or areas of focused study and influence that the occupant is to provide as an academic contribution to the field of evangelism in theological education. Through the "Chair of Fire," Carroll's intent was to increase greatly the kingdom of God through trained evangelists throughout the SBC.

> Its purpose is to bring out the doctrine of soul-winning as seen in God's Word; to discover the spirit and methods used by Jesus Christ and his disciples in "fishing for men"; to find the characteristics and elements of conquest and propagandism in its different organizations and denominations of Christianity and of the false religions of the world, electing and using such of these elements as are good, in the development of this the finest of fine arts—winning men to Christ. It is proposed also to give exhaustive study to the history of revivals, the biography of great soul-winners, their sermons and methods they used and are using in reaching men with the Gospel Light.[59]

Lee Rutland Scarborough's is known as a "pastor, evangelist, seminary president, denominational leader, and author."[60] In May 1908, Scarborough officially joined the family of the Southwestern Baptist

---

57. Carson, *Calling Out,* 17–18.

58. Carroll, "Chair of Fire" address.

59. Naylor, "Southwestern and Evangelism," 25–26.

60. Cox, "Scarborough," *SBE,* 1186–87. Carroll began negotiations with Scarborough in 1906.

Theological Seminary after one and a half years of consistent letter conversations between the seminary founder, B. H. Carroll, and himself as professor of evangelism and field secretary.

Scarborough became the inaugural chairman of the chair of evangelism—the "Chair of Fire." "Scarborough viewed the establishment of the 'Chair of Fire' as a positive innovation in theological education, and thus he credits Carroll with this twentieth-century development in evangelism methodology."[61] He brought to the seminary an evangelistic fire and the working knowledge of pastoring two healthy, growing churches in Texas along with institutional advancement and building project skills gained while serving as the Financial Secretary of Simmons College, now Hardin-Simmons University in Abilene, Texas.

B. H. Carroll desired to see his beloved new seminary produce an evangelistic force throughout the SBC by leading them to a new department of evangelism. Carroll clearly had two candidates in mind, according to letters written between him and Scarborough, but Scarborough was the only choice to head up this important work from his mental inception. "No man among Baptists was better qualified to make it a 'Chair of Fire' than was Lee Rutland Scarborough."[62]

Scarborough and the Evangelism Department

Scarborough's position as the head of a Department of Evangelism at Southwestern Baptist Theological Seminary was a first in theological seminaries. He used the Evangelism Department to begin educating evangelists and future denominational leaders.

> In his leadership inside the seminary itself, Dr. Scarborough's evangelistic influence is immediately recognized. His own statement of the philosophy which gave birth to his seminary service was this: "God has joined evangelism and education in holy marriage." That evangelism should be intelligent and that Christian intellect should be evangelistic were his guiding convictions.[63]

61. Nettles, "Public Figure," 35.
62. Dana, *Scarborough*, 80.
63. Foreman, "Evangelistic Thrust," 58.

The Work of Personal Evangelism

Scarborough taught the art of personal evangelism and mass evangelism at Southwestern Baptist Theological Seminary. He taught his students that prayer served as the key to success in personal soul-winning.[64] A quiet time is essential for those that want to win souls, because it keeps the heart right and burdened before God.[65] The personal prayer life of the evangelist, according to Scarborough's teaching, should invite God's presence to go before the witness, speak through the witness, and follow up after the witness.[66]

Scarborough taught that Scripture should be heavily used during witnessing. "Make much use of God's word—it is the power of God unto salvation, the sword of the Spirit."[67] Scarborough reminds us that the New Testament was not available for the first-century Christian workers; the early church ministers relied heavily on memorization of Christ's words.[68]

In a message from *Products of Pentecost,* Scarborough states that all evangelistic preachers must keep "The Savior at the center."[69] The evangelistic message is to be a triumphant one, because our Savior is triumphant in his resurrection.[70] Prayer is also a common theme in his writings on evangelistic preaching and revival meetings.

> Prayer prevailed. One cannot think of a Pentecost disassociated from prayer. The prayer ratio at Pentecost is significant. They prayed ten days. Peter preached one hour, there was personal work part of the day, and the harvest of three thousand souls was the result. The mixture of prayer and preaching in our day is often so thin we rarely baptize from it.[71]

Personal evangelism and preaching are not divorced from each other. Scarborough taught that each accompanies the other so that the seed of the gospel might be planted and a harvest can be gathered.

---

64. Scarborough, *With Christ,* 175.

65. Scarborough, *With Christ,* 175.

66. Scarborough, *With Christ,* 175.

67. Scarborough, *With Christ,* 177.

68. Scarborough, *With Christ,* 173–74.

69. Scarborough, *Products of Pentecost,* 73.

70. Scarborough, *Products of Pentecost,* 73.

71. Scarborough, *Products of Pentecost,* 73–74.

The Work of Revivals

One aspect of Scarborough's work allowed for him to broadcast the gospel and to promote the seminary's evangelism program through revival meetings. The entire student body also was trained by Scarborough in the art of leading revival meetings in their second year of coursework at Southwestern Baptist Theological Seminary as a part of the rigorous curriculum.[72] He taught that "God did not mean for Pentecost to be the big end of evangelism: he meant it to be the beginning end and to enjoy an ever enlarging expansion."[73]

While serving on an evangelism committee appointed by the newly formed Co-operative Program, he composed a plan to hold summer revival meetings and sent it to denominational leaders. "It is hoped by the committee appointed by this Co-operative Program Commission on Evangelism that our pastors and denominational workers throughout the whole southland will give themselves to a great soul-winning campaign this summer."[74]

In the proposal, Scarborough outlined methods for planning revival meetings, including in rural communities, suburbs, and cities across the South. He fostered the use of young preachers from the Baptist schools and seminaries. "Assistance can be secured in these meetings by calling on the young preachers in our seminaries and Baptist schools. Many of them, fresh from these institutions, with the fires of evangelism burning in their hearts can be of great assistance to these churches."[75]

During each revival meeting, Scarborough suggested that a day be given to the denomination in order to give reports on the workings of the SBC and to preach on some topic in SBC life. Again, characteristic of his seminary presidency and life, he ties at least one day of the revival meeting to focus on education of Christ's kingdom work within the SBC.

> There ought, some time during this denominational day, to be a discussion of tithing; and it would be a fine time for the pastor to organize the church, and, if he has not already done it, put on the cooperative budget for the support of the denominational [? darkened word]. Of course in all this program prayer, organized, [? darkened word] constant prayer and the plain preaching of

72. Naylor, "Southwestern and Evangelism," 90.
73. Scarborough, *Products of Pentecost,* 71.
74. Scarborough, "Summer Evangelism."
75. Scarborough, "Summer Evangelism."

the old gospel must [? darkened word; could be "have a"] pre-eminent and prominent place.[76]

Scarborough firmly believed that all revival meetings must be well-organized and that revival does not just happen. Successful revival meetings are cogent, bathed in constant prayer, and the Word of God must be preached.

Southwestern Baptist Theological Seminary has been consecrated from its start. As of 2020, the seminary and the "Chair of Fire" are now 112 years old. Evangelism and Southwestern Baptist Theological Seminary are synonymous in theological education in most respects. God has now blessed nine evangelistically noted men to occupy this valuable chair in a needed field of study. Nine occupants have sat in Scarborough's chair during the past seventy-eight years. The occupants are L. R. Scarborough, E. D. Head, C. E. Autrey, Kenneth Chafin, Roy J. Fish, James Eaves, Malcolm McDow, L. Paige Patterson, and Matt Queen. God has richly used each of these men at strategic moments in the life of Southwestern Baptist Theological Seminary, associational, state, institutional, and national levels within the Convention.

L. R. Scarborough was a man whom God chose to teach evangelism and to unite the SBC in cooperation, an instrumental kingdom worker doing good, and always rising to the aid of his beloved Convention. Scarborough sought to make his evangelism students sincere with the gospel, but capable of thinking through theological doctrines and philosophies. Scarborough was distinctively a Southern Baptist, an identity that defined his presidency. After becoming president of the seminary, Scarborough looked for creative methods of cooperation between the local church and the Department of Evangelism at Southwestern Baptist Theological Seminary. "We cannot evangelize the world without preachers and evangelists. We are dependent upon the soul-saving spirit in the churches for the calling and the calling out of these evangels."[77] Carson explained that this cooperative agenda to unite Southwestern Baptist Theological Seminary with the Convention and its local churches is a part of the New Denominationalism or the "brand loyalty" among Southern Baptist entities. He encouraged loyalty from both the seminary and the denomination.[78]

---

76. Scarborough, "Summer Evangelism."

77. Scarborough, "Evangelism in Baptist Schools."

78. Carson, *Calling Out*, 74.

In an article written for *The Baptist Standard* on January 19, 1925, Scarborough pleaded with the leaders of the local churches to love Southwestern Baptist Theological Seminary and to trust the theological education being imparted to their sons and daughters.

> Southern Baptists can send us their sons and daughters, their preacher sons for ministers of the gospel; their laymen sons for teachers, singers, secretaries, and leaders in many lines; their daughters to be trained for missionaries, teaching and singing places, for pastors' wives, and for other church and kingdom work.[79]

He also begged the local churches to create further opportunities for the Southwestern Baptist Theological Seminarians to serve in their churches.[80] Southwestern Baptist Theological Seminary also pioneered in the areas of coeducation: from as early as 1908 the seminary has admitted women for ministry training.[81] During the days of the Seventy-Five Million Campaign, Scarborough encouraged a Convention-wide month of enlistment to ministry. "October 24 in all the Baptist schools and October 26 in the Baptist churches were set apart as days for calling out the called, the seeking of new recruits for the ministry, for mission work, and other phases of special service in the Master's Kingdom."[82] The campaign would cause an outpouring of thousands of Southern Baptist to surrender to ministry.[83] Scarborough had been the chief recruiter as the field secretary for the Southwestern Baptist Theological Seminary since the beginning, so setting the Convention on a new course to call out the "called ones" was a natural action.[84]

From the wild western frontier of West Texas to the classrooms of Fort Worth Hall on the campus of Southwestern Baptist Theological Seminary to the platform of the SBC, Scarborough used his zeal for evangelism to unite the Southern Baptist Convention. Scarborough used the "Chair of Fire" to place evangelism at the forefront of theological education at Southwestern Baptist Theological Seminary. It was not only

79. Scarborough, "What the Seminary Can Do."

80. Scarborough, "What the Seminary Can Do."

81. Barnes, *Southern Baptist Convention*, 206.

82. Scarborough, *Marvels*, 45.

83. Scarborough, *Marvels*, 231.

84. Carroll, "Appointment to SWBTS Faculty."

taught in his classes, but every other course also made some evangelistic application to theological education.

Scarborough as Educator

L. R. Scarborough was an educator. In his early years, he had learned the value of a good Christian education, attributing his theological education to the teaching he received sitting under Carroll during his years at Baylor University.[85] A part of his thirty-four-year role as the "Chair of Fire" was to advocate for soul-winning in education at Southwestern Baptist Theological Seminary and in the Convention, too. Scarborough believed that a role of the Baptist schools and theological seminaries was to better the man of God who would one day lead the local church or follow a call to Christian ministry in the field.[86]

Scarborough taught three main courses within the Department of Evangelism at Southwestern Seminary. The first course he taught was Personal Evangelism.[87] This course walked students through the Scriptures as they learned how to evangelize. The second course was a practical evangelism course in which the soul-winners would be required to get involved in revival meetings, evangelistic conferences, and evangelistic preaching.[88] The third course was the study of how Jesus won men.[89] This third course in particular is the precursor to Roy Fish's "Jesus and Personal Evangelism" course that was taught at Southwestern Baptist Theological Seminary. The classroom notes from these courses would eventually be published as the first textbooks in the discipline of evangelism within the realm of theological education.

Scarborough was always concerned about how evangelism methods and strategies learned in the classroom affected these future leaders of the local churches and the denomination. He was mindful of the biblical mandate given by the Apostle Paul in 2 Timothy 2:2 (NASB): "The things which you have heard from me in the presence of many witnesses, entrust these to faithful men who will be able to teach others also."[90] He

---

85. Dana, *Scarborough*, 42–43.

86. Scarborough, "Evangelism in Baptist Schools."

87. Naylor, "Southwestern and Evangelism," 90.

88. Naylor, "Southwestern and Evangelism," 90.

89. Naylor, "Southwestern and Evangelism," 90.

90. 2 Tim 2:2.

was concerned about the quality of the men entrusted with the knowledge of the Word of God and the acquired skills of evangelism. In his presidential inaugural address titled "The Primal Test of Theological Education," Scarborough provides the following five spiritual marks that he believes "theological education should place on the character and life of our rising ministry."[91] The spiritual marks are: 1. The True Stamp of Character; 2. Spirituality; 3. Scholarship; 4. Doctrinal Conviction; and 5. Denominational Sympathy and Cooperation.[92] In other words, theological education should mark the life of its students with these five qualities and should significantly impact the chosen ministry field and their leadership skills in the place of service to the Lord.

Education in Soul-Winning

In general, theological education is a most valuable asset to a man of God. "It is not maintained in this discussion that untrained preachers cannot win the lost to Christ, but it is maintained that the right sort of education and training greatly strengthens the soul-winning powers of preachers and evangelists."[93] Scarborough made certain that Southwestern Baptist Theological Seminary was poised to educate Southern Baptist preachers in evangelism. The curriculum at Southwestern Baptist Theological Seminary required two years of evangelism coursework for every student.[94]

> The entire method, doctrine, teachings, spirit, and power of evangelism in the New Testament, following Christ and Paul and the early churches through two years of study, are set out, and practical demonstrations of soul-winning are required on the part of the students.[95]

Scarborough understood Carroll's urgency to use the theological seminary to equip men and women in evangelism training fully, to strengthen the local churches of the SBC and to grow their numbers.[96] With personal conviction that the evangelist is the key minister for the

91. Scarborough, *Modern School*, 174.
92. Scarborough, *Modern School*, 174–85.
93. Scarborough, "Evangelism in Baptist Schools."
94. Muncy, *History of Evangelism*, 161.
95. Nettles, "Public Figure," 35.
96. Scarborough, *Modern School*, 57–58.

lost world, apart from a "Damascus Road" experience like that of the Apostle Paul, Scarborough writes,

> Denominational leaders, secretaries, teachers, missionaries, and song leaders are great assets. But after all values are properly placed on these and worthy praise heaped on them, it yet remains that preacher-prophets are God's pivotal men. This old sinning world needs more of them in every section of the world's spiritual needs, a better quality of them, better prepared, more thoroughly devoted to the high calling of gospel preaching. The lost world will not be saved from sin's deepest guilt and yawning destiny to social reformers, defenders of science, philosophic discussions, but only by the glorious preaching of the everlasting gospel of a crucified, risen, returning Christ.[97]

Scarborough attempted to multiply himself through the evangelism teaching ministry of Southwestern Baptist Theological Seminary.

CONCLUSIONS

Scarborough had the divine hand of God upon his life and ministry. He modeled in his educational capacities the desired approaches to soul-winning, discipleship, and print. He loved lost people and sincerely gave himself to educating and multiplying his passion and evangelistic zeal in others. Scarborough taught so that the gospel of Jesus Christ would reach many lost people.

Scarborough lived a life of great purpose and drive. He preached and shepherded the seminary through the Great Depression. Scarborough educated and proliferated evangelism in theological seminaries through his teaching, fundraising, denominational leadership, publishing, and preaching ministries. He completed B. H. Carroll's dream of establishing a world-renowned Baptist seminary that is distinctly loyal to the Southern Baptist Convention.

The next chapter continues with an exploration of the "Chair of Fire's" evolution as new occupants take their seat as professor of evangelism in the L. R. Scarborough Chair of Evangelism, "Chair of Fire." Each subsequent chair brings new zeal and fervor for the art of evangelism, while promoting the advancement of Southern Baptist evangelism throughout the Southwestern Baptist Theological Seminary and the denomination by

97. Nettles, "Public Figure," 37–38.

following the tenets established by Carroll and exemplified by the fiery soul-winning passion of Scarborough. Each of the eight subsequent occupants have been held in high esteem due to the legacy of the chair.

3

The Subsequent Occupants

The "Chair of Fire" stands as a testament to Carroll's conviction of the unique and separate office of *evangelist* and to his desire to see the word preached that some might be saved. In chapter 3, the history and expansion of the "Chair of Fire's" reach is developed through detailed consideration of the evangelistic men who followed in the footsteps of L. R. Scarborough's noble task of instructing every ministerial student at Southwestern Baptist Theological Seminary in the applied theology of evangelism. These professors of evangelism wrote the textbooks, shaped the curricula to meet ever-changing needs, modeled evangelistic revival preaching, developed theological courses on Great Awakenings and revivals, promoted personal soul-winning, provided denominational leadership, and further raised the legacy of the chair.

E. D. HEAD (1942 TO 1950)

E. D. Head, a native of Sparta, Louisiana, was sought out by a seminary board of trustees interested in finding "a man who could carry on not only as president but as a teacher in the great 'Chair of Fire.'"[1] Head followed Scarborough in 1942 as both president and "Chair of Fire." He was called away from his pastorate at the First Baptist Church of Houston, Texas, to serve as the third president of Southwestern Baptist Theological Seminary and the second occupant of the "Chair of Fire." Prior to his call

---

1. White, "Evangelism Class," 3.

to the seminary, Head served as an associate professor in the School of Religion at Baylor University, a position that he accepted in 1931.[2]

Head earned both his Master of Theology and Doctorate of Theology from Southwestern Baptist Theological Seminary.[3] "H. E. Dana was the supervisor for his doctoral dissertation, which was written in the area of New Testament in the study of the elephante [*sic*] papyri discovered in Egypt."[4] Head was highly regarded as a scholar and Baptist preacher. Joe Morrow, who published a dissertation titled "The Life and Ministry of Eldred Douglas Head," records that Head earned a bachelor's, two masters' degrees, and a doctorate degree with high marks, teaching at Waco University while pastoring a local church.[5]

> B. H. Carroll was respected for being a self-educated scholar in his own right. L. R. Scarborough was a Phi Beta Kappa law graduate of Yale University and was also considered a scholar in his own right. However, E. D. Head was the first president of Southwestern to have completed the rigors of a formal seminary training.[6]

For the first eight years, he taught evangelism "carrying on in the traditional 'Chair of Fire' established by his predecessor, Dr. L. R. Scarborough."[7] Head also authored four books, including a revision of Scarborough's first evangelism textbook, *With Christ after the Lost*, in 1952.

Head's Work as Professor of Evangelism

Head was a student of Scarborough's while a student at Southwestern Baptist Theological Seminary. "Traditionally, the subject of evangelism in the seminary curriculum was taught by the president," and so Head was set to continue the practice established by Scarborough.[8] *With Christ after the Lost* and *Endued To Win*, both published works of Scarborough were used to create and outline Head's evangelism classes.[9] Remaining

---

2. Morrow, "Eldred Douglas Head," 16.
3. Morrow, "Eldred Douglas Head," 16.
4. Morrow, "Eldred Douglas Head," 17.
5. Morrow, "Eldred Douglas Head," 17.
6. Morrow, "Eldred Douglas Head," 62.
7. "Funeral Services," 2.
8. Morrow, "Eldred Douglas Head," 71.
9. Morrow, "Eldred Douglas Head," 71,

faithful to the design precepts of the "Chair of Fire," "E. D. Head also continued in the tradition of Carroll and Scarborough by teaching the importance of the Holy Spirit in all aspects of the work of evangelism."[10]

Head's evangelism class was a rigorous course of study at Southwestern Baptist Theological Seminary. "The course in evangelism then was largely consisted of learning—memorizing scripture and how to use scripture texts in personal witness. That was the focus of the course."[11] Head, in an interview for *Southwestern News,* stated, "This class boils down to this: A saved soul seeks out an unsaved soul and tells that unsaved soul what Jesus has done for him."[12] He required students to practice personal evangelism throughout each semester, but his courses also required fifteen hundred pages of reading.[13]

For six years Head would teach evangelism and serve the seminary as its president. "On March 10, 1948, President Head, who had been teaching evangelism since September 1942, requested the trustees to secure a professor for this course since his numerous administrative duties made it difficult for him to continue teaching it."[14] The growth of the seminary student body and faculty were the main causes for this shift in his roles at the seminary. A *Southwestern News* article stated, "During his eleven-year administration seminary enrollment grew from 760 to over 2000; faculty members from twenty-seven to forty-one."[15]

C. E. AUTREY (1955 TO 1960)

Born September 17, 1904, in Marion County, Mississippi, to a farmer and his wife, Elijah Adam and Rosa Lee Yates Autrey, C. E. Autrey would become the older of two boys from this marriage. At age six, his mother would pass away from tuberculosis and he and his younger brother, Ernest Lindsey Autrey would be placed in the home of his father's sister, Jenny Smith, until his father remarried a few years later.[16] "In the midst of an unstable environment that included his mother's death and poor

---

10. Morrow, "Eldred Douglas Head," 72.

11. Kiesling, "Investigation," 210.

12. White, "Evangelism Class," 3.

13. White, "Evangelism Class," 3.

14. Baker, *Tell the Generations,* 310–11.

15. "Funeral Services," 2.

16. Leavell, "Autrey's Concepts of Evangelism," 47–48.

economic conditions, E. A. Autrey was a positive, abiding influence in C. E. Autrey's life."[17]

Autrey's life was influenced for Christ by his father's reading the Bible aloud to him, and also by a Baptist preacher from Autrey's youth.[18] Shortly after his family had relocated to Georgetown, Louisiana, the Autrey family began attending Zion Baptist Church. The young pastor was a student from Louisiana College. He gave regular invitations to receive Jesus and took a particular interest in the young people of his church. "At the age of fourteen, primarily through the witness of his father and a Baptist pastor, C. E. Autrey committed his life to Jesus Christ as his personal Savior and requested church membership."[19]

Autrey married his high school sweetheart, May Bradford, following graduation. While working at a box factory to support his family, he began to sense a call to ministry. At first, he resisted the call and began attending both Methodist and Baptist services.

> Finally, I just decided I had to do something. So I went out in the woods, across the road from the farm, and started praying. I was asking the Lord to come into my life, to purify, and to give me the power to do what I ought to do and to see what I should do. I got to praying and the Spirit came down on me.[20]

Following the surrender to ministry, Autrey was licensed to the gospel ministry and began to preach regularly at any opportunity. Autrey's grandson, J. Denny Autrey, retells a story:

> And he [C. E. Autrey] told me [J. Denny Autrey] the story of traveling on train to hear Dr. Scarborough preach in a revival setting. And he said after he heard him preach—I think it was, I think 1923—he said God put a fire in his heart like Dr. Scarborough's for evangelism and for just sharing the gospel, no matter what it took. And he realized then that he needed to pursue his education.[21]

From 1926–34, Autrey pursued his formal education. He received his Bachelor of Arts degree from Louisiana College, his Master of Theology degree from the Baptist Bible Institute, and his Doctor of Theology in

17. Leavell, "Autrey's Concepts of Evangelism," 49.

18. Leavell, "Autrey's Concepts of Evangelism," 50.

19. Leavell, "Autrey's Concepts of Evangelism," 51.

20. Leavell, "Autrey's Concepts of Evangelism," 54–55.

21. Autrey, interview with the author, Appendix 1.

Greek New Testament, studying under Elmer Haight, from New Orleans Baptist Theological Seminary.[22] During this time of formal education, Autrey served as a local church pastor at Tullos Baptist Church in Tullos, Louisiana.

The inauguration of Autrey into the Chair of Evangelism created hope and vision for the future of Southwestern Baptist Theological Seminary's Department of Evangelism. "He [Autrey] met Dr. Williams through his work in Louisiana, as a State Evangelism Exec."[23] President Williams's heartbeat was consistent with the evangelistic fervor of the previous three presidents. Williams sought to increase the emphasis in evangelism at Southwestern Baptist Theological Seminary through the support of seminary trustees to expand the faculty and administration. "On May 20, 1955, C. E. Autrey was named professor of evangelism."[24] He was the first full-time professor of evangelism at Southwestern Baptist Theological Seminary to hold the post as the "Chair of Fire."[25]

Autrey revived the Department of Evangelism by beginning fresh work in personal evangelism and discipleship courses. He brought into the classroom a spirit of cooperation and a desire to work with and through the local churches surrounding the seminary. Alongside personal evangelism, an emphasis on revival preaching returned under his tutelage.[26] "It is the plan of Dr. Autrey to ask the pastors in and near Fort Worth to submit to him the names of lost persons in their communities. The students will select from such lists those they wish to work with."[27] He occupied the "Chair of Fire" four years before resigning to head the Evangelism Department of the HMB in January 1960. "Autrey Resigns 'Chair of Fire,'" read the headline in *Southwestern News* announcing his departure from Southwestern Baptist Theological Seminary in December 1959.[28]

22. Leavell, "Autrey's Concepts of Evangelism," 57–58.

23. Autrey, interview with the author, Appendix 1.

24. Baker, *Tell the Generations*, 355.

25. Autrey, interview with the author, Appendix 1.

26. "'Chair of Fire' Revived," 8.

27. "'Chair of Fire' Revived," 8.

28. "Autrey Resigns," 3.

Autrey's Concept of Church Evangelism

The HMB lost an Associate Director within the Evangelism Department when Autrey accepted the teaching post at Southwestern Baptist Theological Seminary. Evangelism of the local church was always on his mind and heart. "In his present position at Southwestern Baptist Theological Seminary, he is influencing for good many young men going out into the ministry."[29] Autrey sought to better train his seminary students to evangelize, which by reason of logic would better equip the local churches of their assignments to do the work of evangelism within their churches.

Basic Evangelism, Autrey's first book, came from a burden to improve the local church in evangelism. Autrey writes, "The church is a living body, and a living body must renew its life or die."[30] Evangelism, when done properly, will result in new thriving local church membership. Autrey believed, "Evangelism is essential to growth. God has no other plan for the growth of his churches and the expansion of Christianity."[31] All evangelism requires follow-up and discipleship.

> It is common knowledge that almost ninety-five percent of our members never win anyone outside the church to Christ. This is a tragedy and it is not the fault of the average church member. The failure lies in the church. It has failed to teach and direct the new convert to the main task of every believer.[32]

The aim of *Basic Evangelism* was to inspire the local church to be more evangelistic, to be a living New Testament church. Autrey did not have a poor opinion of Christians or the local church: rather, he desired to better equip both members and local churches to saturate the communities with the gospel of Jesus Christ. In chapter 9, Autrey discusses the evangelistic invitation. He believed whole-heartedly that the focus of a worship service is the invitation. He taught that two invitations should be given: "the invitation to the Christians, and the invitation to the unsaved."[33] Autrey provides further keen insights into the "best methods" of conducting the evangelistic invitation. He completes the work with a thought on personal follow-up as the immediate next step to evangelism.

29. Autrey, *Basic Evangelism.*

30. Autrey, *Basic Evangelism,* 58.

31. Autrey, *Basic Evangelism,* 54.

32. Autrey, *Basic Evangelism,* 142.

33. Autrey, *Basic Evangelism,* 134.

Autrey's Concept of Personal Evangelism

Autrey came into the classroom with similar biblical viewpoints to Scarborough's about soul-winning. In his book on personal evangelism, *You Can Win Souls*, Autrey outlines five basic qualifications of a soul-winner that prove to be valuable as you practice personal evangelism. The basic qualifications are:

1. The soul-winner must be converted.

2. The soul-winner's life must be above reproach.

3. A soul-winner must be a vessel unto honor.

4. The soul-winner must possess a passion for the lost.

5. The soul-winner needs the ability that only the Holy Spirit can provide.[34]

Autrey understood that God has set a high and holy standard in Scripture for his people. Soul-winning requires personal sacrifices in order to be effective witnesses for Jesus Christ. His examples for personal evangelism came from Jesus Christ himself. "Autrey's concepts of personal evangelism developed from his understanding of Scripture. In the Bible, Jesus Christ set an example of leading individuals to a saving knowledge of himself."[35]

In chapter 5 of *You Can Win Souls*, Autrey deals with the approach and the appeal of personal evangelism. "Jesus began at a point of interest."[36] By this statement, Autrey is referring to the example of Jesus as the Master Personal Evangelist. Jesus' approach always fit the context of the situation in which he and the person shared a gospel conversation. Jesus' approach started at the point of their understanding of his message.

Autrey also describes: "Christ was not detoured. The soul-winner must not be sidetracked."[37] The point of the appeal was to clearly explain to a lost person how to know God personally. "The one prime question which must be answered is the relation of the sinner to God."[38] Autrey's appeal was direct. He argued that knowing your audience and how best

---

34. Autrey, *You Can Win Souls*, 11–22.

35. Leavell, "Autrey's Concepts of Evangelism," 70.

36. Autrey, *You Can Win Souls*, 65.

37. Autrey, *You Can Win Souls*, 70.

38. Autrey, *You Can Win Souls*, 70.

to convey the gospel, with Christ, was key to a successful presentation. In a pamphlet which Autrey co-authored with Jack Stanton and Kenneth Chafin in 1968 for the HMB titled *We Are Witnesses*, Autrey shrinks the great concepts of his personal evangelism text into a few pages for a much larger audience. Autrey states, "The operation of winning a soul to Christ may be broken down into four steps for clarification. They are: the approach, instructions, appeal, and follow-up."[39]

The remainder of this work demonstrates his pastoral nature. Autrey guides the reader through several "test case" scenarios: for example, Chapter 9: *How to Win the Catholics,* or Chapter 10: *How to Win the Spiritists,* with the singular desire to motivate the Christians to overcome difficulties with fear and nervousness during soul-winning.[40] The book draws inspiration in material from L. R. Scarborough's work, *With Christ after the Lost,* which also instructs the reader how to share Christ with people of other faiths.[41]

KENNETH CHAFIN (1959 TO 1965)

Kenneth Leon Chafin was born on November 18, 1926, in Cherokee County, Oklahoma.[42] "He earned his divinity degrees from Southwestern, including a Doctor of Theology, and was a graduate of the University of New Mexico."[43] Chafin served as a pastor, professor, and denominational worker.

Chafin As Professor

Chafin was installed into the "Chair of Fire" at Southwestern Baptist Theological Seminary upon Autrey's resignation from the seminary in 1959.[44] Chafin joined the evangelism faculty while Autrey still occupied the "Chair of Fire." Malcolm McDow has stated,

---

39. Stanton, Autrey, and Chafin, *We Are Witnesses*, 16.

40. Stanton, Autrey, and Chafin, *We Are Witnesses*, 116–36. (Chapter titles selected at random for illustrative purposes only.)

41. Scarborough, *With Christ.*

42. "Leukemia," 30.

43. "Leukemia," 30.

44. Baker, *Tell the Generations*, 397.

> When Ken Chafin came on the faculty, the fire of Autrey domi-
> nated. But that when Autrey went to the omission [*sic*] board
> that left Chafin, uh, in as a major evangelism professor. And the
> fire and evangelism begin to wane under Chafin. And you did
> not have the prominence of evangelism at Southwestern under
> Chafin that you had under Autrey.[45]

While little is written about Chafin's tenure in the "Chair of Fire," it is recorded in Robert Baker's *Tell the Generations Following* that during Chafin's brief stint as the elected occupant of the "Chair of Fire," the board of trustees strengthened the financial endowment for the chair. The initial endowment was established through profits gained from the sale of a history book about the first thirty years of Southwestern Baptist Theological Seminary, written by L. R. Scarborough and titled *A Modern School of the Prophets*.[46] "The chair of evangelism was further financially endowed by a gift of William and Bessie Fleming on February 26, 1957."[47]

In an oral interview with L. Paige Patterson, the eighth occupant of the "Chair of Fire," Brandon Kiesling documented the following remarks about Chafin: "He was probably the most gifted of all of us that have been in the chair. He was a gifted communicator. He was a very fine thinker and had read widely, far more than most people do outside of their field, and he had a way of making things happen."[48] Chafin authored six books in the field of preaching and evangelism.[49]

Chafin would depart Southwestern Baptist Theological Seminary in 1965 to join the faculty at Southern Baptist Theological Seminary and to be elected as the inaugural occupant of the Billy Graham Chair of Evangelism. In his book *History of Evangelism: Three Hundred Years of Evangelism in Germany, Great Britain, and the United States of America*, Paulus Scharpff stated, "In 1965 Southern Baptist Theological Seminary in Louisville, Kentucky, established the Billy Graham Chair of Evangelism. Kenneth Chafin, who had been head of the Department of Evangelism

---

45. Dickard, "Man between the Times," Appendix 4.

46. Scarborough, *Modern School*, frontmatter.

47. Scarborough, *Modern School*, 356.

48 Kiesling, "Investigation," Appendix 6

49. Chafin books in publication order: *Help! I'm A Layman* (1972); *The Reluctant Witness* (1975); *Tell All the Little Children* (1976); *Is There a Family in the House?: Personal Strategies for Strengthening Your Marriage and Family Life* (1979); *The Communicator's Commentary: 1, 2 Corinthians* (1985); *The Communicator's Commentary: 1, 2 Samuel, Old Testament* (1989); and *A Rhythm for My Life* (2003).

at Southwestern Baptist Theological Seminary, is the first to occupy this chair."[50] Chafin later returned as a seminary trustee from 1975 to 1980.[51]

Chafin's Denominational Service

More notably, Chafin would later become a leader for the moderate and theologically liberal sect within the Southern Baptist Convention during the Convention's conservative resurgence. Gregory Wills in his updated history book titled *Southern Baptist Seminary 1859–2009* states,

> With Cecil Sherman, he tried to mobilize moderate leaders to oppose the conservatives. He was responsible for some of the small number of moderate victories in the early years of the controversy. In 1982 and 1983, for example, he successfully moved the Southern Baptist Convention to replace several fundamentalist nominees to trustee boards with moderates.[52]

Chafin appeared on *The Phil Donahue Show* in June of 1985, where he openly denied that salvation is found in Jesus Christ alone. On the television talk show,

> Chafin, like some other moderates, however, believed that Jesus would save good-hearted persons with or without conscious faith in Jesus Christ. Chafin said: "Jesus said to love the Lord God and to love your neighbor as yourself, and that sums it all up." He said that his friend, a retired rabbi, who evidently rejected faith in Christ, would be in heaven, "probably because of what God has done in Christ."[53]

In his obituary he is remembered for his founding contributions and convictions that led him to assist in the creation of the Cooperative Baptist Fellowship (CBF): "Chafin was among the founders of the Cooperative Baptist Fellowship, a Baptist organization opposed to the SBC leadership elected by the Convention since 1979."[54]

Roy Fish would be appointed to the "Chair of Fire" following Chafin's resignation and departure to Southern Baptist Theological Seminary in

---

50. Scharpff, *History of Evangelism*, 329.

51. Baker, *Tell the Generations*, 495.

52. Wills, *Southern Baptist Seminary*, 460.

53. Wills, *Southern Baptist Seminary*, 460.

54. "Leukemia," 30.

1965. Chafin's zeal for evangelism was not hot-hearted like his predecessors in the "Chair of Fire." Fish became the longest occupant of the "Chair of Fire," and professor of evangelism at Southwestern Baptist Theological Seminary. During Fish's tenure, he would revitalize the effectiveness of the chair and the evangelistic spirit of the seminary. "Naylor brought on Fish and it really resurrected the Evangelism Department. Because it was dead with Chafin," stated Malcolm McDow in an oral interview with Brandon Kiesling.[55]

ADMINISTRATIVE CHANGES TO THE "CHAIR OF FIRE"

Between the years 1982 to 1990, the Seminary Board of Trustees decreed that all academic chairs would rotate through the faculty at the direction of then-president Russell Dilday Jr. and the presiding dean of each school, to provide diversity of ideas and administrative refreshment for the programs and educational processes within each school. The 1980s provided three different evangelism faculty members the distinct opportunity to share the "Chair of Fire." Unfortunately, adequate records were not kept of the chair's eight-year chairman rotation, so defining who occupied the chair during which years is difficult. In 1980, the Board of Trustees at Southwestern Baptist Theological Seminary approved a dramatic adjustment in the organizational structure for all schools.

> Division chairmen and/or department chairmen are appointed by the president on the recommendation of the vice president for academic affairs and provost and the dean of the school. The chairmanship is for a rotating term. The chairman is to be the convening and presiding officer for that division or department in matters of divisional or department decision.[56]

During this time in the chair's history, it was occupied by Roy Fish, James Eaves, and Malcolm McDow in rotation.

Though dates of their occupancy were not well recorded, their leadership did diversify the impact of the "Chair of Fire." Each of these men provided different emphasis on evangelism and service as the "Chair of Fire" during his time of appointment. Dilday and the trustees intended for this new approach in organizational structure to "encourage both

---

55. Kiesling, "Investigation," 234.
56. Minutes of the Board, March 18–19, 1980, 10.

widespread leadership participation and functional efficiency."[57] The rotation of chairmanship would redistribute creative controls and power over each department, creating an environment of fresh ideas and zeal within each school.

ROY J. FISH (1965 TO 2006)

Roy Jason Fish was born on February 7, 1930, in Star City, Arkansas, to Effie and Curtis Wayne Fish.[58] In 1938, the Fish family relocated to Abilene, Texas, where Curtis Fish could provide a better life for his wife and three children. Roy Fish "blossomed in Abilene, making top grades in elementary school. By the fifth grade, he was among the top three in the class declamation contest—the stirring of his love for language and rhetoric."[59] Fish would attend and graduate from Abilene High School.

In 1947, Fish began college at McMurry College in Abilene. One year later he attended the University of Arkansas and ran track. While away at college, Fish sought the Lord. He attended church and approached the ministers seeking the way of salvation, only to be turned away empty-handed, without answers.

> On Wednesday of that week in July 1949, he walked outside his home, feeling a mighty weight on his shoulders. As he stood on the front porch at noon, the words of the invitation hymn the church had sung on Sunday came to him: "Only trust him, only trust him, / only trust him now. / He will save you, he will save you, / he will save you now." The "him" in the verse was Jesus; this he knew. For the first time he understood that Jesus was the way to God. He told Jesus at that moment, "I trust you as Savior and will trust you to take me to heaven. The huge burden rolled away from his shoulders, and the nineteen-year-old knew in his spirit that he had come to know God.[60]

---

57. Minutes of the Board, June 11, 1980, 10.

58. Fish, "Profile," 264.

59. Fish, "Profile," 264.

60. Fish, "Profile," 267.

Roy Fish as Educator

Roy Fish returned to his seminary alma mater in Fort Worth, Texas, in 1965 from First Baptist Church in Fairborn, Ohio, to join the faculty as professor of evangelism. He had pastored five churches. Fish earned a Bachelor of Arts in 1952 from the University of Arkansas, a Bachelor of Divinity in 1957 and a Doctor of Theology in 1963 from Southwestern Baptist Theological Seminary.[61] Fish taught evangelism to students from a heart of compassion for lost people.

> Fish claims his motivation for evangelism is threefold. "Evangelism is done first to the glory of God; God deeply yearns for people to be saved," he said. "Secondly, people around us have needs. We live in a world of hurting people, and I know the basic answer to those hurts is a saving faith, a relationship with Jesus," he added. "Thirdly, my own life. I'm greatly enriched when I share the Gospel. My own life is fulfilled in a way it's not fulfilled otherwise."[62]

Fish was known throughout the SBC for his evangelistic zeal and promoted personal evangelism, evangelistic preaching, and revival meetings. In an oral interview by Brandon Kiesling with one of Fish's former professors, James Leo Garrett states, "Roy had the biggest influence in the denomination, as a public speaker, as a man of influence in Southern Baptist life, and for a brief time as interim, as you know, president of the Home Mission Board, now North American Mission Board."[63] Fish served in several different administrative capacities during his tenure at Southwestern Baptist Theological Seminary. The administration introduced an era of academic chair rotations. He occupied two different academic chairs on a rotational basis of service during this time.

> Roy J. Fish was named to the inaugural George W. Truett Chair of Ministry. The chair, a one-year responsibility for the Pioneer Penetration Spring Revival Program. Fish was named to the L. R. Scarborough Chair of Evangelism ("Chair of Fire") which was officially approved by the board of trustees in 1982.[64]

---

61. "Begin Teaching," 2.
62. Hooker, "Writers Honor," 13.
63. Kiesling, "Investigation," 211.
64. Dilday, *President's Report*, 3.

The Pioneer Penetration Spring Revival Program was managed by Kenneth Chafin, but Fish fine-tuned it. In the fall of 2019 the program was rebranded as the Reach This Nation (RTN); these revival meeting began in 1959, while Fish was a student.[65] Reach This Nation annually sends seminarians to all fifty states to preach the gospel of Jesus Christ in Southern Baptist churches during spring break each year. These revival meetings provide young, inexperienced preachers with opportunities to preach and provide smaller churches with limited budgets the opportunities to hold a series of revival meetings.

In 1982, the trustees officially changed the name of the "Chair of Fire," and in that same meeting Roy Fish was reappointed to the chair for that following academic year. The minutes from the October 1982 trustee meeting state,

> Recommendation: That the legendary "Chair of Fire" be designated as THE L. R. SCARBOROUGH CHAIR OF EVANGELISM ("Chair of Fire"). Motion was seconded by Melvin Faulkner and unanimously carried . . . That the trustees approve the establishing of the L. R. Scarborough Chair of Evangelism ("Chair of Fire") and that Roy Fish be appointed to this chair for the academic year 1982–83.[66]

It would not be until a decade later that Fish would be permanently appointed to the "Chair of Fire," a position that he alone would occupy until his retirement in 2006. McDow recalls, "I believe it was in the early nineties. We did a revision and restructure of [sic] Evangelism Department. And the 'Chair of Fire' went to Roy Fish and I got the George W. Truett Chair of Ministry."[67]

At the time of his retirement, Fish celebrated serving Southwestern Baptist Theological Seminary for forty-one years, thirty-three of those years as the "Chair of Fire." From 1982–90, Fish occupied the chair on a rotation and his specific years of occupancy are not well recorded. An article in *Southwestern News* stated, "Southwestern Seminary trustees honored Fish on April 5, 2005, by naming the seminary's school of

65. The Spring Break Revival Program at Southwestern Baptist Theological Seminary began in 1959 under C. E. Autrey and became known as Pioneer Penetration Mission Thrusts in 1980 under Roy Fish. The evangelism program was renamed Revive This Nation in 2008 under L. Paige Patterson, and is now called Reach This Nation as of fall 2019.

66. Minutes of the Board of Trustees, October 19–20, 1982, 7, 11.

67. Kiesling, "Investigation," 228.

evangelism and missions after him."[68] Fish continued to teach evangelism courses as distinguished professor of evangelism emeritus at Southwestern Baptist Theological Seminary until his death on September 10, 2012.

JAMES EAVES (1973 TO 90)

James Franklin Eaves was born October 29, 1925, in Gibson, Tennessee, to parents Dudley and Ladie Eaves. He was reared in both Edinburg, Texas, and Jackson, Tennessee. Eaves was one of four children.[69] Eaves served his country during both World War II and the Korean War as a pilot and officer for the United States Air Force.[70] "Eaves (ThD, 1962) is a graduate of Union University, Jackson, Tenn., and holds the bachelor of divinity degree from Southwestern as well as the doctor of theology."[71] He served numerous local Baptist churches in Texas, Tennessee, and New Mexico as well as serving the SBC in various denominational roles which included Director of Evangelism and Church Growth Development for the North American Mission Board (NAMB).[72]

Eaves's Seminary Service

Eaves arrived on the campus of Southwestern Baptist Theological Seminary in the fall of 1973 during what church history professor and seminary historian Robert A. Baker described as "unprecedented growth" and an "administrative restructuring."[73] Robert Naylor, president of Southwestern Baptist Theological Seminary, led the seminary to new worldwide recognition and global expansion of its ministry reach during his administration. Eaves joined Roy Fish as a professor of evangelism. "James Eaves's major, had his PhD in New Testament. And Eaves was really a scholar. And he blended academics with the pragmatic aspects of evangelism."[74] Patterson noted that Eaves was a "consistent witness."[75]

68. "Faculty Retirements: Roy Fish," 43.

69. "Obituary: James Eaves."

70. "Obituary: James Eaves."

71. "Trustees Elect Eaves and Debord," 3.

72. "Obituary: James Eaves."

73. Baker, *Tell The Generations*, 396.

74. Kiesling, "Investigation," 234.

75. Kiesling, "Investigation," 249.

Eaves had initially received an invitation and election to join the faculty of the School of Theology as associate professor of biblical backgrounds and archaeology in 1964. This offer was declined due to family health concerns.[76]

Eaves served Southwestern Baptist Theological Seminary for seventeen years beginning in 1973. In *Evangelism for a Changing World*, contributing author Steve Gaines states, "Fish and colleagues James Eaves and Malcolm McDow were catalysts in instituting a PhD major in evangelism at Southwestern Seminary."[77] He was a personal evangelist as well as an academic professor; Eaves promoted personal evangelism in his teaching. In 1979, Eaves joined colleague and fellow professor of evangelism at Southwestern Baptist Theological Seminary Oscar Thompson in a new evangelism campaign, "Witnessing with the Word."[78] *Southwestern News* reported, "The evangelistic program will enable the more than eight hundred students of personal evangelism to use the Bible in sharing their testimony and gospel witness to hundreds of lost people."[79] Alvin Reid, former professor of evangelism and occupant of the Bailey Smith Chair of Evangelism at Southeastern Baptist Theological Seminary in Wake Forest, North Carolina, recalls Eaves's passion for personal evangelism in his *Evangelism Handbook*:

> James Eaves, one of my evangelism professors at Southwestern Seminary, used to say that two barriers keep many Christians from going further in their walk with God: tithing and soul-winning. Why? They affect two things that matter so much— our comfort in material things and our reputation. Crossing these barriers requires faith, without which it is impossible to please God (Heb 11:6).[80]

Eaves retired as professor emeritus in 1990. He passed December 14, 2015, in Houston, Texas, at age ninety.

76. Minutes of the Board, November 24, 1964, 4.

77. Gaines, "Professional History," 281.

78. "Evangelism Dept."

79. "Evangelism Dept."

80. Reid, *Evangelism Handbook*, 39.

MALCOLM MCDOW (1982 TO 2005)

McDow joined the Evangelism Department as an associate professor of evangelism on May 1, 1982. Having earned degrees from Baylor University, Southwestern Baptist Theological Seminary, and New Orleans Baptist Theological Seminary, he provided a diverse prospective on practical theology. Seminary president Russell Dilday Jr. stated, "McDow's combination of church-related and state-level denominational experience in evangelism will add a complimentary dimension to our faculty."[81]

He, James Eaves, and Roy Fish would rotate the chairmanship of the Evangelism division for the next decade. "I believe it was in the early nineties. We did a revision and restructure of [sic] Evangelism Department. And the 'Chair of Fire' went to Roy Fish and I got the George W. Truett Chair of Ministry. And I occupied that until I retired."[82] The George W. Truett Chair of Ministry, established in 1976 to honor the late pastor of the First Baptist Church in Dallas, Texas, promotes "emphasis in pastoral ministry and cross-disciplines in evangelism, field education, missions and preaching. Major funding for the Truett chair was provided by A. Webb Roberts of Dallas, a member of the seminary's Advisory Council."[83] McDow served for twenty-three years in the George W. Truett Chair of Ministry, a chair now occupied by David Allen (2005–), distinguished professor of preaching at Southwestern Baptist Theological Seminary.[84]

McDow as Educator

McDow focused on the history of revivals and spiritual awakenings. In 1995, John Avant, a Southwestern Baptist Theological Seminary alumnus, invited former classmate Alvin Reid and McDow to collect and tell of their experiences of a local and regional awakening. This book is titled *Revival!: The Story of the Current Awakening in Brownwood, Ft. Worth, Wheaton, and Beyond*. This awakening began at Coggin Avenue Baptist Church of Brownwood, Texas, where John Avant served as pastor. The church reportedly experienced repentance and forgiveness and a fresh movement of the Holy Spirit, and this movement of God spread to

81. "Malcolm McDow," 3.
82. "Malcolm McDow," 228.
83. "Fish Is Truett Proff."
84. Tomlin, "Eight SWBTS Professors."

Southwestern Baptist Theological Seminary, then to Wheaton College by way of students and faculty members traveling and preaching the gospel of Jesus Christ and sharing testimonies. In 1997, McDow again collaborated and co-authored a second work with former evangelism student and then-associate professor of evangelism at Southeastern Baptist Theological Seminary Alvin Reid, titled *Firefall: How God Has Shaped History through Revivals.*

McDow contributed to training Southwestern Baptist Theological Seminary students for the spring break revival services. He lectured and authored many journal articles on the work of the revival preacher and the evangelists. In a chapter contribution to *Before Revival Begins* by Dan Crawford in 1996, McDow writes,

> Indeed, preaching in a revival meeting is more than simply an exercise that a preacher fulfills at the appointed times throughout the revival week. It is not some oratorical relic of the past that was relevant for Paul, Bernard, Luther, Whitefield, Finney, and Moody. Evangelistic preaching is God's method of proclaiming the revealed gospel in Jesus Christ to estranged, alienated, and lost members of the human race for the purpose of reconciliation to the Holy God.[85]

McDow further demonstrates his passion for active revival preaching, a characteristic of one who serves as an occupant of the "Chair of Fire." Carl Lane, one of McDow's students and former Southwestern Baptist Theological Seminary trustee, stated, "I learned from this man that the purpose of the church is evangelism, and that everything else is function. His passion became my passion!"[86] McDow's exuberance for evangelism and church growth inspired students to carry a deep love for evangelism and church growth with them into their ministries.

McDow and Fish co-labored together in the Department of Evangelism at Southwestern Baptist Theological Seminary for more than twenty years. Malcolm McDow held that his philosophy of evangelism is that "evangelism is the gospel and evangelizing is the act of sharing the gospel."[87] In separate oral interviews with Brandon Kiesling (2015) and Daniel Dickard (2017), McDow admitted that he and Fish did not

---

85. Crawford, *Before Revival Begins*, 37.

86. "Fishers of Men."

87. Kiesling, "Investigation," 227.

agree on this interpretation of evangelism, but that they had many years of beneficial faculty service together.[88]

McDow as Administrator

James Leo Garrett attributed much of the PhD major in evangelism and the creation of the School of Evangelism and Missions at Southwestern Baptist Theological Seminary named in honor of Roy J. Fish to the diligent and consistent push of Malcolm McDow.

> Malcolm McDow and I shared an office when we first came here in 1980, and I've had many associations with Malcolm. It was my privilege to work with him and Roy to establish the PhD program in evangelism. When I became the associate dean for PhD studies in 1981, I soon discovered that we had a PhD program for every department in the school of theology except for evangelism. And we worked to change that, and that involved setting up a curriculum.[89]

Former president L. Paige Patterson, under whose leadership the Roy J. Fish School of Evangelism and Missions came into existence in 2005, remarks of McDow's influence on the decision: "But, this important feature of Malcolm McDow . . . when I came here as president, he was still here, and he was the one that internally, from the faculty, put enormous pressure on the president of this institution to establish the School of Missions of [sic] Evangelism and name it for Roy Fish."[90]

L. PAIGE PATTERSON (2007 TO 2014)

Leighton Paige Patterson was born to Thomas Armour (T. A.) and Roberta Patterson on October 19, 1942. His father was a doctoral student at Southwestern Baptist Theological Seminary. Patterson spent his early years on the Fort Worth campus. At age four, his family would relocate to the First Baptist Church of Beaumont, Texas, where T. A. Patterson would serve as pastor.[91]

---

88. Dickard, "Man between the Times, 232.
89. Kiesling, "Investigation," 211.
90. Kiesling, "Investigation," 250.
91. "Celebrating 100 Years," 123.

During a revival meeting in 1951 at the First Baptist Church of Beaumont, young Paige "rushed down the aisle into his father's arms. Too emotional to speak, Patterson nodded as his father asked him if he wanted to receive Christ and be baptized."[92] Young Paige later committed his life to ministry.

He earned an undergraduate degree in Biblical Studies from Hardin-Simmons University in Abilene, Texas.

> From there, he and his wife, Dorothy, both enrolled at Southwestern Baptist Theological Seminary. They were both prepared to enter the seminary, but changed their minds at the last minute and instead enrolled at New Orleans Baptist Theological Seminary in New Orleans, Louisiana, at the urging of H. Leo Eddleman (Patterson, July 30, 1991).[93]

Patterson earned both a Master of Theology and Doctor of Theology from New Orleans Baptist Theological Seminary.

Patterson pastored churches in Texas, Louisiana, and Arkansas. He led one Baptist college, two Baptist seminaries, and served as president of the Southern Baptist Convention. Patterson was an architect of what later became known as the "conservative resurgence." "Patterson also fought for Biblical inerrancy within the Southern Baptist Convention (SBC)."[94] Bobby Lewis in his 2009 dissertation quotes Patterson saying, "The controversy has been widely described as the 'inerrancy controversy.' While that is an apt description, the real issue is not whether one chooses to use the world 'inerrant' in his description of the Bible, but whether he finds inconsistencies, anachronisms, blunders, and errors in the Scriptures."[95] Patterson is considered a modern reformer of the SBC today and celebrated by many for his firm stances and leadership in the conservative resurgence movement.

The Fire Returns to the Presidency

On June 24, 2003, L. Paige Patterson would be selected as the eighth president of Southwestern Baptist Theological Seminary. As the newly-elected president, Patterson was welcomed as an institution builder.

92. "Celebrating 100 Years," 123.
93. Jacobs, "Criswell College," 38.
94. "Celebrating 100 Years," 124.
95. Lewis, "Hogue's Concepts of Evangelism," 182.

"'Patterson's previous posts and influence among Southern Baptists prove that he has a track record for success in theological education and church life,' according to Denny Autrey, a Southwestern Seminary trustee and chairman of the seminary's presidential search committee."[96]

With Roy Fish's official retirement in 2006, the "Chair of Fire" would once more return to the office of the president of Southwestern Baptist Theological Seminary. Patterson became the first president since E. D. Head to be installed into the seminary's first academic chair, the "Chair of Fire."

> To fill this vacancy, the trustees accepted the recommendation of the Academic Administration Committee and unanimously selected Paige Patterson to occupy the Scarborough "Chair of Fire." In a letter recommending Patterson to the board, Executive Vice President and Provost Craig Blaising noted that Patterson is known across the Convention for his work in evangelism.[97]

Patterson was officially a professor of theology, but he did teach a Theology of Evangelism course during his tenure as the "Chair of Fire," which is in keeping with the promotion of evangelism in theological education.[98]

> In the case of this chair, however, perhaps it carried an obligation that was not in the written documents, and it was in that unwritten portion of the assignment that I probably made whatever contribution that there was to make. I did teach evangelism a couple of times, but I primarily contributed by attempting to infuse the entire campus with an evangelistic zeal.[99]

On August 21, 2014, Patterson divested himself of the chair and installed Matt Queen as the ninth, and current, occupant of the "Chair of Fire." Queen came to Southwestern Baptist Theological Seminary from Friendly Avenue Baptist Church in Greensboro, North Carolina, on August 1, 2010 to serve as associate professor of evangelism.[100]

---

96. Tomlin, "Paige Patterson," 2.

97. "L. R. Scarborough Chair," 39.

98. Kiesling, "Investigation," 245.

99. Kiesling, "Investigation," 244.

100. Matt Queen, the ninth occupant of the "Chair of Fire," is currently serving on faculty in this role. His tenure will not be examined.

CONCLUSION

Since 1908, Southwestern Baptist Theological Seminary has boasted of the first academic chair of evangelism in the world. From the inception of the chair in the mind of the seminary founder, B. H. Carroll, this chair's occupants have sought to keep evangelism in the forefront of theological education at Southwestern Baptist Theological Seminary. Each of the chair's nine occupants have come to this position from a variety of educational backgrounds and have emphasized different evangelistic components; however, most have demonstrated a strong conviction of the necessity of evangelism both in theological education and local churches.

In the next chapter, research will seek to examine the contributions of the "Chair of Fire" to theological education. The examination will begin with a study of Carroll's conviction of the New Testament "Office of the Evangelist," as seen and interpreted in Ephesians 4:11–12. Careful historical research discloses the historical context of events in 1906 with which Carroll determined that a Southern Baptist seminary should include evangelism as an independent academic discipline.

4

THE "CHAIR OF FIRE'S" CONTRIBUTIONS TO THEOLOGICAL EDUCATION

THE FLEDGLING, NEW, SOUTHERN Baptist seminary was launched in Waco, Texas, on the campus of Baylor University, founded by President Benajah Harvey (B. H.) Carroll with an initial enrollment of 175 students.[1] Seven men are listed as faculty members alongside Carroll in the 1908 Annual Catalogue.[2] Southwestern Baptist Theological Seminary's *First Annual Catalogue* states, "From the beginning and through all of its mutations this institution has steadily grown in favor with the people, in spiritual power, and in attendance of students."[3] The 1908 Annual Catalogue of Southwestern Baptist Theological Seminary shares the parameter of the newly formed Department of Evangelism and the genesis

---

1. "First Annual Catalogue 1908–1909," 16.

2. "First Annual Catalogue 1908–1909," 3. The original seven faculty members of Southwestern Baptist Theological Seminary in 1908 listed in the *Annual Catalogue* were Benajah Harvey Carroll, president and professor of English Bible; Albert Henry Newman, dean and professor of church history and history of doctrines; Charles Bray Williams, professor of biblical Greek and biblical theology of the New Testament; Calvin Goodspeed, professor of systematic theology, apologetics, polemics, and ecclesiology; Jefferson Davis Ray, professor of homiletics, elocution, missions, pastoral duties, history of preaching, and treasurer of the Students' Aid Fund; Lee Rutland Scarborough, professor of evangelism and field secretary; James Josiah Reeve, professor of Hebrew and cognate languages and biblical theology of the Old Testament; and John William Jent, registrar and secretary of the faculty.

3. "First Annual Catalogue 1908–1909," 19.

of the "Chair of Fire" in the classroom as Professor L. R. Scarborough begins his historic journey in theological education. It records:

> This is an entirely new department of theological instruction. At no time or place before in the world has a man been employed to give his entire time to training ministers in the doctrine and methods of Evangelism. This "Chair of Fire" was born in the brain and heart of Dr. B. H. Carroll, the founder of this Seminary, and has become for the first time a permanent and important branch of theological training.[4]

Carroll is credited with the architecture of this particular innovation; that is, establishing a professorship of evangelism in a theological, educational institution.

On March 14, 2020, Southwestern Baptist Theological Seminary and its first endowed chair, the L. R. Scarborough Chair of Evangelism, the "Chair of Fire," celebrated their 112th anniversaries. This chapter briefly provides an overview of the study of missions in theological education as precursors to the "Chair of Fire" through an examination of the lives and work of three distinct pioneering missiologists: Charles Breckenridge of Princeton Theological Seminary, Princeton, New Jersey, United States of America; Alexander Duff of New College, Edinburgh, Scotland; and Gustav Warneck of University of Halle, Halle, Germany. Following this overview, the research will trace the earliest developments of the Southern Baptist missiology teachings of W. O. Carver at Southern Baptist Theological Seminary, Louisville, Kentucky. The research argues that Breckenridge, Duff, Warneck, and Carver laid a foundation in theological education to further establish the precedence of the "Chair of Fire's" demand and contributions to evangelism in theological education by examining the training in personal evangelism, revivals, and the publication of evangelism resources thereby fulfilling the Southern Baptist Convention's (SBC) Program of Evangelism.

PRECURSORS TO THE "CHAIR OF FIRE"

Applied theology, which includes the study of missions and evangelism, was not permanently integrated into a regular curriculum and course of study within theological education until the early 1800s. The establishment of missiology as an independent theological discipline took more

---

4. "First Annual Catalogue 1908–1909," 31.

than sixty years of successes and failures to gain appropriate respect worldwide. The history of missiology in theological education prepared Southern Baptists to lead a second time in a theological institution and establish a chair of evangelism, the "Chair of Fire," and the first department of evangelism in a seminary.

A Chair of Pastoral Theology and Missionary Instruction

Beginning as early as 1811, the General Assembly of Presbyterians in the United States of America felt "the need for making provision in theological education for the teaching of Missions."[5] Olav Myklebust, a Norwegian Lutheran missiologist and author of *The Study of Missions in Theological Education,* continues, "The design of 'Princeton' is in part defined thus: 'to found a nursery for missionaries to the heathen, and to such as are destitute of the stated preaching of the gospel: in which youth may receive that appropriate training which may lay a foundation for their ultimately becoming eminently qualified for missionary work.'"[6]

Nearly thirty years later, Princeton Theological Seminary actuated its design plans. Former professor and head of the Department of Missiology at the University of South Africa David Bosch, in *Transforming Mission,* states, "Charles Breckenridge became the first person appointed specifically to teach missionary instruction (at Princeton Theological Seminary, in 1836), although he was, at the same time, professor of pastoral theology."[7] Myklebust's research proves that Breckenridge served as the first professor of missiology in the world and taught the first courses on missions in the United States of America. Myklebust states, "Of this [missiological] study a detailed account will be given of Alexander Duff's Chair of Evangelistic Theology established in 1867 in Presbyterian New College, Edinburgh. Duff's Chair is the first of its kind in the world. Thirty years earlier, however, there had been established at Presbyterian Princeton the first part professorship of missions in the world."[8]

Breckenridge would serve in this role at Princeton Theological Seminary from 1836 to 1839, a total of three years, before resigning to

---

5. Myklebust, *Study of Missions,* 146.

6. Myklebust, *Study of Missions,* 146.

7. Bosch, *Transforming Mission,* 491.

8. Myklebust, *Study of Missions,* 146–47.

become secretary and general agent of the Board of Foreign Missions.[9] The seminary did not fill his chair of pastoral theology and missionary instruction or his position; thus the chair was discontinued. Missiological study was continued for a time.[10]

A Chair of Evangelistic Theology

In 1867, Alexander Duff, former missionary to India of the Free Church of Scotland, called for the establishment of a chair of evangelistic theology at New College, Edinburgh, Scotland. "Central in the story is Alexander Duff, the first missionary to be formally commissioned by the Church of Scotland. He was at the time the most celebrated missionary after Carey," states Andrew Walls, professor of World Christianity at the University of Edinburgh.[11] The Duff Chair was the first chair of missiology in the world, though not the first professorship.

> This chair of missiology (as it would probably be called today) was only the first stage of Duff's scheme. Associated with the chair would be a "missionary institute," which would address the questions arising from the encounter with other cultures. It would develop a study of what Duff called "the geography, history, ethnology, mythology, habits, manners and practices of unevangelized peoples and nations."[12]

At New College under the tutelage of Duff, missiology was taught as an independent subject in its own right.[13] "The specific purpose of the chair of evangelistic theology was, as Duff himself put it, 'to infuse the missionary spirit into the minds of our students and young ministers; and through them into the minds of the people, and to secure a larger supply alike of men and pecuniary means.'"[14] The Alexander Duff Chair of Evangelistic Theology was abolished by the General Assembly of the Free Church of Scotland in 1892 following Duff's death and several faculty rotations of the chair. In 1909, the Alexander Duff Chair of Evangelistic Theology came to an official end. All monies from its endowment

---

9. Myklebust, *Study of Missions*, 149.

10. Myklebust, *Study of Missions*, 149.

11. Walls, "Missiological Education," 12.

12. Walls, "Missiological Education," 13.

13. Bosch, *Transforming Mission*, 491.

14. Myklebust, *Study of Missions*, 190.

were dispersed to respective educational bodies of the Free Church of Scotland.

The Father of Missions

Gustav Adolf Warneck was born March 6, 1834, to parents Gustav Traugott Leberecht and his wife Johanne Sophie Warneck in Naumburg near Halle.[15] In 1896, Gustav Warneck, at the University of Halle, Germany, according to Bosch and Myklebust, established missiology as a discipline in its own right. Warneck, a German scholar, is considered "the father of German missiology."[16] Stan Nussbaum, a student of David Bosch and a staff missiologist at Global Mapping International in Colorado Springs, Colorado, writes, "Poor health prevented him from becoming a missionary himself, but he served as an administrator for the Rhenish Mission and was a key figure in establishing mission periodicals, mission conferences, and associations."[17] He also authored a theology of mission.[18] Hans Kasdorf, professor of world mission at the Mennonite Brethren Biblical Seminary, Fresno, California, argues, "Warneck's five-volume *Evangelische Missionslehre* was his magnum opus."[19] The publication of this book substantiated missiology as a standard theological discipline in education. Bosch stated, "It was, however, mainly due to the indefatigable efforts of Gustav Warneck—who taught at the University of Halle (1896 to 1910)—that missiology was eventually established as a discipline in its own right, not just as a guest but as having the right of domicile in theology, as Warneck himself put it."[20]

The First Department of Missions

William Owen Carver was born April 10, 1868, in Wilson County, Tennessee, to parents Alexander Jefferson and Almeda Adaline Binkley Carver. At eighteen years old, Carver entered the Master of Arts (MA) degree program at Richmond College in Virginia. He graduated in 1891

15. Kasdorf, "Gustav Warneck," 102.
16. Kasdorf, "Gustav Warneck," 106.
17. Nussbaum, *Reader's Guide*, 162.
18. Warneck, *Evangelische Missionslehre*.
19. Kasdorf, "Gustav Warneck," 106.
20. Bosch, *Transforming Mission*, 491.

with his degree. Carver then enrolled at Southern Baptist Theological Seminary and earned both his Master of Theology (ThM) in 1895 and Doctor of Theology (ThD) in 1896.

Carver pastored churches in Tennessee and Kentucky before joining the faculty at Southern Baptist Theological Seminary, Louisville, Kentucky, in 1898. He served as professor of missions from 1898 to 1943. He is attributed with the establishment of "the oldest continuing department of missions in America" in 1899, called the Department of Comparative Religion and Missions.[21] Alan Culpepper, former dean of the McAfee School of Theology at Mercer University, Macon, Georgia, in his article, "Reflections on Baptist Theological Education in the Twentieth Century," states,

> In 1902, the trustees voted to allow women to attend classes and take exams, but not to matriculate as students. Forty-eight women, most of whom were wives of current students, attended lectures regularly in 1903–04. Carver began teaching aspecial training class in mission methods for women, and in 1907 the Woman's Missionary Union Training School was established.[22]

Culpepper acknowledges that Southern Baptist Theological Seminary and Carver's contributions include first missionary training for women and second the establishment of the Women's Missionary Union (WMU). Carver's contribution to Southern Baptists was his enduring work of missiology in theological education. "Carver's *Missions and Modern Thought* (1910) was an extended justification of the missionary enterprise based on the new modernist form of Christianity," states Gregory Wills, former professor of church history at Southern Baptist Theological Seminary.[23] William Mueller, professor of historical theology and author of the centennial history of Southern Baptist Theological Seminary, recalls Carver's struggle with the people's perception of theological education.

> Southern Baptists were a rather small and divided group when serious interest in theological education first emerged among some of their leaders . . . The financial strength of the newly established body was also comparatively weak. The Foreign Mission Board reported in 1846 receipts of $11,735.22. A year

21. Culpepper, "William Owen Carver," 119.

22. Culpepper, "Reflections," 25.

23. Wills, *Southern Baptist Seminary*, 256.

later, the Domestic Board of Missions for the Southern Baptist Convention had received only $9,594.60 for all its work. In view of these conditions W. O. Carver has rightly said that "missions and theological education had to do their work of building a denomination in the face of retarding and opposing forces."[24]

Carver suffered from illness that caused bodily weaknesses, to the degree that he took a leave in 1900 and 1907.[25] "Dr. Carver had intended pursuing advanced studies at the University of Berlin during his sabbatical of 1907–08; however, illness shattered his plans. Despite his sickness, he visited Gustav Warneck, pioneer of missions at Halle University, and met other distinguished men of affairs."[26] No specific records were kept of their meeting and conversations in Berlin, except that Mueller records that Carver produced two books, *Missions in the Plan of the Ages* and *Missions and Modern Thought*, as fruit from his stay in Europe.[27]

Charles Breckenridge, Alexander Duff, Gustav Warneck, and W. O. Carver set the stage for B. H. Carroll to lay the groundwork for a new foundational discipline in theological education with a new seminary in 1908. The study of missiology as a discipline in theological education made a sufficient primer for the inclusion of evangelism as a standard course of study in theological institutions. Duff's chair of evangelistic theology, the first chair of missiology, did include a shared common methodology with the discipline of evangelism in the course curriculum at New College. Missions education has been defined for the training of missionaries who will serve on foreign fields and distinguishing evangelism education for pastors serving in Western domestic fields. David Bosch, in his book *Transforming Mission*, reiterates, "'Home missions (evangelism) is judged to be *theologically* distinct from (foreign) mission."[28] With this concept, an effortless connection is drawn between the disciplines of missions and evangelism in theological education.

In the next section, research will further establish the precedence of the "Chair of Fire's" demand and contributions of evangelism through personal evangelism, revivals and academic publication in theological education.

24. Mueller, *History of Southern*, 2–3.
25. Mueller, *History of Southern*, 199.
26. Mueller, *History of Southern*, 199.
27. Mueller, *History of Southern*, 199.
28. Bosch, *Transforming Mission*, 410.

CURRICULAR CONTRIBUTIONS OF THE "CHAIR OF FIRE" TO THEOLOGICAL EDUCATION

B. H. Carroll launched Southwestern Baptist Theological Seminary and placed L. R. Scarborough at the helm of his major enterprise: the new Texas seminary. He was the first occupant of the "Chair of Fire" and head of the school's Department of Evangelism from 1908. The academic catalog of the seminary from that year forward provides the opening parameter of the newly-formed Department of Evangelism and the genesis of the "Chair of Fire" in the classroom as Professor L. R. Scarborough began his historic journey in theological education.

> This is an entirely new department of theological instruction. At no time or place before in the world has a man been employed to give his entire time to training ministers in the doctrine and methods of Evangelism. This "Chair of Fire" was born in the brain and heart of Dr. B. H. Carroll, the founder of this Seminary, and has become for the first time a permanent and important branch of theological training.[29]

B. H. Carroll and L. R. Scarborough were like-minded in their commitment to the seminary, as well as the place of evangelism in theological education. The commitment to evangelism was a demonstration of Scarborough's deep affection for Carroll in that he fought to sustain both the seminary and the "Chair of Fire." Scarborough, in *A Modern School of the Prophets*, speaks of their relationship and the strength that their relationship gave to him to lead Southwestern Baptist Theological Seminary:

> By his side and under the loving, tender, helpful guidance of this great soul I began the work of my part of the seminary building. Because of these things and because of our conferences, travels together, far and wide, our campaigns for money-raising and soul-winning, and speaking engagements, because of our prayers together, and common burdens we were thrown together for many years, and thus my life was interwoven with his. Thus I knew, I saw in all relationships and amid all sorts of difficulties, facing all kinds of problems, this mighty man. Because he baptized me, taught me, trained me, called me, as I trust by God's will, into my life's major task, put burdens on me, prayed for and with me, loved me, trusted me, and by his expressed will

---

29. "First Annual Catalogue 1908–1909," 31.

left his responsibilities on me, no wonder I loved him, trusted him, valued him at the topmost place of all men I ever knew.[30]

The "First Annual Catalogue" outlined two of three basic contributions of evangelism in theological education: instruction in personal evangelism and revivals.

1. Lectures.

> The work of the first year will be to follow Christ through the Gospels as he made his disciples to "become fishers of men," and to go with the apostolic workers in their campaigns for souls. The New Testament will be covered in twenty-four lectures, with class work. Conferences and round-tables in soul-winning methods will be held from time to time. All the students in the seminary will be expected to attend these lectures, and other preachers and Christian workers of Baylor University, and of the city of Waco are cordially invited to attend. It will thus be sought to put the evangelistic spirit, note, and methods deep in the lives of every possible Christian worker in and out of the seminary. It is our hope to fan into a glorious flame the fires of a sane and New Testament evangelism in the hearts of thousands of workers.

2. Practical Work in Evangelism.

> Practical work in soul-winning will be done in three directions:
>
> 1. A soul-winners band will be organized at the opening of the session including such students in the seminary, Baylor University, and the churches in Waco, as desire to do practical work in the city of Waco in winning lost men to Christ and to engage in prayer for the power of the Holy Spirit for special service.
>
> 2. The professor of this department will seek personally and through other evangelists and evangelistic pastors to have vital touch with the mission and evangelistic conferences, assemblies, encampments, Bible schools, and also all of the Baptist colleges throughout the Southwest, seeking by addresses and round tables on soul-winning to stir our people and leaders on the doctrine and methods of evangelism.
>
> 3. The professor of this department will be at liberty to hold a number of evangelistic meeting throughout the year in the church desiring

30. Scarborough, *Modern School*, 86.

his services, and as the Divine Spirit may direct. He wishes not only to work through others but also to go directly himself after the lost. Much of his time will be spent on the field with the church in evangelistic campaigns.

It is expected that this department will soon have under its direction a number of evangelists all the time engaged in evangelistic campaigns, thus cooperating with the State Boards and Home Mission Board in bringing in the kingdom of our Savior.

This department asks for the prayers and cooperations of our kingdom forces in making this Seminary a center of world-wide evangelism.[31]

Scarborough understood Carroll's curriculum expectations. The "Chair of Fire," its ideals, principles, and tenets were Carroll's master plan, but the curriculum was to be Scarborough's intendment and implementation. The department courses and the literature in evangelism that he generated would be his great legacy to perpetuate a lasting discipline of evangelism in theological education. Scarborough states in his inaugural address as the second president of Southwestern Baptist Theological Seminary in May 1915:

> Our preachers should have the priestly quality of intercession as well as the prophet power of teaching. In order to do this there should be in every theological seminary a "chair of fire"—a department of evangelism, through which there can be fused the flames of compassionate zeal into the lives of the students and faculty. There is no inconsistency between the profoundest learning and the zeal of the hottest evangelism.[32]

Scarborough had hoped that the fires of evangelism through theological education would ignite in the other seminaries through the training of evangelists and pastors.

Robert Naylor served as the fifth president from 1958 to 1978 at Southwestern Baptist Theological Seminary. In his 1976 Founder's Day Address, he stated, "In the catalogue for 1914–15, the title of Dr. Scarborough in the faculty is listed as 'assistant to the president and professor of evangelism.' Though the catalogue statement on evangelism is not changed, it is to be noted that by that time, courses in world religions and

---

31. "First Annual Catalogue 1908–1909," 31–32.
32. Scarborough, "Primal Test," 9.

in missions had been added."[33] Charles T. Ball was added to the faculty as professor of missions and secretary of the seminary extension division.[34] In Naylor's address, he continues to discuss the Department of Evangelism's expansion through noting that Scarborough's *With Christ after the Lost* was listed in the 1921–22 Annual Catalogue as textbook.[35]

Personal Evangelism and Revivals

From its beginning, a consistent feature of Southwestern Baptist Theological Seminary's Department of Evangelism has been course work in personal evangelism and revivals. Charles Kelley Jr., in his 1993 book *How Did They Do It?: The Story of Southern Baptist Evangelism*, notes that historically, Southern Baptists have identified four trends of current evangelism: personal soul-winning, evangelism through the Sunday school, decisional preaching, and simultaneous evangelistic campaigns.[36] Kelley further explains that personal evangelism has been accurately positioned under the comportment of theological education.

> Theological education has been another source of emphasis on personal evangelism in Southern Baptist life. Evangelism was not included in normal theological education until B. H. Carroll established Southwestern Seminary in Fort Worth, Texas. Carroll, a great Southern Baptist theologian and educator, was a key figure in the struggle to create a national department of evangelism. When he founded Southwestern, shortly after that denominational battle, he decided that evangelism needed to be included in the regular course of theological studies. Carroll apparently established the first chair of evangelism for any seminary in the world.[37]

Kelley also provides three different approaches of personal evangelism that the SBC has utilized: proactive, reactive, and passive.[38] Door-to-door evangelism is considered a proactive approach because the Christian initiates the gospel-sharing opportunity. This method was taught by

33. Naylor, "Southwestern and Evangelism," 90.

34. "Annual Catalogue 1913–1914," 5.

35. Naylor, "Southwestern and Evangelism," 90.

36. Kelley, *How Did They Do It?*

37. Kelley, *How Did They Do It?*, 72–73.

38. Kelley, *How Did They Do It?*, 75.

Scarborough from the beginning, through downtown witnessing, visiting jails, elderly visitation, and home visits. Second, the reactive approach requires some practice and an attentive ear to transition a conversation to a gospel-sharing conversation. Scarborough's book *With Christ after the Lost* includes an entire chapter devoted to educational evangelism, teaching students how to practice a reactive approach.[39] Both of these approaches require intentionality, which is a watermark of Southern Baptist evangelism. The third approach Kelley identifies is a passive program of personal evangelism. Leaving a gospel tract on a door step without the opportunity to speak with the residents is a prime example of a passive evangelism approach. Scarborough used tracts and encouraged them. He said, "They [tracts] are valuable for soul-winning, soul-building, for indoctrination, teaching the truths of God's Word."[40]

An Evangelism Curriculum

B. H. Carroll is known as the "father of theological education in Texas."[41] As early as 1880, he began teaching theology to small gatherings of students in conjunction with his duties at Baylor University, which was Waco University at this time. Jeff Ray observed Carroll's earnest desires to teach ministerial students, "At that time the twelve or fifteen young preachers in the University would gather on Friday nights at his little cottage with Pendleton's Church Manual in their hands. We had the one small textbook, the one teacher, and once a week recitations [*sic*], but the instruction covered or (to speak more accurately) touched upon nearly everything taught in the seminary today."[42]

With the establishment of Southwestern Baptist Theological Seminary, Scarborough was able to organize his course work between personal evangelism and training in revivals. In his inaugural address, Scarborough speaks about the expansion of theological education because of the establishment of the Department of Evangelism and the "Chair of Fire."

> It had two phases: one local and conducted by students and faculty which looked after soul-winning in the downtown areas and in suburban and nearby mission places, in the jails, in the

39. Scarborough, *With Christ*, 133–36.

40. Scarborough, *With Christ*, 139.

41. LeFever, "Theological Education," 164.

42. Ray, *B. H. Carroll*, 134.

rescue homes, in good-will centers, in old people's homes, and
work among the Negroes, Mexicans, and other races. The other
was wider and looked to evangelistic meetings out in Texas
and other states . . . This department of evangelistic extension
work did great good, brought thousands of people to Christ,
widely advertised our Seminary, brought many students to the
seminary, raised some money for its support, and helped to
keep the fires of evangelism burning in the hearts of students
and faculty.[43]

Scarborough's first-year course taught the foundations of evangelism, the
theology of evangelism, the methods of evangelism, and encouraged an
application to evangelism in theological education.

The evangelistic spirit and fires for evangelism that Scarborough
diligently sought to instill in the hearts of seminary students were carried
into the pulpits across the churches of the SBC where alumni served the
Lord. L. Paige Patterson, past president of Southwestern Baptist Theological Seminary, retells of the zeal for evangelism and revivals of his father, T. A. Patterson, a prominent Texas pastor of the First Baptist Church
of Beaumont, Executive Secretary of the Baptist General Convention of
Texas (BGCT), and Alumnus of Southwestern Baptist Theological Seminary, stating,

> He never actually had a class from him [L. R. Scarborough],
> but he was nevertheless profoundly impressed as were all stu-
> dents who came to Southwestern. It led him, for example, to
> schedule three revivals every year in churches that he pastored.
> For example, during the years at First Baptist Beaumont when
> Dad was there for fourteen years, and during that fourteen-year
> period there were three revivals every year. One would always
> be with a vocational evangelist; one would use a notable pastor
> who was a strong preacher; and the third one would make use
> of somebody who was perhaps a missionary or some other area
> like that, professor of evangelism or whatever, and those would
> come to the church and we would have great revival meetings,
> through which we saw a tremendous number of people come
> to Christ.[44]

One substantial facet of the seventies and eighties at Southwestern Baptist Theological Seminary was an expansion in the number of

---

43. Scarborough, *Modern School*, 136.
44. Patterson, interview with the author, Appendix 15.

professors of evangelism. Due to increasing student enrollment, a larger faculty served in the Department of Evangelism. According to Malcolm McDow, James Eaves predominantly taught personal evangelism courses. "He taught contemporary evangelism. In other words, he applied it."[45] In 1978, as a part of Eaves's emphasis on personal evangelism, fellow evangelism professor Oscar Thompson and he introduced David Stockwell's new witnessing program to the seminary. The campus news service wrote: "The Evangelism Department at Southwestern Seminary has announced the institution of a program entitled 'Witnessing with the Word.'"[46] Eaves and Thompson taught students to use the Bible and Scriptures to share the gospel through personal witness.

With regard to the evangelism curriculum, during these days in 1984, McDow, Fish, and Eaves spoke with James Leo Garrett, then-associate dean of doctoral programs for the School of Theology at Southwestern Baptist Theological Seminary, about producing a Doctor of Philosophy in Evangelism. McDow states, "One of the things that I saw that we could do was to implement a PhD in evangelism. But if we implemented a PhD in evangelism, I wanted it to be a full-fledged PhD in evangelism. I did not want it to be hybrid."[47] By full-fledged, McDow means he wanted all coursework to be in evangelism at the PhD level. McDow, Fish, and Eaves determined that the best direction to take the program was to teach in their strengths. McDow and Fish had PhDs in church history, while Eaves had his degree in New Testament. McDow states,

> My approach was in order to make it academic, we would approach it from the historical perspective. We would cover the total history of evangelism from the time of Christ up until the modern times, from the historical perspective . . . So we decided that I would offer the PhD seminar in the early church, from the time of Christ to the death of Augustine in 430 AD, and also a PhD seminar in the Middle Ages and the Reformation, from the death of Augustine to the death of John Knox . . . Roy Fish would offer a PhD seminar in the history of spiritual awakening, picking up with Knox.[48]

In the end McDow stated, "I offered two, Evangelism and the Early Church, from the Time of Christ to the Death of Augustine in 430 AD.

45. McDow, interview with the author, Appendix 12.

46. "Evangelism Dept.," 2.

47. McDow, interview with the author, Appendix 12.

48. McDow, interview with the author, Appendix 12.

The second was Evangelism in the Middle Ages and the Reformation, from 430 AD to the death of John Knox on November the twenty-fourth of 1572."[49]

Fish taught profound, theologically-filled courses such as Jesus and Personal Evangelism. Fish used this course to model for the evangelism student the evangelistic practices of the Master Evangel, Jesus. The Southwestern Baptist Theological Seminary Academic Catalogue provided the following course description: "A detailed study of evangelism in the life and ministry of Jesus. A thorough investigation of the strategy of Jesus along with case studies of his efforts in personal evangelism. Three hours."[50]

Pioneer Penetration Program to Reach This Nation

In 1959 a new revival initiative was introduced at Southwestern Baptist Theological Seminary by C. E. Autrey, then "Chair of Fire." He chose an evangelistic student at the seminary named Roy Fish to lead this initiative, called the "Pioneer Penetration Program." Robert Baker records that "One of the activities of the students illustrating the strong spirit of evangelism and missions among them was the Pioneer Penetration Program, in which they voluntarily used their spring break each year to go into the pioneer areas of the Convention to preach, hold Bible schools, conduct revivals, and perform similar activities."[51] Autrey, who initiated the Pioneer Penetration Program, handed the program over to Kenneth Chafin in 1960. Chafin then left the program in the capable hands of Roy Fish in 1965, when Fish was elected to faculty status and became the "Chair of Fire." An article released by *Southwestern News* in March of 1970 states, "Roy Fish, professor of evangelism and director of the project, reported that during the last four years over one thousand professions of faith have been recorded in services conducted by students. Fish explained the project as an effort to see that churches and missions in the pioneer areas have at least one revival a year."[52]

In 1999 a *Baptist Press* article covering the spring break revivals at Southwestern Baptist Theological Seminary stated, "Spring break for

49. McDow, interview with the author, Appendix 12.
50. "School of Evangelism and Missions," 238.
51. Baker, *Tell the Generations*, 468.
52. "'Field' Revivals Set for Spring," 2.

Southwestern Baptist Theological Seminary students might be a break from school, but it's not a break from ministry. And more than 100 churches and 900 people who made decisions for Christ, including 206 who made professions of faith, are grateful."[53] The significance of the article is that it stressed the importance of this revival program. The Spring Evangelism Practicum was in its fortieth year serving in multiple states in small churches outside the "Bible Belt" that likely did not have means to afford any revival services for their church.

Over these sixty-one years, Pioneer Penetration has been rebranded a few times. The revival program was later renamed the "Spring Evangelism Practicum"; then, in 2006, the initiative was renamed "Revive the Nation" (RTN). Information acquired by an email from the program's new director, Brent S. Ray, adjunct professor of missions and director of the World Missions Center for the Roy J. Fish School of Evangelism and Missions at Southwestern Baptist Theological Seminary, verified that as of fall 2019, the evangelism initiative was rebranded again and is now "Reach This Nation." Ray states, "This change in nomenclature also gives us the opportunity to engage SWBTS women in RTN ministry, given that the focus is broader than just preaching."[54]

According to meticulous records kept by Roy Fish and Dan Crawford, professors of evangelism who supervised the revivals during 1965 to 2008: "The Spring Evangelism Practicum has had 5,523 total students participate; 4,839 churches served (not including 1965, 1979); and 13,898 reported professions of faith."[55] Crawford attributes much of his success as a director of the Spring Break Revival Practicum to his experience and background work with college students. Crawford states, "I came in from having worked with college students for fifteen years, and then being a national consultant with college students, and I came to work with students."[56] These spring break revivals continue today.

The Contribution to Evangelism Literature

The third basic contribution of evangelism in theological education came through Carroll's encouragement to Scarborough to widely publish

53. Little, "Seminarians' Spring Ministries," 1.
54. Ray, email message to the author, Appendix 17.
55. Pioneer Penetration Totals, Appendix 21.
56. Crawford, interview with the author, Appendix 3.

evangelism textbooks and other literature. Scarborough began publishing literature in the academic discipline of evangelism as early as 1914. "In this role, Scarborough taught courses on evangelism and produced such texts as *Recruits for World Conquests* and *With Christ after the Lost*—cornerstones of the seminary's evangelism curriculum for many years."[57] *Recruits for World Conquests*, a soul-stirring book, is evidence of Scarborough's commitment to call for men and women to be educated in theology and evangelism and to give their lives to the work of the gospel ministry.[58] Carroll encouraged Scarborough, telling him

> that while traveling and doing field work you carefully study book by book and prepare one by one the lectures that will make your fame, taking full time in preparation of each lecture, making each one a masterpiece individually, and so prepared as to fit into a series for publication as a text book.[59]

Carroll conveyed to Scarborough that without proper distribution of evangelistic literature to students and the denomination that there would be no "kindling everywhere, in all the churches and in the hearts of all the preachers, holy fires of evangelism and a passionate concern for the salvation of the lost and for New Testament soul-winning."[60] Carroll understood the difficulty that Scarborough would have as he began teaching and the ability to have expansion in a new theological discipline at a seminary without textbooks and curricula to guide and shape the teaching of courses.

Beginning as early as 1914, with *Recruits for World Conquests,* Scarborough followed Carroll's directive and began to publish his seventeen works in the academic discipline of evangelism for theological education. He authored the first textbook on personal evangelism, *With Christ after the Lost,* in 1919. Scarborough followed up with a second volume on evangelism with *Endued to Win* in 1922.[61] Both textbooks were required and used in the Department of Evangelism for many years at Southwestern Baptist Theological Seminary.

Scarborough would publish a few volumes of his evangelistic sermons that were preached on the field while he was the field secretary for

57. Sibley, "L. R. Scarborough," 3.

58. Scarborough, *Recruits.*

59. Carroll, Letter Offering Chair of Evangelism, 1908.

60. Dana, *Scarborough*, 86.

61. Dana, *Scarborough*, 86–87.

the seminary. In 1942, he published a New Testament doctrinal study on Jesus' ministry of the forty days between Resurrection Sunday and Pentecost called *After the Resurrection, What?*[62] Muncy provided evidence that authorship of books had a wider reach than simply classroom instruction only.

> Hundreds of men and women whose lives have been invested in the furtherance of the gospel around the world have received inspiration and vitally important information in these classes. But the professor's influence did not and does not stop with the lives of the people who have had the privilege of studying in his classes and the many lives touched by them. Dr. Carroll charged him with the responsibility of producing an evangelistic literature. He has written books which have had and are having a wide reading.[63]

Scarborough published literature that flooded the seminary and eventually the Convention. Carroll had achieved the objective set and anticipated with the inauguration of this great "Chair of Fire."

Each of the subsequent occupants of the "Chair of Fire" have authored books in the field of evangelism. The second occupant of the "Chair of Fire" and third president of Southwestern Baptist Theological Seminary, E. D. Head, was deeply committed to continuing Scarborough's legacy, and revised *With Christ after the Lost.*[64] The revision of this first evangelism textbook at the seminary reorganized and combined repetitious chapters and condensed them into one. A bibliography was included for further reading in evangelism and analogous subject areas. Head also published other books.[65]

Another example, in 1966, was C. E. Autrey, the first full-time professor of evangelism and third occupant, who wrote *The Theology of Evangelism*, a book that provided theological validity to evangelism as a discipline in theological education.[66] In the preface, Autrey states, "*The Theology of Evangelism* portrays evangelism as a vital issue which

---

62. Scarborough, *After the Resurrection*.

63. Muncy, *History of Evangelism*, 161.

64. Scarborough, *With Christ*, rev. ed.

65. Head books in publication order: "The Indian Renaissance" (1927); *Burning Hearts* (1947); *Coradoes Abrasados* (1950); "Reflections from the Papyri on New Testament Life and Literature" (1952); *Evangelism In Acts* (1952); *Revivals In the Bible* (1952); *Why All This Suffering?* (1941); and *With Christ after the Lost*, rev. ed. (1952).

66. Autrey, *Theology of Evangelism*.

cannot be separated from the very nature and purpose of Christianity. This portrayal is verified by the fact that evangelism is involved in every activity of the church."[67] Autrey's book, a first on the topic of the theology of evangelism, sought to further provide understanding of the discipline of evangelism through academic and biblical parity in theological education. He published several other books.[68]

Kenneth Chafin published books on personal evangelism and a few biblical preaching commentaries.[69] His authorship further demonstrates his commitment to personal evangelism as a viable practice for every member of the church. The commitment to personal evangelism is best demonstrated through his denominational work at the HMB, when as the head of the Evangelism Department he led the Convention in record salvations and baptisms through his personal evangelism method introduced as Witness Involvement Now (WIN). Charles Kelley stated, "In 1972 the SBC set a new record in baptisms reported by the churches, with more than 445,000 people being baptized during the church year."[70]

Roy Fish and Malcolm McDow made a few contributions through published works in the field of evangelism through historical theology. Fish and McDow both published books on revivals. According to Paige Patterson, the eighth president and former occupant of the "Chair of Fire," "Nobody, I do not think even among Southern Baptists, was a student of the history of revivalism like Roy Fish was."[71] Fish was an expert on revivals. In 1996, Fish published *When Heaven Touched Earth: The Awakening of 1858 and Its Effects on Baptists*.[72] Known also as the Layman Prayer Revival of 1858, Fish provides a work on a little-known national revival, making his book both a meaningful contribution to church history and

67. Autrey, *Theology of Evangelism*, 9.

68. Autrey books in publication order: *Basic Evangelism* (1959); *Revivals of the Old Testament* (1960); *Renewals before Pentecost: How God's Spirit Revitalized His People in Old Testament Times* (1960); *You Can Win Souls* (1961); *Evangelistic Sermons* (1962); *Evangelism in the Acts* (1964); *The Theology of Evangelism* (1966); and *We Are Witnesses* (1968).

69. Chafin books in publication order: *Help! I'm A Layman* (1972); *The Reluctant Witness* (1975); *Tell All the Little Children* (1976); *Is There a Family in the House?: Personal Strategies for Strengthening Your Marriage and Family Life* (1979); *The Communicator's Commentary: 1, 2 Corinthians* (1985); *The Communicator's Commentary: 1, 2 Samuel, Old Testament.* (1989); and *A Rhythm for My Life* (2003).

70. Kelley, *How Did They Do It?*, 46.

71. Patterson, interview with the author, Appendix 15.

72. Fish, *When Heaven Touched Earth*.

to the discipline of evangelism through research on a revival. This book gives the reader insights into the importance of praying lay people and their work within the local church. Fish discusses the social climate surrounding the revival, the preparation for revival, the awareness of revival, and then after-effect of revival. Fish also published *Giving a Good Invitation,* a small pastor help book on the invitation or a "time of response." Fish defines what the pastor is inviting people to do and its importance and then works through best practices for giving a good invitation. Fish further published books on personal evangelism, giving an invitation, and the history of revivals.[73]

Malcolm McDow, also a historical theologian and occupant of the "Chair of Fire," published two books on revival history. The first, *Revival!: The Story of the Current Awakening in Brownwood, Fort Worth, and Beyond,* and the second, *Firefall: How God Has Shaped History Through Revivals,* each record and trace God's working through the Holy Spirit to bring specifically marked eras of revivals.[74] McDow collaborated with former students John Avant and Alvin Reid. Fish used *Firefall* as a main course textbook for "Spiritual Awakenings."

Both Fish and McDow were contributors to a textbook for the Pioneer Penetration Program, *Before Revival Begins: The Preacher's Preparation for a Revival Meeting,* edited by Dan Crawford, professor of evangelism and then director of the Spring Evangelism Practicum in 1996.[75] Sixteen Southwestern Baptist Theological Seminary alumni collaborated and contributed chapters to a textbook that has been used to prepare students for their spring break revival assignment.

Paige Patterson, a committed scholar and evangelist, contributed many articles and chapters to books on evangelism. When asked in an interview, he stated, "I have a couple of chapters in books as well as articles and shorter pieces. Thom Rainer edited a *festschrift* for Lewis Drummond, my predecessor in the presidency at Southeastern Seminary, asked me to

---

73. Fish books in publication order: *Giving a Good Invitation* (1974); *Every Member Evangelism for Today* (1976); *Dare to Share* (1982); *When Heaven Touched Earth: The Awakening of 1858 and Its Effect on Baptists* (1996); and a posthumous publication, *Coming to Jesus: Giving a Good Invitation* (2015).

74. Avant, McDow, and Reid, *Revival!,* and McDow and Reid, *Firefall.*

75. Crawford, *Before Revival Begins.*

do the chapter on 'lifestyle evangelism' in it."[76] Patterson has published fifteen articles and books on evangelism.[77]

This call to publish literature in evangelism is a tenet of the "Chair of Fire" carried on until today by each of the chair's occupants. In most recent days, the current occupant of the "Chair of Fire" has published four works on personal and local church evangelism.[78] These works have been distributed Convention-wide and are also used as supplemental textbooks in evangelism courses. The methods promoted in these resources are easily adopted as personal and local church models of evangelism.

The Southern Baptist Professors of Evangelism Fellowship (SBPEF)

An intimate fellowship of cooperation exists between the six Southern Baptist seminaries and their professors of evangelism. Beginning as an informal corridor gathering of the professors of evangelism at each annual meeting of the SBC in 2000, a microcosm, named the Southern Baptist Professors of Evangelism Fellowship (SBPEF), was formed. Thomas Johnston, senior professor of evangelism at Midwestern Baptist Theological Seminary and current president of SBPEF, stated in a personal telephone interview, "That fellowship was founded many years ago under Lewis Drummond and others when they would meet at the summer state leadership meeting of the Southern Baptist Home Mission Board, the North American Mission Board."[79] A leader of the group, Roy Fish, then-

---

76. Patterson, interview with the author, Appendix 15.

77. Patterson contributions to evangelism in published order: "Miracle at Love Field" (1971); "The Evangelist" (1981); "Lifestyle Evangelism," in *Evangelism in the Twenty-First Century: The Critical Issues* (1989); Review of *Effective Evangelistic Churches* (1996); "A Theology of Evangelism," in *The Gospel for the New Millennium: A Collection of Essays* (2001); "The Ultimate Hunt," *The Christian Sportsman* (2007); *Hunting the Most Dangerous Game: A Tract* (2008); Review of *With Christ after the Lost* (2008); Foreword for *Urban Impact: Reaching the World through Effective Urban Ministry* (2010); "Billy Graham e a Pregação Evangelística," (2012); "Why Southern Baptists Declined and What to Do, Part 1" (2014); and "Why Southern Baptists Declined and What to Do, Part 2" (2014).

78. Queen books in publication order: *A Passion for the Great Commission: Essays in Honor of Alvin L. Reid* (2013); *Everyday Evangelism* (2016); *Mobilize to Evangelize: The Pastor and Effective Congregational Evangelism* (2018); and *And You Will Be My Witnesses* (2019).

79. Johnston, interview with the author, Appendix 9.

professor of evangelism and occupant of the L. R. Scarborough Chair of Evangelism, the "Chair of Fire," asked Johnston to lead the organization of evangelism professors in 2001.[80] The SBPEF convene at the SBC annual meeting.

Johnston worked with NAMB to secure a place of meeting and all professors of evangelism from Baptist schools and seminaries are welcome to attend. Johnston explained the internal organizational structure of the group: "The president and the executive committee, which is president, vice president, and secretary." According to Johnston, currently Carl Bradford, assistant professor of evangelism at Southwestern Baptist Theological Seminary, serves the organization on the Executive Committee as SBPEF Secretary.[81] "He's very able in that area. You have to be at a Southern Baptist seminary. One of the six. And you have to be full-time teaching as a professor of evangelism in order to be seated in one of those executive committee spots, just to make sure it stays with the SBC seminaries," stated Johnston.[82]

In 2011 Johnston edited a book and led the SBPEF in a cooperative effort of contributing a work on SBC evangelism titled *Mobilizing a Great Commission Church for Harvest: Voices and Views from the Southern Baptist Professors of Evangelism Fellowship*.[83] In his foreword to the book, Philip Roberts, former president of Midwestern Baptist Theological Seminary, states, "Evangelism is the theme of *Mobilizing a Great Commission Church for Harvest*. And that is why this volume is so vitally important. It addresses the concept of how the entire people of God can be involved in sharing the great news of God's gift of eternal life offered to all."[84] This book is an academic treatise on the theological discipline of evangelism, but is purposed to encourage these professors' students, who will one day become the future pastors, evangelists, missionaries, and Christian workers in evangelism through the local SBC churches they lead.

80. Johnston, interview with the author, Appendix 9.
81. Johnston, interview with the author, Appendix 9.
82. Johnston, interview with the author, Appendix 9.
83. Johnston, *Mobilizing a Great Commission*.
84. Johnston, *Mobilizing a Great Commission*, ix.

CONCLUSION

Carroll's dream of a "Chair of Fire" draws from a deep conviction to follow God's heart. His selection of the man of God to administrate the task of developing the academic standard of evangelism in theological education was not taken lightly. Carroll's lasting legacy has been the seminary to which he gave his final years. "The creation of Southwestern Seminary and its Evangelism Department led to thousands of men and women being equipped for gospel ministry."[85] However, Carroll's vision of establishing an evangelistic seminary located on the western pioneering frontiers of Texas may not have been realized without the astute and capable mind and evangelistic character of L. R. Scarborough.

L. R. Scarborough accomplished for Southern Baptist evangelism what W. O. Carver had done for missions. He took away any assumptions that Southern Baptist pastors would simply "know" how to share the gospel message and make converts through soul-winning. Instead, Scarborough taught from the Scriptures how to share Jesus with others and challenged students and faculty at Southwestern Baptist Theological Seminary to be personal soul-winners. He tasked his students with the responsibility to practice evangelism through an applied evangelism practicum. The Seminary was infused with the fires of evangelism.

The "Chair of Fire" occupants have kept evangelism in the consciousness of Southern Baptists through revivals. The occupants have often preached and called for men and women to surrender their lives to the call of ministry. Each man has published many books, chapters, and articles on evangelism and dispersed them throughout the Convention and its seminaries. Every occupant of the L. R. Scarborough Chair of Evangelism, the "Chair of Fire," finds their charge in Carroll's words to Scarborough.

> My greatest concern is not for myself. My spiritual horizon is cloudless. The way up to the fellowship of Christ and the redeemed is clear. But my deep concern is about the seminary. He said: "Your life will be given largely to it. It is an institution born in the prayer of faith and in the faith of prayer. You will need faith and prayer ahead. It was born for Christ; keep it lashed to him. It will need love. As a baby needs the love of its mother, so somebody will have to mother the seminary. I believe you and some of the other men connected with it love it. Keep the fires of

85. Kiesling, "Investigation," 191.

love burning on all the altars about the seminary. Faith, prayer, and love will bring the money and keep the enduring elements around it. These will have to save it. Keep it on a hot trail after the lost. That is why I started the chair of evangelism and chose you as its professor. Never let it get away from the compassion of Calvary. Keep it missionary and true to the truth. Give it the best of your life.[86]

Carroll offered Scarborough the aforementioned charge from his death bed. Through excellence in academia, the "Chair of Fire" has acquired a status of respect and equality with all other theological disciplines among scholars, though some have doubted the validity of the discipline of evangelism in theological education.

86. Scarborough, *Modern School*, 90.

5

THE SPREADING FIRES OF EVANGELISM

FOR FIFTY-ONE YEARS, the Southwestern Baptist Theological Seminary in Fort Worth, Texas, and its L. R. Scarborough Chair of Evangelism, the "Chair of Fire," singularly led the Southern Baptist Convention (SBC) in formal theological education of evangelism. The "Chair of Fire" provided a significant educational platform of promotion of the seminary's Evangelism and Missions Departments and through the chair's occupants providing a training ground for men and women in the applied art of evangelism. B. H. Carroll's vision for his evangelistic seminary had been realized.

The formal instruction in evangelism in areas such as personal soul-winning, decisional preaching, revivals, and church evangelism gave Southwestern Baptist Theological Seminary students advanced exposure and familiarity with the national programs of evangelism being used and developed out of the Home Mission Board (HMB), now the North American Mission Board (NAMB). The professors of evangelism at Southwestern Baptist Theological Seminary introduced formal evangelism training through both classroom instruction and field practicums. The "Chair of Fire" and its Department of Evangelism provided the HMB with equipped evangelists properly prepared and ready to assist the local churches of the SBC in kingdom expansion through the work of evangelism.

Since the inception of the "Chair of Fire" in 1908, much progress has been made throughout the Convention as the other five seminaries have created departments of evangelism, hired evangelistic faculty to teach in the field of evangelism, created an evangelism curriculum, and published textbooks in evangelism. Each of the six SBC seminaries now have both endowed chairs of evangelism and departments of evangelism, each designed to further equip their students and the future Southern Baptist ministry force in the work of evangelism. The professors who have occupied these academic chairs have contributed to their seminaries and to the Convention through textbook publications, scholarly authorship, services to the denomination, and by keeping an evangelistic consciousness about the SBC.[1] This chapter will introduce each of the additional chairs of evangelism with brief historical sketches. These academic chairs are as unique as the men after whom they are named and their occupants.

NEW ORLEANS BAPTIST THEOLOGICAL SEMINARY'S ROLAND Q. LEAVELL CHAIR OF EVANGELISM (ESTABLISHED 1959)

Roland Quinche Leavell was born on December 21, 1891. Reared in Oxford, Mississippi, "he followed his mother's wishes and entered the ministry of the Southern Baptist Convention. As a pastor, he not only served well in a number of churches, but become renowned throughout the Convention for his success in evangelism."[2] During his career, Leavell's passion and skill in the art of evangelism would bring appointments to the Director of Evangelism for the HMB and the presidency of New Orleans Baptist Theological Seminary.

Roland Q. Leavell served as fourth president of New Orleans Baptist Theological Seminary. Leavell was searching for new challenges in ministry. "He was aware of the centrality of theological education in the Baptist scheme of things and therefore knew that such a position would bring him added honor; besides he was attracted by a place of leadership with more prestige than the pastorate. He was now fifty-two

---

1. The sequence of the subsequent chairs of evangelism are as follows: the Roland Q. Leavell Chair of Evangelism at New Orleans Baptist Theological Seminary, New Orleans, Louisiana (1959); the Billy Graham Chair of Evangelism at Southern Baptist Theological Seminary, Louisville, Kentucky (1965); the E. Hermond Westmoreland Chair of Evangelism at Gateway Seminary, Ontario, California (1966); the Bailey Smith Chair of Evangelism at Southeastern Baptist Theological Seminary, Wake Forest, North Carolina (1994); and the Gary Taylor Chair of Missions and Evangelism at Midwestern Baptist Theological Seminary, Kansas City, Missouri (2012).

2. Bowman, "Roland Q. Leavell," v.

years old, and he felt that he was ready for a position with more status and opportunity."[3] Leavell seized the opportunity to become president of the seminary in 1946. Dottie Hudson, his daughter, in her biography of her father, recalled Leavell's charge to the seminary: "In his inaugural address, he challenged his audience, saying, 'Our Seminary has unprecedented and unparalleled opportunities to build evangelism fires that will give revival light around the world.' God had given him the interest in and ability to work hard and long, and this would be required of him."[4] Leavell worked with a seminary committee to change the school's name from New Orleans Baptist Bible Institute to its current name.[5] This was done to give the New Orleans Baptist Theological Seminary equal status with the other seminaries. He immediately commenced with the organization of evangelism education. The program required all students to learn methods of personal evangelism and to participate in field exercises each week.[6] "The seminary presidency may well have been the crowning achievement in his ministry, since he took a fledgling school and led it to unprecedented growth."[7] Leavell was forced into an early retirement by a massive stroke in 1958.

While exact records have not been kept pertaining to the creation, inauguration, and subsequent occupants of the Roland Q. Leavell Chair of Evangelism, historical information and records have been gleaned through personal telephone interviews. In an email from a New Orleans Baptist Theological Seminary (NOBTS) former president, Charles S. Kelley Jr. states,

> I can now confirm that the Roland Q. Leavell Chair of Evangelism was established by the NOBTS trustees to honor him upon the occasion of his retirement, I believe in 1959. However, they did not fund the chair at the time it was established or in the following years. Dr. Landrum P. Leavell II, my predecessor, raised the money necessary to activate it and several other unfunded chairs in other departments of the seminary.[8]

---

3. Bowman, "Roland Q. Leavell," 217.

4. Hudson, *He Still Stands Tall*, 120–21.

5. Hudson, *He Still Stands Tall*, 119.

6. Hudson, *He Still Stands Tall*, 121.

7. Gibson, "Leavell's Preaching," 31.

8. Kelley, email correspondence with the author, Appendix 11.

The endowment and activation for the Chair came some twenty-four years later in 1983. Conflicting research states that C. C. Randall was the first occupant of the Roland Q. Leavell Chair of Evangelism, such as this *Baptist Press* statement: "C. C. Randall, pastor of First Baptist Church of Tuscaloosa, Ala., for the past 20 years, became the first person to occupy an endowed chair at New Orleans Seminary: The Roland Q. Leavell Chair of Evangelism."[9] However, B. Gray Allison was verified by the Office of the Provost at New Orleans Baptist Theological Seminary to be the inaugural occupant of the chair from 1959–66.

B. Gray Allison (1959 to 1966)

Beverly Gray Allison was born in Ida, Louisiana on May 7, 1924. Allison served during World War II in the US Army Air Force as a pilot.[10] "He married his wife Voncille in 1946, earned an undergraduate degree at Louisiana Tech, and initially was an insurance salesman until entering New Orleans Seminary, where he earned a divinity degree in 1952 and a doctorate in theology in 1954."[11]

Allison served as pastor, evangelist, professor of evangelism, seminary founder, and president during his career. Roland Q. Leavell was president when he joined the faculty at New Orleans Baptist Theological Seminary as a professor of evangelism. Allison was the inaugural occupant of the Roland Q. Leavell Chair of Evangelism, which he occupied until 1966. In a press release dated August 12, 1966, "B. Gray Allison occupied the chair of evangelism until his resignation earlier this year to accept a position with the Southern Baptist Home Mission Board's division of evangelism."[12] Allison founded Mid-America Baptist Theological Seminary in Memphis, Tennessee, in 1972 as an alternative to the six Southern Baptist Seminaries prior to the conservative resurgence.

Eugene N. Patterson (1966 to 1974)

Eugene N. Patterson was a two-time faculty member at New Orleans Baptist Theological Seminary. He initially served the Louisiana seminary

9. "New Orleans Trustees," 30.

10. "B. Allison," n. p.

11. Toalston, "Gray Allison," n. p.

12. "Patterson Named Professor," 2.

from 1945–59 as professor of homiletics. Patterson resigned to become president of Grand Canyon College in Phoenix, Arizona, then returned to New Orleans Baptist Theological Seminary as professor of evangelism in 1966. A *Baptist Press* release stated, "The returning professor is the second person to occupy the Roland Q. Leavell Chair of Evangelism."[13]

Patterson was a graduate of Howard College in Birmingham, Alabama. He earned the Doctor of Theology from New Orleans Baptist Theological Seminary. The *Baptist Press,* announcing his election to the presidency at Grand Canyon College, stated, "The president-elect has studied at Union Theological Seminary, New York, and at Oxford University in England."[14] With limited records of the Roland Q. Leavell Chair of Evangelism, the academic catalogues provide evidence of an eight-year vacancy following Patterson's resignation.[15]

C. C. Randall (1982 to 1988)

Clarence Cecil Randall was born March 10, 1923, in Wesson, Mississippi, to parents Archie Martin Randall and Mattie Case Randall. He and his wife, Dorothy Lane Britt Randall, had four children.[16] Randall served as a pastor in Tuscaloosa for twenty years before accepting his election and installation to the Roland Q. Leavell Chair of Evangelism and professor of evangelism at New Orleans Baptist Theological Seminary.

> On unanimous recommendation of the committee, the church voted on January 21, 1962, to call Dr. Clarence Cecil Randall, thirty-eight-year-old pastor of Highland Baptist Church of Meridian, Mississippi, to be its new pastor. Dr. Randall began his tenure in Tuscaloosa on February 19, 1962. His warmth, sound preaching, and God-given ability to relate to people seemed to bring the kind of healing the church needed. Dr. and Mrs. Randall (Dot) had four children, three sons and a daughter.[17]

As a Southern Baptist pastor, Randall provided strong leadership during the height of the Civil Rights era.

---

13. "Patterson Named Professor," 2.

14. "E. N. Patterson Named," 1.

15. Phillips, email correspondence with the author, Appendix 16.

16. "Clarence Cecil Randall."

17. Guffin, *Here We Raise Our Ebenezer*, 22.

One Sunday morning in the late 1960s, two black gentlemen attending a convention in town came to the 11:00 a.m. worship service. Before the service, an usher told them that there was a church for them down the street, and they immediately left.

Dr. Randall heard of the incident just before he came into the sanctuary for the service. At a strategic point in the middle of his sermon, he stated emphatically: "This is not my church, and this is not your church, but this is God's church, and whoever chooses to worship here is welcome."[18]

Randall served for twenty years in Tuscaloosa and was a beloved pastor. "On November 10, 1982, Dr. C. C. Randall gave the church his resignation to accept a position as Roland Q. Leavell Chair of Evangelism at New Orleans Baptist Theological Seminary."[19] Randall became the third occupant of the chair at New Orleans Baptist Theological Seminary. He occupied the chair until 1988.

Charles S. Kelley Jr. (1989 to 1996)

Charles "Chuck" Seymoure Kelley Jr. was born in Beaumont, Texas, on July 27, 1952, to Charles S. Kelley Sr. and Doris Rae Weisiger Kelley.[20] He is the fourth of five children born to the couple and their only son. Chuck Kelley's brother-in-law is L. Paige Patterson, who married Dorothy Kelley.

Kelley graduated from Baylor University in Waco, Texas, with a Bachelor of Arts degree in philosophy with a minor in religion. While a student at Baylor, Kelley was instrumental in the Baptist Student Union and pastored a small church in Ireland, Texas. "Chuck met Rhonda Harrington at the first meeting of the freshmen BSU. He was elected president, and she was elected vice president."[21] They were married at First Baptist Church of New Orleans, Louisiana, on June 21, 1974.[22] Kelley continued his education and earned both his Master of Divinity (1978) in Biblical Studies and Doctor of Theology (1983) in preaching at New Orleans Baptist Theological Seminary in New Orleans, Louisiana.

---

18. Guffin, *Here We Raise Our Ebenezer*, 23.

19. Guffin, *Here We Raise Our Ebenezer*, 24.

20. Price, *Engage*, xviii.

21. Price, *Engage*, xx.

22. Price, *Engage*.

Kelley joined the faculty at New Orleans Baptist Theological Seminary during Landrum P. Leavell II's presidency in 1983 as professor of evangelism. In a personal telephone interview, Kelley stated,

> I was a professor of evangelism from 1983 forward. I became the Roland Q. Leavell Chair in 1989. I became president in 1996. I continued my role as a professor of evangelism, but I did not keep the chair for a very particular reason. At NOBTS, any endowed chair includes, for the occupant, a monthly stipend in addition to their salary. I simply did not think it was right for me, as president, to receive that monthly endowment and occupy that chair when I could use it for a faculty member. I gave the chair, at that point, to Preston Nix, who occupies it to this day.[23]

Although Kelley, as president of the institution, installed Preston Nix into the Roland Q. Leavell Chair of Evangelism, evidence provided by archives of New Orleans Baptist Theological Seminary list three occupants that preceded him.[24]

During his occupancy of the chair, Kelley led the Pastoral Ministry Division, which is the largest division of the seminary. "Basically, the Roland Q. Leavell Chair has been the driver for the evangelism curriculum, because it was our first chair."[25] In 1983, Kelley, C. C. Randall, and Ed Thiele created all of the necessary courses for an emphasis in evangelism for the Master of Divinity degree. "We created a Doctorate of Ministry in evangelism, and we created a PhD in evangelism. All of that happened within the first two years the three of us were there."[26]

With regard to seminary-wide curriculum, Kelley fashioned an evangelism class, which is still taught today, that every student in the MDiv program of the seminary must take before graduating.

> It was our first semester-length class in the curriculum. Every student had to take it. They did two things. They were taught how to share their faith, and how to teach other people to share their faith. Then they were divided up into teams of two or three,

23. Kelley, interview with the author, Appendix 10.

24. Through email correspondence, circulation librarian Rebekah Phillips at the John T. Christian Library at the New Orleans Baptist Theological Seminary verified that professors Charles "Chuck" Register, James Cogdill, and David Meacham served between 1996 and 2008. See Appendix 16.

25. Kelley, interview with the author, Appendix 10.

26. Kelley, interview with the author, Appendix 10.

and they had to go out knocking on doors in the city of New Orleans, through one of our local churches, for at least ten weeks during the semester. That became a necessity for graduating.[27]

Kelley served as the eighth president of New Orleans Baptist Theological Seminary from 1996 to 2019. Kelley inherited from his predecessor, Landrum P. Leavell, the newly-founded Angola Penitentiary Extension Center that began in 1995. "The effort led to a church-planting movement at the prison, with many coming to Christ, resulting in a transformation of the prison's culture."[28] Kelley's leadership placed a high emphasis on evangelism both on the main campus in New Orleans and in its extension centers. In 1997, Kelley remarked of the sixteen members of the first class to graduate with degrees at Angola: "Kelley asked the congregation 'to rejoice and celebrate that God is never through with any human life. He always has the power to change and transform a life and make any life useful and productive.'"[29] During his presidency, New Orleans Baptist Theological Seminary experienced student enrollment expansion and two complete campus rebuilds.

> Shortly after Chuck Kelley was elected to follow Leavell as NOBTS president, serious termite damage was discovered throughout the campus. The trustees considered relocation, but in the end approved a massive campus restoration effort. A few years after the campus rehabilitation effort, Hurricane Katrina ripped through the region and inundated the campus with flood water. Recovery was no small task, but the campus was rebuilt and the seminary community renewed its commitment to the city.[30]

In 2014 New Orleans Baptist Theological Seminary, under Kelley's leadership, introduced the Caskey Center for Church Excellence. "The center offers full scholarships and other assistance for bi-vocational and small church ministers. The program, which emphasizes personal evangelism, has resulted in 26,359 gospel conversations and 2,887 new believers."[31]

---

27. Kelley, interview with the author, Appendix 10.

28. Myers, "Chuck Kelley Announces Retirement," 3.

29. Moore, "First Class."

30. Myers, "New Orleans Seminary Celebrates," 4–5.

31. Myers, "Chuck Kelley Announces Retirement," 2.

Kelley retired from the office of the president at New Orleans Baptist Theological Seminary on July 31, 2019. He continues his service today as president emeritus and distinguished research professor of evangelism from his home in Fairhope, Alabama. In his retirement he "plans to begin a renewed focus on research into the SBC's evangelism issues."[32]

Charles L. Register (1996 to 2000)

Charles "Chuck" Register is a native of Starke, Florida. He married his wife, Charlene, in 1982.[33] Together, he and his wife have two children. He is a graduate of the University of Florida and earned both Master of Divinity and Doctor of Theology degrees from New Orleans Baptist Theological Seminary.

In November 1996, the Board of Trustees at New Orleans Baptist Theological Seminary "approved Charles L. Register to occupy the Roland Q. Leavell Chair of Evangelism."[34] Register joined the faculty in 1994. He also served as director of the Leavell Center for Evangelism and Church Growth at New Orleans Baptist Theological Seminary. According to the Baptist State Convention of North Carolina (BSCNC) website, "Register has continued his work in church planting since his resignation from the seminary. Chuck Register has been employed by the BSCNC as executive leader of Church Planting and Missions Partnerships since 2009. Chuck oversees church planting, associational partnerships, Great Commission partnerships and collegiate partnerships."[35]

James Cogdill (2000 to 2003)

James "Jim" Paul Cogdill was born April 27, 1955, in Marion, Illinois, to James and Lillian June Cogdill. He married Debbie Collie on May 25, 1974.[36] "Cogdill completed both his bachelor of arts degree, summa cum laude, and a bachelor of science degree in education, summa cum laude, at Southeast Missouri State University in 1982."[37] He earned his master

32. Myers, "Chuck Kelley Announces Retirement," 2.
33. Jameson, "Chuck Register," 2.
34. Moore, "NOBTS Trustees Focus," 7.
35. Jameson, "Chuck Register."
36. "Dr. James Paul Cogdill."
37. Baker, "New Orleans Trustees add Jim Cogdill," 1.

of divinity (1986) and doctorate of philosophy (1990) from Southern Baptist Theological Seminary, Louisville, Kentucky.

Cogdill served in many capacities, including professor, dean, seminary vice president, and pastor. He served Southeastern Baptist Theological Seminary in Wake Forest, North Carolina; Midwestern Baptist Theological Seminary in Kansas City, Missouri; and New Orleans Baptist Theological Seminary in New Orleans, Louisiana as professor of evangelism and church growth. Cogdill was installed as the Roland Q. Leavell Chair of Evangelism in 2000 following Chuck Register's resignation.

David Meacham (2004 to 2007)

David Meacham was born in Renton, Washington, and reared in Georgia and California. He earned a bachelor of arts in TV and film from San Diego State University. He earned both the master of theology (ThM) and doctor of ministry (DMin) from New Orleans Baptist Theological Seminary.

Meacham served as "a missionary of the Home Mission Board (now North American Mission Board) division of associational missions, serving as director of missions of the Southern Nevada Baptist Association in Las Vegas for eleven years" prior to joining the faculty of New Orleans Baptist Theological Seminary in 2001. He was elected professor of church planting; a part of his service was as director of the Cecil B. Day Center for Church Planting and director of the seminary's Nehemiah Project.[38] According to an article from *Baptist Press*, "NAMB's Nehemiah Project seeks to bring about a dramatically higher percentage of seminary graduates to become church planters across the United States."[39] In 2007, Meacham resigned from New Orleans Baptist Theological Seminary and accepted a position as senior strategist for NAMB's church-planting group. Preston Nix succeeded Meacham in 2008, becoming the eighth occupant of the Roland Q. Leavell Chair of Evangelism.

Preston L. Nix (2008–)

Preston Nix currently serves as the Roland Q. Leavell Chair of Evangelism and Director of the Leavell Center for Evangelism and Church Health

38. Baker, "Nevada Exec David Meacham."
39. Baker, "Nevada Exec David Meacham."

at New Orleans Baptist Theological Seminary. He has occupied this endowed chair since his installation on August 1, 2008. Nix was reared in Waco, Texas. He attended Stephen F. Austin University in Nacogdoches, Texas, where he earned his bachelor of arts degree in 1978.[40] Nix earned his master of divinity in 1984 and doctor of philosophy in evangelism in 1992 from Southwestern Baptist Theological Seminary in Fort Worth, Texas. Nix stated, "My claim to fame at Southwestern Seminary, I was the one who pioneered the brand-new evangelism major [in the PhD program] at Southwestern Seminary. I was the only one that first year."[41] Nix studied under Roy J. Fish, James Eaves, and Malcolm McDow during his degrees at Southwestern Baptist Theological Seminary.

An aspect of his teaching role is modeling personal evangelism practices to his students. Each week, on Thursdays, he accompanies students from personal evangelism classes out to share the gospel door-to-door with the surrounding New Orleans community around the seminary.[42] This outreach is in connection with a course,

> Supervised Ministry One, which was where you do not just take a course and learn about evangelism. You have to do it. For ten of the sixteen weeks, you have to be out with a team. Originally, and for many years, it was what you did in New Orleans, but then after Katrina especially, we became a lot more of a commuter campus and people were scattered. So people are doing their evangelism with their local churches, but you have to have a team. Again, at least one other person, ideally two others. They go out in their church community.[43]

Second, Nix has become the Southern Baptist Convention's Crossover liaison between NAMB and the other seminaries' professors of evangelism. "Crossover is an annual evangelistic event that takes place in the city where the SBC Annual Meeting is held."[44]

> I've been the point person with Crossover and NAMB with the seminaries. Then we started passing it off, as far as coordinating all the seminaries and their involvement in the different areas, and generally it was the seminary closest to that location,

---

40. Nix, interview with the author, Appendix 13.
41. Nix, interview with the author, Appendix 13.
42. Nix, interview with the author, Appendix 13.
43. Nix, interview with the authorr, Appendix 13.
44. Trevillian, "Crossover Report Emphasizes Evangelism," 1.

whatever city where the Convention was held. But I have been the guy that's been the point man for that from almost the very beginning and have continued to serve in that capacity. It's not so much connected to the chair, but it's because of my position.[45]

Nix has been a part of SBC Crossover since the earliest days in 1989, when the Convention was held in Las Vegas, Nevada.

ADDITIONAL CHAIRS OF EVANGELISM AT NEW ORLEANS BAPTIST THEOLOGICAL SEMINARY

The Roland Q. Leavell Chair of Evangelism is New Orleans Baptist Theological Seminary's first endowed chair. The Seminary's evangelistic impetus has led friends of the seminary and supporters of evangelism in theological education to inaugurate two additional chairs of evangelism. In the seminary's 2019–20 graduate catalogue, there are a list of three chairs of evangelism.[46] The aforementioned is the first chair listed; second, the Max and Bonnie Thornhill Chair of Evangelism, currently held by Jake Roudkovski (2014–); and third, the Thomas Gurney Chair of Evangelism and Church Health, currently held by Bill Day (2001–).

The Max and Bonnie Thornhill Chair of Evangelism

The Max and Bonnie Thornhill Chair of Evangelism was established in 1993, and Robert L. Hamblin was installed as the inaugural occupant, occupying the chair from 1994–98. Records from the New Orleans Baptist Theological Seminary academic catalogues show the chair was unoccupied from 1998–2001. The chair was then filled by Will H. McRaney Jr. from 2001–07. The Max and Bonnie Thornhill Chair of Evangelism is currently occupied by Jake Roudkovski. He serves as professor of evangelism and pastoral leadership and as the director of the Doctor of Ministry Program. Roudkovski has occupied the chair since 2007.[47]

Kelley, in a personal interview, recounts the explanation for the creation of this second chair of evangelism at New Orleans Baptist Theological Seminary. He states,

---

45. Nix, interview with the author, Appendix 13.

46. "Graduate Catalog 2019–2020," 246–49.

47. Phillips, email correspondence with the author, Appendix 16.

Well the Thornhills, likeable couple, they got to know a former professor of evangelism who taught with me for several years before he left to go pastor a church, and this couple were involved in his ministry. They knew Dr. Leavell, and known him for a number of years. They decided they wanted to do a chair.

They asked Dr. Leavell to come up and help them make the final arrangements, and Dr. Leavell took my friend, who was teaching with me at that time, he was teaching evangelistic preaching, took him with him because he was such a good friend of these people there. While they're driving up, my friend asked Dr. Leavell, he said, "Well, Dr. Leavell, is there any particular direction that you want to go with this chair?" He said, "Well Don, we want a chair in any area but evangelism," he said, "so we're going to talk with them and see if they would be willing to . . . anything they're interested in, but we will not encourage them to do evangelism because we already have so many evangelism chairs."

They got there, they were chatting, and they said, "Yes, we definitely want to do the chair." They were going to start with $500,000 check. Dr. Leavell said, "Is there an area that you want to do this chair for? Would you like us to make a suggestion?" He said, "We want to do evangelism. That's what we'd like to do." Dr. Leavell said, "That's great. We would love to have that. That will be wonderful."

When they were driving back and my friend said, "Dr. Leavell, I thought you said we didn't need another evangelism chair?" He said, "Don, the gorilla in the room can sit in any chair he wants." Then said, "We are happy to sit. Rule number one is always listen to the donor, whatever the donor wants, it's our job to facilitate. So we'll certainly be able to use it. It would have been nice to have at least one chair in some area of the seminary without a chair, but we can always use another chair of evangelism. So, that's what I would take from them."[48]

The chair is the direct outcome of generous evangelistic lay people devoted to furthering Southern Baptist evangelism through theological education.

---

48. Kelley, interview with the author, Appendix 10.

The Thomas Gurney Chair of Evangelism and Church Health

The Thomas Gurney Chair of Evangelism and Church Health, established in 1997, was created to help grow healthy churches. A strategy of the chair is to research and implement a "purposeful interim." Randy Millwood, the inaugural occupant of the Gurney Chair of Evangelism and Church Health, stated, "An interim specialist also will lead a church to develop and implement an outreach strategy during the interim time, a unique aspect of the purposeful interim."[49] Millwood filled the chair from 1998 to 2000. The current occupant of the chair is William H. Day Jr., who has occupied the chair since 2001. Day is currently titled distinguished research professor and associate director of the Leavell Center for Evangelism and Church Health.

SOUTHERN BAPTIST THEOLOGICAL SEMINARY'S BILLY GRAHAM CHAIR OF EVANGELISM (ESTABLISHED 1965)

Billy Graham is a notable evangelist of the twentieth and twenty-first centuries. Paulus Scharpff, an evangelism historian, has stated,

> The most influential single individual in evangelism in America during this period is Billy Graham of Montreat, North Carolina. Few places and few spheres of influence have remained untouched by this remarkable man who for fifteen years has been in the spotlight and yet appears ever stronger and more powerful in his ministry. He is a friend of presidents and world rulers, yet has the ear of the common man. While he himself did not follow the traditional college-plus-seminary educational route, yet he has been a friend of education. He has identified himself with a broad spectrum of church groups in his evangelistic crusades, but has maintained a simple and positive proclamation.[50]

In 1965 the Billy Graham Chair of Evangelism was established and endowed at Southern Baptist Theological Seminary in Louisville, Kentucky. Adam Greenway, in a telephone interview, recalled the significance of this chair of evangelism, stating, "Well, the Billy Graham Chair of Evangelism was established, I believe, in 1965 at Southern Seminary when

---

49. Zygiel, "NOBTS Completes Interims Pilot," 1.
50. Scharpff, *History of Evangelism*, 322.

Duke McCall was president there. Dr. Graham himself had been in a relationship with Southern Seminary and the Graham organization going back to the fifties, but it took on a new form in 1965 with the inauguration of the Billy Graham Chair."[51]

Albert Mohler, ninth president of Southern Baptist Theological Seminary, made his first initiative the establishment of the Billy Graham School of Evangelism, Missions, and Church Growth. "He announced the initiative at his inauguration in October 1993. Billy Graham endorsed Mohler's vision for the new school and the attachment of his name to it. Graham preached at Mohler's inauguration service at Louisville's Freedom Hall Arena. Graham's support gave the school credibility and momentum."[52] Today, the school is known as the Billy Graham School of Missions, Evangelism, and Ministry.

The Billy Graham Chair of Evangelism has had five occupants. Greenway states, "Every occupant of the Billy Graham Chair of Evangelism at Southern Seminary has been an alumnus of Southwestern Seminary, and that's a neat insight. But the Billy Graham Chair there was their first endowed professorship in evangelism, it certainly is I think, a historic chair there."[53]

Kenneth Chafin (1965 to 1969)

Kenneth Chafin arrived at The Southern Baptist Theological Seminary to become the inaugural occupant of the Billy Graham Chair of Evangelism after serving a five-year tenure at Southwestern Baptist Theological Seminary in Fort Worth, Texas, where he had held the "Chair of Fire" from 1960 to 1965. He is the only professor of evangelism to occupy both the "Chair of Fire" at Southwestern Baptist Theological Seminary and the Billy Graham Chair of Evangelism at Southern Baptist Theological Seminary. Chafin had previously served for many years in the Billy Graham Evangelistic Association.[54] Chafin succeeded Autrey as Director of Evangelism at the HMB in 1970. Chafin believed mass evangelism should utilize the television through mass media.

---

51. Greenway, interview with the author, Appendix 6.

52. Wills, *Southern Baptist Theological Seminary*, 544.

53. Greenway, interview with the author, Appendix 6.

54. Wills, *Southern Baptist Theological Seminary*, 460.

The central feature of Chafin's program, however, was not television. It was a witness training school designed to help laymen become active, effective evangelists, sharing the gospel with others in home or marketplace encounters. The school was introduced as the WIN School (Witness Involvement Now), and has also been called the Lay Evangelism School (LES). Participants in the school were taught to share their personal testimonies and explain the gospel with a tract."[55]

He moved the Department of Evangelism's focus from revivals to personal evangelism.[56] Gregory Wills stated, "He became well known in the Southern Baptist controversy as one of the most vocal opponents of the conservative takeover."[57] Chafin was succeeded by Gordon Clinard, pastor of First Baptist Church of San Angelo, Texas.

Howard Gordon Clinard (1970 to 1972)

Howard Gordon Clinard was born April 14, 1921, in Springfield, Tennessee, to parents Lewis Josephus and Lydia Tucker Clinard. In 1941, he married Christine Browder Clinard and together they had three children. Clinard was a pastor, professor of evangelism, president of the Baptist General Convention of Texas, trustee, and author.

"He [Clinard] received his bachelor of arts degree in 1944 from Union University at Jackson, Tenn. In 1949 he graduated from Southwestern Baptist Theological Seminary at Fort Worth with a bachelor of divinity degree and in 1958 he received a doctor of theology degree."[58] In 1963, while serving on the faculty of Southwestern Baptist Theological Seminary, Clinard partnered with H. C. Brown Jr. and Jesse J. Northcutt to co-author a book on sermon preparations. The book was titled *Steps to the Sermon*.[59] Clinard was also a former editor of the *Southwestern Journal of Theology*.

Clinard left Southwestern Baptist Theological Seminary to become pastor of the First Baptist Church of San Angelo, Texas. He simultaneously served two terms as president of the Baptist General Convention of

55. Kelley, *How Did They Do It?*, 46.
56. Kelley, *How Did They Do It?*, 45.
57. Wills, *Southern Baptist Theological Seminary*, 460.
58. "Dr. Howard Gordon Clinard," 2.
59. "3 Southwestern Profs," 3.

Texas (BGCT). "He was elected president of the Baptist General Convention of Texas in 1967, and re-elected in 1968."[60] Clinard joined the faculty at Southern Baptist Theological Seminary as full professor of evangelism with tenure and filled the Billy Graham Chair of Evangelism for two years of service at the seminary. *Baptist Press* reported, "Clinard succeeds Kenneth L. Chafin, who resigned early this year to become director of the evangelism division for the Southern Baptist Home Mission Board in Atlanta."[61]

In August 1972, Gordon Clinard would return to West Texas to become a distinguished professor of Bible at Hardin-Simmons University of Abilene, Texas.[62] "Dr. Clinard had been interim pastor of University Baptist Church since May."[63] Clinard was killed in a three-car accident in 1973 in Abilene.[64]

Lewis Drummond (1972 to 1988)

Lewis Drummond was the third occupant of the Billy Graham Chair of Evangelism at Southern Baptist Theological Seminary. He is from Dixon, Illinois, and was born in 1927. He took courses at a Lutheran college. Through the witness of college students Drummond made Jesus Lord and Savior.[65] He would accept his calling during his time of Air Force service.

Drummond earned a bachelor of arts degree from Howard College. He then attended Southwestern Baptist Theological Seminary and earned both master of divinity and master of theology. Drummond earned a doctor of philosophy from King's College at the University of London.[66] "Following his graduation from King's College, Drummond served churches in Alabama and Texas 1949–61 until the Ninth and O Baptist Church in Louisville called him as its pastor in 1964."[67]

---

60. "Gordon Clinard Elected," 2–3.

61. "Gordon Clinard Elected," 2.

62. "Dr. Howard Gordon Clinard," 2.

63. "Dr. Howard Gordon Clinard," 2.

64. "Dr. Howard Gordon Clinard," 1.

65. Rainer, *Evangelism*, 4–5.

66. "Our Professors: Lewis Drummond."

67. "Our Professors: Lewis Drummond."

Drummond returned to London, England, to accept his first teaching position at Spurgeon's Theological College after twenty years in the pastorate. "In 1968 he accepted the chair of evangelism and practical theology at Spurgeon's Theological College in London. This position was the first full professorship of evangelism in Europe. After five exciting years in England, he returned to the United States to become Billy Graham Professor of Evangelism at the Southern Baptist Theological Seminary in Louisville, Kentucky."[68]

During his fifteen-year tenure at Southern Baptist Theological Seminary, Drummond provided instruction in various evangelism courses, such as "Introduction to Evangelism, Building an Evangelistic Church, Evangelism and Spiritual Formation, Personal Evangelism, Evangelistic Preaching, Theology of Evangelism, and Principles of Spiritual Awakenings."[69] Furthermore, Drummond pioneered the doctor of philosophy in evangelism at Southern Baptist Theological Seminary. "Southern Seminary, under Dr. Drummond's leadership, was the first school in the world to offer the PhD in evangelism."[70]

Drummond was a prolific author. He published numerous books throughout his career.[71] He resigned as the Billy Graham Professor of Evangelism at Southern Baptist Theological Seminary in 1988 in order to become the fourth president of Southeastern Baptist Theological Seminary in Wake Forest, North Carolina. Drummond retired in 1992, after

68. Rainer, *Evangelism*, 5.

69. Rainer, *Evangelism*, 5.

70. Rainer, *Evangelism*, 5.

71. Drummond books in publication order: *Evangelism: The Counter Revolution* (1972); *Life Can Be Real* (1973); *Leading Your Church in Evangelism* (1975); *What the Bible Says* (1975); *Here They Stand: Sermons from Eastern Europe* (1976); *The Awakening That Must Come* (1978); *Witnessing for God to Men* (1980); *The Revived Life* (1982); *Charles G. Finney: The Birth of Modern Evangelism* (1982); *The Life and Ministry of Charles G. Finney* (1984); *The People of God in Ministry* (1985); *Spiritual Awakening: God's Divine Work* (1985); *How to Respond to a Skeptic* (1986); *The Word of the Cross: A Contemporary Theology of Evangelism* (1989); *Spurgeon: Prince of Preachers* (1992); *Eight Keys to Biblical Revival: The Saga of Scriptural Spiritual Awakenings, How They Shaped the Great Revivals of the Past, and Their Powerful Implications for Today's Church* (1994); *Miss Bertha: Woman of Revival* (1996); *Women of Awakenings: The Historical Contribution of Women to Revival Movements* (1997); *The Spiritual Woman: Ten Principles of Spirituality and Women Who Have Lived Them* (1999); *The Evangelist: The Worldwide Impact of Billy Graham* (2001); *Ripe for Harvest: The Role of Spiritual Awakening in Church Growth* (2001); *Reaching Generation Next: Effective Evangelism in Today's Culture* (2002); and *The Canvas Cathedral: A Complete History of Evangelism from the Apostle Paul to Billy Graham* (2003).

serving for four years as president of Southeastern Baptist Theological Seminary.[72] Following his retirement from Southeastern Baptist Theological Seminary in 1992, Drummond returned to the classroom as the Billy Graham Professor of Evangelism and Church Growth at Samford University's Beeson Divinity School.[73] He retired once more in 2003.

David F. D'Amico (1989 to 1996)

Limited literature exists about David D'Amico, who served as the Billy Graham Chair of Evangelism occupant 1989–96. David D'Amico left the SBC to join the leaders of the moderates, who would later organize themselves as the Cooperative Baptist Fellowship (CBF) during what would later become known as the conservative resurgence of the SBC. "He was formerly Billy Graham Professor of Evangelism at the Southern Baptist Theological Seminary in Louisville, Kentucky, and the former Executive Director of the Metropolitan New York Baptist Association."[74] In 1994, the *Baptist Press* praised D'Amico for his chairmanship of Southern Baptist Theological Seminary's Home Missions Week, stating, "D'Amico, who chaired the committee directing the event, noted thirty-five students made commitments to home missions during the special emphasis."[75] D'Amico's research field has been the study of cross-cultural evangelization to the increasing Asian and Hispanic populations in the United States.[76]

Timothy Beougher (1997–)

Timothy Beougher currently serves as the Billy Graham Chair of Evangelism at Southern Baptist Theological Seminary, a teaching position he has held for twenty-three years. He earned a bachelor of science from Kansas State University, master of divinity at Southwestern Baptist Theological Seminary, and both master of theology and doctor of philosophy (1997)

---

72. "Southeastern's History: Drummond Presidency."
73. Nunnelley, "Drummond, Retired Beeson Professor, Dies at 77."
74. "Our Reviewers."
75. "Lewis Urges Seminarians," 8.
76. Walker, "Christians Urged to Prepare," 4.

at Trinity Evangelical Divinity School. Albert Mohler specifically hired Beougher to occupy the Billy Graham Chair of Evangelism.[77]

> When Dr. Mohler talked to me about coming to Southern, he said that one of the changes that he was making, as president, is that Personal Evangelism would become a required class for all students in all degree programs. At that time, it was a required class for pastors, for ministerial students, those in the pastor track, but if someone was in the music track, they didn't have to take Personal Evangelism. He [Mohler] said, "We're going to change the curriculum." He [Mohler] said, "I want Personal Evangelism to be a required class for every single student." He [Mohler] said, "I want them to actually learn how to do evangelism, actually practice it. I just don't want a theoretical kind of course."[78]

Mohler essentially tasked Beougher with infusing Southern Baptist Theological Seminary with the fires of evangelism. Beougher did so through both classroom instruction and field ministry practicum. Today the course is titled "Personal Evangelism." The course is mandatory for all students at Southern Baptist Theological Seminary, not just those students on the track to become a pastor.

According to Beougher, the Billy Graham Chair of Evangelism oversees Southern Baptist Theological Seminary's student participation in SBC Crossover each year. He also organizes and leads the campus each year in a day of service and sharing called the "1937 Project." Beougher states,

> . . . in 1937, there was a major flood in Louisville. A lot of the downtown area flooded. The seminary here in Louisville sits on a hill kind of like Southwestern. It's a little higher than the surrounding region. Actually, the city hall moved to Southern Seminary's campus in 1937, and the seminary really had an impact in terms of ministering to the Louisville community. Every April, we have an outreach where students, faculty, everyone goes out throughout the city to do service projects, to share the gospel, just connect and show love for our city.[79]

With regard to the impact that the chair of evangelism has had on Southern Baptist evangelism, Beougher states, "I think the primary

---

77. Beougher, interview with the author, Appendix 2.

78. Beougher, interview with the author, Appendix 2.

79. Beougher, interview with the author, Appendix 2.

impact has obviously been through students, sending out students that have been trained in personal evangelism that are going to be pastors and associate pastors, youth pastors, children's directors, worship leaders, with those students going out knowing how to share the gospel and having shared it multiple times. I think that is significant."[80] The greatest impact of the Billy Graham Chair of Evangelism is the imparting of the academic knowledge and practical confidence to share the good news of Jesus Christ with others.

Though not immediately connected with the chair, Beougher discusses the evangelism outreach of the Bevin Center for Mission Mobilization that is housed under the Billy Graham School of Missions, Evangelism, and Ministry. Through the Center, students are provided opportunities to witness in jails, schools, with Fellowship of Christian Athletes (FCA), and on short-term mission trips. Beougher states, "We have regular churches asking for students to come and preach and so we try and set that up and work with the students in terms of some basic training, make sure they are clearly sharing the gospel as they go."[81]

GATEWAY SEMINARY'S E. HERMOND WESTMORELAND CHAIR OF EVANGELISM (ESTABLISHED 1966)

Erwin Hermond Westmoreland was born September 9, 1905, in Booneville, Arkansas. Westmoreland was a prominent Texas pastor. "Dr. Westmoreland graduated from Ouachita Baptist College and received his doctor's degree from Southern Baptist Theological Seminary, Louisville, Kentucky. He also holds honorary doctor of divinity degrees from Ouachita and Baylor University."[82] He served South Main Baptist Church of Houston, Texas, from 1938 until his retirement in 1971. During his thirty-three years of pastoral ministry, "the church's membership had swelled to over six thousand members."[83] Westmoreland's pastoral leadership fueled church-planting efforts as South Main Baptist Church sponsored seven mission congregations in the Houston area. "At home, several important ongoing ministries were inaugurated, including the South Main International Learning Experience (SMILE), a ministry for

---

80. Beougher, interview with the author, Appendix 2.

81. Beougher, interview with the author, Appendix 2.

82. "To God Be the Glory," 16.

83. South Main Baptist Church, "Our History."

internationals living in Houston, and Sojourn House, which provides apartments to patients being treated in the Texas Medical Center."[84] He also served as a chairman of the Board of Trustees at Golden Gate Baptist Theological Seminary in Berkeley, California.[85] E. Hermond Westmoreland died on August 28, 1976, at age seventy.

Golden Gate Baptist Theological Seminary (now Gateway Seminary) initiated the chair of evangelism in 1966 with a fundraising campaign. Gateway Seminary president Jeff Iorg in a telephone interview provided a history of the chair of evangelism: "The chair was ultimately named for E. Hermond Westmoreland, who was a trustee and prominent Texas pastor . . . Over the years, there was about $260,000 donated for the chair in the sixties, seventies, and the eighties. That was not nearly enough to endow the whole chair, but it was a significant number of gifts for which we [the Seminary] were grateful."[86]

Iorg continues,

> But in the 1990s, the seminary invested most of the money for this chair with the Arizona Baptist Foundation. In terms of the grand total of the seminary's investments, it was a token investment, but the seminary does have small investments in Baptist foundations in the West both to demonstrate our partnership to them and to encourage them and also to gain an income for the seminary. We had invested about $300,000 in the Arizona Baptist Foundation . . . The E. Hermond Westmoreland Chair of Evangelism funding was essentially lost.[87]

The E. Hermond Westmoreland Chair at Gateway Seminary has remained insufficiently funded and unoccupied since 2006. Iorg recapped the E. Hermond Westmoreland Chair of Evangelism's current status: "Dr. Crews chaired the investor committee which put us at the end of the line, which meant we got nothing. Today, the chair is in name only with no serious funding attached or no real connection to much, any longer, to the Westmoreland family . . . "[88]

84. South Main Baptist Church, "Our History."

85. South Main Baptist Church, "Our History."

86. Iorg, interview with the author, Appendix 8.

87. Iorg, interview with the author, Appendix 8.

88. Iorg, interview with the author, Appendix 8.

George William "Bill" Schweer (1978 to 1996)

G. William Schweer is from Independence, Missouri. He earned a bachelor of science from the University of Missouri in Columbia, Missouri; and a bachelor of divinity, master of theology, and doctor of theology from Central Baptist Theological Seminaryin Kansas City, Kansas. "During a revival meeting in 1951 he met the woman with whom he would spend the rest of his life, Wanda Beckham. They were married just three months after their first date, adding three children to the family during the next six years."[89]

Schweer served as a pastor of two churches in Missouri before moving his family to the mission field of Indonesia in 1957. As a Foreign Mission Board (FMB) missionary, he served as an educator and was eventually elected president of the Baptist Seminary of Indonesia in Semarang, Java, in 1970.[90] "Dr. Schweer served two years in that capacity before returning to the United States to become pastor of First Baptist Church, Palatine, Ill. He held that position until he came to Golden Gate Seminary in 1975."[91] From 1978 to 1996, Schweer worked as the initial denizen of the E. Hermond Westmoreland Chair of Evangelism. Iorg, speaking of his service and character, states that Schweer was "a fantastic evangelist and professor and Christian gentlemen in every regard."[92] He published several articles and "a textbook for seminary evangelism classes entitled *Personal Evangelism for Today* published by Broadman."[93] George William Schweer died on May 16, 2018, at age ninety-one.

William Lyle "Bill" Wagner (1996 to 2006)

William Lyle Wagner was born on January 23, 1936, in Albuquerque, New Mexico, to William Chauncy and Opal Strayer Wagner. He married Sally Ann Crook Wagner on November 21, 1956. Wagner earned a bachelor of science at the University of New Mexico, Albuquerque, in 1957; a master of divinity at Southwestern Baptist Theological Seminary, Fort Worth, Texas, in 1961; and a doctor of missiology from Fuller

---

89. Green, "George William Schweer," 1.

90. "Dr. G. William Schweer."

91. "Dr. G. William Schweer."

92. Iorg, interview with the author, Appendix 8.

93. Iorg, interview with the author, Appendix 8.

Theological Seminary, Pasadena, California, in 1976. "William Lyle Wagner was named to the Westmoreland Chair of Evangelism as professor of evangelism and church growth. Wagner has served as a Southern Baptist foreign missionary since 1965. He previously was a pastor in New Mexico."[94] He occupied the E. Hermond Westmoreland Chair of Evangelism for ten years. In 1997, *Baptist Press* announced Wagner's nomination for the SBC second vice-president position.[95] Cal Guy, a retired Southern Baptist Missionary and then professor emeritus of Southwestern Baptist Theological Seminary in Texas, nominated him.[96] Cal Guy further commented of Wagner's qualifications, "Dr. Wagner is a rare combination of layman, preacher, scholar, practitioner, American Christian, world Christian, church planter and administrator."[97] Wagner would serve until his retirement in 2006.

SOUTHEASTERN BAPTIST THEOLOGICAL SEMINARY'S BAILEY SMITH CHAIR OF EVANGELISM (ESTABLISHED 1994)

L. Paige Patterson served as president of Southeastern Baptist Theological Seminary from 1992 to 2003. He led the charge of establishing a chair of evangelism at the seminary during his presidency and by doing so set a regular standard of evangelism in theological education at the seminary in Wake Forest, North Carolina. In a personal interview, Patterson states, "The Bailey Smith Chair of Evangelism (the first endowed chair at Southeastern Baptist Theological Seminary) was established in March 1994, only two years after I arrived at Southeastern Seminary. My pattern, of course, was the 'Chair of Fire' at Southwestern Baptist Theological Seminary."[98] Patterson was reared in Beaumont, Texas, the son of a prominent Texas pastor and Baptist statesman, T. A. Patterson. As a student at Southwestern Baptist Theological Seminary, T. A. Patterson was influenced by the Scarborough administration.[99] When Paige Patterson

---

94. Wyatt, "Golden Gate Trustees Approve," 7.

95. "Golden Gate Prof."

96. "Golden Gate Prof."

97. "Golden Gate Prof."

98. Patterson, interview with the author, Appendix 15.

99. Patterson, interview with the author, Appendix 15.

surrendered to ministry, his father gave him a copy of L. R. Scarborough's *With Christ after the Lost.*

Bailey Smith served Southern Baptist churches in Texas, Arkansas, New Mexico, and Oklahoma as pastor from 1961 to 1985 and as a vocational evangelist from 1985 to 2015, a ministerial career spanning sixty-two years. During the early years of the conservative resurgence era, he served from 1981 to 1982 as the simultaneous president of Baptist General Convention of Oklahoma and of the Southern Baptist Convention. His wife, Sandy Smith, in a personal telephone interview said, "I think his philosophy [of evangelism] would have been, everyone is lost until we know by their explanation that they are not. And, never assume that somebody is saved. And so I think with that in mind that is why he spent hours and hours and hours, all day, every Saturday and days of the week, while he was a pastor, to go to people's homes and talk to them about Jesus."[100]

The Smiths and the Pattersons had a friendship forged while working to bring the denomination back to biblical principles. "And we became such good friends, we believed very much the same things. And we had such respect for them that when Dr. Patterson approached Bailey, who [sic] Dr. Patterson is a few years younger than both of us, but when he approached Bailey about this chair of evangelism by Patterson, and he was thrilled to death, because it was such a passion of his."[101]

Smith mentioned that Bailey Smith had a friend named Randy Bates, who funded the chair of evangelism.[102] Bailey Smith was honored that the chair of evangelism considered him a great evangelist of the Southern Baptist Convention. Sandy Smith stated, "And it was a thrill for Bailey because it became even more obvious to him that he was respected for his concentration and his single-mindedness toward evangelism. As far as I know, he did not, I am pretty sure that he did not choose the person who would fill that chair, but I am quite sure that Dr. Patterson talked, spoke together about what it should be, what should be taught, how it should go."[103]

George Robinson, the current occupant of the chair, recollects the historical event on September 4, 1994, at Binkley Chapel, where Bailey

100. Smith, interview with the author, Appendix 19.

101. Smith, interview with the author, Appendix 19.

102. Smith, interview with the author, Appendix 19.

103. Smith, interview with the author, Appendix 19.

Smith preached at the inaugural celebration of the Bailey Smith Chair of Evangelism at the Southeastern Baptist Theological Seminary, stating,

> During the 1994 service in which Smith preached, he passionately spoke on the importance of the Christian call to share the gospel to everyone, no matter their background, emphasizing the heartbeat of the Great Commission focus of SEBTS. Noting Jesus' love for all people, Smith said, "There is only one kind of person in the world: those for whom Jesus shed his precious blood—red, yellow, black, white, rich, poor, illiterate and educated," said Smith, who was quoted in a 1994 *Baptist Press* article reporting on the dedication service. I am convinced that the chair named in Dr. Smith's honor has and continues to cultivate passion for all kinds of people everywhere.[104]

The Bailey Smith Chair, like the L. R. Scarborough Chair of Evangelism, the "Chair of Fire," was designed to teach and promote a working knowledge and zeal for evangelism and to cultivate a passion for reaching the lost. Robinson further defined the chair's tenets:

> The original anticipated impact of the Bailey Smith Chair of Evangelism was that "three thousand God-called men" would be trained in ten years. The initial hope was that in just one year these three thousand could share the Gospel with at least three hundred thousand lost souls. Since the inception of the chair in September of 1994, far more than three thousand men (and women) have been equipped through evangelism training and events led by its occupants.[105]

Alvin L. Reid (1994 to 2018)

Alvin Lee Reid was born April 3, 1959. He served Southeastern Baptist Theological Seminary as professor of evangelism and student ministry. In 1994, Reid was installed as the inaugural occupant of the Bailey Smith Chair of Evangelism, an academic chair he held until his resignation on May 18, 2018. "Before teaching at Southeastern, Reid taught at Houston Baptist University from 1992–95 and had served as director of evangelism and stewardship for the State Convention of Baptist in Indiana."[106]

---

104. Robinson, email message to the author, Appendix 18.
105. Robinson, email message to the author, Appendix 18.
106. "Alvin Reid Resigns at Southeastern."

Reid earned a bachelor of arts from Samford University, Birmingham, Alabama, and both master of divinity and doctor of philosophy (1991) from Southwestern Baptist Theological Seminary, Fort Worth, Texas. His dissertation was supervised by Roy Fish, then-professor of evangelism and occupant of the "Chair of Fire," at Southwestern Baptist Theological Seminary, and was titled "The Impact of the Jesus Movement on Evangelism among Southern Baptists."[107] In 2013 a *festschrift* in his honor entitled *A Passion for the Great Commission: Essays in Honor of Alvin L. Reid* noted that he was "a dynamic teacher, inspiring speaker, and accomplished author."[108] Roy Fish provided definition and clarity in his foreword to the book, stating, "A *festschrift* is usually dedicated to a professor and is usually composed of essays written by friends, colleagues, and former students."[109] Reid published several books.[110] "Reid's website previously had stated he had spoken at more than two thousand churches, colleges, conferences, and events."[111] He was involved with the Gospel Coalition and the youth program Student Leadership University. In a *Baptist Press* release on May 24, 2018, Reid stated, "I have resigned from teaching and public ministry to address personal and spiritual issues in my life."[112]

107. Reid, "Impact of the Jesus Movement."

108. McDonald and Queen, *Passion,* back cover.

109. McDonald and Queen, *Passion,* xv.

110. Reid books in publication order: *evival!: The Story of the Current Awakening in Brownwood, Fort Worth, Wheaton, and Beyond* (1996); *Firefall: How God Has Shaped History through Revivals* (1997); *Introduction to Evangelism* (1998); *The Net Mentor Handbook* (2000); *Servanthood Evangelism Manual* (2000); *Light the Fire: Raising Up a Generation to Live Radically for Jesus Christ* (2001); *It's All Good* (2002); *Radically Unchurched: Who They Are and How to Reach Them* (2002); *Evangelism for a Changing World: Essays in Honor of Roy J. Fish* (2002); *Raising the Bar: Ministry to Youth in the New Millennium* (2004); *What Can We Do* (2006); *Join the Movement* (2007); *The Convergent Church: Missional Worshippers in an Emerging Culture* (2009); *Evangelism Handbook: Biblical, Spiritual, Intentional, and Missional* (2009); *Advance: Gospel-Centered Movements Change the World* (2010); *Roar: The Deafening Thunder of Spiritual Awakening* (2010); *With: A Guide to Informal Mentoring* (2010); *Book of Matches* (2012); *As You Go: Creating A Missional Culture of Gospel-Centered Students* (2013); *Pursuing God: A 40-Day Guide to Personal Revival* (2013); *Revitalize: Your Church Through Gospel Recovery* (2013); *Stronger: A Practical Guide to Physical and Spiritual Discipline* (2013); and *Sharing Jesus Without Freaking Out: Evangelism the Way You Were Born to Do It* (2017).

111. "Alvin Reid Resigns at Southeastern."

112. "Alvin Reid Resigns at Southeastern."

George G. Robinson IV (2019–)

George Robinson was born February 7, 1969, in Atlanta, Georgia. In 1991, Robinson graduated with both a bachelor of arts in political science and in 1993 with a master of arts (non-degree program), and Georgia Department of Education Social Sciences Secondary Education Teaching Certification from the University of Georgia. In 2001, he earned a master of divinity from Southeastern Baptist Theological Seminary in Wake Forest, North Carolina. Robinson attended Western Seminary in Portland, Oregon, in 2007, receiving his Doctor of Missiology.[113]

Prior to accepting a professorship at Southeastern Baptist Theological Seminary, Robinson served as a social sciences teacher for Gwinnett County Public Schools and an ISC Missionary with the International Mission Board to South Asia (Pakistan). His international service from 1999 to 2000 was in partial fulfillment of the Two Plus Two missions degree program crafted by Keith Eitel at Southeastern Baptist Theological Seminary. Eitel would later bring the Two Plus Two program to Southwestern Baptist Theological Seminary in 2005. Robinson has served as an Associate Pastor and with e3 Partners Ministries in Plano, Texas. Robinson was elected to faculty service in 2008 at Southeastern Baptist Theological Seminary. His faculty rank is associate professor of evangelism and missions. Prior to the Bailey Smith Chair of Evangelism occupancy, he was the Richard and Gina Headrick Chair of World Missions. In the fall of 2019, Robinson was installed as the Bailey Smith Chair of Evangelism at Southeastern Baptist Theological Seminary. Robinson followed Alvin Reid, former professor of evangelism, as the Bailey Smith Chair of Evangelism's second occupant since its formation in 1994.

Robinson's philosophy of evangelism is "that God has uniquely gifted some to serve the church so that all may joyfully participate in the sacred task of bearing witness to Christ among our neighbors and the nations until Jesus returns and makes all things new."[114] This philosophy provides a perspective of the man leading the campus through evangelism consciousness. Robinson states, "I would have to say that the depth of impact is rooted in my investment in equipping, coaching, and mentoring my students at SEBTS."[115]

---

113. "Elected Faculty," 34.

114. Robinson, email message to the author, Appendix 18.

115. Robinson, email message to the author, Appendix 18.

MIDWESTERN BAPTIST THEOLOGICAL SEMINARY'S GARY TAYLOR CHAIR OF MISSIONS AND EVANGELISM (ESTABLISHED 2012)

At the 2011 Missouri Baptist State Convention annual meeting, Kent Cochran made a motion calling for a review of process for the creation and installation for a chair of evangelism at Midwestern Baptist Theological Seminary. The Missouri messengers had moved five years prior to raise $500,000 in funding to be matched by the seminary for the purposes of creating such a chair of evangelism at the institution.[116] In 2012, Midwestern Baptist Theological Seminary confirms through *The Pathway*, "The chair has been operational since April 25, with $577,728 in funding contributed by the MBC. It has since grown to more than $1 million due to investments and other gifts."[117] Then-interim president Robin D. Hadaway announced, "The Gary Taylor Chair of Missions and Evangelism embodies the ideals of sharing the gospel in the Midwest and throughout the world."[118] The name of the chair of missions and evangelism was officially announced at the 2012 Annual June Meeting of the SBC Convention.

Raymond Gary Taylor served the Missouri Baptist Convention (MBC) in multiple capacities. He was a former president and evangelism director of the MBC. From 1989–2007, Taylor pastored First Baptist Church of O'Fallon, Missouri.[119] Taylor pastored six churches in Missouri and Tennessee from 1963 to 2007. From 2007 to 2012, Taylor served as Director of Evangelism at the MBC in Jefferson City, Missouri.[120] Raymond Gary Taylor died on May 29, 2012 at the age of seventy.

---

116. An examination of key meeting minutes and newsprint concerning the chair of evangelism at Midwestern Baptist Theological Seminary appear to support this view. See Missouri Baptist Convention, *2011 Annual Reports and Statistics*. In addition Greg Warner wrote an article titled "Seminary Trustees to Confront President over Audit, Management Issues." However, three days later on February 10, 2012, the Missouri Baptist Convention's (MBC) Journal, *The Pathway*, announced, "Roberts resigns as MBTS president." Then, an article on this chair of evangelism came out on May 15, 2012, three months later. *The Pathway* published a brief article stating that an agreement had been made between Midwestern Baptist Theological Seminary (MBTS) and MBC titled "MBTS, MBC Launch Chair." The plans to fill the chair are uncertain.

117. "New MBTS Chair Named for Taylor."

118. "New MBTS Chair Named for Taylor."

119. "New MBTS Chair Named for Taylor."

120. "Rev. Raymond Gary Taylor," 2.

Robin D. Hadaway (2012–)

Robin Hadaway was reared in Tallahassee, Florida. He is married to
Kathy Baze Hadaway. Together they have three grown children.[121] Ha-
daway completed a bachelor of arts (1971) at Memphis State University.
He earned a master of divinity (1978) from Southwestern Baptist Theo-
logical Seminary, Fort Worth, Texas; the doctor of ministry (1986) from
Golden Gate Baptist Theological Seminary (now Gateway Seminary, On-
tario, California); and Doctor of Theology (2011) from the University of
South Africa. Hadaway is a retired captain of the United States Air Force.
Hadaway served with the International Mission Board for eighteen years
before being elected to the faculty of Midwestern Baptist Theological
Seminary. Hadaway, a polyglot, is fluent in Arabic, Swahili, and Portu-
guese, having also served as a pioneer church planter in North Africa and
Tanzania.[122]

Robin Hadaway joined the faculty at Midwestern Baptist Theological Seminary in 2003 as a professor of missions. In 2012, Hadaway was
installed as the inaugural occupant of the Gary Taylor Chair of Missions
and Evangelism. Thomas Johnston, senior professor of evangelism at
Midwestern Baptist Theological Seminary, said, "And the monies and
the chair was named chair of missions and evangelism and was given to
Dr. Robin Hadaway, a longtime missionary with the IMB and also missions professor. And he's done very well in that chair and I'm grateful
for him. So that's how the monies were dispersed back when they were
given."[123] Hadaway, while serving as the seminary's interim president in
2012, worked to finalize the chair's endowment and activate this unique
academic chair. Hadaway still occupies the Gary Taylor Chair of Missions
and Evangelism. In 2020, Hadaway published a textbook, *A Survey of
World Missions*.[124]

CONCLUSION

The L. R. Scarborough Chair of Evangelism, the "Chair of Fire," founded
in 1908 by Carroll along with the beginning of Southwestern Baptist

121. "Robin D. Hadaway."
122. "Resources by Robin D. Hadaway."
123. Johnston, interview with the author, Appendix 9.
124. Hadaway, *Survey of World Missions*.

Theological Seminary, furnished an innovation in theological education that has shaped Southern Baptist evangelism. The "Chair of Fire" created both the blueprint and the template for evangelism and theological education through a means of training and preparation of pastors, church workers, denominational leaders, and parachurch workers through rigorous classroom instruction and practical application in theological education. Malcolm McDow, former occupant of the "Chair of Fire," argues,

> Academic chairs bring status to an institution. This is the major contribution of a chair. Anytime an institution has a chair, it augments the academic standing, standard, and whatever you want to call it, and consequently, when you have a chair and you mention that this is a chair, even to the lay person, it creates more respect for the institution. And really, it creates respect for them as an occupant. In certain circles, it opens doors for ministry that you may not have otherwise. So therefore, a chair is very significant for education.[125]

Southwestern Baptist Theological Seminary stood alone in this unique evangelistic fervor for half a century. The "Chair of Fire" anchored the seminary to soul-winning in an unparalleled fashion: "Keep it on a hot trail after the lost."[126]

Each seminary is governed autonomously by its own administration and SBC-elected trustees; therefore the addition of a chair of evangelism at another seminary did not come from Southwestern Baptist Theological Seminary through direct imposition. Strong connections are evident between the "Chair of Fire" at Southwestern Baptist Theological Seminary and the creation of the subsequent chairs of evangelism at the other five Southern Baptist seminaries. The evidence is easily seen through similar structure patterns and evangelistic emphasis. Each chair of evangelism shares three basic commonalities: faculty, curriculum, and publication. First, many of the occupants of the chairs are Southwestern Baptist Theological Seminary alumni. For example, in two separate interviews, Adam Greenway and Timothy Beougher acknowledged that each occupant of the Billy Graham Chair of Evangelism at Southern Baptist Theological Seminary have been graduates of Southwestern Baptist Theological Seminary.[127] The present Roland Q. Leavell Chair of Evangelism occu-

125. McDow, interview with the author, Appendix 12.

126. Scarborough, *Modern School*, 90.

127. Greenway, interview with the author, Appendix 6; and Beougher, interview with the author, Appendix 2.

pant at New Orleans Baptist Theological Seminary is also a graduate of the Southwestern Baptist Theological Seminary. These men each studied evangelism under an occupant of the "Chair of Fire."

Second, each chair of evangelism has orchestrated curriculum in personal evangelism and revivals. A series of courses in the history of evangelism, personal evangelism, church evangelism and growth, as well as evangelistic preaching, are a part of each seminary's curriculum. This demonstrates a further watermark of contributions from the "Chair of Fire," who forged a path for evangelism in theological education. Thirdly, SBC seminaries have seen a marked increase of publications within the discipline of evangelism. Preston Nix commented about the importance of evangelism literature,

> Dr. Scarborough's book, *With Christ after the Lost*, was used for so many years and then *Evangelism: Christ's Imperative Commission* by Dr. Leavell. So both [sic] our presidents that the chairs were established with presidents, both were a [sic] pastors who had seen success in their churches in evangelism. Of course, Dr. Leavell was at the domestic ministry for home mission work, I guess it was, by that time. Both wrote books that became textbooks for evangelists. Those are some of the connections I see. I don't know if there's a direct connection of the actual chair itself, but the purpose of the chair, who it was established for, and both writers, I think those are significant.[128]

A historical overview of Southern Baptist chairs of evangelism and their occupants directly place the "Chair of Fire" as the central blueprint though educational initiatives and attachment to the establishment of each additional chairs of evangelism.

---

128. Nix, interview with the author, Appendix 13.

6

Conclusion

This book has been a historical analysis of the formation and contributions of the L. R. Scarborough Chair of Evangelism, the "Chair of Fire," to evangelism in theological education within the Southern Baptist seminaries. The study presented the "Chair of Fire's" specific contributions to the scholarship and education that Southern Baptists have received through trainings in evangelism from 1908 to 2020. After careful examination of both Carroll and Scarborough's correspondence and writings, with a review of the founding principles of the chair examining the formation, the inner workings, and fundamental functions of this academic chair, the findings were presented in order to establish the chair's equal standing in theological education. The presentation of Carroll and Scarborough's role in the formation of the chair of evangelism, the "Chair of Fire," are also linked to the subsequent occupants at Southwestern Baptist Theological Seminary, curricula, and the spread of evangelism in theological education throughout the five Southern Baptist seminaries.

SOME OBSERVATIONS

Muncy writes, "Since the establishment of 'the Chair of Fire' in the Southwestern Baptist Theological Seminary in 1908, other seminaries throughout the country have added courses in evangelism to their curricula."[1] This book sought to investigate the "Chair of Fire's" contribution to the

---

1. Muncy, *History of Evangelism*, 163.

inclusion and subsequent implementation of evangelism as an academic discipline and to examine the "Chair of Fire's" impact on the other Southern Baptist seminaries from 1908 to 2020. Muncy identified four main curricula of evangelism in theological education that have been utilized by the "Chair of Fire" and Southern Baptists seminaries. The four main courses that shaped the curriculum of evangelism were to teach exposition of the kingdom of God drawn from the Old and New Testaments, a history of evangelism, a study of propaganda methods of major religions, and practical and scriptural methods in evangelism. The primary ways that these goals are achieved through the "Chair of Fire" in theological education are through personal evangelism and revivals.

The establishment of the L. R. Scarborough Chair of Evangelism, the "Chair of Fire," in correlation to the founding of the Department of Evangelism at Southwestern Baptist Theological Seminary and the Home Mission Board (HMB), ensured first that the seminary would remain evangelistic and that the HMB would have trained evangelists for the purposes of personal and public evangelism. The North American Mission Board Department of Evangelism had shifted its focus from the distinct work of the evangelist to church planting. This may be one reason for Convention-wide decline in salvations and baptisms.

The founding of the "Chair of Fire" as the first academic chair at Southwestern Baptist Theological Seminary was significant in that Carroll ensured that the subject of evangelism would never cease at his seminary. Timothy Beougher stated,

> It was saying evangelism is a field that's worthy of academic study. It's not simply practice. It's not just pragmatism. There are academic issues related to the study of evangelism. I think the Scarborough Chair and Southwestern, for many years, just reminded people of that. It isn't just something that you practice. There's a whole history. There's a theology. There's a biblical basis just like there would be for preaching. That's very important to understand.[2]

Scarborough created a curriculum of two full years at the seminary in the discipline of evangelism. Students were taught the methods of sharing the gospel message personally and then through practicums and other applied theology courses were provided opportunities to exercise their learned skills of evangelism through theological education.

---

2. Beougher, interview with the author, Appendix 2.

Scarborough's influence in the teaching of young men to preach evangelistically through revivals is also seen through the establishment of the "Chair of Fire." Scarborough provided both classroom instruction on revivals and also led students to preach revivals. These revivals were the teaching labs for training up evangelists and evangelistic preachers who made the greatest impact on Southern Baptist evangelism by utilizing the education acquired at Southwestern Baptist Theological Seminary in their local churches. Students still preach revivals during their spring break during the seminary's annual revival campaign, "Reach This Nation." These revival campaigns have been a part of seminary life for more than sixty years and have been opportunities for faculty and students alike to practice both personal evangelism and revival preaching. Since 2010, Southwestern Baptist Theology Seminary has required students enrolled in its basic evangelism class, Contemporary Evangelism, to present no less than twelve complete gospel presentations through its practicum.

Since the founding of the subsequent chairs of evangelism at the other five Southern Baptist seminaries beginning in 1959, similar curricula and evangelism outreach have produced a cascade of evangelistic theology throughout our Convention. Each seminary has included evangelism practicums attached to the coursework in personal evangelism. Charles Kelley stated,

> You couldn't graduate NOBTS if you didn't have that class. Personal Evangelism was a course in the curriculum, but that course was called Field Education, Today's Supervised Ministry. We just taught our students that everybody in ministry has at least one job, and that's telling other people about Jesus.[3]

Timothy Beougher at Southern Baptist Theological Seminary stated, "From the time that I came in 1996, every student in every degree program has to take Personal Evangelism, and they're required to submit at least seven witnessing reports over the course of the semester, where they've shared the gospel with someone."[4] Southeastern Baptist Theological Seminary has utilized the Bailey Smith Chair of Evangelism by equipping students in evangelism methods and sending them out to share the gospel. Each student is required to share the complete gospel and provide an opportunity for personal response to Jesus with ten lost people. The Bailey Smith Professor of Evangelism, George Robinson, stated,

3. Kelley, interview with the author, Appendix 10.
4. Beougher, interview with the author, Appendix 2.

Since the inception of the chair in September of 1994, far more than three thousand men (and women) have been equipped through evangelism training and events led by its occupants. Each semester as many as 250 Southeastern Baptist Theological Seminary students have been equipped and required to share the gospel through personal evangelism with a minimum of ten people who are far from God. Conservatively speaking, in the roughly fifty semesters since the chair's endowment, some ten thousand students have gone through that one-semester training, sharing the gospel with more than one hundred thousand people during the single semester of training. Those students are now serving churches and on the mission field the world over, multiplying the number impacted exponentially.[5]

At Gateway Seminary, professor of evangelism Edsel Pate teaches a course with similar course requirements titled Basic Evangelism, which has a field practicum requirement. Pate stated, "We have one required evangelism class and that's it. It is just Basic Evangelism. The emphasis in that class is really personal evangelism. So that's eight evangelism verbatims in the semester. And that could either be a six- or an eight-session semester, or a fifteen-session. But they're required to do eight evangelism verbatims."[6] Thomas Johnston, senior professor of evangelism at Midwestern Baptist Theological Seminary, is also committed to personal evangelism and has implemented a practicum for his students. He stated, "So my emphasis is two-fold at Midwestern. One is to teach New Testament evangelism, and two is to have students go out and do it. And so I go out and do door-to-door and street evangelism anywhere from once a week up to, I've even gone up five to six times a week with students. I don't practice that all the time."[7]

The fundamentals of evangelism in theological education continue to be taught at the seminaries through the various professors of evangelism. New Orleans Baptist Theological Seminary has multiple chairs of evangelism which have been established during the past sixty-one years, providing what appears to be a strong commitment to evangelism in theological education. The chairs of evangelism continue to promote the highest standards in academic study and practical experience in the discipline of evangelism.

5. Robinson, email to the author, Appendix 18.

6. Pate, interview with the author, Appendix 14.

7. Johnston, interview with the author, Appendix 9.

FINAL CONCLUSIONS

The primary impact that this book should have on Southern Baptist evangelism is evangelism consciousness throughout the SBC. The L. R. Scarborough Chair of Evangelism, the "Chair of Fire," serves as much more than just an academic chair; the chair is a custodian of evangelism in the SBC. The "Chair of Fire" occupant at Southwestern Baptist Theological Seminary continues the legacy of infusing the Fort Worth seminary campus with an evangelistic spirit, leading by example both in and out of the classroom. The chair still calls administration, faculty, staff, and students to fulfill the Great Commission.

The "Chair of Fire's" contribution to Southern Baptist evangelism in theological education has been one of immeasurable value to the souls won to Jesus through the evangelistic fervor of students who have caught the fires of evangelism while studying personal evangelism, re-vivalism, and discipleship at Southwestern Baptist Theological Seminary. The "Chair of Fire" has provided biblical training for men and women through regular evangelistic opportunities throughout the local community, state, and country. Students of evangelism at Southwestern Baptist Theological Seminary have developed keen knowledge of how to share the good news of Jesus with others, in all circumstances, using the Bible or through evangelism methods like Continuing Witness Training's *Eternal Life* or *Satisfied?*, a gospel tract written by the current occupant.[8] Students graduate from Southwestern Baptist Theological Seminary hot-hearted and passionate about evangelism and take this motivation to the local churches where they are called by God for service.

The chair has also promoted the national programs of evangelism through classes and through cooperative publication, such as works produced by the Southern Baptist Professors of Evangelism Fellowship. Each professor of evangelism has strengthened the SBC in the task of keeping evangelism central in the hearts and minds of Southern Baptists. Further, publication of evangelism literature has assisted in keeping the local Southern Baptist churches engrossed with evangelism education throughout their church education programs.

With these aforementioned accomplishments of the "Chair of Fire's" impact on Southern Baptist evangelism, the Convention should acknowledge the continued need for educated men and women in the art of evangelism and employ evangelists throughout the churches. On a

8. *Eternal Life*, and Queen, *Satisfied?*.

national level of our denomination, research has proven that evangelism is fundamental in a struggle against the liberal drift. Preston Nix states,

> We don't quite have the advantage of structure nor the program approach to help us. I'm not all for thinking programs are what's going to save us, but the way that the Home Mission Board, Domestic Mission Board before that, NAMB was set up, we had a greater focus and we were producing more literature and training materials and helps. We just we don't have that. It's almost nobody's business anymore. It went to Lifeway for a while. Who's producing the materials?[9]

This refocus has left many local Southern Baptist churches in decline and without consistent revivals from seminary-educated, -trained, and -called evangelists.

Scholarship on Fire should motivate Southern Baptist scholarship to demand continued centrality of evangelism as a hallmark and guard against doctrinal infidelity within the SBC. This study has proven the importance of the "Chair of Fire's" contributions to Southern Baptist evangelism in theological education and has strengthened the argument of its status as a regular discipline of study within Southern Baptist Seminaries. The endgame of this historical overview is that Southern Baptist seminaries will continue to promote evangelism and teach connectedly the New Testament doctrines of the office of the evangelist as outlined by the "Chair of Fire's" founder, B. H. Carroll.

9. Nix, interview with the author, Appendix 13.

Appendix 1

Personal Interview with
J. Denny Autrey, March 21, 2016

This is a complete and accurate transcript of the oral history interview of Dr. J. Denny Autrey by Beau Brewer over the phone. No spoken words which were recorded were omitted, except for any non-English phrases which could not be understood by the transcriber. This is a transcript of spoken English, which of course follows a different rhythm and rule than written English. In very few cases, words were too unclear to be distinguished. In these cases, [unclear] or [?] was inserted. Both interviewee and interviewer would interject "Uh hmm" or "Uh huh" frequently, but these were not transcribed unless they came at a definite break in the conversation. In some sections of the tape, the microphone was apparently frequently bumped and every occasion of this has not been noted.

. . .   Three dots indicate an interruption or break in the train of thought within the sentence of the speaker.

. . . .   Four dots indicate what the transcriber believes to be the end of an incomplete sentence.

( )   Words in parentheses are asides made by the speaker.

[ ]   Words in brackets are comments made by the transcriber.

    This transcription was made by Pioneer Transcription Services and was completed in March 2016.

Beau Brewer:	Good afternoon. My name is Beau Brewer. I am a PhD student in evangelism at Southwestern Baptist Theological Seminary in Fort Worth, Texas. Today, I am conducting a telephone interview in fulfillment of my dissertation research, which will

assess contributions of the L. R. Scarborough Chair of Evangelism, famously known as the "Chair of Fire," on the theological education and the discipline of evangelism. Today's interview will focus on the work of Dr. C. E. Autrey, the third occupant of the "Chair of Fire." This cell phone recording is being done on Monday, March 21, 2016, at 3 p.m., and I am located in the World Mission Center on the campus of Southwestern Baptist Theological Seminary. I have the privilege and honor of interviewing Dr. J. Denny Autrey, Professor of Pastoral Ministries and Dean of the J. Dalton Havard School for Theological Studies. This is Southwestern Seminary's Houston campus. Good afternoon, Dr. Autrey.

Denny Autrey: Good afternoon, Beau.

Beau Brewer: First, will you briefly tell us about yourself and any significant memory you have of your grandfather's influence on your present work for the seminary?

Denny Autrey: Be happy to. Of course, I am the first Resident Dean of Southwestern Seminary's campus here in Houston. Southwestern began to offer classes here in Houston in 1975, and from 1975 until 2001, we met on the campus of Houston Baptist University. In 2001, we moved to our present Havard campus at the Park Place Baptist Church, which donated their facility to us in the spring of 2002. At our 2001 board meeting and accreditation meeting, the accrediting board faxed an ATS, determined that Houston was doing everything to be able to be a free-standing degree-granting institution on their own underneath the authority of Southwestern. So the trustees in 2003 began to discuss placing a Resident Dean in the Houston area, and in April of 2004, I was elected to that position as the first Resident Dean.

Prior to that timeframe, they had had an Associate Dean for extension work and Associate Dean for the Houston campus who would come down on Mondays from Fort Worth and stay the day and then fly back. And that changed in 2004. So I've held this position for the last twelve years, and it's been a good experience and one I've really enjoyed. The reason I was elected—one of the reasons I was elected is because I too did my master's work here at the extension in Houston at HBU from 1979 until 1984. Received my MDiv in '84, and then began my work in the DMin work in preaching, and proclamation and family ministry in the spring of '85, and finished that in the spring of 1987.

So long heritage with Southwestern. My grandfather always encouraged me to pursue my theological education because he said, you know, preparing your heart and your head will—God will use to open other doors for you in preaching. So he was a great influence in my educational aspect and always continued to challenge me to do further study. It was his desire for me to do a PhD, so he was a little bit distraught when I decided to do the DMin. But he said that would be still a good degree for somebody in the pastorate, and I thought that I would be in the pastorate the rest of my life. So it turned out that I did finish my PhD. So in 1981 he wrote me a letter indicating he'd be praying that I would finish my master's but pursue a PhD, and he would be very happy to know that I have both DMin and PhD now.

Beau Brewer: All right. Well, can you provide any insights into the selection of Cassius Elijah Autrey? That's C. Autrey from this point forward because there's just too many Autreys here. By presiding this Southwestern Seminary President J. Howard Williams, 1953 to 1958, into the chair of evangelism. Your grandfather served for ten years, did he not?

Denny Autrey: No, he served from 1955 to 1960, so he served five years in the chair of evangelism. He—the reason he had come in contact with Dr. Williams—he had served as the chairman of evangelism for the state of Louisiana from 1946 until about 19—I would think '50 or '51. He had pastored prior to that from early 1930s until 1946, and then was asked to move to the to move to the Department of Evangelism, the denominational heading of the state of Evangelism for Louisiana. And evangelism was always his heart. That came from Dr. Scarborough. When he was, I think about nineteen, he first got saved and then was working at a sawmill in Louisiana where he grew up. And he told me the story of traveling on train to hear Dr. Scarborough preach in a revival setting. And he said after he heard him preach—I think it was, I think 1923—he said God put a fire in his heart like Dr. Scarborough's for evangelism and for just sharing the gospel, no matter what it took. And he realized then that he needed to pursue his education.

And he was closest to, at that time, the Bible Baptist Institute, which was in New Orleans and did not become New Orleans Baptist Theological Seminary until 1929. So he began his work there at Bible Baptist Institute in the undergraduate program in 1928. By the time he finished, he had a BD from New Orleans, and then he went ahead and did his master's work there and his PhD in evangelism, all in evangelism. That was just his heartbeat. But it was Dr. Scarborough's preaching that really lit a fire in his heart to get his theological education and move on there.

He met Dr. Williams through his work in Louisiana, as the state evangelism exec. And then from that position, he was asked to come on board of the Home Mission Board in 1951 to work with the executive director—I'm trying to think of his name at this point. And he was his associate. So he became the associate executive director of the Home

Mission Board Evangelism Department from 1951 to 1954. It was also during that timeframe that Dr. Williams had met him and asked him if he would come. And I think the chair of evangelism had not been—the chair of evangelism or "Chair of Fire" had not been—no one was sitting in it at that time. I think—you mentioned he was the third one. I can't remember if it was Dr.—

Beau Brewer: He is the third. It was—E. D. Head was the second one.

Denny Autrey: Okay. So Dr. Head was the second one. So after his death, then Dr. Williams was trying to fill that position there.

Beau Brewer: Correct.

Denny Autrey: And I believe that when my grandfather came in 1955, he was the first full-time professor of evangelism.

Beau Brewer: That is correct.

Denny Autrey: At that point—yeah, after that point, Dr. Scarborough, Dr. Head were—they were systematic theology or—and then they were at—additional professors of evangelism. But my grandfather was the first full-time professor of evangelism for Southwestern Seminary and the "Chair of Fire."

Beau Brewer: That is correct. So your grandfather authored many books, and you mentioned that he had been influenced greatly by Dr. Scarborough, the first occupant of the "Chair of Fire," whom the chair is named after, many books on evangelism, such as *You Can Win Souls*. This book carries much of the same ideals as Dr. L. R. Scarborough, especially with his views on the soul-winner, on the character of the soul-winner. Would you be willing to speak to Scarborough's influence on this evangelistic fervor?

Denny Autrey: Sure. My grandfather's first book was *Basic Evangelism*. He wrote that in 1959. And that's while he was in Southwestern. And that book became a textbook for evangelism for probably the next thirty years, and it's probably still on the reading list of some. But it's on church evangelism. It's basically an overview of how to do church evangelism. There's a very significant chapter in there—I believe it's chapter 9—on how to give an evangelistic invitation for pastors.

But he wrote *You Can Win Souls* in 1961. It was in 1961 that he began his work as the executive director of the Home Mission Board for the Department of Evangelism. And he held that position from 1960 until 1969. So this is the first book that he wrote, and it's on personal evangelism. How does somebody develop a desire to win people to Christ there? It's a great book. He was influenced by Scarborough because Scarborough had such a desire to win people to Christ. He was an academic, but he was really an evangelist. And everywhere he went, he preached revivals. And so my grandfather followed in that same vein of being a revival preacher, teacher, and had a real heart for evangelism. So he wanted to try to put in print a tool that would help students and pastors to be soul-winners—to be personal soul-winners. So that influence from Scarborough really prompted him to write that book on personal evangelism.

So church evangelism is basic evangelism. *You Can Win Souls* is personal evangelism. And then in 1966 he headed a delegation of seventy southern Baptists that went to the Berlin Evangelism Conference that was chaired by Dr. Billy Graham, and as a result of being the chair of that group, he wrote *The Theology of Evangelism* that was published by B&H in that timeframe there. So all three are really excellent books there on the basis of why we do evangelism and how we think Dr. Scarborough had a great influence on his writing as well as his preaching as well.

Beau Brewer: Now, do you know if your grandfather ever sat under Dr. Scarborough in the classroom?

Denny Autrey: He did not, but he told me that, every time, if he had the opportunity to hear Dr. Scarborough preach, he would go and take a bus, take a train, take a whatever and just go to where he was to hear him preach. And he heard him preach often in the thirties. He finished his undergraduate degree at Louisiana College, and then he went to New Orleans and received his master's and his PhD. And he began pastoring, I think in around 1932 or 33, and he pastored until 1946. So during the times of his pastorate, especially in Louisiana, he would drive over to Texas and hear Dr. Scarborough as often as possible. That was just one of his favorite preachers.

Beau Brewer: All right. Your grandfather had quite a plethora of ministry. He started off as a pastor; he became an educator. He left Southwestern to become the director of the North—or not the director, but the president of the North American Mission Board. Then he left there and went to—went back to his alma mater at New Orleans as an educator, and then became a church planter. Can you talk a little bit about that transition in his life, I mean just going from these different—what motivated these moves?

Denny Autrey: Well, my grandfather felt like, that number one, understanding the call to ministry was the first thing that any minister needs to understand. If God's called you to ministry, he's called you to prepare for ministry. And that's something we at something we at Southwestern believe, and he believes that as well. That was his heart. But he also felt like that the call to ministry meant, whatever you call me to, Lord, that's what I want to do. So he saw in the call, not just to be a preacher, but to be whatever God opened the door for him to do. So he was willing to tackle whatever. He pastored from, again, 1933 to 1946, so those thirteen or fourteen years after his education, he pastored.

And then he received a call to come to do denominational work there in Louisiana. And because of his heart for the local church and became of his heart for evangelism, he took that position very seriously. And of course, that opened up the door to the Home Mission Board, and to work there, and then that opened up the door for him to bring that fervor and that fire to Southwestern. And so he came there to talk for a number of years, and then again, back at the Home Mission Board, and then back to New Orleans, back to mid-America. And he taught there as well. He helped them get established in their early days, in the early seventies.

So he just felt like that when you respond to say yes to the Lord in ministry, that could be preaching, but it meant evangelism no matter what. And that's the way he viewed his call. He didn't think that he was called from just the—to be a pastor, or called to be an evangelist, or called to be a professor. He was called by God, and whatever God opened the door for him, he was willing to say, yes Lord, I'll be willing to do what you want me to do. So that's kind of what motivated him to make those changes and really have that varied plethora of work during his career.

Beau Brewer: I might add a question to you because you kind of stirred something. What do you feel like his greatest attribute to the "Chair of Fire" was? What was his greatest contribution to the "Chair of Fire" during those five years?

Denny Autrey: Well, I think—not only to the "Chair of Fire," but also to the Home Mission Board—he brought a real fervor that it was the responsibility of every pastor to prepare his people for evangelism. And so when he came to the "Chair of Fire" at Southwestern, I think Dr. Head, Dr. Williams, and surely in the light of Dr. Scarborough, they wanted to transfer that fire, that fervor for personal evangelism to the student. And my grandfather was the perfect example of wanting that, an academic mind who had a pastor's heart, but who was really an evangelist at heart, to really rekindle that flame there. And so I think the emphasis or the great significance of asking him to be "Chair of Fire" there was to rekindle that and really get that moving again in the right direction.

He moved from that to the Home Mission Board again, and the simultaneous revivals were something that had been done in previous timeframes. But he brought, you know, soul-winning commitment Sunday back to the Southern Baptist calendar. He brought the simultaneous revivals back to the associational meetings. I mean, he was serious about getting pastors back into the role of being soul-winners and not just preachers on Sunday.

Beau Brewer: Well, do you have anything else that you'd like to add to this interview about your grandfather?

Denny Autrey: Well, I just have to say, he was a great influence on many for sure, but he was a great influence on me. He was a man who I thought to be not only a man who practiced what he preached. He would get up every morning, and even in his later years in life, he would study, just study God's word, whether it be meditation for preaching Sunday or whatever, he would be—he'd stay in the study in the mornings there. And then he would evangelize; he would go out and witness. He would go out and knock on doors in the afternoon whether it be for church members or just cold-calling, whatever. He was— even until the age of seventy-six and seventy-seven, he was still fulfilling that responsibility of knocking on doors, winning people to Jesus, sharing his faith. He was just a great example of that.

And so what it brought to my ministry, and what it brought to me was the importance of being—having a sharp head, but having a heart that's really submitted to the spirit of God and obedient to being a witness for Jesus. So I think that's the greatest contribution that he's not only had on Southern Baptists for the "Chair of Fire," but me personally as well.

Beau Brewer: Well, thank you very much, Dr. Autrey.

Appendix 2

PERSONAL INTERVIEW WITH
TIMOTHY BEOUGHER, MAY 27, 2020

THIS IS A COMPLETE and accurate transcript of the oral history interview of Dr. Timothy Beougher by Beau Brewer over the phone. No spoken words which were recorded were omitted, except for any non-English phrases which could not be understood by the transcriber. This is a transcript of spoken English, which of course follows a different rhythm and rule than written English. In very few cases, words were too unclear to be distinguished. In these cases, [unclear] or [?] was inserted. Both interviewee and interviewer would interject "Uh hmm" or "Uh huh" frequently, but these were not transcribed unless they came at a definite break in the conversation. In some sections of the tape, the microphone was apparently frequently bumped and every occasion of this has not been noted.

... Three dots indicate an interruption or break in the train of thought within the sentence of the speaker.

.... Four dots indicate what the transcriber believes to be the end of an incomplete sentence.

( ) Words in parentheses are asides made by the speaker.

[ ] Words in brackets are comments made by the transcriber.

This transcription was made by Rev.com Transcription Services and was completed in May 2020.

Beau Brewer:	This is Beau Brewer. I am a PhD candidate at Southwestern Baptist Theological Seminary in Fort Worth, Texas. I am on a live telephone interview with Dr. Timothy Beougher, professor

of evangelism and occupant of the Billy Graham
Chair of Evangelism at Southern Baptist Theological Seminary in Louisville, Kentucky. Today is May
27, 2020.

Dr. Beougher, thank you for being with me this
morning.

Timothy Beougher: You're very welcome.

Beau Brewer: Well, I am very excited about this interview, one,
because you are holding probably the second-most
famous chair in all of Southern Baptist evangelism
named after one of the greatest evangelists of the
twenty-first century. Researching your academic
career, you are the fifth occupant and the fifth professor of evangelism to occupy the Billy Graham
Chair of Evangelism at Southern Seminary. Would
you give me the dates of your particular service in
this institution and the dates that you were installed
to this particular chair?

Timothy Beougher: Yes. Looking up here at the certificate of installation on my wall, I was officially installed in the
chair on August 26, 1997.

Beau Brewer: Okay, so that's about twenty-five years now.

Timothy Beougher: Yeah. I started teaching the year before in 1996.

Beau Brewer: At Southern Seminary?

Timothy Beougher: At Southern.

Beau Brewer: Now, you had—

Timothy Beougher: I taught here for one year as professor of evangelism before I was officially installed in the chair.

Beau Brewer: How wonderful. Before you came to Southern, you
were at Mid-America?

Timothy Beougher: No, at Wheaton College.

Beau Brewer: Wheaton College. That's right, and you—

Timothy Beougher: I taught at Wheaton Graduate School and also was
the associate director of the Billy Graham Institute
of Evangelism at Wheaton.

Beau Brewer: Oh, that's right, so you have a long-standing connection with Dr. Graham.

Timothy Beougher: I do.

Beau Brewer: Have you actually met Dr. Graham? I'm just curious. I know this isn't a question—

Timothy Beougher: Yes, many times.

Beau Brewer: Okay. I just was curious. You definitely have a long-standing connection with Dr. Graham. That's really neat. Would you please articulate your philosophy of evangelism?

Timothy Beougher: Yeah. Let me give you my definition. That might spark any further questions. Here's how I define evangelism: the compassionate sharing of the good news of Jesus Christ with lost people in the power of the Holy Spirit for the purpose of bringing them to Christ as Savior and Lord that they, in turn, might share him with others.

Breaking that down in terms of my philosophy, I began with compassion. Matthew chapter 9, it said, "When Jesus saw the multitudes, He felt compassion for them." Too often, I think, as believers, when we look upon the sinful multitudes, our first response is not compassion. It's criticism or even condemnation, so really beginning with that heart of compassion that the people are lost. We shouldn't expect them to act any differently because they are lost. To me, personal evangelism really begins by asking God to cultivate in us that heart of compassion for the lost.

The second part of that, our audience are lost people. They are lost. They need Christ. They're without hope, without God in this world. They're headed towards a crisis, eternity in hell. The reminder, what I always challenge my students with, is that when someone is lost . . . We may think that everybody, at least in America, has heard the gospel at least a hundred times and is just rejecting it.

I've found, even here in Louisville, Kentucky, where someone once said, "The Bible Belt buckles in Louisville, Kentucky," nine out of ten people that I'm witness to here in Louisville do not understand the biblical gospel. They're on their religious ritual plan or the good works plan. They don't really understand the gospel, so we're sharing with lost people the . . . I talk, in the definition, that is the good news of Jesus Christ. When we share the gospel, we're not sharing something that's going to ruin somebody's life, but it's going to transform it for now and for all eternity.

Talk about the necessity of doing this in the power of the Holy Spirit. As Paul talks about in 2 Corinthians 4:7, we have this treasure in the earthen vessels, that the surpassing greatness of the power might be from God and not from we ourselves. It's not our human ingenuity or our human skills as we witness. It's being empowered by the Holy Spirit.

The purpose is to bring them to Christ. We're not trying to win people to a church even though we hope that they will become faithful church members. We're not trying to win them to a denomination even though we hope they will become loyal Southern Baptists. We want to being them to Christ because he is the Savior.

A lot of people have given up on the church. A lot of people say they want nothing to do with Christianity because they have witnessed the ungodly behavior of Christians. Part of the reality is that Christians are hypocrites. All of us are hypocrites. A hypocrite is somebody who says one thing and does something else. There are many days I accomplish that before breakfast, so I always just point people to Christ. Christ was not a hypocrite. He's the one we need to look towards.

Just a quick story of that. Recently, my wife and I were riding in an Uber. I was engaging the driver in conversation. He had the music real loud when we got in. I asked if we would turn it down. We started talking, and he realized this was a gospel conversation. He said, "No offense, but I'm done with religion. I've seen too much hypocrisy in the church. You're just wasting your time. I'm not interested."

I went back to the fact that he was a musician and mentioned that my wife, Sharon, teaches piano students. She has forty different piano students. I asked this driver, his name was John, I said, "If someone misplays Mozart's Ninth Symphony, just really butchers it, do we say that Mozart was a bad composer?" He said, "Absolutely not. That's not on Mozart. That's on the student." Then he stopped and said, "Whoa." He said, "I see where this is going." I said, "John, there are a lot of Christians who don't play Christ's music very well. I'll readily acknowledge that, but that doesn't diminish who Christ was." Anyway, we had a wonderful conversation. We got to our destination. He said, "I'm turning off the meter, but can you just pray for me and pray with me?"

Anyway, just a reminder that our goal is to point people to Christ. Jesus said, "If I be lifted up, I will draw all persons to me." One of my goals in evangelism is to lift up Christ, to point people to him and then that they, in turn, might share him with others. I realize that evangelism is the first phase in making disciples. The goal of the Great Commission is not to make decisions. It's to make disciples. Part of my definition of evangelism includes that ongoing follow-up of this new believer so that this new believer will then begin to share his or her faith with others. That's my basic definition which summarizes my basic approach and philosophy.

Beau Brewer: Oh, yes, sir. That's excellent. You have been seated as the occupant of the Billy Graham Chair since 1997. Correct?

Timothy Beougher: Correct.

Beau Brewer: That's almost twenty-five years if I'm doing my math correct. I'm a theologian because I don't do math well.

Timothy Beougher: I understand.

Beau Brewer: In that occupancy of your chair, do you feel like there are specific tenets that are outlined by Dr. Graham for the chair, or does each individual occupant define the role and the purpose of the chair in his own abilities, his own personality, his own strengths, his own teaching styles? Does that make sense?

Timothy Beougher: It does. I think it's very definitely the latter. I know, when I stepped into this role . . . Well, my situation was a little bit different because I was hired by Dr. Mohler specifically for this. The previous chairs basically, as they stepped into this, they utilized their own approach, their own philosophy.

When Dr. Mohler talked to me about coming to Southern, he said one of the changes that he was making, as president, is that Personal Evangelism would become a required class for all students in all degree programs. At that time, it was a required class for pastors, for ministerial students, those in the pastor tack, but if someone was in the music track, they didn't have to take personal evangelism. He said, "We're going to change the curriculum." He said, "I want personal evangelism to be a required class for every single student." He said, "I want them to actually learn how to do evangelism, actually practice it. I just don't want a theoretical kind of course."

Here's the challenge that he gave me. He said, "When I hand the student a diploma at graduation, I have to know not only that that student knows how to share the gospel but has done it multiple times." He said, "Would you come to Southern and help make that happen?" That was really the vision, and so the challenge that I was given, which is what I was already doing at Wheaton . . . To me, the whole notion of having a personal evangelism class without required witnessing reports is like having a swimming class where people just sit on the deck chairs and never get in the pool. You can't learn how to swim unless you get in the pool. You can't learn personal evangelism unless you're actually witnessing.

That was a component. I don't know what my predecessors did in that regard as to whether or not there were required witnessing reports or not or it was more theoretical. I just know, from the time that I came in 1996, every student in every degree program has to take personal evangelism and they're required to submit at least seven witnessing reports over the course of the semester where they've shared the gospel with someone.

Beau Brewer: That's about a fifteen-week semester. Correct?

Timothy Beougher: Yeah. It's thirteen actual weeks of classes with breaks and everything, so it's basically one every other week which, to me, is . . . With students being in full-time students, many of them working other jobs—

Beau Brewer: Absolutely.

Timothy Beougher: . . . We settled on that amount. When I was teaching at Wheaton, we required one a week. Little bit easier, I think, for college students in their environment. Many of them did not have outside jobs. We do . . . . It's basically one witnessing report every other week, which is very doable and very manageable. I want these to be worthwhile reports. I want them to be significant and not just something somebody's checking off a box of a course requirement.

Beau Brewer:	Sure. Dr. Beougher, so you personally teach the contemporary evangelism, the personal evangelism class?
Timothy Beougher:	Yeah. The required class for every student is called Personal Evangelism.
Beau Brewer:	Personal Evangelism? I'm just curious. What is your main textbook for that class?
Timothy Beougher:	The main textbook that I use is the book *Tell the Truth* by Will Metzger.
Beau Brewer:	That's an excellent book. I was just curious if there were other Southern Baptist authors that you were using.
Timothy Beougher:	Well, I use a little booklet that I wrote, *Overcoming Walls to Witnessing*, as one of the textbooks. I use Greg Gilbert, Greg's a local church pastor here in Louisville at Third Avenue, *What Is the Gospel?*
Beau Brewer:	I've read that one, yes. It's excellent.
Timothy Beougher:	Then I use J. I. Packer's *Evangelism and the Sovereignty of God*. Dr. Packer was my dissertation supervisor. I use his book, and we discuss evangelism and the sovereignty of God and how a strong belief in the sovereignty of God should not hinder evangelism but actually fuel it.
Beau Brewer:	That's some motivation, sure is.
Timothy Beougher:	Then I use the book by Greg Koukl, *Tactics*, a book on apologetics and world views. They're very, very helpful in a post-modern context of witnessing.
Beau Brewer:	Fantastic. What other insights to the workings of the Billy Graham Chair might you provide? What other kinds of activities do you do? Do you lead the campus in evangelism weekends, Crossover, SBC Crossover, a big campaign here in the summer? I'm assuming that you do other things besides just teach the one course at Southern Seminary.
Timothy Beougher	Yes. Well, we have multiple sections of that one course. I do lead the crossover for Southern

students every summer. We have a day of service and sharing every April where we call it the "1937 Project" because, in 1937, there was a major flood in Louisville. A lot of the downtown area flooded. Seminary here in Louisville sits on a hill kind of like Southwestern. It's a little higher than the surrounding region. Actually, the city hall moved to Southern Seminary's campus in 1937, and the seminary really had an impact in terms of ministering to the Louisville community. Every April, we have an outreach where students, faculty, everyone goes out throughout the city to do service projects, to share the gospel, just connect and show love for our city.

We also have, here on our campus that's under the Billy Graham School, the Bevin Center for Mission Mobilization. I don't direct that, one of my colleagues does, but we provide avenues, through the Bevin Center, for local evangelism in jails here, in schools, with FCA, short-term mission trips. We provide training for all of that, so just multiple ways for our students to be engaged, be involved in evangelism.

We have regular churches asking for students to come and preach, and so we try and set that up and work with the students in terms of some basic training, make sure they're clearly sharing the gospel as they go, so a lot of different functions housed under the Billy Graham School. I don't directly oversee the Bevin Center. I give input to it, but that's done by one of my colleagues.

Beau Brewer: Sure. What kind of connections, if any, did or does the Billy Graham Chair of Evangelism have with Southwestern Seminary's "Chair of Fire?" Now, the L. R. Scarborough "Chair of Fire" is the first of its kind. According to all the research that I can possibly find on the chair, I've found multiple outside of Southwestern historical accounts that the "Chair of

Fire" was the first of its kind. B. H. Carroll created it in . . . I think it was in his mind in 1904, 1905, certainly 1906 when he made his extremely famous address to the Southern Baptist Convention. In 1908, he created the "Chair of Fire." It was later renamed the "L. R. Scarborough Chair of Evangelism," still nicknamed the "Chair of Fire," but it is the first professorship, the first endowed chair of evangelism in the world.

What kind of connections does the Billy Graham Chair that was created in 1965 have to Southwestern's "Chair of Fire," and what are some of the differences, if there are any, in terms of the chair's function, emphasis, and purpose?

Timothy Beougher: Yeah. I think the obvious initial connection was Ken Chafin coming from Southwestern. Did Ken hold the "Chair of Fire" when he was at Southwestern?

Beau Brewer: He did from 1960 to 1965, and then he resigned from Southwestern to go to Southern Seminary to occupy the inaugural occupancy of the Billy Graham Chair of Evangelism.

Timothy Beougher: Yeah, yeah. I thought that was the case. Obviously, there's that initial connection. I think a second connection not necessarily directly with the "Chair of Fire" but with Southwestern . . . I believe Lewis Drummond told me this once, and I didn't follow up by doing the research myself, but he said that every single occupant of the chair, including me, were Southwestern grads.

Beau Brewer: That is correct. Every one of you have—

Timothy Beougher: Yeah, David D'Amico and others.

Beau Brewer: Yes.

Timothy Beougher: There actually hasn't been a Southern grad to hold this chair. Now, part of that has been that Southern didn't start its PhD program, actually, in evangelism until under Dr. Drummond. We had others like Thom Rainer who graduated, Chuck Wallace.

We've had many. Tom Johnson at Midwestern, your president there, Adam Greenway, have come through our program. My guess is that, whenever the Lord calls me home or I retire, that the next occupant will be a Southern Seminary grad. I'm assuming that, but yeah, all of us are Southwestern-ers. Lewis Drummond loved that fact because he dearly loved Southwestern even though he taught at Southern and at Southeastern, became president there at Southeastern and then went on to Beeson. He always loved Southwestern.

Beau Brewer: Well, it would be almost impossible to be from any other school considering Southwestern kind of held that bedrock for fifty years all by itself.

Timothy Beougher: Right, right.

Beau Brewer: I mean it wasn't until 1959 when the Roland Q. Leavell Chair of Evangelism at New Orleans was created by their board of trustees and then, what, six years later, the Billy Graham Chair there at Southern was created, so quite an interesting history. Southwestern Seminary almost held the "Chair of Fire" and the Department of Evangelism exclusively for fifty years, and so—

Timothy Beougher: Right. I don't think that necessarily means that evangelism wasn't being taught at the other seminaries.

Beau Brewer: No, that's not what I was saying, but—

Timothy Beougher: Leavell was teaching evangelism at New Orleans, but certainly, in terms of the visibility of having the chair, that's true. Southwestern was the anchor for decades.

Beau Brewer: Yes. Well, no, I admit all the other seminaries were teaching some courses in evangelism. I just think that Southwestern was leading in terms of visibility and graduates, people in that area, in that field of study.

As a fellow Southwesterner, who did you study evangelism under at Southwestern Seminary?

Timothy Beougher: Took Personal Evangelism under Roy Fish, took Church Evangelism under James Eaves.

Beau Brewer: Oh, wonderful, so you had the twin towers.

Timothy Beougher: I did.

Beau Brewer: You really did. I used to attend church with Dr. Eaves. What a godly, godly man, an incredible, incredible scholar, truly a sharp, sharp mind all the way to the very end. Unfortunately, I never had him for class, but I did have Dr. Roy Fish in my master of divinity degree. I took Jesus and Personal Evangelism with him and Great Awakenings or Revivals with him. Both of those classes were just jam-packed with kids. I've never seen anything like it. Of course, he taught those courses after his official retirement at Southwestern.

Can you discuss the L. R. Scarborough Chair of Evangelism and its importance in theological education?

Timothy Beougher: Well, I think keeping the banner held high for evangelism, there's the tendency . . . well, I'll just . . . Let me share something with you that's off the record. Okay? I know we're recording all of this, but . . . Well, I'll put it on the record. I just won't name the faculty member.

Beau Brewer: Okay.

Timothy Beougher: When I taught at Wheaton, every day, I would drive by the sign "For Christ and His Kingdom." That's the motto of Wheaton College, "For Christ and His Kingdom," and yet when I was hired as professor of evangelism there in 1990, I could tell that there were some faculty members that weren't really keen on having evangelism taught on their campus. They would say, "Well, that's something the church ought to do," or, "That's something Moody Bible Institute ought to do." There was sort of the sense that evangelism isn't academic. Wheaton College is the leading academic evangelical institution. It's kind of like evangelism is vacation Bible school. It's not truly academic, et cetera, et cetera.

I talked to one of my colleagues there and just asked him about it. He said, "Tim, just keep the flag flying high." He said, "The reason that some people are critical is because they're not doing evangelism, and it's easier to criticize it than for them to change their life and try and do it themselves." The very visibility of the Billy Graham Center there on Wheaton College's campus, the fact that they started an MA in evangelism that I came in to help lead in 1990, just raising that visibility was huge.

It was saying evangelism is a field that's worthy of academic study. It's not simply practice. It's not just pragmatism. There are academic issues related to the study of evangelism. I think the Scarborough Chair and Southwestern, for many years, just reminded people of that. It isn't just something that you practice. There's a whole history. There's a theology. There's a biblical basis just like there would be for preaching. That's very important to understand.

Beau Brewer: By the way, you did your PhD in evangelism?

Timothy Beougher: No. I did a ThM in evangelism under Robert Coleman at Trinity, author of *Master Plan of Evangelism*, actually wrote my ThM thesis on the 1970 revival that started at Asbury where Robert Coleman was teaching, made his way to Southwestern where Dr. Fish was. The two of them were my committee for that, with Dr. Fish giving the Southwestern side, Dr. Coleman the Asbury side.

My PhD is actually in historical theology. I left Southwestern. I graduated with my MDiv at Southwestern in 1986, went through the qualifying exams for the PhD. I was actually going to do my PhD in theology as opposed to evangelism simply because my desire that our practice ought to be based on a solid theological basis. I'd been accepted into the PhD program in theology at Southwestern. I went to Trinity for a year to work on my ThM fully expecting to come back to Southwestern and study in the doctoral program there.

While I was at Trinity in 1986, Trinity started their PhD program, so I was part of the inaugural class in 1997 in historical theology, so my PhD is actually in historical theology, not evangelism. I geared all of my seminars and writings towards how the gospel was understood and how evangelism was practiced in the different epochs of the church. My ThM's in evangelism. My PhD's actually in historical theology.

Beau Brewer: Well, don't sweat it, Dr. Beougher. Dr. Queen is the first occupant of the "Chair of Fire" to actually have a PhD in evangelism, so you're not missing anything. Dr. Fish—

Timothy Beougher: I was actually on Dr. Queen's committee.

Beau Brewer: Oh, you were! That's right. I forgot about that.

Timothy Beougher: I was the external reader.

Beau Brewer: That's right. You were. Dr. Fish and Dr. Eaves and, I believe, Dr. McDow were all historical theologians. Well, no. I'm sorry. Dr. Eaves was a New Testament guy, but Dr. McDow and, of course, Dr. Fish were both historical theologians, so it makes perfectly good sense.

Timothy Beougher: It did.

Beau Brewer: You can be a good evangelist and serve in other fields. I would say that Dr. Fish served splendidly for forty-one years.

Timothy Beougher: He did.

Beau Brewer: It was incredible. Well, so how have these many chairs, specifically the Billy Graham Chair of Evangelism at Southern and, if you can speak to

Southwestern's chair of evangelism, how have they . . . but, obviously, all six of our seminaries have chairs now. How have these chairs of evangelism impacted Southern Baptist evangelism as a whole?

Timothy Beougher: Well, I think the primary impact has obviously been through students, sending out students that have been trained in personal evangelism that are going to be pastors and associate pastors, youth pastors, children's directors, worship leaders, with those students going out knowing how to share the gospel having shared it multiple times. I think that's significant.

I think, in terms of writing on the field of evangelism, the works that have been produced continue to have an impact today. I think reminding Southern Baptists the . . . I grew up in a different denomination, very liberal denomination. When I met Christ and talked to my pastor and discovered he was a universalist, I jumped ship, and I jumped from that denomination to Southern Baptist because I'd been attending a Southern Baptist church in college, and I discovered two things about Southern Baptists. They love the Bible, and they love evangelism and missions.

Beau Brewer: Yes, we do.

Timothy Beougher: In fact, a lot of the issue in the conservative resurgence was centered around those two things. We're getting away from the scripture, and we're getting away from our primary task. I would say that these chairs have helped keep Southern Baptists focused on evangelism. I think that's partly true, but I also think that Southern Baptists have helped remind seminaries of the need for this.

Beau Brewer: Well, Dr. Chuck Kelley, in his book . . . well, both of his books, 1993, *How Did They Do It?* and then 2018, *Fuel the Fire*, mentions the "Chair of Fire" and its creation by B. H. Carroll, Southwestern Seminary's first president and founder. The creation of the "Chair of Fire" really falls under the umbrella of personal evangelism in the sense that the occupant of the chair here at Southwestern, one of its major tenets was to infuse this campus with an evangelistic spirit. I can hear it in your voice, Dr. Beougher, that, in some connected way, that's also your responsibility at Southern Seminary, to continually infuse your seminary and its faculty and its students and administration, to keep them focused on the Great Commission and also on the task of reaching lostness.

Timothy Beougher: Yeah, that's true.

Beau Brewer: Is there anything further that I haven't even thought of pertaining to the Billy Graham Chair of Evangelism that you think I should know for this kind of research?

Timothy Beougher: Don't really think so. I think you've covered most of the basics there. Well, the one sort of slight addition here and what makes Southern a little bit different than the chairs at Beeson is that, back in 1993 when Dr. Mohler came to Southern, Billy Graham agreed to give his name to a school, so the Billy Graham Chair preceded the Billy Graham School of Evangelism here, but Southern is the only school that Billy Graham allowed to carry his name not just for a chair but with an entire school. That was something that I personally heard him say he would never do.

When I was teaching at Wheaton, there was a donor that offered a huge amount of money to actually start a Billy Graham school of evangelism there, and Billy Graham said, "Thank you, but no thanks. I don't want to attach my name to a school." He reflected how John Harvard had given his life and his family fortune to found Harvard University, back then Harvard College, to train ministers for the gospel and how very little of that was going on now. In fact, things were antithetical to the gospel, and Billy Graham didn't want to give his name to a school that, two or three hundred years from now, would be attacking the gospel instead of promoting it.

Billy Graham said, "I trust Al Mohler. I trust Southern Baptists, and so I am going to give my name to the founding of a new school here at Southern Seminary," so that for the past now . . . We just celebrated the twenty-fifth anniversary of the Billy Graham School last year. It was founded in 1994, a year after Dr. Mohler became president. I think that dovetails into the chair. The chair of evangelism obviously preceded it, but now we have the entire Billy Graham School here, mission's evangelism and ministry all focused on Great Commission studies.

Beau Brewer: That's incredible. Can you talk a little bit about your relationship with Dr. Billy Graham?

Timothy Beougher: Yeah. I first met him when I was hired to teach there at Wheaton. He came and he had . . . I had not met him personally but, obviously, I was going to be coming in to teach at his alma mater. I was going to be, as part of that, made the associate director of the Billy Graham Institute of Evangelism, so he sent his right-hand man, T. W. Wilson, to talk to me. He was a part of the interview process. Robert Coleman had given me a very strong recommendation, so I became very close to T. W. Wilson.

He served in an advisory capacity. He was the liaison between the Billy Graham Association and the Billy Graham Center there at Wheaton College. Basically, T. W. Wilson made sure that, any time that Billy Graham came to Wheaton, that I had a chance to talk with him because he was so excited about what was happening there. T. W. wanted Billy to hear that from me personally, so I had that opportunity on different occasions to be able to talk to Billy about what was going on.

Just to show you Billy Graham's humility, the very first time that I met him, he came there to Wheaton, and I introduced myself to him, talked for a minute, and he said, "I so wish that I could come study evangelism under you." I'm thinking that's the craziest thing anybody's ever said. Billy Graham saying he wants to come study evangelism, and he's Mr. Evangelism. Billy, he was genuinely serious, though. He said, "Tim, I've never had a class in evangelism."

Beau Brewer: What incredible humility.

Timothy Beougher: He said, "I'm just trying to figure all this out on my own." He said, "I would love to come and study under you." Well, that had nothing to do with me. That had everything to do with Billy Graham's humility.

Beau Brewer: That's exactly right. I was going to say that's tremendous humility because when you think about how many people he had led to Christ, even by then, through his crusades and through just his organization, my goodness. Wow, that is incredible.

Have you ever . . . well, did you . . . Sorry. Let me stop stuttering over my words. Did you ever participate in any of his crusades as part of your responsibility with the Billy Graham Chair either at Wheaton or . . .

Timothy Beougher: Yes, at Wheaton I did. I was involved in a Pittsburgh crusade and one . . . oh, gosh, one of the . . . there was Portland, Oregon; Pittsburgh, and then one in one of the California . . . I can't remember. It was in the Los Angeles area, Anaheim maybe, so got to be a part of that, got to be a part of the Billy Graham Schools of Evangelism that BGA used to host for pastors, different locations all over the country including in Canada.

| Beau Brewer: | That's incredible. Well, thank you so much for sharing this little piece of history with me. I know that it's going to have a tremendous impact on my research moving forward. Thank you again, Dr. Beougher, for sharing. |

Thank you. God bless.

Appendix 3

Personal Interview with Dan R. Crawford, May 15, 2020

This is a complete and accurate transcript of the oral history interview of Dr. Dan R. Crawford by Beau Brewer over the phone. No spoken words which were recorded were omitted, except for any non-English phrases which could not be understood by the transcriber. This is a transcript of spoken English, which of course follows a different rhythm and rule than written English. In very few cases, words were too unclear to be distinguished. In these cases, [unclear] or [?] was inserted. Both interviewee and interviewer would interject "Uh hmm" or "Uh huh" frequently, but these were not transcribed unless they came at a definite break in the conversation. In some sections of the tape, the microphone was apparently frequently bumped and every occasion of this has not been noted.

. . .   Three dots indicate an interruption or break in the train of thought within the sentence of the speaker.

. . . .   Four dots indicate what the transcriber believes to be the end of an incomplete sentence.

( )   Words in parentheses are asides made by the speaker.

[ ]   Words in brackets are comments made by the transcriber.

This transcription was made by Rev.com Transcription Services and was completed in May 2020.

Beau Brewer:	This is Beau Brewer. I'm the PhD Student in evangelism at Southwestern Baptist Theological Seminary. Today is May 15, 2020. I am on a telephone interview with Dr. Dan Crawford, senior professor of evangelism and missions (retired), and the Fred

	and Edith Hale Chair of Prayer Emeritus. Welcome, Dr. Crawford.
Dan Crawford:	Thank you.
Beau Brewer:	Would you first articulate your philosophy of evangelism?
Dan Crawford:	I think when you reduce it down to its most simple definition, it's the sharing of the good news of Jesus Christ with those who have not yet discovered it. And then that would be all the way from sharing one-on-one, which we would call personal evangelism, to the sharing in large groups, which we might call corporate evangelism.
Beau Brewer:	Okay. Researching your academic career, you have served in multiple capacities, including, I believe, you're a trustee at Howard Payne University, correct?
Dan Crawford:	No.
Beau Brewer:	No.
Dan Crawford:	I was on the Board of Directors for the Alumni Association—
Beau Brewer:	Okay.
Dan Crawford:	. . . and served twice as president of that board.
Beau Brewer:	Oh, wow. Would you give specific dates of any places that you have served leading up to your service at Southwestern Seminary?
Dan Crawford:	Sure. To start with, I was pastor of a church while I was in college at Howard Payne University, and then I was pastor of another church when I was a student at Southwestern Baptist Seminary. Those are both part-time student-type pastorates.
	When I graduated from Southwestern Seminary in 1967, I became employed by the Baptist General Convention of Texas as the director of Baptist Student Ministries and professor of Bible at the Pan American University in Edinburg, Texas. That

school is now called the University of Texas Rio Grande Valley.

Six years there, then three years at East Texas State University, same title. Commerce, Texas. That school is now called Texas A & M at Commerce. Then six years at the University of Texas as the director of Baptist Student Ministries there. Did not occupy the chair of prayer at that institution.

Then I went to the Home Mission Board, which now is the North American Mission Board, as the national evangelism consultant with students, single adults, and young families. That was 1982 until 1985.

1985, I joined the faculty at Southwestern Baptist Theological Seminary. Served until 2007, at which time I retired and became an adjunct professor, and that continued for four years.

My current title is senior professor and I discovered at a dinner meeting with Dr. Adam Greenway that that title, senior professor, means that I am always connected to the seminary. I didn't know that. I thought "senior" just simply was a fancy way of saying you're retired, but he said, "No, there's a difference in being retired and being senior professor," so I'm still connected somehow. I don't know exactly how, but I'd asked him what happened to my adjunct professor status, and he said, "You don't need that. You're always connected." So that's me. That's who I am.

Beau Brewer: That's very nice. Can you give dates of service with regard to your directorship of the Spring Revival Practicum program?

Dan Crawford: Yeah, when I joined the faculty August of '85, it was with the understanding that approximately half of my job would be directing of what was then called Operation Penetration, which we changed to Spring Revival Evangelism Practicum, which is now called Revive This Nation. So I came with the understanding that I would teach half-time and half the time I would direct that program, which after one year, in realizing what we were looking at, with the advice of the other people in the Evangelism Department, we turned that into an academic course instead of just a volunteer program, so my teaching load then became full-time professor, but with half of the classes being that Spring Revival Practicum, which took up twelve months out of the year, but only actually involved students in the one week of spring break.

Beau Brewer: Okay. So how many years do you think you served as the director for that program?

Dan Crawford: Twenty-two.

Beau Brewer: Twenty-two?

Dan Crawford: Twenty-two years, from 1985 to 2007, and then they asked me in the first year of being an adjunct professor, if I would train my successor, so I taught it another year with him sitting in the classroom.

Beau Brewer: And who was your successor?

Dan Crawford: You called his name a while ago.

Beau Brewer: Oh, Dr. Cky Carrigan.

Dan Crawford: Cky Carrigan? Yes.

Beau Brewer: Yes. Okay.

Dan Crawford: He sat in the room the first year, the next year he taught it and then he was gone.

Beau Brewer: That's right. Okay. Can you give me just a rough estimate of the responsibilities and teaching methods that were yours during your time as director?

Dan Crawford: Sure. Let's look at it a one year at a time. We would start in August recruiting churches to participate. We purchased the mailing list from the still-then Home Mission Board of every church outside of the Bible Belt with under one hundred members, I believe. Something like that. We bought mailing labels for all those churches, and we did a bulk mail out of about fifteen thousand copies. This took most of August and into September asking them to consider participating in our program, sent them an application form to return. All of this was prior to everything going internet.

Of course, as soon as school started, we were busy recruiting students, at least informing students of the possibilities of being in the program, and trying to get that word out. That took a lot of work in the fall semester, going to other people's classes and making announcements and all kinds of things that you would do to promote a program.

Meanwhile, working with churches, trying to get churches lined up, clearing those churches, "vetting" I think is a more popular name for that, just to be sure we knew what we had, clarifying things.

For instance, we would ask on the application, would you be willing to take a student who's been through a divorce? And then if they checked yes, that always required a phone call for me to talk to them about it. We also asked if they would take a student from another nationality or a black student, so we had to follow up on all those. That took most of my fall semester working with that.

When the teaching time came, it was a January J-term for the benefit of students who lived off-campus and went to our extensions, and then we taught one course on Monday night, and went one section on Monday night, one section on Tuesday afternoon, requiring every student to take the course the first time they participated. If they went a second year or third year, they didn't have to take the class again, but it was a three-hour course.

Beau Brewer: And what kind of curriculum did you . . .

Dan Crawford: We started with, of course, giving them a brief history of the program and summarizing for them what all this was about. Then we moved to the personal, spiritual preparation of the student. I'm not sure the exact order of this, but we covered the uniqueness of revival preaching versus just sermon preparation. You knew how to prepare a revival sermon, that would be a bit different from just basic sermon preparation.

When we discovered that most of them hadn't taken preaching yet, we had to back up and do a quick review of how to prepare a sermon in general, and then how to prepare revival sermons.

We talked about how to give an evangelistic invitation. Dr. Fish was always willing to come in and do that or videotape it so we could use him when he wasn't in town because he was the expert on that.

We talked to them about the role of personal evangelism as the guest evangelist. And we talked to them about a number of practical things like how to act as a guest, the temptations that Satan would likely throw at them and how to be ready for those, talked about the role of prayer in sermon preparation and in sermon delivery, talked about how to be a guest in a home because most of them were going to stay in a home. We covered a lot of things that you wouldn't think need to be covered in how to preach a revival.

We also compiled a book using mostly seminary professors and recent graduates, a book called *Before Revival Begins*, which covered all of those subjects, and then had five, I think, five sample revival sermons in the back of the book from the men who were in the Evangelism Department, plus the current president at that time, who was Ken Hemphill.

Beau Brewer: Yes. I own that book. It's a fantastic edition.

Dan Crawford: It's being revised.

Beau Brewer: Is it?

Dan Crawford:	They changed the program. This is now going to be a year-round program. They changed the name from Revive This Nation to—
Beau Brewer:	Reach This Nation.
Dan Crawford:	. . . Reach This Nation, but I changed it again for them. I said, "I understand what you're doing. Are you limiting it only to America?" "Oh, well, no." I said, "Well, then why are you getting singular 'nation'? What about 'nations'?" "Oh yeah, that's good. We'll change it." So it's now "nations." Whatever. It's still RTN. They did want to keep RTN. But the book is being revised and expanded and I'm supposed to be the one compiling that.
Beau Brewer:	Can you, without breach of your contract with the publisher, give us some insights as to what you are adding to it?
Dan Crawford:	Well, we haven't even met yet. A team of people . . . I've just talked to Brent Ray about it, and finally, two days ago, agreed to do what he'd asked me to do, [which] is compile it.
	Then it'll broaden the whole perspective because what students will now be doing is not just preaching revivals, although that's part of it, but they'll be going on mission-type projects and doing various kinds of evangelism projects, I suppose, summer and fall break and Christmas and every other time. So it will broaden it more beyond revival preparation, to personal preparation, to revitalization of churches, which is a big deal these days. We'll have a little bit in there on the history of Southwestern Seminary, which we may use some of your stuff now that I know you're doing it.
Beau Brewer:	Yes, well, it should be done—
Dan Crawford:	History of Southwestern and evangelism and "Chair of Fire" and all that.
Beau Brewer:	Yes.

Dan Crawford:	So just a broader perspective, and I think we have a section on target group evangelism, which we also had in that revival book, not just how to preach to Asians and blacks and so forth, but how to evangelize people of other persuasions, how to evangelize international students, for instance, and things like that.
Beau Brewer:	Wonderful.
Dan Crawford:	How to evangelize youth, how to evangelize children, et cetera.
Beau Brewer:	You just mentioned that during different years of directorship of this program, you had Dr. Fish come in and give guest lectures in the class pertaining to giving an evangelistic invitation, which I'm very familiar with Dr. Fish and that particular book, especially. Can you talk about your years with Dr. Eaves and Dr. McDow and the chair, as well? Because, of course, there's about a ten-year gap . . . Actually, you were hired in the middle of that gap where that chair was in rotation between the three.
Dan Crawford:	It was. It was, but it only rotated once to Dr. McDow.
Beau Brewer:	Oh, okay.
Dan Crawford:	He only did it one time.
Beau Brewer:	Okay.
Dan Crawford:	And I don't know if it was jokingly or seriously, he said he would never do it again. So he set out to hire somebody to do it all the time, which ended up being me. Dr. Eaves had it several times, but it would rotate among the three of them.
Beau Brewer:	Okay.
Dan Crawford:	I don't know if it went ten years or not, but it could have.
Beau Brewer:	About eight years, actually, from about 1982 to about 1990 is the estimated time I have found in records.

Dan Crawford:	No, I took it over in '85.
Beau Brewer:	Oh, '85.
Dan Crawford:	My first spring would have been spring of '86.
Beau Brewer:	Okay.
Dan Crawford:	From that point on, it was all me.
Beau Brewer:	Okay.
Dan Crawford:	Yeah.
Beau Brewer:	Can you talk about the "Chair of Fire" and their influences on the revival practicum, on Operation Penetration, then Spring Break Revival?
Dan Crawford:	From the perspective of Dr. Fish and his occupancy of the "Chair of Fire," my first semester . . . My first class as a seminary student was Dr. Fish's first class to teach, so we go back to the beginnings for both of us.
Beau Brewer:	Yes, you do.
Dan Crawford:	Then, obviously, he became a great friend, as well as a colleague, and tremendous help in the program because even though Dr. Eaves had it by title, it really boiled down to Dr. Fish doing it, and I don't think he ever really turned loose of the program until I arrived, and that gave me a great bit of confidence to know that he would turn it all over to me.
Beau Brewer:	Yes.
Dan Crawford:	Specifically, "Chair of Fire" and its relationship to the revival program? I don't know that there was any kind of direct relationship, just the support.
Beau Brewer:	Just the support. Sure.
Dan Crawford:	Yeah, and the fact that the other guys in the department knew what I was going through, in terms of being up all night some nights, and what happens when, on Saturday, when guys are flying out and all the planes start canceling because of ice in Chicago, and those kinds of things.
Beau Brewer:	Yes.

Dan Crawford:	And by the way, before I took it, nobody flew anywhere. It was all carpools.
Beau Brewer:	Oh, goodness.
Dan Crawford:	That's one of the changes we made.
Beau Brewer:	I guess so.
Dan Crawford:	They'd drive three days and drive to the state of Washington.
Beau Brewer:	To preach for four days and come home.
Dan Crawford:	Yeah, right. Without a spring break. There was no spring break.
Beau Brewer:	For sure.
Dan Crawford:	Just take the week out of school.
Beau Brewer:	That's for sure. Can you discuss the "Chair of Fire's" importance in theological education from your perspective?
Dan Crawford:	The whole idea of a chair, of an endowed chair, is that it guarantees that that subject, that discipline, will be taught forever at that institution, because supposedly all the money it takes to teach evangelism is spun off of the chair endowment, so that gives you an assurance that your discipline is always going to be taught.
	You've been around enough to see some disciplines at Southwestern disappear and had there been a chair, legally that couldn't be done. It was done, but it's not legal. For one thing, to have a "Chair of Fire" meant that we knew that forever and ever and ever, evangelism would be taught at Southwestern Seminary.
Beau Brewer:	Yes.
Dan Crawford:	I think the fact that the . . . . Was it the first occupant was the president?
Beau Brewer:	Yes, L. R. Scarborough was the first occupant.
Dan Crawford:	Yes. The fact that presidents have occupied that chair raises the significance of it. Dr. Head occupied

	it for a semester or two, a year or two, when they were without a professor of evangelism. Of course, Dr. Patterson occupied it. I don't know if any of the others did or not, but that's highly significant. You don't see presidents occupying the chair of archeology.
Beau Brewer:	That's true.
Dan Crawford:	I don't even know if we have a chair of archeology.
Beau Brewer:	I'm not sure either, but—
Dan Crawford:	But that's the significance, to me at least, is that it says not only is this permanent, it's high-priority at Southwestern. And, of course, we've always been known as the seminary of evangelism and missions until Mid-America decided to claim it.
Beau Brewer:	Would you talk a little bit about that journal article? I haven't had the opportunity to read it.
Dan Crawford:	*Mid-America Seminary Academic Journal* a few years ago had an article where they claimed to be the new evangelism seminary among Southern Baptists and proceeded to talk about how Southwestern had become liberal, and the emphasis on evangelism had declined, and the programs that we had, such as the revival program, had declined over the years. At the time of that article, which I was still on the faculty so this would have been maybe twelve or fifteen years ago when that article came out . . . . We were still growing in numbers of participants in the Spring Revival Practicum, so we certainly weren't in decline at that time.

We had declined because there were years we sent 250, and we were probably down to 200, but certainly [it] wasn't in a tailspin. The enrollment had declined, so it was harder and harder to find preachers, and the number of students enrolled in Southwestern preparing for a preaching ministry had declined. That was a significant negative blow

	to the revival practicum. I could talk about that if you want me to.
Beau Brewer:	Sure. If you'd like, go for it.
Dan Crawford:	They were correct that there had been decline, but it certainly wasn't in the revival program.

Yeah, I thought for years that we were declining in the number of preaching-type students, just simply because it was harder and harder to get students to sign up for that. Then there was a survey done as to what students were preparing for, and number one on that list was missions. That has always been true at Southwestern.

| Beau Brewer: | I'm sure. |
| Dan Crawford: | Number two was church planting, which was a result of our emphasis over the last few years, a big emphasis on church planting, so we were preparing students who were going to go out and start a church. They didn't think that they were going to preach because they thought, "Well, I'll just start a church and then I'll go somewhere else and start another one." |

Number three, I think, I don't remember the exact order, but counseling was in there, youth ministry was in there, chaplaincy was in there, and then pastoral ministry. I think we came in sixth of students who actually felt like when they graduated, they were going to be preaching on a regular basis.

That affected our program. If you're not going to preach, then why would you want to take a practicum?

| Beau Brewer: | Right. |
| Dan Crawford: | I think the idea that revivals had seen their best days had an effect on us, although that's not necessarily true, it's just how you go about it. I think Sunday morning to Sunday morning, with every night of the week, noonday services, those kinds of |

revivals have probably seen their best days. But all of that Mid-America tried to take the claim and we challenged it.

Beau Brewer: We're still thriving in the Evangelism Department, even under current occupant, Dr. Matt Queen. So.

Dan Crawford: Who was mentored by Alvin Reid.

Beau Brewer: Yes, who was—

Dan Crawford: Who was mentored by yours truly.

Beau Brewer: By yours truly and Dr. Fish and others. Yes.

Dan Crawford: Alvin was my graduate assistant . . .

Beau Brewer: Oh, my goodness.

Dan Crawford: . . . and grader who helped me teach the practicum.

Beau Brewer: So there you are. So you can see—

Dan Crawford: Matt Queen is my grandson in the ministry.

Beau Brewer: Yes he is. Yes he is. And it's a good thing to be your grandson.

Dan Crawford: I don't think he's claiming that, but I told him once, that's what he was.

Beau Brewer: That's all right. Revivals have been a longstanding part of Southwestern's heritage, and really our history, and, obviously, the Pioneer Penetration or the Operation Penetration and the spring break revival rracticum, that all started around 1959 with Chafin, officially, but we know that there's evidence that, of course, Dr. Scarborough preached revivals continuously. We know that his successor, C. E. Autrey, was also a big proponent of revivals. Can you talk a little bit about revivals prior to the Operation Penetration? Do you know much about that?

Dan Crawford: I don't really. I only knew C. E. Autrey by reputation. I had Dr. Chafin for class—

Beau Brewer: Oh, you did? Okay.

Dan Crawford: One class.

Beau Brewer: And what was that like?

Dan Crawford:	There were two evangelism courses back then before they merged them into one. There was a course in personal evangelism where I had Dr. Fish and then Church Evangelism. And I had Church Evangelism with Dr. Chafin.
Beau Brewer:	How was that? Tell me a little bit about that.
Dan Crawford:	Dr. Chafin, while evangelistic, was cut out of a different mold, I think you could say. I think, basically, he was for anything that worked, even if it was strange. He's the one that went on to the Home Mission Board and developed the Lay Evangelism School.
Beau Brewer:	Yes. LES.
Dan Crawford:	Yes. And if you go back and look at the numbers of baptisms amongst Southern Baptists, still our highest years were when Chafin was vice president of evangelism for the Home Mission Board.
Beau Brewer:	Yes, that is true.
Dan Crawford:	We were doing the WIN Clinics and the Lay Evangelism School. Now the purists among the evangelism people would not look upon him as another Roy Fish or C. E. Autrey. He wasn't in that style. His concept was [that] everybody needs to be an evangelist.
	I don't know if Dr. Chafin preached a lot of revivals. I know he eventually ended up being pastor of a church in Houston where I was baptized long before he got there, South Main Baptist Church, which used to be [a] very conservative, very evangelical church.
Beau Brewer:	Unfortunately, that's not the case now.
Dan Crawford:	It's taken a wrong turn or wrong direction or whatever. I went several months ago because I was in Houston for a wedding, and I went on Sunday morning and I jokingly said, "When I left, I had to

go back out and look at the sign and see if 'Baptist' was still in it."

Beau Brewer: Unfortunately.

Dan Crawford: He became pastor of that church and did some pretty unique things. I enjoyed him because it was totally different from Dr. Fish but they blended together. They didn't clash. It wasn't like they were in opposition, they just had two different approaches to evangelism. And as you say the spring revival, the Pioneer Penetration really started under Chafin. I don't know why or how or what, but when Dr. Fish came on board in '65, it all went to him.

Beau Brewer: Dr. Crawford, do you have anything else that you would like to add to this interview? Anything that you think I've missed?

Dan Crawford: From the perspective of the "Chair of Fire" or the overall perspective of evangelism . . . .

Beau Brewer: Okay.

Dan Crawford: I just thought my contribution to the spring revival program was again different from any of the others, because my background had been to work with students; whereas all the other people that came into the Evangelism Department came as a pastor or a state evangelism director, as in the case of Dr. McDow. They came in from that perspective.

I came in from having worked with college students for fifteen years, and then being a national consultant with college students, and I came to work with students.

Beau Brewer: That's a great perspective.

Dan Crawford: My idea was, if you sign up for this course, I'm going to send you somewhere because my belief is I need to kick you out of the nest and see if you can fly. And when you get back, I'll weep with you or I'll rejoice with you, but get out there, go do it. I'm going to help you get prepared as much as I can help you in the time we've got, and I'm going to trust you that you can do your job. Otherwise, what are you doing here?

Beau Brewer: Absolutely.

Dan Crawford: That was a little different. I think some students were shocked by it. Some others were challenged by it. And the feedback I'm getting ten, twenty, thirty years later is that, for many of them, it changed their whole perspective on ministry and gave them a boost of confidence that they really didn't have. And really a majority of students who took that course in my years did not have preaching experience, maybe home church and one time at the nursing home or something. They sure didn't have five revival sermons.

Beau Brewer: Yes, sir.

Dan Crawford: I think that my contribution was indirectly to the churches, directly to the students. I think the students appreciated what I told them the first class: "This is the way we do it. When I get ready to make all the assignments, the praying and fasting starts on Thursday. I don't go anywhere for the whole weekend. I pretty well lock myself in my office and I stay in the word and in prayer and in fasting until God says, 'It's time.'"

I looked for a go word. Once I found that word in scripture where I said, "Now God is in this with me," then I made the assignments. So what I could say to the students was, "As far as I know, this is where God wants you to be." I didn't just throw them all up in the air and let them fall on a map. I really worked at putting people where I thought God wanted them to be.

Some of them didn't turn out too well, but most of them did, but I think it gave students a boost. And I really think that was my kind of unique contribution was at the point of relating to the students versus the bigger picture of revival and churches, and so forth. So do whatever you want to with that, but that's from me.

Beau Brewer: Thank you. No, that's terrific insight. Thank you so much. And again, I'd like to thank you for your time this morning. If you could, would you send me your copy of the list of numbers and possibly that article from Midwestern—

Dan Crawford: Yeah, I'll do that.

Beau Brewer: I'm sorry, not Midwestern, Mid-America, Mid-America.

Dan Crawford: Mid-America. Yeah.

Beau Brewer: That would be terrific. Oh, sorry. One more thing. Would you talk a little bit about Tom Brooks Riza?

Dan Crawford: Todd. Todd Brooks Riza was a seminary student who signed up for the Spring Revival Practicum. I assigned him to a church in International Falls, Minnesota. He had never preached a revival. In fact, he had never preached before period.

He was dating a seminary student, Korean girl, who took him to her church the week before our spring break, where they were having a revival, and the pastor at the end of the service formed a healing line for people that wanted to be healed, and Todd got in line because he had suffered for many years with juvenile diabetes.

When he told the pastor, the pastor prayed over him and told him that he was now healed and he need not take any more medication. Todd died on Thursday night prior to flying to Minnesota on Saturday.

In talking with his parents, they said, "Did he write any sermons? Because he never preached before." I said, "Yes, he turned in five outlines." They said, "Would you come and preach his funeral and preach one of his sermons?" It was really the only time I've been able to justify preaching somebody else's sermon. It really was only an outline. I think I had them write the purpose of the sermon and the opening sentence and outline and the closing sentence or something like that.

But I preached his sermon, his revival sermon. Then his parents set up a memorial in his memory, the Todd Brooks Riza Memorial Award, to be given to the participating student who demonstrates a passion for personal evangelism, to be elected by fellow students. That's not the exact wording on the plaque, but it's pretty close.

So every year when we'd get back and we'd have our testimony time and all the students would get told their stories and all, the students would do one of two things: they would vote on who gets to speak in chapel and they would vote on who they thought deserved the Todd Brooks Riza Award. And that award was always presented in chapel. The Riza family would be present in chapel that day, and as they could work it out, we would take the student to lunch sometime that day. And that award went on for a number of years after I retired, but it just disappeared. The plaque disappeared and the award disappeared. I think we found the plaque somewhere.

Beau Brewer: Do you happen to know what year that was initiated or roughly? Because I'm going to go look for it.

Dan Crawford: I don't but I'm going to guess around 1990 or '91.

The big plaque has his picture on it and it has a small name plate for the award winner each year. There would be seven or eight or nine names on there, so I'm guessing, I don't know, mid-nineties, somewhere in there, maybe.

I have a one-page document that you may have seen on the history of the Spring Revival Practicum.

Beau Brewer: I would love to have that if you have it.

Dan Crawford: Okay. I know where that is. It was in the notebook.
                 All right. Thank you.

Beau Brewer: God bless you, sir.

Appendix 4

Personal Notes from Dan R. Crawford

HISTORY OF THE SPRING EVANGELISM PRACTICUM

PIONEER PENETRATION, AS THE Spring Evangelism Practicum was initially called, began with approximately sixty students on their knees in prayer in the winter of 1959. An idea was formulated in the heart and mind of one student that Southwestern Seminary students could take a week out of classes in order to preach revival services in small churches in Ohio.

Among those praying for direction that winter day in 1959 at the Gambrell Street Baptist Church were Seminary students Roy Fish and Larry Lewis. Dr. Lewis, retired president of the Southern Baptist Home Mission Board, went to Marysville, Ohio, that spring. In a chapel address at Southwestern, he later stated, "I spent fifteen years on the mission field, planting churches and as a mission pastor, but I look back to that one week of Pioneer Penetration as the one experience that God used more than any other to direct me toward a mission career."

Dr. Roy Fish, who would later join the evangelism faculty at Southwestern, said recently, "Over the years it has been very exciting to see what God has done both in touching hundreds of lives of people and also what God has done in the lives of those who go."

As the years went by the program grew in both student and church participation. In the early sixties Dr. Kenneth Chaffin took over the direction of the program followed in the mid-sixties by Dr. Roy Fish and later by Dr. James Eaves and Dr. Malcolm McDow. Since 1985 the program has been under the direction of Dr. Dan Crawford. For many years the program was funded by gracious gifts from the Panhandle Baptist

Foundation of Amarillo, Texas, under the leadership of the late C. J. Humphrey. More recently, funds have been provided by the Joe F. Hayes family of Travelers Rest, South Carolina.

In the years since 1959 the name of the program was changed briefly to Operation Penetration in the early eighties and to its present name, Spring Evangelism Practicum, in 1987 when it became an academic course offered by the Evangelism Department.

Early records are non-existent, but since 1965, records show participation by over five thousand students, leading revival services in approximately 4350 churches, in forty-three states, the District of Columbia, Canada, England, Puerto Rico, Mexico, and American Samoa. Professions of faith have been recorded by more than 13,400 people.

Through the years many students have echoed the statement by SWBTS student Sammy Ravelo, who said, "If we are willing to obey Jesus' command to reach the lost, God will send us to places where people can only be touched by the peculiarities of the personality God has given us." Likewise, numerous pastors have agreed with pastor Don Chandler of Inwood, West Virginia, who wrote, "In my opinion, this is the finest program to come out of our seminaries. The Spring Evangelism Practicum is one more example (and a good one) of how 'investment' in the Cooperative Program keeps returning to the local church."

God has richly blessed the evangelistic outreach of the Spring Evangelism Practicum with every indication that the blessing will continue for many years to come.

Appendix 5

EMAIL MESSAGE FROM SUZANNE DAVIS, MAY 28, 2020

From: Suzanne Davis
Sent: Thursday, May 28, 2020, 11:15 a.m.
To: Brewer, Beau
Subject: Roland Q. Leavell Chair of Evangelism

Hi Beau,

I have some good news and some not as good news for you regarding the information you requested about the Roland Q. Leavell Chair of Evangelism.

First, Dr. C. C. Randall did occupy the chair from November 22, 1982, through his retirement on July 31, 1988.

For Dr. Robert L. (Bob) Hamblin, I could find no record that he had ever been named the Roland Q. Leavell Chair of Evangelism. He was first elected to the faculty in the spring of 1982 and began serving on August 1, 1980. His title was associate professor of evangelism—none of the memos or correspondence regarding his election gave any other title besides associate professor. He left the seminary in the fall of 1982 when he was elected as vice president for evangelism at the SBC's Home Mission Board (now called NAMB). (For your reference, I've attached an article about his election to that position.) Dr. Hamblin returned to the NOBTS faculty in September of 1994, when he was elected to serve as professor of evangelism and occupied the Max and Bonnie Thornhill Chair of Evangelism—which he held until his retirement in July 1998.

I hope the information is helpful. Please let me know if you have any questions.

Thanks.

Suzanne Davis
Administrative Assistant to Dr. Norris Grubbs, Provost
New Orleans Baptist Theological Seminary

Appendix 6

Personal Interview with Adam W. Greenway, May 21, 2020

This is a complete and accurate transcript of the oral history interview of Dr. Adam W. Greenway by Beau Brewer over the phone. No spoken words which were recorded were omitted, except for any non-English phrases which could not be understood by the transcriber. This is a transcript of spoken English, which of course follows a different rhythm and rule than written English. In very few cases, words were too unclear to be distinguished. In these cases, [unclear] or [?] was inserted. Both interviewee and interviewer would interject "Uh hmm" or "Uh huh" frequently, but these were not transcribed unless they came at a definite break in the conversation. In some sections of the tape, the microphone was apparently frequently bumped and every occasion of this has not been noted.

. . .   Three dots indicate an interruption or break in the train of thought within the sentence of the speaker.

. . . .   Four dots indicate what the transcriber believes to be the end of an incomplete sentence.

( )   Words in parentheses are asides made by the speaker.

[ ]   Words in brackets are comments made by the transcriber.

This transcription was made by Rev.com Transcription Services and was completed in May 2020.

Beau Brewer:	This is Beau Brewer. I'm a PhD Candidate at Southwestern Baptist Theological Seminary in Evangelism. I am on a live telephone interview with Dr. Adam Greenway, president of Southwestern Baptist

Theological Seminary, and the former dean of the Billy Graham School of Missions, Evangelism, and Ministry at Southern Baptist Theological Seminary. Today is May 21, 2020.

Dr. Greenway, thank you for being with me.

Adam Greenway: Thank you for having me, it's good to be with you.

Beau Brewer: Researching your academic career, you are the ninth president of Southwestern Baptist Theological Seminary. Would you give me the dates of your service at each institution leading up to your service at Southwestern?

Adam Greenway: Sure. So I was elected the ninth president of Southwestern Seminary, February 27, 2019, 11:15 a.m., central time is when I officially assumed office.

Prior to that, I served from 2007, June 1, until that time as a faculty member at Southern Baptist Theological Seminary in Louisville, Kentucky, through the variety of things through administratively before becoming the dean of the Billy Graham School of Missions, Evangelism, and Ministry June 1, 2013.

Prior to serving at Southern Seminary, I was a pastor of the Baptist Church at Andover in Lexington, Kentucky from 2002 until 2007. And before that I was a master of divinity student here at Southwestern Seminary. So in a sense, I left Texas to go to Kentucky and then God in his kindness allowed me to come back here as the president in 2019.

Beau Brewer: Fantastic. Thank you so much for sharing that. Would you articulate your philosophy of evangelism?

Adam Greenway: Yes. My philosophy of evangelism is that we need to do it. That we have a responsibility and the privilege of being able to be instruments in the hands of the Lord to connect all people to Jesus Christ. We do this in word, we do this through verbal proclamation of the gospel, talking about who God is, who Christ is, what we have done, our need, how we respond to the gospel.

It is a biblical imperative. It is an existential joy to think about being the instruments through which God uses to bring men and women and boys and girls saving faith of Jesus Christ. It is the main reason that we are left here on the earth. It is to do what we can to tell others how they too can be saved. As one definition of evangelism goes, evangelism is simply one beggar telling another beggar where he found bread.

I think there is great encouragement and credibility to that. And so my philosophy of evangelism is [that] I'm all for it. Believe in it. I did a PhD in it. I was deeply impacted in my master's studies here studying particularly the men like Roy Fish and Malcolm McDow. And for the last number of years, in addition to whatever administrative title I've held, I have been a professor of evangelism in some form or fashion since 2007, including now here as a full professor of evangelism and apologetics.

So it is very intrinsic to my not only academic ministry but my understanding of what New Testament Christianity is all about.

Beau Brewer:	Dr. Greenway, that leads me to a sidebar. You would be, I believe, the third president to serve in the Evangelism Department. I believe the last president to actually serve in the Evangelism Department at Southwestern Seminary was Dr. Head and so that's—
Adam Greenway:	In fairness it would be Dr. Hemphill because his faculty title was professor of evangelism and church growth, so in fairness—
Beau Brewer:	Well, I stand corrected, my apologies.
Adam Greenway:	Our seventh president, my president, the man who signed my diploma that I'm looking at here in my office, in addition to being president, he held the

faculty title of professor of evangelism and church growth. So I think I would be in addition to Dr. Head and Dr. Scarborough, obviously, Dr. Hemphill, and then now yours truly.

Beau Brewer:

That's excellent, thank you so much for correcting me. Before coming to Southwestern Seminary, you did serve as the dean of the Billy Graham School of Missions, Evangelism, and Ministry at Southern Seminary. Would you provide any insights to the workings of the Billy Graham Chair of Evangelism?

Adam Greenway:

Well, the Billy Graham Chair of Evangelism was established, I believe, [in] 1965 at Southern Seminary when Duke McCall was president there. Dr. Graham himself had been in a relationship with Southern Seminary and the Graham organization going back to the fifties, but it took on a new form in 1965 with the inauguration of the Billy Graham Chair. And it's been held by different people down through the years. The first occupant was Kenneth Chafin and then Gordon Clinard, and then Lewis Drummond, who held the chair for many years, [and] after that David D'Amico. And for the last twenty-something years, it's been held by my former colleague, Tim Beougher.

Fun fact, every occupant of the Billy Graham Chair of Evangelism at Southern Seminary has been an alumnus of Southwestern Seminary, and that's a neat insight. But the Billy Graham Chair there was their first endowed professorship in evangelism, it certainly is, I think, a historic chair there.

And it was that relationship that eventually gave rise to the support from Dr. Graham for the naming of the school of missions and evangelism there, that's had different names because of the way the school was configured over the years for Dr. Graham. Billy Graham had often said he would not allow his name to be used at any particular institution because he had ties to multiple institutions. But when Albert

Mohler was elected president of Southern in 1993, he was able to, through some intermediaries, to present a vision to Dr. Graham about establishing the school of missions, evangelism, and it was then called "church growth" at Southern Seminary, and Dr. Graham, who spoke at Dr. Mohler's Inauguration in the fall of 1993, endorsed that vision and said that he would allow his name to be attached to it, which was a significant coup . . .

Beau Brewer: Yes, it is.

Adam Greenway: . . . For the seminary at that time. And another fun fact, the deanship of the Billy Graham School has never been held by the person who was the Billy Graham Chair of Evangelism, that's always been two separate roles. So Thom Rainer was the founding dean and then Chuck Lawless and then a briefly Zane Pratt and then I was dean for six years and now Paul Akin is the dean there.

Beau Brewer: Okay. Well, is there any particular reason why there's a separation between the two?

Adam Greenway: I don't know if it's been intentional in most academic contexts, [but] endowed chairs are usually seen as significant faculty honors. And so you've reserved those for faculty; for administrators you have deans, provosts, presidents. It is less typical that they hold endowed positions. Now, some places you'll see an endowed deanship, but it's not typical if I can say it that way.

When I was dean in an endowed chair there that I was elected to by the board of trustees, because that was an honor that the institution wanted to bestow upon me, which I was very grateful for, but it's not typical.

Just in some cases, it's just a timing issue. The chairs already occupied by a faculty member and a new dean is named, well, they're not going to usually vacate the chair and dishonor the faculty member to give it to the dean at that point.

Beau Brewer: What was the name of your chair that you occupied?

Adam Greenway: Yeah, the chair I occupied was the William Walker Brooks Endowed Chair. It had had different faculty positions attached to it over the years, but at Southern the chair sort of goes with the position. So my title was William Walker Brooks Associate Professor of Evangelism and Apologetics.

Beau Brewer: Okay. So it was also a chair of evangelism?

Adam Greenway: Well, not technically. It was an endowed chair but it was an evangelism chair because I was an evangelism faculty member. It was not tied to any specific discipline per se.

So if it had different, in fact, every occupant of that chair had a slightly different faculty title. So Bill Leonard had held that chair when he was the William Walker Brooks Professor of American Christianity. John Debert held that chair when he was the William Walker Brooks Professor of Church and Community. Some chairs are not tied to a specific discipline, but will be assigned to whatever the discipline of the faculty member may be at school or general area.

Beau Brewer: Okay. Well, thank you for that clarification. That's exciting.

So you mentioned that every occupant of the Billy Graham Chair of Evangelism was a Southwesterner or at least a Southwestern alumnus; that would be a very strong connection. So what other connections, if any, did or does the Billy Graham Chair of Evangelism have with Southwestern Seminary's "Chair of Fire," and, at the same time, would you share what the difference is?

Adam Greenway: No direct ties, but I can attest to other than obviously the "Chair of Fire" was established with really the founding of the institution by Dr. Carroll,

Dr. Scarborough being the first full-time professor of evangelism at any seminary in North America in 1908. You'd have to wait more than a half century until you have the establishment of a chair at Southern Seminary.

I think it was Southwestern had long been the leading seminary in evangelism in the SBC. I think Southern Seminary saw an opportunity there, with their ties with Dr. Graham, and they had the opportunity to launch that chair. But I don't know that there was any real organic connection or thoughtfulness. Again, other than the interesting tidbit that every occupant of the chair at Southern was a product of Southwestern.

Beau Brewer: You just—

Adam Greenway: And, in fairness, Dr. Graham always had a strong connection to Southwestern. He was an honorary life member of Southwestern Advisory Council; he had close ties here. I'm told that at some point he was asked about regrets he had in ministry, in life. And one of those regrets was that he didn't go to seminary and that he said further, if he would've gone to seminary, he would've gone to Southwestern Seminary.

Beau Brewer: Well, that's incredible. You just mentioned that the "Chair of Fire" was the first in North America. Do you know of another chair? Because, of course, B. H. Carroll claimed that it was the first chair of evangelism in the world, and I believe W. L. Muncy in his book titled *A History of Evangelism in the United States* also claims the same premise. I just want to make sure that my facts are correct.

Adam Greenway: Yeah. There is chair in an informal sense that simply means a professorship.

Beau Brewer: Yes.

Adam Greenway: Then there is chair in a formal sense, which means an endowed professorship. Like, so sometimes the language will become cloudy here because Southern and New Orleans Seminaries had people who were teaching evangelism before the establishment of the Billy Graham Chair in 1965. But Southwestern was the first seminary to have a professorship, if I can be more direct on that, of any seminary in North America full-time. And it was a chair in a sense by being a professorship that later became a chair in terms of formal inauguration when it became the "Chair of Fire," of course now the L. R. Scarborough Chair of Evangelism.

So in that sense, there were other seminaries that would eventually come along with teaching evangelism and have professorships, but in terms of actual endowed chairs in evangelism to this day, there's still only a handful. There's the Bailey Smith Chair at Southeastern Seminary. The Billy Graham Chair at Southern, the chair that I held, which could be repurposed, but was used in evangelism when I was there.

: Obviously the Scarborough Chair here, I believe there are evangelism chairs or professorships at New Orleans Seminary now, but I wouldn't know the names of those, but every institution has a little different policy about how they use the term "chair" and how that's named or funded. So sometimes you use the old line, we maybe using the same vocabulary, but using a different dictionary.

Beau Brewer: Sure. So can you discuss the L. R. Scarborough Chair of Evangelism's importance in theological education?

Adam Greenway: Well, I mean, to be blunt, it was an academic innovation unprecedented at the time. The history of American theological education, freestanding seminaries, the first one, Andover Newton, was not even a hundred years old by the time that Southwestern Seminary was chartered March 14, 1908, and the founding faculty were assembled together.

And so the entire enterprise of freestanding theological education was still a novelty in many ways. And so it represented, I think, a positive development of recognizing that evangelism was an academic discipline that was worthy of that kind of faculty recognition and faculty position. It was a way by which Dr. Carroll wanted to make a distinct contribution in terms of what Southwestern Seminary was going to be, particularly as a second seminary in Southern Baptist life after Southern Seminary.

Beau Brewer: Yes.

Adam Greenway: There were voices who did not believe we needed a second seminary and that Southern Baptist only had one and only needed one. And Dr. Carroll believed that we needed more than one, and that we needed one here in Texas especially, and that it needed to, in a sense, be a preservation and perpetuation of the best of Southern, but with some correctives, I can say it that way, of things that he thought were missing; he'd been a trustee of Southern. And so he had a pretty close view to see what was happening there. And since that time, certainly in Southern Baptist life, other seminaries have followed that lead in wanting to give higher elevation to practical disciplines, if I can say it that way.

Beau Brewer: Excellent. And what would you say is the most significant way that the "Chair of Fire" has impacted Southern Baptist Evangelism?

Adam Greenway: Well, I mean, I think the occupants of that chair have been among the faculty who have taught more students evangelism than any other institution anywhere. I mean, you think about people like Dr. Scarborough, Dr. Head, you look at, of course, Roy Fish, Malcolm McDow, these are people who are synonymous with evangelism, evangelistic teaching, evangelistic training; it's incalculable the number of students that they impacted and through them, the churches.

I think that the L. R. Scarborough Chair probably has done more to advance the cause of evangelistic training and evangelistic consciousness in Southern Baptist life than perhaps any other academic entity, or academic innovation.

Beau Brewer: That's excellent. You know, of course Scarborough wrote seventeen books, most of which were based on evangelism and theological education. Can you speak to the importance of publication, of printing textbooks as a contribution to theological education?

Adam Greenway: Well, I mean, providing resources, I think, is important to theological education. Obviously, resources that can be used as textbooks or materials in academic contexts, classrooms and the like, but also beyond that. The resources that students can take with them into the churches or that churches themselves can procure. And you think back to Scarborough's own works, *With Christ after the Lost* and *Recruits for World Conquests* and other resources.

And then, of course, Dr. Fish on the invitation, Dr. McDow on revival and awakening, Dr. Queen on *Everyday Evangelism*. The people who have held the Scarborough Chair here have been scholar practitioners, they've been teachers, they've been preachers, they've been writers, they've been evangelists.

And I think that represents the best heart and commitment about what an academic institution, certainly within a Southern Baptist Convention seminary context, ought to be characterized by and known for, that we're working to do things to be able to teach and to train and to equip and to mentor and to resource our folks, to be able to get the task done, which of course the task is the fulfill-ment of the Great Commission in our time.

Beau Brewer: That's excellent. Anything further that you would like to share about the "Chair of Fire" and/or the Billy Graham Chair of Evangelism?

Adam Greenway: No. Other than it gives me a sense of pride and gratitude from the Lord that by account, the cur-rent occupant of the Billy Graham Chair of Evan-gelism is a very dear personal friend, Southwestern Seminary alumnus, and somebody that I have great respect for. Tim Beougher and his work at South-ern Seminary is extraordinary. And the fact that Dr. Graham felt led to allow his name to be car-ried on the chair of evangelism at Southern Semi-nary I think was a wonderful thing for Southern Seminary.

As president of Southwestern Seminary I'm thank-ful for Dr. Queen, what he does; I think he is im-minently qualified to hold the Scarborough Chair. What he's doing continuing in that line of faithful-ness, going back [to] Scarborough himself.

And certainly, all we can do to promote a culture and a consciousness for evangelism across theolog-ical education in the Southern Baptist Convention. I think that's important, I think that's healthy and needful. I think it's something that we should be doing, because again, there are always those voices who want to say you don't need the practical in theological education. All you need is kind of the classical disciplines, Bible theology, history, you can get all that other stuff somewhere else. I reject that point of view very strenuously and believe that theological education, serving the Southern Baptist context, ought to be holistic and ought to see the value in both the classical and the applied or practi-cal disciplines.

I think that's been the genius of Southwestern Seminary since Dr. Carroll and Dr. Scarborough back in 1908 and as an alumnus, I'm very committed to doing what I can to see that vision perpetuated, continued moving forward until Christ comes again.

Beau Brewer: I couldn't have said it better. Thank you so much, Dr. Greenway for your time. I know you've had a busy day.

I look forward to publishing your work with my dissertation and yes, I'll send you a copy of the transcript when it's finished.

Adam Greenway: Fantastic. Look forward, and blessing be with you as you continue in your labors.

Beau Brewer: Thank you, sir. Have a blessed day, sir.

Adam Greenway: You too. Goodbye.

Appendix 7

Personal Interview with Richard Headrick, May 19, 2020

This is a complete and accurate transcript of the oral history interview of Mr. Richard Headrick by Beau Brewer over the phone. No spoken words which were recorded were omitted, except for any non-English phrases which could not be understood by the transcriber. This is a transcript of spoken English, which of course follows a different rhythm and rule than written English. In very few cases, words were too unclear to be distinguished. In these cases, [unclear] or [?] was inserted. Both interviewee and interviewer would interject "Uh hmm" or "Uh huh" frequently, but these were not transcribed unless they came at a definite break in the conversation. In some sections of the tape, the microphone was apparently frequently bumped and every occasion of this has not been noted.

. . .   Three dots indicate an interruption or break in the train of thought within the sentence of the speaker.

. . . .   Four dots indicate what the transcriber believes to be the end of an incomplete sentence.

( )   Words in parentheses are asides made by the speaker.

[ ]   Words in brackets are comments made by the transcriber.

This transcription was made by Rev.com Transcription Services and was completed in May 2020.

| Beau Brewer: | This is Beau Brewer. I'm a PhD candidate at Southwestern Baptist theological seminary in Fort Worth, Texas. I'm on a live phone interview on May 19, 2020, with Mr. Richard Headrick. He is a dear |

friend of Dr. Paige Patterson and a friend to South-eastern Seminary and also a friend to the Southern Baptist Convention.

Beau Brewer: Glad to have you with me, Mr. Headrick.

Richard Headrick: Hey, thank you, Beau. I appreciate the opportunity to share with you.

Beau Brewer: Well, would you first articulate maybe your philosophy of evangelism?

Richard Headrick: Well, hit the streets to tell people about Jesus.

Beau Brewer: Okay. Can you elaborate on your relationship with Bailey Smith?

Richard Headrick: Yeah, sure. I met Bailey, gosh, I can't remember the years, but he came to Laurel to do, I think it was called a Starlight Crusade in our football stadium. And our business, in outdoor advertising, and so I was a good fit to help put up some billboards and have artists and stuff like that. So, I handled the PR for the crusade, even though I was lost and Bailey just treated me wonderfully and we became friends. And through the years we just stayed in touch a little bit.

And then when I got saved, I went and became a member of his board of directors and was chairman of that board for, good gracious, I don't know how many years, but it was a wonderful relationship. The guys that he had on the board are just good, godly men and we never saw any gray in Bailey Smith. He was always a black and white preacher. Just shelled the corn like it's supposed to be shelled and we just watched people get saved by the thousands. So it was a privilege to become part of that ministry and then become personal friends with Bailey and Sandy and the boys. And it's just ongoing. Even though Bailey's gone on to be with the Lord, we still stay in close contact with Sandy, probably text her four and five times a . . . Let me cut off a phone call here, okay?

Beau Brewer: Sure.

Richard Headrick: Okay. But we text back and forth and encourage her. We have a hotel down in Central America and Bailey has been there several times, Sandy has been several times, and we like to shoot the bull about that. And she has good memories there and so forth. So, that relationship has gone on for, shoot, thirty, thirty-five years perhaps? And my wife and I've been married now twenty-seven and it's been a close relationship during all of that as well. So, that's about the Bailey Smith tale, you know?

Beau Brewer: Okay. So, what was your role at Southeastern Seminary and how did that come about?

Richard Headrick: Paige came and spoke at one of Bailey Smith's board meetings. And in those days I had a ponytail, had long hair and a ponytail about halfway down my back, and my handle, so to speak, in the biker community is Rhino Man, and Paige had heard about me through Bailey and came up with this story he told the board that a rhinoceros grows the horn out the front of his head and the rhinoceros's horn is actually made out of hair that is just spun up there on the rhinoceros horn. And he told the board, he said, "Now, Richard's handle is Rhino Man," and said, "He loves rhinoceroses. And all he was trying to do was grow a horn out the front of his head, but it backfired and grew out the back."

And so he kind of captured our fancy there and we became a little more involved, a little more involved with him. And then when he got up to a point there, he asked Gina and I to come and be part of the board of visitors and that was simply a little old thing, you'd go up a couple times a year, I forget, send a few dollars up there and that gave you the title of "board of visitor." And then after some years, I don't remember how many, they asked us to be, or me, to be a trustee there. And so we consented, they have allowed us to come and I was a trustee there for several years and it's gotten to a point that it was time for me to not continue and I resigned from that position, but still stayed on as a board of visitor.

And in the latter years of our association, there was Southeastern. I had sold a business. We didn't need to work and Paige was promoting the Two Plus Two program and you're very familiar with that, I'm sure.

Beau Brewer: I am.

Richard Headrick: Okay. Well, a lot of the students were getting out there and these, gosh, God-forsaken countries and by themselves in hostile territory and so forth and I used to be a smuggler back years ago in Central America and knew ins and outs of how to get in and all this kind of stuff. So, Paige, let me back up, he knew I had that experience and we had a ministry over in Vietnam working with the underground church there and the lepers and handicapped children and so forth, and we had come back in one time from one of those trips and stopped by Southeastern to visit Paige and Dorothy or just say hello and they were packing to head over to Indonesia where a couple of their students had got in trouble over there and almost gotten killed. And J. D. Greear was one of them. And we asked them where they were going and said, "Well, we've got some students over there that's in trouble and we're going to get them out of trouble." And I said, "No, me and Gina will go get them out of trouble."

And so, to make a long story short, all four of us went over there. And we got there and it was a pretty bad situation there. There had been a lot of killing and all and some of the churches were still burning, roadblocks, some viciousness in Jakarta. They had took the heads of Christians and put them on stakes alongside the road and so forth. And we were able to go in and J. D. has a very interesting story about that, what got him in that trouble. And so we had a pretty good tie that built a real strong tie with Paige and Dorothy and after that event was over, we went on to another Indonesian island for a few days of rest and while we were there at dinner one night, Paige and them, they broached the subject, would we consider traveling and visiting the Two Plus Two students scattered around the world and encourage them to keep on keeping on? And they asked us, would we pray about it?

Well, prior to that, Gina and I, at home at night when we say our prayers, we would always pray, "Lord, we need to be doing something to help. There's something that helps that I know you want us to do." And one night Gina said, "Wouldn't it be great if we could just go and travel and visit missionaries and so forth?" And here we were sitting at a table in a foreign country being asked to go visit missionaries. And it was an answer to prayer that we experienced that night. And so Paige told us, he said, "Now what we're going to do, we're going to pay you nothing, we're not going to give you any money to travel with, but we're going to double your salary every year." So that the salary made me really interested even though it was nothing.

So we consented to do that and for the next four years Gina and I traveled all over the world and we stayed gone nine months out of the year visiting Two Plus Two students and other career missionaries, friends that we'd made along the way throughout the world. And it was an incredible adventure that we got to do. We also, as we visited the Two Plus Two students, Gina would make her report of the condition they were in, whether they were lonely, tired, disgusted, wanting to go home, wanted to stay forever, whatever their situation was. And I would make a similar report, but we wouldn't discuss it with each other. And then when we got back, we wrote that up and gave it to Paige and Dorothy so they could see how that program was going on.

So, like I said, we did that for four years and then a little after that Paige moved on out to Southwestern and we got back pretty heavy in business and that kind of ended that. But what an experience to be able to go and do and see and become friends with folks out there on the frontlines, brother. It was a good time.

Beau Brewer: Mr. Headrick, do you happen to have any of those reports that you would share?

Richard Headrick: I'd have to ask Paige.

Beau Brewer: Okay. I will double back around and ask him.

Richard Headrick: Sure.

Beau Brewer: But of course, he's only going to share if you give approval. So, how much do you know about my dissertation topic?

Richard Headrick: None.

Beau Brewer: Did he share much with it? Okay. Well, my dissertation is about the L. R. Scarborough "Chair of Fire," which is the chair of evangelism, the very first academic chair for evangelism in the world, which means that Southwestern holds the very first professor of evangelism, which his name was L. R. Scarborough. He was a pioneer, a cowboy off the Western frontier of Texas as a young man and then educated at Yale and at Baylor or Baylor and then Yale and then came to Southern for about two semesters and then was called to the pastorate in Texas again. And then eventually called by the father of theological education in Texas, his name is B. H. Carroll, which was the first president of the seminary. And so my dissertation is recording all this great history about the chair. And what I'd like to ask you is with limited knowledge about the Bailey Smith Chair of Evangelism, what do you see that are some of the responsibilities of that chair? Do you know any?

Richard Headrick: No, sir. I do not.

Beau Brewer: Okay. I just didn't know and I thought I'd ask.

Richard Headrick: I'm sorry.

Beau Brewer: No, you're fine. You don't have to apologize at all. And so, you were not part of the fundraising at all for the Bailey Smith Chair, is that correct?

Richard Headrick: No, sir. No.

Beau Brewer: Okay. All right.

Richard Headrick: The way I understand it, Randy gave it all.

Beau Brewer: Randy Bates. Okay.

Richard Headrick: Now I could be wrong on that.

Beau Brewer: Okay.

Richard Headrick: But that's the way I understood it. Yes, sir.

Beau Brewer: That's fine. That's good to know.

Richard Headrick: Okay.

Beau Brewer: Well, brother, I really don't have anything extra. I was going to just drill you and have you tell the story about how you funded the chair, but as you're not the funder, the funder for it.

Richard Headrick: No.

Beau Brewer: That kind of does away with that part, but thank you for sharing your testimony, your connection to our students at Two Plus Two Program.

Richard Headrick: Yes, sir.

Beau Brewer: Of course, Dr. Keith Eitel created the Two Plus Two Program at Southeastern and brought it to Southwestern.

Richard Headrick: Correct.

Beau Brewer: And it is a highly successful program, even today. Still places students all over the world.

Richard Headrick: Awesome.

Beau Brewer:	Serving and learning how to be a missionary in an apprenticeship pattern. So, all things that you contributed to.
Richard Headrick:	And it's been a real good experience. Paige Patterson and Dorothy, oh my goodness, what contributions they made to our lives.
Beau Brewer:	Absolutely.
Richard Headrick:	So, I'm telling you it's been incredible. I just hate he got dumped on like he did, but being the man of integrity that he is, he never lashed back or nothing. I just stand amazed at how courageous he's been through it. So thank you for standing by my friend.
Beau Brewer:	Absolutely. I'm a two-time graduate of Dr. Patterson's and I'll be finishing a doctorate this December under our new president, but have deep, deep respect and appreciation for Dr. Patterson and Mrs. Patterson.
Richard Headrick:	Amen.
Beau Brewer:	So, thank you for your time.
Richard Headrick:	You bet, Beau.
Beau Brewer:	And I pray you have a blessed evening.
Richard Headrick:	Well, thank you. Well, let me pray for you before we hang up. How's that?
Beau Brewer:	Absolutely.
Richard Headrick:	All right.

APPENDIX 8

PERSONAL INTERVIEW WITH JEFF IORG, MAY 27, 2020

THIS IS A COMPLETE and accurate transcript of the oral history interview of Dr. Jeff Iorg by Beau Brewer over the phone. No spoken words which were recorded were omitted, except for any non-English phrases which could not be understood by the transcriber. This is a transcript of spoken English, which of course follows a different rhythm and rule than written English. In very few cases, words were too unclear to be distinguished. In these cases, [unclear] or [?] was inserted. Both interviewee and interviewer would interject "Uh hmm" or "Uh huh" frequently, but these were not transcribed unless they came at a definite break in the conversation. In some sections of the tape, the microphone was apparently frequently bumped and every occasion of this has not been noted.

. . .   Three dots indicate an interruption or break in the train of thought within the sentence of the speaker.

. . . .   Four dots indicate what the transcriber believes to be the end of an incomplete sentence.

( )   Words in parentheses are asides made by the speaker.

[ ]   Words in brackets are comments made by the transcriber.

This transcription was made by Rev.com Transcription Services and was completed in May 2020.

Beau Brewer:	This is Beau Brewer. I am a PhD Candidate at Southwestern Baptist Theological Seminary in Fort Worth, Texas. I am on a live telephone interview with Dr. Jeff Iorg of Gateway Seminary in Ontario, California. Today is May 27, 2020.

	Dr. Iorg, thank you for joining me.
Jeff Iorg:	You're welcome.
Beau Brewer:	Well, I have been researching your academic career. You are the seventh president of Gateway Seminary.
Jeff Iorg:	That is correct.
Beau Brewer:	Would you provide your academic credentials and give me a sense of the dates of your service leading up to your presidency at Gateway Seminary?
Jeff Iorg:	Well, in terms of my academic credentials, I graduated from Hardin-Simmons University in 1980 with a major in Bible. I graduated from Midwestern Baptist Theological Seminary in 1984 with a master of mivinity degree and Southwestern Seminary in 1990 with a doctor of ministry with a focus on missions and evangelism.
Beau Brewer:	Oh, fantastic.
Jeff Iorg:	That's the summation of my academic credentials.

Jeff Iorg:

In terms of my ministry service, my first ministry assignment really was as a staff pastor. I was the minister to children at Elmcrest Baptist Church in Abilene, Texas. That was probably from about 1978 until 1981. Then I was the pastor of Green Valley Baptist Church in St. Joseph, Missouri, from 1982 until 1989. Then I was the founding pastor of Pathway Church, as it's currently named, in Gresham, Oregon, which is a suburb of Portland. I was there from 1989 until 1995. In 1995, I became the executive director of the Northwest Baptist Convention and served there for almost ten years before becoming the president of Gateway. It was then, of course, known as Golden Gate Seminary, and I became the president in 2004, so I am just now completing my sixteenth year at Gateway. I've been a pastor, a church planter, a state executive director, and a seminary president over the last forty years.

Beau Brewer:	My goodness, that's an incredible career. You said that you have a DMin in evangelism and missions from Southwestern Seminary?
Jeff Iorg:	Correct.
Beau Brewer:	I am just curious. I know this wasn't one of your questions, but who was your evangelism professor?
Jeff Iorg:	Well, I had several. I actually attended Southwestern for about a third of my MDiv before I transferred to Midwestern when I was called to the pastorate in Missouri. In my DMin studies, my doctoral supervisor was Roy Fish and my project report was entitled "Developing Effective Listening Skills for Personal Evangelism."
Beau Brewer:	Oh, man.
Jeff Iorg:	The purpose of my report was to . . . At the time, *Evangelism Explosion* and *Continuing Witness Training* were very prominent training tools in evangelical churches, and my goal was to take that next step and move from what I called a "go-tell approach" to a dialogical approach converting or building on those, if you research them, and I'm sure you have, those lengthy memorized presentations that were part of *EE* and *CWT* and taking them to the next level where people became much more capable of having conversational gospel presentations built on those foundations. Dr. Fish supervised me, and I did that work back in the late 1980s.
Beau Brewer:	Oh, man. That is incredible. Would you articulate for me, real quick, your philosophy of evangelism?
Jeff Iorg:	Well, I borrow the same definition I've been using since the "Continuous Witness Training" days. Evangelism is sharing the good news of Jesus Christ and the power of the Holy Spirit and leaving the results to God. I can expound on any part of that you want, but that's my basic definition of personal

evangelism, and I think that can also be extended to public or pulpit evangelism.

I believe that evangelism is verbally sharing the gospel or, in some way, communicating the gospel story and doing that in the power of the Holy Spirit, recognizing that God is at work in the life of the witness, the life of the lost person, and in the orchestration of the circumstances and then recognizing that I am powerless to bring about a conversion but that God must act in the context of my witness to bring about a conversion. That's a fast and short summary of my philosophy of evangelism and what it means.

Beau Brewer: That's incredible. Thank you. Can you tell me more about the E. Hermond Westmoreland Chair of Evangelism at Gateway Seminary?

Jeff Iorg: I can tell you more about it, and this may be where our interview stops because, unlike Southwestern's "Chair of Fire" with L. R. Scarborough, our chair has some more dubious history associated with it.

Beau Brewer: Okay.

Jeff Iorg: The chair was actually initiated in 1966 with a fundraising campaign that was launched by the seminary. We have the brochures of that and the printed material that was used in that campaign. The chair was ultimately named for E. Hermond Westmoreland, who was a trustee and prominent Texas pastor. That all was good news. Over the years, there was about $260,000 donated for the chair in the sixties, seventies, and eighties. That was not nearly enough to endow the whole chair, but it was a significant amount of gifts for which we were grateful.

Then a professor named George Schweer, S-C-H-W-E-E-R, held the chair for many years and was a fantastic evangelist and professor and Christian gentlemen in every regard, but in the 1990s, the seminary invested most of the money for this chair with the Arizona Baptist Foundation. In terms of the grand total of the seminary's investments, it was a token investment, but the seminary does have small investments in Baptist foundations in the West both to demonstrate our partnership to them and to encourage them and also to gain an income for the seminary.

We had invested about $300,000 in the Arizona Baptist Foundation. Of course, you may not know this story, Beau. I don't know how old you are, but in the late 1990s, the Arizona Baptist Foundation failed, failed dramatically, and the president was convicted and sent to prison. In that context, the seminary, of course, had its investment jeopardized because that was part of the problem, is the inflated and fraudulent accounting that was going on, et cetera.

Then, when the foundation failed, of course, it went into court, and the judge appointed what was called an investors' committee, which was to represent the people who had lost money in the foundation. Most of the foundation's investments were in real estate, and so if that real estate was being liquidated, there was going to be some return back to the investors, but, of course, not nearly all of it was going to be returned, and there had to be some means by which there were recommendations made to the court about how this money was going to be distributed as it was received.

Well, Dr. William O. Crews was the president of Golden Gate Seminary at the time, and was considered by almost everyone in the western United States to be our most significant and trusted leader, and so, through a process, the judge asked Dr. Crews to chair the investors' committee. Now, the good news was that they picked a person of sterling integrity to chair the investors' committee and to go to the meetings and listen to the horrible stories of people who lost everything to the foundation's collapse. Dr. Crews did his normal, masterful, integrity-filled leadership job of getting that investor group through that crisis.

The other corollary to that, though, was that Dr. Crews knew, when he accepted the responsibility, that meant that Golden Gate went to the end of the line, so to speak, on ever recouping any money from that source. I think, Beau, you can probably understand what I mean. You know?

Beau Brewer: Yes.

Jeff Iorg: You chair the investors' committee and you reward your own organization money, that doesn't work.

Beau Brewer: Right.

Jeff Iorg: Dr. Crews knew what that meant, and so the seminary never got any money restored from the Arizona Baptist Foundation collapse. They ultimately wound up paying about ... I don't know how much, but I've heard different estimates. The first people who got their money were individual investors, pastors, and others [who] had their retirement accounts there and put all their money into the foundation. They received as much as they could, and then the institutions like Gateway didn't really get much, and we got nothing.

The E. Hermond Westmoreland Chair of Evangelism funding was essentially lost. Because of that, when Dr. Schweer retired, just because of the scandal associated with the foundation's failure and how the seminary and got involved in trying to help investors get the best deal they could from the court and how the ultimate awards were decided and how the seminary really received nothing, we did not name anyone to that chair for a number of years.

When I became president, there was no one serving in the E. Westmoreland Chair of Evangelism, and we left it that way for quite a number of years. I don't remember when, but at some point, we designated Dr. Pate in that role again and, today, it's fine. There's no negative stigma attached to the thing. The story I'm telling you is now fifteen or twenty years old and is dead history to a lot of people, but it was really a raw time in the West when the Arizona Baptist Foundation failed. It was a $300 million foundation.

Beau Brewer: Goodness.

Jeff Iorg: Everybody that invested in it lost millions.

Beau Brewer: Yes.

Jeff Iorg: Because of that, we just haven't made a big deal about the chair or didn't for a number of years. Now, there has been money given to the chair after the foundation collapsed. There was some money the seminary held that was not put in the foundation, and so we currently have a little over $100,000 that support the chair, which only generates about five to six thousand dollars of earnings a year, but nevertheless, it's a little bit of an amount that we still retain. If anyone were to give to the chair or there was some estate that matured that we didn't know anything about that maybe they'd put it in there twenty-five or thirty years ago, we'd still be able to receive those funds for the chair, but we're not actively fundraising for it any longer.

Beau Brewer: Okay.

Jeff Iorg: That's the history. It was started in 1966, funded in the seventies and eighties. The seminary made one investment in the Arizona Baptist Foundation, which was moving the funds for this chair to that foundation sometime in the early nineties. The foundation failed in the late nineties. Dr. Crews chaired the investor committee which put us at the

	end of the line, which meant we got nothing. Today, the chair is in name only with no serious funding attached or no real connection to much, any longer, to the Westmoreland family or anything like that, not any that we know of at least.
Beau Brewer:	Okay. May I clarify? May I ask some questions for clarification?
Jeff Iorg:	Oh, sure. No, none of this is secret.
Beau Brewer:	Well—
Jeff Iorg	It's not talked about because it's kind of ancient history now, so go ahead.
Beau Brewer:	Who was the first occupant? Do you know?
Jeff Iorg:	No. I would say it was probably . . . I said George a minute a go. That was his legal name. Everyone knows him as Bill Schweer. I should clarify that. I would say it was Bill Schweer. I mean I don't know that, but I would say that probably was the first one because he was evangelism professor here for, gosh, twenty-five years. I'm sure that he was the first.
Beau Brewer:	Okay, and then from what I have found to be true, Bill Wagner was the next occupant, and he held it from '96 to 2006 if only by title.
Jeff Iorg:	I would say that's probably true. I came in '04 and Dr. Wagner was retiring about the time I got here, and so that's probably true, but we didn't make a . . . . I mean it wasn't a high-profile appointment. Dr. Wagner was also an Islam specialist, and I think that's what he's more well-known for. He wrote books on Islam and things like that, so yeah, that's probably true.
Beau Brewer:	Okay. You said that you believe Dr. Pate is actually installed in this chair?
Jeff Iorg:	He is our lead professor of evangelism, and so, again, we don't . . . . Because of the history of it, we haven't made a big thing out of this chair like we do some of our other ones, but now that you brought

	this up to me, I mean it's revived in me a desire to say, "Hey, we should probably reclaim this now."
Beau Brewer:	Well, because—
Jeff Iorg:	When I came to seminary and I raised the question . . . . I heard all these stories about the Arizona Baptist Foundation, and that had only happened five years before I got [to] the seminary. I mean emotions . . . I mean, look, I don't know. What happened was lots of people in the West took their money out of GuideStone and other things because the Arizona Foundation was achieving these remarkable returns on investments. They were doing so well because the real estate market was booming, and they were buying real estate all over the West and, really, all over the country.
	When the dot-com bubble burst in the late 1990s and real estate values plummeted in the West, the foundation turned out to be a house of cards built on all kinds of dubious promises and other things, and so hundreds of pastors in California lost everything they had. It was well known that the seminary lost the investment on this. I mean no one blamed the seminary. I mean everyone else was investing it appropriately, they thought, just as the seminary was, but because of that, there was just not a lot of attention drawn to the E. Westmoreland Chair for a while. I do think those days are gone and we ought to make more of it now than we do, but anyway, that's the history of it.
Beau Brewer:	Sure. Well, I am rooting for Dr. Pate. Just go on and install him. That'll be great. No, because my—
Jeff Iorg:	Yes. Well, there's no reason we could not do that. Frankly, your email kind of . . . I mean you know how it goes when you're in an institution like this. Things happen, and then they get put on a shelf, and then you think, "Well, do we really want to deal with that?" I haven't even thought about it

in a couple of years, quite honestly, since we've been through so many other changes here at the seminary, but your research and your email got me motivated, and we're talking about . . . . I had some people go back and re-find files and pull out information for me, so it's a good thing. Maybe we can reinvigorate this a little bit and see where it goes there for us.

Beau Brewer: Yeah. Well, praise the Lord. I'm all for promoting evangelism and theological education.

Jeff Iorg: Sure, absolutely.

Beau Brewer: I am looking at what I have been able to find through Google searches and Dr. Pate giving me some information and some leads. To my knowledge and to Dr. Pate's knowledge, the chair has been unoccupied since 2006, so that gives you a little bit of reference. It would be terrific if it were reinstalled and reinstated. Maybe it won't bring up the ill feelings that it once did.

Jeff Iorg: Yes. I think you're right. We still have a prominent plaque displayed here on the wall. The thing's probably two feet wide and four feet tall, and it's a huge sign which has the original donors listed. It is not like we've kept it a secret or been ashamed of it in that sense. We just have not carried through with following through, like you're describing, with promoting it. Anyway, thank you for bringing that up to me. That is good.

Beau Brewer: Well, you are welcome. Any time, any time. Well, so, assuming that you and your administration do decide to reinstate the Westmoreland Chair of Evangelism at Gateway Seminary, what kind of tenets would the chair of evangelism have at your seminary? I mean what kind of teaching parameters and—

Jeff Iorg: The priority would be the evangelism instruction and building the evangelism program through our curriculum. We have required evangelism courses and evangelism practicums and things like that already.

This might be a little self-serving, but I think one of the reasons that there hasn't been as much urgency about this is because my background is evangelism and, within the seminary, not by my insistence but just by default, I have become the voice of evangelism at Gateway. We recently wrote a seventy-fifth anniversary history. Two faculty members wrote the book for us and not at my insistence. I did not have anything to do with it, but they actually wrote about the fact that I brought a new evangelism focus to the seminary by my lifestyle, by my ministry experiences, and by my training.

I suppose that, in terms of outside the classroom in terms of preaching, conferencing, and other things, I have probably done more about that than any faculty member would have in this chair of evangelism because I think we've seen our academic chairs here . . . . We have two or three others. We have seen them as focused mainly on building the academic program and building what we do in curriculum design and what we do in making sure that things are not only in the classroom taught but where the subject is taught but also infiltrated through the curriculum in meaningful ways and things like that. That is what we would look for as the focus of this chair, and it would be similar to what we're already looking for in our lead evangelism professor, which is Dr. Pate.

Beau Brewer:	Well, Dr. Pate is a fine man. I really enjoyed our conversation. You can—
Jeff Iorg:	He's the best.
Beau Brewer:	You can read his interview in the appendices of my dissertation later.
Jeff Iorg:	Great.

Beau Brewer:	It will be published this year. What kind of connections, if any, does the E. Hermond Westmoreland Chair of Evangelism have with Southwestern Seminary's "Chair of Fire?"
Jeff Iorg:	Well, I do not know of any connection except that Southwestern has been an example of this. Southwestern has been an example of prioritizing evangelism in theological education for a hundred years now, and it is hard for me to imagine that that influence did not have some impact on Golden Gate in 1966. I do not know of any direct connection, but the organic connection seems, to me, to be fairly reasonable to assume existed because of the strength of Southwestern and its influence throughout the denomination.
Beau Brewer:	Well, it is interesting that, in 1966 . . . I am sorry. In 1966, your school named a chair after Westmoreland for evangelism and, in 1976, Southwestern Seminary named a chair after Westmoreland for preaching, so—
Jeff Iorg:	Really?
Beau Brewer:	Yes. Southwestern also has an E. Hermond Westmoreland Chair of Preaching and so it's interesting that they are both named after the same person.
Jeff Iorg:	Right, right.
Beau Brewer:	Of course, you're right. He was a—
Jeff Iorg:	I was surprised that there's a connection in the regard of Southwestern to Gateway. I am surprised about the both of us having the same someone named for the same. That's great.
Beau Brewer:	Yes. Both chairs are named after the same person and, well, of course, he was a very well-known Texas pastor at South Main Baptist Church in Houston. For a number of years, in fact, he was followed by Dr. Kenneth Chafin, who also was a professor of evangelism both here at Southwestern and at Southern as the first Billy Graham Chair of

	Evangelism in '65, and then he went to South Main in '70, I believe it is '72, as the pastor that followed as the one that succeeded Westmoreland.
Jeff Iorg:	Wow, that's interesting.
Beau Brewer:	That's a little interesting tidbit you probably didn't need to pay for, but so you can see there's a lot of connections there.
Jeff Iorg:	Correct.
Beau Brewer:	What kind of differences would exist? If the chair existed today, there are obviously going to be some differences. Your school's evangelism programs are different from ours. I mean, of course, they share some commonalities, but your campus's focus is different from ours. What are some differences that would exist in the chair's function and emphasis and purpose?
Jeff Iorg:	Well, the biggest difference between Gateway and the other Southern Baptist seminaries is the multicultural environment in which we work. 65 percent of our students are not Anglo, and so that means that we have to learn how to do things and teach how to do things in a lot of different ways. Evangelism, for us, is a multi-faceted approach to getting the gospel into the lives of people.
	Our Seminary is located in five different urban areas. We're in five of the seven largest cities in the West, and so in order to do evangelism in a multicultural and an urban environment, you do have to approach some aspects of it differently, but I would say those differences are methodological. They are not, certainly, differences in the gospel or in the message that we're trying to communicate, and so I think the commonality is the passion and urgency about the message of the gospel. The differences would be in the methodologies that are required because of the different settings in which we train people.

Those are, in my view, the commonalities and the differences between what historically may have been done through the chair at Southwestern or in some other Southern Baptist seminary and what is done here at our school.

Beau Brewer: Excellent. You discussed, just a moment ago, that you did your DMin. here at Southwestern Baptist Theological Seminary and your major supervisor, your project supervisor was Dr. Roy Fish. Correct?

Jeff Iorg: Correct.

Beau Brewer: He is the longest occupant of the "Chair of Fire" here at Southwestern. Can you speak a little bit about the L. R. Scarborough Chair of Evangelism and its importance in theological education?

Jeff Iorg: Well, there's probably not any person who has meant more to evangelism in the Southern Baptist Convention than Roy Fish. I mean for, what, almost fifty years, he towered over Southwestern Seminary with his character, his influence, his scholarship, and his passion for evangelism.

His impact and his impact through the chair of evangelism or the "Chair of Fire," I should say, it is almost impossible to put it into words. For me, the reason I went back to Southwestern for my doctoral studies was to study with Dr. Fish. I was accepted into both the PhD and DMin programs and, by God's direction and my circumstances at the time, I chose the DMin program, but he still took me all the way through, and then he had actually also preached my inauguration message as president of Gateway.

Beau Brewer: Oh, wonderful.

Jeff Iorg: He had a profound impact on me and as he has on thousands of others, but I think, in that regard, even a personal impact on me and in my desire to bring to Gateway a strong emphasis on getting the gospel to as many people as possible and letting that be interwoven throughout everything we're doing here at the school.

Beau Brewer: Fantastic. I would say you can't really determine a chair's influence, but you could always demonstrate contributions, and Dr. Fish certainly made many contributions. Can you speak to some of those contributions that he made?

Jeff Iorg: Well, I think Dr. Fish, for me, his most significant contribution was combining scholarship about evangelism with passion for evangelism. Evangelism sometimes gets a bad reputation for being emotionalism, revivalism, anti-intellectualism, a feeling-oriented approach to faith. In its most extreme expressions, maybe some of those things are true, or I would say they're caricatures of what is true about evangelism. On the other extreme, you have people who are intellectuals who would like to discuss evangelism as if it's a theory or if it is an academic study or discipline only.

Dr. Fish was masterful in that he was the serious academic who really cared about the study of evangelism and all things related to it but, at the same time, had a personal warmth and a passion and a practice of evangelism that made him genuine and real and approachable and personable. For me, that is what drew me to him, was the excellence and thoroughness of what I experienced in the classroom because I actually had him for evangelism as an MDiv student before I transferred to Midwestern, so I had him at the master's level, and then I came back and took him again in the DMin and had him as my supervisor.

I just saw it from multiple angles of how he impacted and changed me by combining both scholarship and practice in a way that made me want to be like him. I mean if I could live my life over and if I could have done anything, I would have wanted to be Roy Fish and try to accomplish what he accomplished, but he was a one-of-a-kind, and no one else ever is going to do that again, but he certainly had that kind of impact on me.

Beau Brewer: Yes. I would agree. I was one of Dr. Fish's last students. I had Jesus and Personal Evangelism and Spiritual Awakenings with Dr. Fish in the MDiv level. It was actually after he had already officially retired. He was just teaching adjunctively, but those classes were still packing out. I mean they couldn't get enough room in a room for him because there were so many students that wanted to sit at his feet and learn from the master, really.

What would you say is the most significant way the "Chair of Fire" has impacted Southern Baptist evangelism?

Jeff Iorg: Well, I honestly think it is by inspiring and motivating pastors and people like you and me. I mean, how many hundreds of people went through Roy Fish's classrooms and came out inspired, motivated, trained, and committed to being evangelistic leaders, whether they are pastors or missionaries or in any other kind of Christian leadership? I think that is the most significant contribution.

The second contribution would be the way he was able to inspire and really gather other faculty around him at Southwestern. I mean there were other good faculty members, Ebbie Smith, Dan Crawford, other good men in evangelism that I also took for classes. I was always astounded that, while they may not have been as well-known as Roy Fish, they really were, in their own right, just as dynamic and just as impactful.

Then the third thing I think the chair has done is for the Southwestern has for probably the longest . . . I'm sure you research if this is true or not, but for the longest, Southwestern had PhD programs that turned out people who could go and teach evangelism at other places. I think those are the three primary contributions, inspiring students to evangelism in whatever field of ministry they were going to lead, gathering an evangelism faculty around Dr. Fish that was remarkable, and then, three, training through the PhD program and even the DMin program other leaders like you and me who are going to go out and do this in an academic way and at a training level for the next generations.

Beau Brewer: Couldn't say it better. Anything further you think that I have missed pertaining to the E. Hermond Westmoreland Chair or to the "Chair of Fire?" Anything else that you'd like to add?

Jeff Iorg: No. You know more about my Seminary than I do, so I've been motivated to get after it here and see if we can't reclaim the actual use of this terminology and re-elevate some of this. Like we say, it's now been ten years since the worst of this has gone away, I think, so we probably have no reason we shouldn't move ahead and just go ahead and do it.

Beau Brewer: Well, I look forward to hearing and reading about that in *Baptist Press* because I would say that having a chair . . . . Just from my research, having a chair on any discipline, especially the field of evangelism, adds confidence, adds a significant weight of importance to not only the faculty but to students.

I spoke with Dr. McDow. I'm sure you also had him when you were at Southwestern. Dr. McDow talked about the value and the weight of importance that a chair endues to a professor who is occupying that chair. It gives a significant seat of importance to that person. It also empowers that person to do a specific work. I would encourage you, yes, absolutely, not only as a Southern Baptist but also as somebody that is studying the effects of evangelism and theological training, to continue on. Get that chair back up and running, because I believe Dr. Pate would be a fantastic professor of evangelism

	and . . . well, I've never had a class with him, but from what . . . My conversation with him was excellent and then—
Jeff Iorg:	Well, he's extremely popular here. He's the real deal in every way, so yeah, you read him right. He's awesome.
Beau Brewer:	Yeah. He seems very awesome. I would just encourage you to continue in planning, and I look forward to hearing more about the advancement of the Westmoreland Chair of Evangelism at Gateway Seminary.
Jeff Iorg:	All right, brother. Well, thanks for that.
Beau Brewer:	Well, thank you for sharing with me just a little bit of this history. I will make sure that you get a copy of this in the next day or so after I get it transcribed and so we can talk through it. If there's anything you need to change or want to clarify, we'll do that. I will look forward to—
Jeff Iorg:	Sure. Okay. Thanks, brother.
Beau Brewer:	I look forward to talking to you again soon.
Jeff Iorg:	Thank you. Bye.
Beau Brewer:	Have a blessed one.
Jeff Iorg:	Bye.
Beau Brewer:	Bye-bye.

Appendix 9

Personal Interview with
Thomas P. Johnston, May 21, 2020

THIS IS A COMPLETE and accurate transcript of the oral history interview of Dr. Thomas Johnston by Beau Brewer over the phone. No spoken words which were recorded were omitted, except for any non-English phrases which could not be understood by the transcriber. This is a transcript of spoken English, which of course follows a different rhythm and rule than written English. In very few cases, words were too unclear to be distinguished. In these cases, [unclear] or [?] was inserted. Both interviewee and interviewer would interject "Uh hmm" or "Uh huh" frequently, but these were not transcribed unless they came at a definite break in the conversation. In some sections of the tape, the microphone was apparently frequently bumped and every occasion of this has not been noted.

. . .   Three dots indicate an interruption or break in the train of thought within the sentence of the speaker.

. . . .   Four dots indicate what the transcriber believes to be the end of an incomplete sentence.

( )   Words in parentheses are asides made by the speaker.

[ ]   Words in brackets are comments made by the transcriber.

This transcription was made by Rev.com Transcription Services and was completed in May 2020.

Beau Brewer:	This is Beau Brewer. I'm a PhD Candidate of Evangelism at Southwestern Baptist Theological Seminary in Fort Worth, Texas. I am on a live telephone interview with Dr. Thomas Johnston, a professor of evangelism at Midwestern Baptist Theological

Seminary in Kansas City, Missouri. Dr. Johnston, welcome.

Thomas Johnston: Thank you, Beau. It's a privilege to be here. And I wanted you to know that soon I'll be senior professor of evangelism here.

Beau Brewer: Oh. Excellent.

Thomas Johnston: Yes.

Beau Brewer: Well, correct that for the form. He is senior professor of evangelism at Midwestern Baptist Theological Seminary.

Thomas Johnston: Yes. Thank you.

Beau Brewer: So, Dr. Johnston, we are researching the "Chair of Fire" and its influences on the Southern Baptist Convention, but specifically it's contributions to evangelism and theological education. And I have eagerly been wanting to interview all of the professors of evangelism at our different seminaries to discuss this chair with them, because the premise of dissertation and historical data show that Southwestern was the bedrock of evangelism in theological education.

B. H. Carroll created the chair in 1908 along with the seminary here in Fort . . . Well, at that time it was in Waco at Baylor University and then sheltered there until 1910. But we want to discuss you and your work at Midwestern Baptist Theological Seminary and the chair's influences on your program there. So researching your academic career at Midwestern Baptist Theological Seminary, would you give me the dates of your service and do you currently hold a chair?

Thomas Johnston: Okay. I do not technically hold a chair . . . . By the way, thank you, Beau, for this opportunity and privilege to be interviewed and I'm really look forward to this time. And I've been really encouraged by talking with you here and preparing for this time.

: First of all, I was all-but-dissertation at Southern Seminary, and Dr. Blaising, whom you know because you went to Southwestern, said you can't leave Louisville until you've written your first draft.

So in 2001, I wrote my first draft, in the spring of 2001. And I came and taught my first class here at Midwestern in July. July 15, 2001. It was a doctoral seminar with Dr. Phil Roberts. And then I began my official first year in August of 2001 as, I think, assistant professor of evangelism.

So I've been here nineteen full academic years. I'll finish that off in, I think, July 31 is the year end for us. So I've been able to be here for a long time and I'm grateful for the honor and privilege of having served that long at this school. In the meantime, I've become a full professor. And we did get monies for a chair of missions and evangelism. The chair was given to Dr. Robin Hadaway, a long-time missionary with the IMB and also missions professor. And he's done very well in that chair and I'm grateful for him. So that's how the monies were dispersed back when they were given.

It's called the Gary Taylor Chair of Evangelism. Gary Taylor was the DOE, director of evangelism, for the Missouri Baptist Convention and, unfortunately, died of cancer. And so in honor of him and his service to Missouri, they named the chair in his honor.

Beau Brewer: So that's the Gary Taylor Chair of Evangelism and Missions?

Thomas Johnston: Correct. Missions and Evangelism.

Beau Brewer: Oh. Missions and Evangelism.

Thomas Johnston: Missions comes first. Missions and Evangelism. Yes.

Beau Brewer: Okay. All right. So Dr. Johnston, would you please articulate your philosophy of evangelism?

Thomas Johnston: My philosophy of evangelism has shifted over the years. I used to be so red-hot for evangelism that I would put evangelism as primary over discipleship. I read Dr. L. R. Scarborough's 1914 book where he says that soul-winning and soul-building are "Siamese twins" of God's Great Commission, of Christ's Great Commission. And so, from that point on actually, having read that, I began to see his wisdom. And I see that in Ezekiel 3, specifically verses 15, 16, all the way to 21. Where both soul-winning and soul-building as it were, the ministry to the wicked, the ministry to the righteous. They use the same verbs, have the same commands, have the same results. And so therefore I put them at fifty-fifty.

However, that said, the Great Commission in Matthew says, "Teaching them to observe all that I commanded you." The "them" is clearly those that are saved through winning disciples in verse 19. So, "them" is a phenomenal word in Matthew's Great Commission. Because who are you baptizing? You're baptizing "them." Not the nations, "nations" being neuter plural. But the "baptized," masculine plural. He baptized the saved disciples, from completed "disciple-making." I like to translate that verb "win disciples." Anyways, so the main purpose of the church is to teach "them," a particular group of people who are saved and baptized, to observe all things that I have commanded you.

That being said, the "them" is a very small group in relation to the world. So, we have a very small group of people whom we are called on to disciple. But then, the church is called to go out and proclaim the good news. So, we have, say, the 95 percent to 98 percent of the world that's unsaved and in my estimation that needs to hear the gospel. And then we have the 2 to 5 percent that are truly, regenerate, born-again Christians who love Jesus and are baptized and so forth. And they need to be discipled. The weight of following Scarborough and his balance, the Siamese twins of God's gospel, are evangelism or soul-winning, and soul-building. And yet how that takes place is a bit more complicated because some things happen inside the church, some things happen outside the church.

Beau Brewer: Okay. Man, that's wonderful. So, you mentioned that the Midwestern Seminary does have a chair of missions and evangelism.

Thomas Johnston: Yes, yes.

Beau Brewer: Can you talk about some of the tenets? What does that chair represent at Midwestern? Of course, the Scarborough Chair of Evangelism, known as the "Chair of Fire," has certain tenets that were set forth in its creation by B. H. Carroll. One of which being that the occupant of "Chair of Fire" at Southwestern would teach the distinctive office of the evangelists as was Dr. Carroll's interpretation of Ephesians chapter 4, verses 11–13, where he saw the office of the evangelists listed in scripture. So that is a tenet that is still taught. Yes, I know the Baptist faith and message only lists two specific offices, but we still teach that the role of the evangelist is a primary position inside the church. For an inter-church ministry, not just to one particular congregation.

Thomas Johnston: We live in an interesting time when the so-called charismatic movement might emphasize the five-fold role of the ministry, that is the apostle, prophet, evangelist, pastor, and teacher. So, we do have in the Church Growth Movement, as well as in the charismatic and Pentecostal movements, we have right now today a strong push-pull toward all five roles or all five leadership roles being a part of church leadership. In the missions movement, the contemporary missions movement, we have a movement toward calling an apostle, a "sent one," or a missionary.

My father was a missionary in France, and so I grew up in France. I understand how apostle comes from the Greek word ἀποστέλλω, which is the verb "to send." "I send" in Greek. So, I understand where that comes from. I do have hesitation because of abuses of the world "apostle." However, it's interesting to compare this concept with the Great Commission with the five roles. You can see the process and procedure of the Great Commission happening. You have the apostle being sent out. You have the prophet or revivalist. And I think your former president Dr. Paige Patterson would like to call it "the revivalist who awakens a person's soul by preaching of the law."

Then you have the evangelist come in with the gospel and providing the response to the bad news of the law that was broken. The gospel . . . . Then you have the new believer being taught. Pardon me, the evangelist pastor. He's being pastored, shepherded, often by being baptized and entering into a church. And then he's being taught the rest of his life. You actually have in those five roles a beautifully-chronologically developed in the Great Commission. Sent ones, revivalists, evangelists . . . . Or sent ones, prophetic ministry, evangelism, pastoring, and teaching. It's very interesting.

So yes. I agree with your assessment and Dr. Carroll's assessment that the evangelist is part of today's church. I don't believe it's ceased. I don't think it's a ceased office. I think the office manifests itself sometimes without the name "evangelist" because of the practice in various languages, various places, various countries, various denominations and groupings. I know the old Methodists had an "exhorter" who would be exhorting. And that was an actually church office. The office of the exhorter. I'm not sure if it's from the Methodist movement. So, you have a different term here. He was doing

exhortation to awaken people to their need for salvation. Also, he was a youth pastor, I think, or a
pastor in training. So, your question is, do we have
a chair of evangelism, or do we as a school respect
and honor the ministry of the evangelists?

Beau Brewer: Yes.

Thomas Johnston: And I cannot speak for anybody else, but I do. I
wrote a book called *The Worth and Work of the
Evangelist*. I actually reorganized and rewrote a
book by Keith Fordham and then published it
also using his name. Keith Fordham and myself,
The Worth and Work of the Evangelist. I feel very
strongly that the evangelist is needed. Now, how
the ministry of the evangelist looks might be different in different cultures and contexts. But it is still a
needed role.

Do we have a chair of evangelism? We do. We do,
it's a chair of missions and evangelism. And it's not
focused like you would be to train evangelists other
than to train missionaries to go forth on the mission field and evangelize there. Which IMB's very
good at, by the way. Do we have one? In practice
but not in name—other than what's already been
created. Does that answer your question, Beau?

Beau Brewer: Yes. Yes it does. Thank you. So do you know if a
connection exists between Midwestern Seminary's
Department of Evangelism and Southwestern
Seminary's "Chair of Fire" and our department?

Thomas Johnston: Yes. Yes. I love Matt Queen. The connection exists through a spirit of fellowship as brothers in
the Lord and at the Southern Baptist Convention.
And as well as through the SBPEF—the Southern
Baptist Professors of Evangelism Fellowship. That
fellowship was founded many years ago under
Lewis Drummond and others when they would
meet at the Summer State Leadership Meeting
(SSLM) of the Southern Baptist Home Mission

Board, the North American Mission Board. At the SSLM, which gathered together state directors of evangelism, the state execs, and other leaders, such as . . . let me see, Love Loud directors, etc. They would all come together. We used to have massive meetings. The professors of evangelism were invited to that.

And at first, we were not listed among the breakout sessions. So, my goal, after I was asked to be president of the SBPEF, actually by Dr. Roy Fish . . . . It was in 2004. I thought that it would be nice for us to have a room to gather together. So, I worked with the North American Mission Board so we had a room and a time slot in the schedule when other people gathered in their affinity groups. We would meet as an affinity group. Prior to that time we used to meet in the hallway. After this way we started meeting in a meeting room. And the SBPEF grew in size. So now we have about forty-two professors of evangelism. A Southern Baptist professor of evangelism is someone who teaches evangelism at a Southern Baptist school. It could be a seminary or a college, a Baptist college. The president and the executive committee, which is president, vice president, and secretary . . . . By the way, the secretary right now is your own Dr. Bradford.

Beau Brewer:	Carl Bradford.
Thomas Johnston:	Yes, yes, yes.
Beau Brewer:	Oh, wonderful.
Thomas Johnston:	He's very able in that area. In order to be seated in one of those executive committee spots, you have to be at a Southern Baptist seminary. One of the six. And you have to be full-time teaching as a professor of evangelism there. This is to make sure that the SBPEF stays controlled by the SBC seminaries.
Beau Brewer:	Sure.

Thomas Johnston: So we're connected through that and we get to meet each other and we work together. We began working together. I actually began cooperative teaching. I taught a group of Southwestern students in Orlando. At the SBC in Orlando about 2006 or so.

Beau Brewer: Actually 2007.

Thomas Johnston: 2007?

Beau Brewer: I was in that class and that's when I first met you.

Thomas Johnston: You were?

Beau Brewer: Yes sir.

Thomas Johnston: Praise the Lord. That was a good time. What was it, 2007?

Beau Brewer: 2007.

Thomas Johnston: And that began that year, Beau, began a movement of all the seminaries now working together to teach a class together. So, we've been doing it ever since that time. Where especially myself, and Dr. Preston Nix, worked together, but we grew in cooperation when we met in Louisville with Dr. Tim Beougher. We began to cooperate very effectively. And so now NAMB pays for and organizes every year a crossover seminary evangelism class. And they house us in a certain location and provide the classroom space. And we share the plenary session and we have breakout sessions. So it's very, very effective. I'm very grateful for that.

This class allows us as seminary students and professors to rub shoulders. And what I saw is that early on, among some of the professor of evangelism, there can sometimes seem to be a spirit of rivalry. It really shouldn't be that way. So, my goal in really working hard to promote the SBPEF was to promote a spirit of cooperative evangelism and love for one another. And I think we've really had that. It's been very effective. So yes, there is a link. And the link between Midwestern and Southwestern's

"Chair of Fire" is the clearest and the most up-to
date-one in the SBPEF. And I'm very grateful for
that.

Beau Brewer: Well, I hate to draw you back to Dr. Fish, but
                          you did mention him. So he helped establish this
                          organization?

Thomas Johnston: Dr. Fish?

Beau Brewer: Yes.

Thomas Johnston: Dr. Fish. Yes. Now it was before my time. I think it
                          was back to Dr. Drummond, who along with Dr.
                          Fish and others . . . . Yes, Dr. Fish. See, they were
                          meeting together as literally a loose fellowship of
                          professors. When I began as president and I got a
                          room, I started getting a list of names of who was
                          part of it. And then we started encouraging coop-
                          erative work.

                          We actually wrote a book together. I think it was
                          2011. It was called *Mobilizing Great Commission
                          Churches for Harvest*. Nineteen SBPEF professors
                          of evangelism wrote chapters. And I remember I
                          had one dean tell me, "There aren't even nineteen
                          professors of evangelism in the SBC." So I said,
                          "Well, I think there are." Anyway, it was very inter-
                          esting. So, just working our cooperative strategies
                          to encourage one another in evangelism. Yes, Dr.
                          Fish was clearly a part of that. A wonderful man of
                          God.

Beau Brewer: Yes, he was. So can you discuss the L. R. Scarbor-
                          ough Chair of Evangelism, the "Chair of Fire," and
                          its importance in theological education?

Thomas Johnston: Yes. Thank you, Beau. What a great question. This
                          is a question that has blessed me this morning with
                          thinking. First of all, if you don't mind, the name
                          "Chair of Fire." Fire burns. What does fire burn?
                          Fire burns chaff. In academic institutions, there is
                          a chaff of intellectual arrogance. 1 Corinthians 8:1
                          says knowledge puffs up, love edifies.

Secondly, there's the chaff of cultural relevancy. And true New Testament evangelism, in my estimation, runs counter-intellectual and counter-cultural. What do I mean by counter-intellectual? It does not run on rationalistic lines. It runs on spiritual lines. Teaching how lost souls need to hear the gospel and believing in the need to be saved is a spiritual activity. Souls hearing the gospel and hardening their hearts and rejecting Jesus is also a spiritual activity.

So in that sense, evangelism is counter-academic. I've heard it called a redheaded stepchild of theological education because it doesn't fit the academic paradigm. In that way, it is a siloed activity. It is difficult to sit in the chair of evangelism because, in a way, we're running contrary to the academic tide. Just like your founder, Dr. Carroll, said, "Why not give fins to fish who swim against the stream and wings to birds who fly against the wind?" In academia, the professor of evangelism, in a way, flies against the wind and swims against the tide or against the flow of the current. So yes. The "Chair of Fire" is vitally important. And it's amazing. And when I say counter-cultural, when we evangelize, we're going against culture. I think the book called *Christ and Culture* by Niebuhr, I think it's Richard or Reinhold . . . . Whichever one it is.

Beau Brewer: It's Richard.

Thomas Johnston: Yes. It's unfortunate. It's very unfortunate because it frames it as "Christ against culture," but really, it's "culture against Christ." I mean, they killed him on a cross. It isn't Christ against culture. It's culture against Christ. So, when we do evangelism, we find out the culture is against Christ. We get criticized. We get spat on. We get mocked, ridiculed, sworn at for Jesus. For the name of Jesus. And we need that to happen because that lets us know that Jesus was a man of sorrow acquainted with grief, reviled, and rejected by men.

If we don't experience that, we don't think that's the case and therefore we try to accommodate culture and we try to, unfortunately, I think we hybridize evangelism's culture and we end up with all these funny hybrids that are far from New Testament Evangelism. And we put adjectives in front of their names. We put adjectives like "lifestyle" evangelism, "friendship" evangelism. Let me see. "Servant" evangelism. And they sound good and they're not bad things. But we end up sometimes with an evangelism that doesn't resemble New Testament evangelism.

Plus, on the intellectual side, we have apologetics. And apologetics is fine, as long as biblical apologetics like I know Southwestern is doing. But apologetics can end being just another excuse for being overly intellectual and wanting to sound smart, instead merely sharing a gospel that is smart. Anyways, the "Chair of Fire" is phenomenally important. And the "Chair of Fire," as you mentioned, and I agree, Southwestern was the first school to inaugurate a professor of evangelism. So, in that way, there's a mile marker in the history of theological education that says, "We're going to have someone who's fully devoted to teaching evangelism."

And is that easy? Not at all. It's not easy at all. I've been here nineteen years. I've heard from other professors. It's not easy, but it's necessary. Just like the evangelist is the only church leader in the church focused on ministry outside the church, soul-winning. So, the professor of evangelism is the only one who is called to move his students to go out and share the gospel and lead people to Christ. And is that easy? No, it's not easy at all. I have students who'd rather write a thirty-five-page paper than cross the street and talk for five minutes to their neighbor about Jesus. A lot of students like that. It's very, very difficult in that way sometimes.

So yes, I'm very grateful for Southwestern in taking in Dr. Scarborough and also Dr. Carroll. Really being, I think, open to the work of the Holy Spirit in terms of how to keep theological education on track. So, if I'm still on question five, can I bring up another thing?

Beau Brewer: Please.

Thomas Johnston: I believe that's there two reasons for the conservative resurgence. Reason number one is divine. It's God's word, Christ's blood, the powerful gospel, and the gracious work of the Holy Spirit among us. So that's my first reason. The second reason is I believe [in] an emphasis on soul-winning and evangelism. From the human side of the conservative resurgence, it's my thought that it's the evangelistic mandate given to the church. That makes us the only counter-cultural because we're trying to lead people to Christ. To proselytize. There's nothing wrong with the word "proselytize." To proselytize people to follow Jesus. To make them disciples. That's what we want to do. And so that's our focus. And because of that, we're countered to the world, countered to the culture. And I believe that in the work of Dr. Paige Patterson and others who were leaders in the conservative resurgence, lost souls and evangelism were important to keeping us leashed to the cross of Christ and tied to his ministry to seek and to save the lost.

Beau Brewer: That's wonderful. Thank you. What would you say is the most significant way the "Chair of Fire" has impacted southern Baptist evangelism?

Thomas Johnston: I think, as I mentioned before, I think evangelism is a bellwether for the health of the church. If souls are genuinely being saved, repenting and being saved . . . . If genuinely repenting of sins, turning to Jesus, and being saved. If that's really happening, I think it's a bellwether of the health of the church.

If it's not happening, there's something wrong with the church.

In that way, the "Chair of Fire," I think, helps keep the main thing the main thing. Every generation has to fight its own battles against modernism, secularism, cultural accommodation, and anything else that stands in the way of the Great Commission. Any kind of an arrogance or -ism. It's the "Chair of Fire." Now, I'm a faculty member at and SBC seminary, and I can have an impact on the broader evangelism knowledge of the SBC. If you've read Chuck Kelly's book on *How Did They Do It?* as I read that book, and as I look at the history of evangelism. By the way, I am editing a book on the history of North American Evangelism with twenty-two other professors of evangelism right now at this time.

Beau Brewer: Oh wow.

Thomas Johnston: As we look at his history of North American evangelism, there were definitely surges of evangelism. And I would say there's a dual approach. Evangelists, such as R. A. Torrey and maybe John Wilbur Chapman. I'm thinking about the time period when the chair was being inaugurated at SWBTS, and also of Moody, and let me see, Billy Sunday. But at that same time period, God was good enough to provide not only evangelists who were proclamational and as they were [the] crusade-type of evangelists, but he also provided a new thrust in personal evangelism and the training of evangelists through the "Chair of Fire." And so, I think all of twentieth-century evangelism has been definitely hugely impacted by the "Chair of Fire." Especially from an academic point of view and I'm so grateful for that.

Beau Brewer: You mentioned that you are publishing books with the other professors of evangelism.

Thomas Johnston:	Yes.
Beau Brewer:	I would say that that is another way that the "Chair of Fire," and really evangelism and theological education are impacting Southern Baptist evangelism. Wouldn't you say?
Thomas Johnston:	Yes. Yes, yes. There are actually very few good books on evangelism. And when I say very few, I'm thinking R. A. Torrey's *How to Work for Christ*, 1901, and maybe 1897. Yes. I have a massive chronological bibliography of evangelism. And really right about 1900 to 1920, there was a huge surge of interest in evangelism and books on evangelism that took place. Arthur Thwing had a book called *The Working Church*, 1888. There's *Seven Years of Street Preaching in San Francisco*. I believe that's 1892 or something. So, we had books come out prior to that time. But there begins to be a surge of interest in books that are written on evangelism after the "Chair of Fire." Obviously of Scarborough's *With Christ after the Lost . . . .* Is that what it is? *With Christ after the Lost.*
Beau Brewer:	Yes. Yes, in 1919.
Thomas Johnston:	Yes. That's a phenomenal book. So, we have that history. I compare that to, if you don't mind that I'm saying this, I compare that to how many times L. R. Scarborough's book has been reprinted to another book published the same year, which is Walter Rauschenbusch's *A Theology for the Social Gospel*. That last book has literally been republished hundreds of times, unfortunately. It's a very unhelpful book. But anyways, I'm grateful for the terebinth or the remnant that actually is excited about evangelism. And I pray that we might continue to be excited about evangelism.
Beau Brewer:	Yes, I agree. Really, is there anything further you would like to share about the "Chair of Fire" or

Midwestern's Department of Evangelism? What are some of the things that you teach in your classes?

Thomas Johnston: I was blessed by God's sovereign grace as it were to teach evangelism for five years at a place called Crown College. And at that time, that was an old Bible college and it had become a regular four-year liberal arts college. But they had five required Bible classes. And the board of Crown wanted an evangelism class. So what they did is they combined an evangelism class and a Bible class together. So it was really biblical evangelism. So I was given the name "biblical evangelism" when I taught at Crown up in Minnesota for five years. And I thought, "I can't think of a better name than that." Well, the only better name I could think of was I read when I was a doctoral student at Southern. I saw the words "New Testament Evangelism" put together. Those three words, "New Testament Evangelism." It may seem like something very natural and normal to you, but it wasn't until I was getting my PhD that I actually encountered those words together in a way that really spoke to me. And I thought, "Praise God. That's what I've been trying to teach the whole time."

So my emphasis is twofold at Midwestern. One is to teach New Testament evangelism and two is to have students go out and do it. And so I go out and door to door and street evangelism anywhere from once to week to two. I've even gone up five to six times a week with students. I don't practice that all the time. It's actually very exhausting.

Beau Brewer: I'm sure.

Thomas Johnston: But, I scheduled myself last semester and also this semester (before the coronavirus) with three outreaches every week. And that is workable and effective for me. I can handle that. In my schedule, with my family and everything else, I can handle that. And my wife is open to it. I now go out on Saturday mornings also. So, I have a twofold thrust: first, biblical New Testament evangelism, what the Bible teaches. And the main textbook we use is the Bible. For example, there are fifty-five personal evangelism conversations in the New Testament: fifteen in the book of Acts and the remainder, forty or so, in the Gospels. Twenty-one of those conversations are in John, most of which are with lost souls, but some of them with the disciples, such as Peter being reinstated. Anyways, we have a phenomenal amount of material on evangelism in the New Testament, not only in the message of evangelism, but also in the urgency and a practice of it. For example, I have my "Evangeliziology" text, which maybe you've heard of.

Beau Brewer: Yes.

Thomas Johnston: It's three volumes now.

Beau Brewer: It's three volumes now? I need to buy the third volume. I only have two.

Thomas Johnston: Out of the three volumes, in the third volume, what I've done is I've reorganized the 2019 version. And so, what I've done is I expanded it too much. They only allow me to print six hundred pages per volume. And so, I have chapters like 1 through 7 in volume 1. Which are roughly equivalent to the 2014 volume 1. One difference is I've taken the "Work of the Evangelist" and made it chapter 3. I wanted to move the work of the evangelist up toward the front of my notes, and not keep it in the back in chapter 30. I want the "Work of the Evangelist" to be toward the front so that people will see it. And they don't fall asleep before they get to it.

The first volume is really kind of prolegomena, including such foundational elements as motivations, definition, and so forth. And then the second volume is mainly on the evangelism proper. The third volume is on follow-up and the church, follow-up and discipleship in the church. So that's how it's roughly split up in the 2019 version. I'm sorry that the volume 3 is not totally new. In the 2014 edition it's included in a portion of the volume 2, but even last night I was adding material into the chapter on the Parable of the Sower as I came across it in my teaching and preaching. I'm constantly trying to grow those volumes. And I thought, "Well, some people might be interested." There may be a few people that might be interested in evangelism, such as much as I am. Praise God. So, thank you for asking.

That's my goal at Midwestern. My original goal was to try to raise up an army of evangelists. Literally, I was praying that God would do that. In a small part, I think I've had some impact in that way. And then my second goal was that everybody who took my class had the privilege and opportunity to share the gospel with somebody and bring them to the point of commitment. And praise God, maybe even be saved. Now we have so many online students and the requirements for online are different than the requirements for on campus. So it's been a bit of a struggle for me personally to be able to meet those goals, but I'm sure trying to meet it.

Beau Brewer: So you would say an aspect of your role on your campus at Midwestern is to infuse your campus and its students and faculty members and fellow faculty members with a spirit of evangelism?

Thomas Johnston: Correct.

Beau Brewer: That right there is one of the tenants of the "Chair of Fire," so I can see there's another connection there that you guys share. That's wonderful. Would you talk a little bit about your preaching? Do you preach a lot?

Thomas Johnston: Yes sir. Right now, I'm interim pastor at a small urban church in a very difficult area, a changing area.

It is called Bethany Baptist Church. We do a lot of evangelism there. It's actually twelve minutes from the seminary. So, I bring some students there to do evangelism. The area is possibly 40 percent Hispanic and includes Iraqis, Vietnamese, Thai, and others—also Anglos. So, I bring students there a lot for door to door evangelism. So that evangelism is tied to a local church. It's a very difficult area. A lot of meth and crack and homelessness. So that's kind of like my Petri dish of evangelistic fervor. It mainly takes place in that area for me.

On Saturday mornings, I go out with other churches. It's my Saturday morning team. I call it the Visiting . . . Or what is it? It's the Traveling Evangelism Team. We travel to different churches. I'll schedule churches other than Bethany for Saturday morning, because that's a good time for churches to have an outreach. And we would go with their people. But during the week, we go out in the Bethany area and knock on doors. I think I've probably easily knocked on every door once, I'm sure within about . . . I would say . . . it has to be about six blocks from the church. And then some doors I have knocked on up to five, six, seven, eight times in the last three and half years that I've been doing evangelism there. So, I find that going back even a month later is not too much, especially to reach a lost soul.

Beau Brewer: Absolutely.

Thomas Johnston: I, like right now, the T4T movement going on. Searching for "houses of peace." Our area's so laden with crime that house meetings or home bible studies are difficult because no one trusts their neighbors. And literally, I had a student come up to me and said, "Let's go visit one of the church members." And we went and he had a gun on his dining room table. The student was kind of caught off-guard by that. But hey, that's the neighborhood. You've got to protect yourself. It's amazing. While that student hasn't gone out with me again, he has never gotten over evangelism. Amen.

Beau Brewer: Amen.

Thomas Johnston: God is good. Thank you so much, Beau. This has been such a blessing to meet with you and I thank you for asking these questions. And I'm glad you've been able to record it too so you can listen later.

Beau Brewer: Yes. Thank you. This interview, once it's transcribed, it will be placed in the back of my dissertation for posterity and hopefully to inspire somebody to come along and write about the Gary Taylor Chair of Missions and Evangelism. I'm looking forward to including that information in the dissertation as well as other things that you have brought forth. This is really good.

Thomas Johnston: Thank you.

Beau Brewer: Thank you so much.

Goodbye.

Thomas Johnston: Goodbye.

APPENDIX 10

PERSONAL INTERVIEW WITH CHARLES S. KELLEY JR., MAY 26, 2020

THIS IS A COMPLETE and accurate transcript of the oral history interview of Dr. Charles S. Kelley Jr. by Beau Brewer over the phone. No spoken words which were recorded were omitted, except for any non-English phrases which could not be understood by the transcriber. This is a transcript of spoken English, which of course follows a different rhythm and rule than written English. In very few cases, words were too unclear to be distinguished. In these cases, [unclear] or [?] was inserted. Both interviewee and interviewer would interject "Uh hmm" or "Uh huh" frequently, but these were not transcribed unless they came at a definite break in the conversation. In some sections of the tape, the microphone was apparently frequently bumped and every occasion of this has not been noted.

...   Three dots indicate an interruption or break in the train of thought within the sentence of the speaker.

....   Four dots indicate what the transcriber believes to be the end of an incomplete sentence.

( )   Words in parentheses are asides made by the speaker.

[ ]   Words in brackets are comments made by the transcriber.

This transcription was made by Rev.com Transcription Services and was completed in May 2020.

Beau Brewer: This is Beau Brewer. I'm a PhD candidate at Southwestern Baptist Theological Seminary in Fort Worth, Texas. Today is May 26, 2020. I am on a live telephone interview with Dr. Charles Kelley Jr., former president of New Orleans Baptist Theological Seminary in New Orleans, Louisiana. Dr. Kelley, thank you so much for being with me.

Charles Kelley Jr.:   Sure. Glad to participate.

Beau Brewer: Wonderful. Today we're discussing the Roland Q. Leavell Chair of Evangelism, which you held, I believe, from 1989 to 1996. I would like for you to back up, and researching your academic career, you have been the president of New Orleans Baptist Theological Seminary in New Orleans. Would you give me the specific dates that you were installed as the president, and then would you also give me any titles of chairs that you have held at New Orleans during your tenure there?

Charles Kelley Jr.:   Okay. I was a professor of evangelism from 1983 forward. I became the Roland Q. Leavell Chair in 1989. I became president in 1996. I continued my role as a professor of evangelism, but I did not keep the chair for a very particular reason. At NOBTS, any endowed chair includes, for the occupant, a monthly stipend in addition to their salary. I simply did not think it was right for me, as president, to receive that monthly endowment and occupy that chair when I could use it for a faculty member. I gave the chair, at that point, to Preston Nix, who occupies it to this day.

I continued as a professor of evangelism. I retired July 31, 2019, and I am currently serving as a distinguished research professor of evangelism at the seminary.

Beau Brewer: That's wonderful. Did you just say that you had Dr. Preston Nix installed at the end of your term?

Charles Kelley Jr.:   Yes. When we hired him, I made him the Roland Q. Leavell Professor of Evangelism on the occasion of his hiring, and I thought it was the best thing to do for me to give up that chair, and to give it to a full-time professor and let that full-time professor have the stipend that came with the chair.

Beau Brewer: Well, the reason I ask is because I believe I may have the incorrect date there for him, because I think I read that he was installed in 2008, which means that the Roland Q. Leavell Chair would have been unoccupied for about, I don't know, six or seven years.

Charles Kelley Jr.: Well, it would have been me until there was somebody to give it to. I gave it to somebody. I think it was Preston. I'll have to . . . I'm just not certain. We may have had Bob Hamblin back before then. I'm just not . . . or Charles Harvey. It may have been Charles Harvey. I just don't have the sequence. Again, I'm in our home in Fairhope, but I don't have access to a lot of my records.

Beau Brewer: No, it's okay.

Charles Kelley Jr.: I gave up the chair as soon as I became professor of evangelism. We had two people that came to our faculty before Preston, and I'm sure one, or both of them, was in that chair. One of them was Charles Harvey Sr. Charles Harvey Sr. had been a very successful pastor in Louisiana for a number of years, one of our most beloved pastors. He stepped down from the pastoring to become head of evangelism for the state convention of Louisiana. Then I hired him to become a professor of evangelism for us.

Another NOBTS, actually professor alumnus, Dr. Bob Hamblin, who was the first occupant of the chair, and I can tell you that whole story in a minute, but when he retired from the North American Mission Board (NAMB), he came to teach evangelism for us. He may very well have put it in that year. I would tell you, to get a source of primary information, probably the thing to do is to contact the administrative assistant of the provost at NOBTS, Suzanne Davis is her name. Just ask her if she could

	look up the professorships of Charles Harvey, and Robert Hamblin, when they were there, and did either, or both of them, have that chair.
Beau Brewer:	Okay.
Charles Kelley Jr.:	As soon as I became president, and I turned over my responsibility . . . The third name is Chuck Register. Chuck Register was also somebody who very well could have been an occupant of that chair.
Beau Brewer:	Okay.
Charles Kelley Jr.:	So just ask about the tenured time, the time of service, and whether or not any of them held the Roland Q. Leavell. That would give you a primary source, the seminary's documented records. Either Suzanne Davis, who's an administrative assistant to the provost, or the graduate dean's office would also have those records. Dr. Bo Rice, who's also a professor of evangelism, would also have those records. His assistant could look that up.
Beau Brewer:	Wonderful. Dr. Kelley, would you articulate your philosophy of evangelism?
Charles Kelley Jr.:	Well, that's a matter of . . . . That's a very big question. Let me just say, very simply, and then we'll go any direction you want to go. Number one, evangelism is every Christian's job, every believer, that we are all follow Jesus, or called upon, to bear witness to him. That is that we see that from the people Jesus led to Christ, all the way through the New Testament, teachings of the New Testament, as well as the illustrations. It's the responsibility of every believer that has long been a Southern Baptist congregation.
	Secondly, I would say evangelism is the lifeblood of the church. What gasoline is to a car, what a plug is to a hairdryer, so evangelism is to the life of the church. If there's not a stream of converts coming in, that church will die because we lose everybody we have. Everybody we have leaves the church one

way or another. They pass away, they move someplace else, or they just drop out. There has to be a steady stream of new Christians coming in. The church is never more than one generation away from extinction. That's the simple reality. Evangelism is the lifeblood of the church.

The third thing that I would say is kind of a cornerstone of my convictions is what Paul said about "becoming all things to all men, so that by all means, I might reach some," that there is not a silver bullet. There is not one methodology. This is not one path to pursuit of evangelism, but you do everything and anything that will help reach people for Christ. That's preservationism, mass evangelism, today's world, social media, conversations, articles, billboards, tracks, scripture distribution, evangelists preaching revival meetings and crusades, any and every means possible to share the gospel of Jesus Christ and invite people to make a response is appropriate. Those are kind of the three main pillars of my philosophy of evangelism.

Beau Brewer: That's terrific. Do you happen to know what year the Roland Q. Leavell Chair of Evangelism was inaugurated?

Charles Kelley Jr.:   No. That's what I'd said to you before you started the recording. I do not know. I'm in Alabama, and away from all my stuff. I've been here for more than a month now, and it's just amazing to me that's the only chair whose story, origin story, I can't tell you. It's really ironic. Just appears I never got around to asking Dr. Leavell of the story behind the Roland Q. Leavell Chair.

I think that there are two to three possible ways it came into be. To the best of my knowledge, it was launched by Dr. Leavell about 1982, with Dr. Bob Hamblin. Dr. Leavell was a very evangelistic, very successful Southern Baptist pastor for many years before he came to be president of the seminary. This is Landrum P Leavell II . . .

Beau Brewer: Right.

Charles Kelley Jr.: . . . before he came to be president of the seminary. When he arrived in January of 1975, he started emphasizing evangelism his very first semester, and he taught . . . There's only one course in the curriculum, this is why I'm pretty confident, there was no professor of evangelism. There was only one course in the curriculum. Introduction to Evangelism 355. To this day, that's the only evangelism course that I've ever had for formal training in my whole life. Dr. Leavell would teach that once a semester, once a term. We were on a term system then. Then it was passed around to whoever was the low guy on the totem pole for the rest of the year, all the time. So there was no evangelism program. There was no evangelism chair. However, in 1982, Dr. Leavell launched the Roland Q. Leavell Chair of Evangelism, and its first occupant was Dr. Bob Hamblin.

Dr. Bob Hamblin was a graduate of Southwestern. Majored in New Testament. Very evangelistic. Very very evangelistic. He was the long-time pastor of a church in Tupelo, the biggest church in Tupelo, not First Baptist, it was a different church, but he had a wonderful ministry there. Basically, he retired from there. He was older by then, but still had lots of gas in the tank. I think he must have been around sixty years old, or so, when he came. He served for one year, and did a terrific job. In that year, he started our evangelism curriculum for the seminary, getting beyond just that one simple introduction course. At the end of a year, he was hired as vice president for evangelism for the whole mission board. He left us to go to Atlanta.

That one year was extremely important, although I had just finished all of my seminar work, and he did not have time to make any doctoral seminars anyway, but he was the chairman of my committee for that one year, and that's when I wrote my dissertation. I had a real fight. The professor in charge of our doctoral program then did not think evangelism was academically working. He did not want me to do a dissertation on evangelism. He told me it was unworthy of a dissertation.

Dr. Hamblin fought the fight to allow . . . . I majored in preaching because that was as close to evangelism as I could get. I majored in preaching, but because of Dr. Hamblin, I was allowed to do a dissertation on evangelism that turned out to be a pretty seminal work for the rest of my life. He was very important in my life. We were very close. Then he went to the North American Mission Board.

After he'd left in 1983, I graduated, yeah, in '83, in May of '83, and in 1983, Dr. Leavell hired three evangelism professors. He hired Dr. C. C. Randall to be the next Roland Q. Leavell Chair of Evangelism. He launched the Broadmoor Chair of Discipleship, which was the first discipleship chair of the SBC, and believed very strongly that that was a part of evangelism, that evangelism and discipleship are two sides of the same coin, which I think is an extremely important perspective. Then he hired me. I was the third one. There was not a chair that I occupied, but I was the third evangelism professor. In one year, we went from no professors after Dr. Hamblin resigned to three professors. That was all Dr. Leavell's passion for evangelism, and that was really the launch of what became a very broad, large, program of evangelism, touching just about every aspect of it.

I can't tell you exactly when the chair was started. I think it may have been started in the sense of an account receiving gifts being opened in memory of Dr. Roland Q. Leavell upon the occasion of his death, his passing, which happened rather unexpectedly as a result of some serious heart problems. He was such a giant in Southern Baptist Evangelism, I have no trouble at all imagining that people who knew him and loved him would have been interested in doing that, but if that was the case, they did not raise enough money to launch the chair, initiate the chair. They just started the fundraising megabit. But for sure, when Dr. Leavell got there, Dr. Leavell is the one who initiated the chair, launched the chair, and made Dr. Bob Hamblin its first occupant.

Beau Brewer: Wonderful. What are some of the responsibilities of occupying the Roland Q. Leavell Chair of Evangelism, or do you believe that each occupant defines the role of that chair?

Charles Kelley Jr.: I think there's a sense in which each occupant defines the role of a chair, and there've been some things that were not done because of the chair, but just happened by coincidence. I was chairman of the Pastoral Ministry's Division, which is the largest division of the seminary, when I was occupying the chair. Preston Nix is now the chairman of the Pastoral Ministry's Division, and he's the Roland Q. Leavell Professor of Evangelism, but that's just a matter of leadership skills and timing. It's not a responsibility of the chair.

Basically, the Roland Q. Leavell Chair has been a driver for the evangelism curriculum, because it was our first chair. The first occupant, Dr. Hamblin, created about four or five courses in evangelism. Probably not five, maybe three to four courses in evangelism during that one year that he was there.

Then when I joined the faculty in 1983, I was not the Roland Q. Leavell chair, but I and Cecil Randall, who was the chair, and then our Broadmoor Discipleship Professor, Ed Thiele, the three of us created all the necessary courses that remain for a master of divinity evangelism major. We created a doctorate of ministry in evangelism, and we created a PhD in evangelism. All of that happened within the first two years the three of us were there.

Beau Brewer: What kind of courses did you have, just out of curiosity? I'm trying to put together the materials, the coursework, and such.

Charles Kelley Jr.: Well, we taught a broad range of things. Of course, the Introduction to Evangelism, that had always been there. New Testament, Evangelism, the Evangelism of Jesus, Prayer in the New Testament, Evangelistic Preaching. We did things, all the Great Awakenings and Revivals, a history class on the great revivals and awakenings of history. Things like that.

Beau Brewer: Okay.

Charles Kelley Jr.: Again, you could look, again, the best thing as a PhD student, for your primary sources, would be the catalogs of the seminary.

Beau Brewer: Yes.

Charles Kelley Jr.: You would know, you could look at the academic catalogs, beginning in 1982, and you would not see anything but Introduction to Evangelism in the catalog before 1982 when Bob Hamblin arrived. He was only there a year. So the courses he created would not have been printed in the catalog until 1983. So really, beginning in 1983, you then will see the development of the evangelism curriculum, and you will see it in all of its nuances and things that have come and gone.

Beau Brewer: Excellent.

Charles Kelley Jr.: Also, the distinctive thing for our program that was very important, not connected with the Roland Q. Leavell Chair, because I created this the first year I was hired, and I was not the Roland Q. Leavell chair, but this was a cornerstone of our program. As I told you, I think every believer is a witness. I had a very interesting experience. I was thirty years old and had just finished my dissertation when Dr. Leavell offered me the position of an evangelism professor on the faculty of one of the largest seminaries in the world. I did not want to do it. I really did not want to do it. I was at, been in school for twenty-five consecutive years, through all my growing up, and I was ready to be out of school.

All I wanted to do was get out there. I'm an evangelist by calling. I just want to get out there and preach and be a full-time evangelist. God made it very, very plain for me. I had one of the deepest experiences I've ever had with God, and he wanted me to take that evangelism position. I had a choice of either obey the Lord, or choose to disobey him. So I accepted the position, but I was mad about it. I literally showed up for my first day of faculty workshop mad because I did not want to be doing this.

I went to my first day of class, and on my first day of class, I asked, I did a survey of the class. I had thirty, forty students. I did a little survey just to see what their background was. I asked these questions. Do you witness sometimes, often, seldom, or never? Can you give me a simple plan of salvation with just measure points and what scripture reference? That's all. Maybe one or two other questions. I went back to my office after that class, and I sat at my desk, and I started going through those survey forms. I discovered that about 70 percent of the students said they witnessed seldom or never.

The real shocker was 35 percent of the students, I'll never forget this, 35 percent of the students could not give a coherent plan of salvation with major points as a scripture reference. These were guys who were so deeply in love with Jesus, and so passionate about following Jesus, that they were devoting the rest of their life to ministry, and they had come to earn a seminary degree, and yet they could not give a coherent plan of salvation. That broke my heart. That's when I understood why God had me on that faculty.

When I got over being angry and I got to work, I created a class that was required of every single student in the MDiv program of the seminary. It was a semester-length class. It was our first semester-length class in the curriculum. Every student had to take it. They did two things. They were taught how to share their faith, and how to teach other people to share their faith. Then they were divided up into teams of two or three, and they had to go out knocking on doors, in the city of New Orleans, through one of our local churches, for at least ten weeks during the semester.

That became a necessity for graduating. You couldn't graduate NOBTS if you didn't have that class. Personal Evangelism was a course in the curriculum, but that course was called Field Education, Today's Supervised Ministry. We just taught our students that everybody in ministry has at least one job, and that's telling other people about Jesus. So the Roland Q. Leavell Professor has taught that class ever since I gave it up.

Beau Brewer: That's a great class. I love the concept. Personal evangelism is, I believe, the active ingredient for real daily evangelism, especially for a Southern Baptist.

Charles Kelley Jr.: Well, it is, Beau. Then this may touch a little bit on your research, it's why having evangelism professors is so very important, because here's the reality. You must never underestimate the power of human nature. When somebody is a student, everybody understands they don't know things, they're not good at things, they're learning things, they may stumble over some things. But when you graduate, it's assumed that now you know all that stuff. When a person graduates from seminary, with a seminary degree, the assumption of people in the churches is, "Our pastor knows how to share his faith. Our pastor is a confident witness." The reality is that's not true.

After all my years in the classroom, I will tell you, when I taught that class, this breakdown of the class was true every section of that class I ever taught. Ten percent of the class were eager, excited, thrilled. "Finally, a class that I can make . . . This is what seminary should be all about." Ten percent, sitting in the front row. Ten percent of the class hugely angry, hugely angry at being forced to take this class. Put it off as long as they could. This crew, or almost always, take it their very last semester of seminary because they finally figured there was no way across the stage unless they went through that class, and they were very angry, very resentful that they were having to take it. Eighty of the class, scared to death. Scared to death. Having virtually no experience in evangelism, that's how we'd start.

About the sixth or seventh week of class, every class session we started with an opportunity for students to report on their witness experiences they had during the week. About week six or seven, students would begin to lead people to Christ. The whole timbre and atmosphere of the class changed. Students would begin to talk about what Jesus did when they got into a conversation, by leading. Somebody question . . . . I had so many students tell me that the first time they ever led anybody to Christ was in that class. Here's . . . [crosstalk]

Beau Brewer: Praise the Lord.

Charles Kelley Jr.: . . . when a pastor is serving a church, and he hasn't gotten over the fear and reluctance and intimidation barrier, and he doesn't have confidence as a witness, is he ever going to take the lay people of his church out to witness with him?

Beau Brewer: No.

Charles Kelley Jr.:	No. He doesn't want them to see that he's inadequate. He's afraid, he's uncertain, he's not good at this. He will never teach anybody how to witness. How is he going to get there? Because the problem is if you go out to share your faith one time, you may lead somebody to Christ, but that's not the way consistent witnessing is. Sometimes you lead people to Christ. A lot of times you don't. You may go out one time and not find anybody who wants to have a conversation, but that's not the way witnessing is. Sometimes people want to talk, sometimes they don't want to talk.
	You may go out one time and you may encounter somebody who's really angry, really ticked off, really upset, and they get really mad at you. But that's not the way witnessing is. That happens rarely, in my experience. It happens, but it's not very common, but if that happens to you, when you go out one time, you'll say, "That's the way it always is." It takes time. It takes repeated experiences to get people really rooted in the evangelistic task so they understand, "I can do this." Hopefully they get to the point where they realize, "I must do this." The seminary world is an artificial world.
Beau Brewer:	Yes it is.
Charles Kelley Jr.:	You could create rules, people will do things in order to learn that nobody else could make them do, because I approach any pastor in American and say to that pastor, "You have to go out every week for the next ten weeks and knock on doors and attempt to share your faith with somebody." Can I do that? No. No. Rare is the pastor who would ever undertake that himself just because he wanted to learn how to witness. But in a seminary environment, I can give people assignments and they have to do them, so I'm not only transferring knowledge, I'm enhancing skills, developing skills. I'm not only transferring knowledge and enhancing skills, I'm

passing on the passion. This was the genius of B. H. Carroll. To my knowledge, that "Chair of Fire" established by B. H. Carroll was the first academic chair in evangelism in the history of the world.

Beau Brewer: That is correct.

Charles Kelley Jr.: I do not know of anything before then. That's when evangelism entered the academy. The academy had been, and still largely does outside of Southern Baptist life, function with the understanding that people are ministers, of course they will talk to people about the gospel, of course they will know how to lead somebody to Christ, and that is a wrong assumption. Based on what I saw, most of the people who got calls into ministry have never been trained, had never been mentored, never been taught to witness before they got to seminary, and if they don't get it while they're at seminary, they're not going to get it when they get out.

Those seminary professors of evangelism are exceedingly important in rooting a passion, a knowledge, and skills for evangelism in the lives of students, because it's the last shot we have to do so. Otherwise, they finish school and they go out with everybody looking at them like they're a finished product, and that student forever being embarrassed about not knowing how to share his faith, and therefore doing little of it.

Beau Brewer: Can you further discuss the connection that you've already mentioned between the Roland Q. Leavell Chair of Evangelism at New Orleans and the L. R. Scarborough Chair, the "Chair of Fire," at Southwestern Seminary? You've already made mention to it.

Charles Kelley Jr.: Yes, I don't know of a direct connection other than influence. As I said, Dr. Leavell was the one, as far as I can tell, Dr. Leavell was the one who launched the Roland Q. Leavell Chair of Evangelism. It may have been started as a funding enterprise earlier, but Dr. Leavell is the one who got the money together to endow it and launched it. Dr. Leavell, I am extremely aware, knew everything that Southwestern did, although he was an NOBTS graduate. But having known that Southwestern had a chair of evangelism, Dr. Leavell would know, "Okay, that's possible, I'm going to have one of those." I know, if nothing else, it was an inspiration for him to have an academic, endowed chair on our faculty like Southwestern had on their faculty.

Beau Brewer: Well, Dr. Kelley, I was just thinking back to the courses that you and the other faculty members, the other professors in evangelism at New Orleans had initiated, and I'm thinking through them. Classes on the history of revivals, the Evangelistic Preaching, Personal Evangelism, Church Evangelism, those courses seem to parallel between your school and Southwestern Seminary's Department of Evangelism. So there's certainly some commonalities there.

Charles Kelley Jr.: Well, remember the first occupant of our Roland Q. Leavell Chair was Dr. Bob Hamblin. Dr. Bob Hamblin was a graduate of Southwestern Seminary.

Beau Brewer: There's another strong connection.

Charles Kelley Jr.: Dr. Hamblin, yes, Dr. Hamblin was not the creator of the chair. That was Dr. Leavell, as far as I know. Dr. Hamblin was the one who figured out, "Now that I'm in this chair, what am I going to do?" He came in, went through Southwestern as a very evangelistic student. I don't know what courses he may have had, but I do know he would have taken whatever was required with joy, and may have had some electives. He loved the Greek New Testament, but he was also very evangelistic. He certainly knew what Southwestern was doing, and he certainly had, whoever was in the "Chair of Fire" when he was a student, he certainly had that professor for at least some of his coursework. That's a direct connection between Southwestern's model and curriculum, and the first occupant of the Roland Q. Leavell Chair.

So the chair didn't give rise to the chair, only presidents can create chairs.

Beau Brewer: Right. Of course.

Charles Kelley Jr.: But the professor who got hired said, "Okay, what do I do now that I am the occupant of this chair, what do I do?" I'm sure a lot of his inspiration and direction came from his experience at Southwestern.

Beau Brewer: Again, the current occupant, Dr. Preston Nix, is a Southwestern grad, and he also sat under Dr. Roy Fish, who is probably the second or third most famous occupant of the "Chair of Fire," certainly the longest standing.

Charles Kelley Jr.: Without a doubt, yes. Without—

Beau Brewer: I'm sure there are influences there, if you can measure influence, but certainly contributions there.

Charles Kelley Jr.: Well, the Southern Baptist world, although it is not as much this way now as it was in the past, is a world in which everybody keeps up with what everybody else is doing. When you have one school do something like create a chair of evangelism, the other schools are eventually going to get around that. I, as I told you, I don't think you could understand Southern Baptists, who we became, without understanding the reality Southern Baptists has a convention put in their academic world, teachers of evangelism for students coming through.

The fact that we have all six of the seminaries now with chairs of evangelism, the fact that those professors, I'm assuming they still get together periodically once a year . . .

Beau Brewer: They do.

Charles Kelley Jr.: . . . or so, that influence the cross-pollination, but the impact of those professors on the students, that would be interesting to see how many of the seminaries have one course required of at least MDiv students in there. I promise you, do you think the Presbyterians have an evangelism professor at all the Presbyterian seminaries?

Beau Brewer: Probably not.

Charles Kelley Jr.: Do you think the Methodist do? Nobody else does. This is distinctive that it was we went from that first effort, and B. H. Carroll, who is just such an incredible person. I do hope that you . . . I read in the appendix, it was in both books, the appendix of B. H. Carroll's address after the debate on whether or not to create a department of evangelism . . .

Beau Brewer: I sure did.

Charles Kelley Jr.: . . . about the role of the evangelist. It was just a magnificent, magnificent address. Carroll being so evangelistic himself, and having the genius to recognize the significance of putting evangelism in the heart of an academic institution, was so very crucial. I think the "Chair of Fire" is well named because that literally, in a world like that, how did trains travel in B. H. Carroll's day? They traveled by steam, fire created the steam that pushed the wheels and pushed everything forward. The factories, how do they run? Fire coming out of full-steam powered factories of that day. Electricity is kind of bottled fire itself. This is a fire that invites Southern Baptist churches in it. It's just one of the reasons why you can't say it's the only reason, but I think a very significant reason for the connection that is distinctive in Southern Baptist life, in Southern Baptists with evangelism.

I think if you were to ask people who know things, distinguishing features of all the major American church families, and you were to say to them,

"Well, what's the distinguishing feature of Southern Baptists?" I think they would probably say, "Well, they're theologically conservative, they're big on the Bible, and they're big on missions and evangelism." That's who we are.

B. H. Carroll, in that early stage of Southern Baptist life, rooting evangelism into theological education of Southern Baptist ministers was crucial for the development of our denominational identity around evangelism. To me, it is no surprise that Carroll was the one who turned the tide. There probably would not be a Department of Evangelism if it were not for B. H. Carroll on that day in 1906. The most interesting thing to me is that it was a huge controversy, three-year controversy on whether or not to create a Department of Evangelism, primarily driven by landmarkism.

After a three-year battle, Carroll finally stood up, gave his impromptu summary of the role of the evangelist in the New Testament and the history of the church, closed with his incredible, "Did I not fence the fish that have to swim against the tide? Did I not [give] wings to birds that have to fly against the wind? Give me evangelists, give me evangelists." He said that and they gave him evangelists, but the remarkable thing is it was never controversial again. Never again. That controversy on that day, with Carroll's address, the department was created, and it was never questioned again in the history of the SBC. There's a Hebrew word for that, and that's wow. Just amazing.

Beau Brewer: Yes. Yes.

Charles Kelley Jr.: The only . . . . what makes me so very frustrated with today's world, with NAMB has just so downgraded evangelism.

Beau Brewer: Yes, they have.

Charles Kelley Jr.:   . . . so little attention, that it's just such a dramatic shift what Southern Baptist have done. It's just not helping us at all. Anyway, that's a different story.

Beau Brewer: Well, no, you're exactly right. I'd like for you to discuss a little bit about how the Roland Q. Leavell of Evangelism has impacted Southern Baptist evangelism through theological education.

Charles Kelley Jr.:   Well, what I was just saying, that it makes evangelism a part of the preparation of its ministers. If you go to a Southern Baptist seminary now, you're going to have at least some training in evangelism, and there is going to be someone in that coffee, who drinks coffee in the cafeteria, the coffee shop with students, talks about evangelism, who is active in faculty discussions, "Are we going to do this, or are we going to do that?" And then bringing that perspective of evangelism. You have woven the thread of evangelism into the tapestry of theological education, and that's a process by which Southern Baptists like to prepare their ministers for service.

That is huge. That is huge when you consider that most students who go to a seminary without evangelism professor, they may hear the word, but they won't . . . . I'll never forget, years ago, I was in Dallas and had some time. I'd never been on the campus of Dallas Theological Seminary, so I went to their bookstore. I was just looking around their bookstore, which was small, but I'm looking around, and I think in their bookstore, I found one, maybe two titles on evangelism in their whole bookstore.

Beau Brewer: Oh good grace.

Charles Kelley Jr.:   It simply was not there. You go to Dallas Theological, you're going to learn about Greek and Hebrew, and you're going to learn about expository preaching and teaching the Bible. You're not going to learn about evangelism. Again, I don't think you can understand the denominational identity of Southern

Baptists, and the distinctive role of evangelism in Southern Baptist life, if you don't understand the role of evangelism in Southern Baptist seminaries, and that was all set in motion by B. H. Carroll and that chair.

That chair demonstrated that it could be done, and once that chair demonstrated, yeah, you can make this a part of theological education, then you just get to work on that. I got to see a little taste, as I said, the professor who was in the Roland Q. Leavell Chair fought a very important battle for me. My dissertation was on the changing role of the revival meeting in the Southern Baptist program of evangelism over a period of time. I knew to do that I was going to have to do some different kinds of research to find the material. I knew the material was there, but it was not going to be easy to find, and I was going to have to do a lot of work to find it, but I knew where I could get it.

I worked with Dr. Hamblin on that, and he liked what I was doing. It was time to go to the course that you have to take on preparing your dissertation, how to do a dissertation, and you prepare a prospectus as a part of that course. The professor who teaches that course gives you a thumbs-up or a thumbs-down on the prospectus. I prepared mine. I went in for my private meeting with the professor, and he told me that this was not worthy of a dissertation. I've never been so crushed in all my life. I was just . . . it was just a huge moment of despair.

I left that class, and I stopped by Dr. Hamblin's office, and he was in, and I walked in and he said, "Who died? You sure look upset." I said, "Well, I've just been told that my dissertation topic is not worthy of a dissertation." He said, "Well Chuck, tell me again, what exactly are you wanting to do in life?" I told him. He said, "Why do you want to do this?" I told him. "How are you going to get the information that you need?" I told him. He said, "I think that is a great idea, and something very significant in the field of evangelism. You just make whatever technical corrections, grammatical technical things that he gave you to do, and I'll take care of the approval of the topic." He said, "I'll take care of that, just make your corrections, and don't worry about it." Sure enough, he took care of it.

For the rest of the tenure of that professor, every time an evangelism student had that course, I made sure I was in my office, because it was normally taught in January between semesters, I made sure I was in my office because that professor would tell any evangelism student that brought any topic for dissertation connected to evangelism, that it was not worthy of a dissertation topic. That student would stop by my office sad and upset like I was, and I would talk to him, listen to him, and I would tell him, "Make the technical corrections that he gave you, any grammatical things, and I'll take care of it." And I did.

That was the microcosm of the academic world about evangelism. Not worthy of attention. Having an academic professor who had the same training, same degrees, same skills, to say, "This is worthy. This is important. This matters. " You can't measure the impact on that. I got to see, in the peculiarities of our institution, what it would have been like for somebody with a passion for evangelism had they been in a seminary without an advocate on the faculty. You just don't . . . There's no way for us to know how much progress in evangelism was made because of Carroll's vision, and because of the people he put in that "Chair of Fire," and that be an example and a challenge to the other seminaries: "We're doing this, you can do this too," and each seminary taking up that torch and getting that voice for evangelism, that value of evangelism, that expertise in evangelism.

I had a very interesting experience one day. I'd been on the faculty for a decade or so, and I was working late. My office was in another building from the rest of the faculty. Our offices are [in the] Leavell Center for Evangelism. I was working late one evening, and there was a knock on the window of my office. I looked up, it was one of our professors from the Biblical Studies Division. I went outside and said, "Hey, come on in." He came on in, he said, "Chuck, I saw your light on," and he said, "I just need to apologize to you." I said, "You don't owe me any apology at all. I don't know any reason that you'd need to apologize to me." He said, "No, no. I need to apologize to you."

He said, "Chuck, every time you do something, it's so simple. It's so clear. You just want to say this is not serious stuff," he said, "but you know, this year I've really been paying attention." He said, "It is not easy to do simple." He said, "Chuck, a breadth of your knowledge, you know more about my field than I know about your field. You know more about most of the disciplines of this seminary, than those professors know about your field, in addition to knowing your field." He said, "I just want you to know, I apologize for not recognizing the scholarship that you bring to the table, and how that helps our whole seminary and what it means. I just want you to know I have deep respect for you, and I'm sorry I haven't always had that."

About a year or so later, we were having a faculty luncheon during exam week, and the topic was on how to work with doctoral students and dissertations. I'm just sitting there in the back of the room, having lunch, the whole programming thing. The guy who was in charge of the doctoral program, at that time, different guy than the one I told you about. He and I were not good buddies. We disagreed on a lot of stuff. He was very different than I was. Not big on evangelism.

He got about halfway into his presentation, and he said, "How many of you know that you have PhD students who are enrolling in at least one evangelism seminar so they can take Chuck? I don't know if you know this or not, but Chuck has people in his seminars from most of our disciplines, and they are doing it against our counsel because they have learned from Chuck's students how he prepares his students to write a dissertation. And they are going to him with their dissertation ideas. They are taking at least one of his seminars because of what he's doing. If you didn't know that, you need to know it."

I nearly fell out of my chair. I had no idea. Again, having that voice for you, because this is what evangel.... most people I know love evangelism. We do tend to be simple in our presentations. We're really working hard on clarity, and we look for emotive power and things like that. But, with your call to this world, you also have academic standards. You have scholarly markers, and you do things right, you do it thoroughly. Having somebody who loves evangelism, who has those high academic standards, who knows his field and knows how it relates to other things, and can talk intelligently about stuff besides "share Jesus now," is very important.

So B. H. Carroll was a very wise man, and what he set in motion couldn't tell it at the time, and it's just hard to grasp its significance now, but I think it was one of the most important things that happened to solidify the identity with evangelism that came to characterize a Southern Baptist Convention. It has been very influential. That domino let many other dominoes fall in place, and a denomination-wide respect and recognition of the importance of evangelism. God bless you, B. H. Carroll.

Beau Brewer:	No kidding. I've read a lot about Dr. Carroll, and a lot of his works thus far because of course the "Chair of Fire" has four major tenets, one being that the occupant of the chair would teach the Inclusion of the Office of the Evangelist. Now I know that the Baptist Faith in Message 2000 only has two offices listed in the church. That would be the office of the pastor, and the office of the deacon, but Carroll's view were that the office of the evangelist was equal to the convention and to its work. So the office of the evangelists, as listed in Ephesians 4, was an inter-church ministry. The evangelist was, of course, responsible to his local church for character and for accountability, but the ministry field was the outside world. It's a fascination that the "Chair of Fire" still teaches this particular standard about the words of the evangelists.
Charles Kelley Jr.:	Yeah, very definitely. It was not a local church office, but it was an office of the church at large.
Beau Brewer:	Yes.
Charles Kelley Jr.:	Boy, his address was just so great.
Beau Brewer:	It is.
Charles Kelley Jr.:	Just so great. Thank goodness somebody wrote it up afterwards. The only account I ever found of it was in the Baptist Standard of Texas the week after the convention.
Beau Brewer:	Yes sir, that is the only account of it. I have not seen it in the archives either at Southwestern Seminary. Well, are there any other pieces of the Roland Q. Leavell Chair that you would like to share with me, of any specific tenets that this chair specifically teaches?
Charles Kelley Jr.:	No.
Beau Brewer:	No.
Charles Kelley Jr.:	But we don't have anything. We just expect somebody who is in that chair to be fully focused, and

excellent, and teach evangelism, and engaging students in learning to share their faith. Other to this day, Preston Nix will go out with students and, if you want to learn how to witness, and you don't know how, we had that one class, but if that kind of whets your appetite, or you want to learn more, most Thursdays he's out taking students here in their faith in the community and doing all of that.

But in terms of curricular-type assignments, we don't have it set up like that. We're very blessed, now, as I said, Dr. Leavell was very evangelistic, and our seminary, we have a stronger heritage of evangelism than just about anybody, maybe even from Southwestern, when you look at our former presidents. Most of our former presidents have a very strong connection to evangelism.

The second president of our seminary was the first head of the Department of Evangelism that Carroll helped to create, W. W. Hamilton. We don't have anybody who didn't like evangelism. Everybody has some strong connection with evangelism who serves as president of our seminary. It's been a very important note for us, and a part of our identity, all the way through. That's what makes it such a . . . having the endowed chair's a good fit. Our donors have recognized that.

Let's see, we now have six chairs connected to evangelism, right now.

Beau Brewer: Six chairs.

Charles Kelley Jr.:   I don't think any seminary has that many evangelic chairs.

Beau Brewer: Can you list those six chairs?

Charles Kelley Jr.:   Let's see, there's the Roland Q. Leavell Chair, the Max and Bonnie Thornhill Chair of Evangelism, great layman. Loved evangelism. The Thomas Gurney Chair of Evangelism and Church Health. Mr. Gurney was an attorney in Orlando, Florida.

Member of First Baptist Church, Orlando, with Jim Henry. Was teaching Evangelism Explosion when he was ninety years old. He was just quite a guy. The Gurney Chair of Evangelism Church held the Broadmoor Chair of Discipleship, and sometimes we have put that occupant in the CE division, and sometimes its pastoral ministries, but we really emphasize the inescapable connection of evangelism and discipleship and consider discipleship a part of our evangelism program. The Cecil B. Day Chair for Church Planting, and then, let's see, what am I leaving out? I know we have another one on the way that's somebody's estate for evangelistic preaching, that's going to be a chair. I'm sorry, there may be one other than that. That's not enough. Oh, well, we want this to say . . .

Roland Q. Leavell, Max and Bonnie Thornhill, Thomas Gurney, Broadmoor Chair of Discipleship, oh, the Caskey Chair of Evangelism in Ministry. The occupant of that chair is the director of our Caskey program. That's one, the Caskey Scholarship Program is for those who are serving in typical churches with the worship attendance of less than 250 people, most of them are only 100 people. It pays all their expenses for seminary. It pays all their tuition and fees and everything. It does some other stuff for them. It's by far our best scholarship program, and it'll follow it all the way through any degree that we offer. But there's one stipulation, you have to share the gospel and invite somebody to receive Christ once every week of the semesters which you have the scholarship.

Beau Brewer:	Oh, that's incredible.
Charles Kelley Jr.:	Yes.
Beau Brewer:	And impacting as well, both for that church, for that pastor, and for the seminary.

Charles Kelley Jr.: Yeah. This is from a family, they do a life commitment to evangelism, and are [inaudible] to evangelism. We sat down together and they were thinking about doing something. They'd done something like this at a different place, and for various reasons, ended that program. They wondered if we were interested in something like that. I said yes, and they said, "Well, is it even possible to require evangelism experience?" I said, "Sir, what you have to understand is that this is an artificial world, this is not the real world. In an artificial world, we make the rules. If you're going to give a full-ride scholarship to somebody through their seminary degree, and you want to require them to share their faith and invite somebody to Jesus once a week, every week during a semester, we can certainly require that and keep up with it." And we do. Our students now, they're running about a 10 percent conversion rate, is what they're running.

Beau Brewer: Right.

Charles Kelley Jr.: I think so far those students have witnessed to more than ten thousand people. So many of their, they're in small churches, and they start off with, they hear that requirement, they're a little intimidated. They wonder, "How am I going to find anybody to witness to?" But their first meeting at the beginning of semester, all the students in that scholarship program meet with the occupants of that chair to talk about the semester and this immense requirement. He says, "Okay, here's your assignment. Every Monday morning when you wake up, I want you to pray this prayer as soon as your feet hit the floor: 'Dear Lord Jesus, I ask you this week, would you give me at least one opportunity to explain the gospel to somebody and invite them to Jesus. Pray that for . . .'" We call it the Monday Morning Prayer.

They start praying that prayer, but by golly, they have witness opportunities. It's been very . . .

because they turn in reports and that's very inspirational reading their reports. I just thank God for
Southern Baptist laypeople, because this is a family.
They're laypeople, but they love evangelism and
their favorite thing in the world is getting those
reports from students.

Beau Brewer:		Well, how could you not enjoy that, reading about
lives being changed, not to mention, the equipping
of a brother or a sister in Christ who will go on to
lead churches.

Charles Kelley Jr.:	Yes indeed.

Beau Brewer:		Are the six chairs that you mentioned, are they all
endowed chairs?

Charles Kelley Jr.:	Yes, they are endowed with different amounts of
money.

Beau Brewer:		Sure.

Charles Kelley Jr.:	Every one of them, except the Day Chair, I believe,
has at least $500,000 in it. They go from $500,000
to more than a billion.

Beau Brewer:		Oh goodness. Whoa, that's a lot of chairs. I didn't
even realize that any one seminary had that many.

Charles Kelley Jr.:	Yes. That's who we are.

Beau Brewer:		I love it.

Charles Kelley Jr.:	That's what we've done. It's just very interesting. Our
donors have recognized this about us, so they've
responded to it. Just a huge story, the Thornhill
Chair, by the way, Dr. Bo Rice is the dean of our
graduate program and a professor of evangelism
and preaching. He's in the Thornhill Chair. Well the
Thornhills, likeable couple, they got to know a former professor of evangelism who taught with me
for several years before he left to go pastor a church,
and this couple were involved in his ministry. They
knew Dr. Leavell, and known him for a number of
years. They decided they wanted to do a chair.

They asked Dr. Leavell to come up and help them make the final arrangements, and Dr. Leavell took my friend, who was teaching with me at that time, he was teaching evangelic preaching, took him with him because he was such a good friend of these people there. While they're driving up, my friend asked Dr. Leavell, he said, "Well Dr. Leavell, is there any particular direction that you want to go with this chair?" He said, "Well, Don, we want a chair in any area but evangelism," he said, "so we're going to talk with them and see if they would be willing to . . . anything they're interested in, but we will not encourage them to do evangelism because we already have so many evangelism chairs."

They got there, they were chatting, and they said, "Yes, we definitely want to do the chair." They were going to start with $500,000 check. Dr. Leavell said, "Is there an area that you want to do this chair for? Would you like us to make a suggestion?" He said, "We want to do evangelism. That's what we'd like to do." Dr. Leavell said, "That's great. We would love to have that. That will be wonderful."

When they were driving back and my friend said, "Dr. Leavell, I thought you said we didn't need another evangelism chair?" He said, "Don, the gorilla in the room can sit in any chair he wants." Then said, "We are happy to sit. Rule number one is always listen to the donor, whatever the donor wants, it's our job to facilitate. So we'll certainly be able to use it. It would have been nice to have at least one chair in some area of the seminary without a chair, but we can always use another chair of evangelism. So, that's what I would take from them."

Beau Brewer: That's great. That is great. Is there any other, any further information that you would like to give containing the seminary, the Roland Q. Leavell Chair, the "Chair of Fire?" Anything that you think I've missed?

Charles Kelley Jr.:   No, I would just say, again by way of summary, if you
                        want to know the greatest significance, the greatest
                        significance to me is by the direct link between the
                        "Chair of Fire" and this, or any of the other chairs.
                        The genius and the incredible significance of the
                        "Chair of Fire" is that it put evangelism in the aca-
                        demic world on academic terms. The highest honor
                        in the academic world, as you well know, is to oc-
                        cupy an endowed chair. Endowed chairs, across
                        all of academia, are very highly respected. To be
                        the occupant of a chair is to be somebody on the
                        faculty.

                        When Carroll said [that] evangelism is so impor-
                        tant, we're going to inaugurate this "Chair of Fire"
                        and put evangelism in the heart of the Southwest-
                        ern curriculum, the reverberations of that are still
                        going on. I think it has resulted in evangelism be-
                        coming a standard part of the preparation of South-
                        ern Baptist ministers. I think it has put a voice for
                        evangelism within the faculties of our seminaries,
                        and that is important in ways you never hear about.
                        Nobody ever knows about it, the discussions that
                        happen because of it.

                        Having coffee one day after chapel, an evangelism
                        professor, and one of the youngest guys on the fac-
                        ulty, about five or six of us are sitting around the
                        table having coffee after chapel. I happened to be
                        sitting next to a theology professor with whom I
                        greatly disagreed, but he said, "Chuck," I'm thinking
                        about how it is he was the editor of the *Theological
                        Journal we* had then. He said, "I'm thinking about
                        theological issues," and he [unclear], "Any particu-
                        lar theological issues in evangelism right now?" I
                        said, "Well, actually, there are, quite significant." He
                        said, "Like what?" I said, "Well, we're in the very
                        early stages of a rise in Calvinism." He was shocked,
                        and this is a theology professor. He was absolutely
                        shocked. This was 1989 or so, something like that.

He said, "You're talking about five points TULIP of Calvinism, there's a resurgence of classic Calvinism?" I said, "Oh yeah. It's very early stages now, but this is eventually going to become something very significant. It's going to divide the conservative resurgence and people who are working together on the conservative resurgence are going to come to alternative view points, and they could end up being more disruptive to denominational life and the conservative research one day."

He said, "Well, what else?" Then I talk about the Lordship of Christ and it ended up he had me do an article for the *Theological Journal* on that. That conversation would have never happened had I not been a professor of evangelism, sitting next to the professor of theology. So just having that voice, that perspective, that experience of evangelism as a part of the theological faculty, serving on committees, supervising doctoral students, engaging in the affairs of the seminary, no one ever knows all the influence that [an] evangelism professor has, but because he's in the room, the room is different. That's the genius of Carroll, and it's a big reason why Southern Baptists are who we are.

Beau Brewer: Well, Dr. Kelley, thank you so much for this interview. It has really been a privilege to sit here and to listen to you talk about a subject that I adore almost as much as you do. I appreciate all the information that you've been able to give me about the Roland Q. Leavell Chair of Evangelism and the evangelism efforts at New Orleans Baptist Theological Seminary. I just really appreciate it.

This dissertation is . . . . I hope the dissertation that I'm writing will become a seminal work for young scholarship, new scholarship in this area as we explore evangelism in theological education moving forward.

Charles Kelley Jr.: Well just remember, Beau, that the most difficult part of a PhD program is the writing of the dissertation. I read a study one time, this was years ago, I don't know what it is now, but at the time, this was a study done at a university that indicated 80 percent of the people who got to the point of a dissertation in completing their doctorate, never finished. When I read that, I was just astounded. I had not yet started on my dissertation. I was just astounded. I said, "How in the world would you get that close, could you not finish?"

But when I got there, I realized I completely understand that. Your glass is full of so much fuel, and you are using that fuel every day, every week, every month, every year, and when you start that dissertation, you start burning through that fuel. When you run out, I mean you've run out. The real world is very intoxicating, and you're so close to the real world again, and getting out of this artificial environment of studies, and if you once stop, it's extremely difficult to ever pick it up again.

I can cut to the point in my own journey on my dissertation. I got to a point . . . I had a very interesting experience with the Lord on my dissertation while I was researching at Southwestern one hot summer day. Nobody was on campus but me, if felt like. I was doing some research in the library of Southwestern for my dissertation. That night, after the library closed, I just realized what a battle I was in, and I didn't know if I would . . . I'd already been offered the position to teach at NOBTS. All I had to do was finish my dissertation. I just didn't know if I was going to get it done. God had to really deal with my soul about this being a part of what he wanted to do with my life.

So, dear friend, the key is to keep plodding. You can do this. Your big battles with dissertations are, number one, getting started. After you have your oral exams, and you've done so much work, just getting started on that . . . psychologically you're ready for a break, and getting back in to the serious work on the dissertation, that's a battle for some students.

Secondly, stopping your research and starting to write, that's the second big battle, because there's always more stuff out there. Research is pulling at threads, and every thread leads to another thread. You keep finding new things to investigate. I finally learned, I started a file folder and I had all of my doctoral students do this, I started a file folder labeled "good stuff," because you come across all this fascinating information, all this wonderful information, it's not germane to your dissertation, it's not essential for your research problem. So you've got to have a place to put good stuff, and you can look at it later, but you can't be distracted by it. You can't keep pulling that thread. It's not the right thread.

My good stuff file was very important for me because you've got to get into that dissertation, you've got to get into the research, but then you've got to stop the research and you've got to start writing. When you get into that writing, you've just got to write all the way through and you have to finish it. That's the last big battle is finishing the task, wrapping it up and saying, "It's done. There's more that I can do. There's more that I can say. There's more that I could find, but this is enough, and this is where it stops." That's a more difficult battle than most people realize. But you can do this. You have a great professor to work with you in Dr. Queen. He's one of my favorite people on the face of the earth. You've got a great professor to work with. You've got all the ability and skill and talent that you need, so let's just get this thing done.

Beau Brewer: Thank you so much for saying that. I agree whole-heartedly. Dr. Queen is truly a Southern Baptist church man. Most people don't even know. He is truly an encouragement to my heart. He keeps the fires of evangelism hot on Southwestern Seminary, and we are blessed to have him there.

Charles Kelley Jr.: Indeed.

Beau Brewer: Well, thank you so much, Dr. Kelley, for this incredible interview. I look forward to getting it transcribed and sending it back to you for your review, and then getting it into the dissertation.

APPENDIX 11

EMAIL CORRESPONDENCE FROM CHARLES S. KELLEY JR., MAY 27, 2020

From: Charles S. Kelley Jr.
Sent: Wednesday, May 27, 2020, 1:33 a.m.
To: Brewer, Beau
Subject: Roland Q. Leavell Chair of Evangelism

Beau, I can now confirm that the Roland Q. Leavell Chair of Evangelism was established by the NOBTS trustees to honor him upon the occasion of his retirement, I believe in 1959. However, they did not fund the chair at the time it was established or in the following years. Dr. Leavell P. Leavell II, my predecessor, raised the money necessary to activate it and several other unfunded chairs in other departments of the seminary. The Leavell Chair was activated about 1982, with the hiring of Dr. Robert Hamblin, who had served successfully for many years as pastor at Harrisburg Baptist Church in Tupelo, MS. Dr. Hamblin was a very evangelistic and fruitful pastor. He loved the Greek New Testament and was a wonderful expository preacher. He returned to our faculty a second time as a professor of evangelism when he retired from the HMB. Friends of Dr. Hamblin established a chair of New Testament exposition in his honor upon the occasion of his final retirement from our faculty. Bless you!

CHUCK KELLEY, ThD
President Emeritus
Distinguished Research Professor of Evangelism
New Orleans Baptist Theological Seminary

Appendix 12

PERSONAL INTERVIEW WITH
MALCOLM MCDOW, MAY 19, 2020

THIS IS A COMPLETE and accurate transcript of the oral history interview of Dr. Malcolm McDow by Beau Brewer over the phone. No spoken words which were recorded were omitted, except for any non-English phrases which could not be understood by the transcriber. This is a transcript of spoken English, which of course follows a different rhythm and rule than written English. In very few cases, words were too unclear to be distinguished. In these cases, [unclear] or [?] was inserted. Both interviewee and interviewer would interject "Uh hmm" or "Uh huh" frequently, but these were not transcribed unless they came at a definite break in the conversation. In some sections of the tape, the microphone was apparently frequently bumped and every occasion of this has not been noted.

...   Three dots indicate an interruption or break in the train of thought within the sentence of the speaker.

....   Four dots indicate what the transcriber believes to be the end of an incomplete sentence.

( )   Words in parentheses are asides made by the speaker.

[ ]   Words in brackets are comments made by the transcriber.

This transcription was made by Rev.com Transcription Services and was completed in May 2020.

Beau Brewer: This is Beau Brewer. I am a PhD candidate at South-western Baptist Theological Seminary. I'm on a live phone interview with Dr. Malcolm McDow, who served in the fourth or the fifth occupancy of the L. R. Scarborough Chair of Evangelism, otherwise known as the "Chair of Fire," here at Southwestern Seminary. Good day, Dr. McDow.

Malcolm McDow: Hi. It's good to talk with you, Beau.

Beau Brewer: All right. Would you tell me about the two chairs that you occupied during your service to Southwestern Seminary?

Malcolm McDow: I occupied the L. R. Scarborough Chair of Evangelism and I also occupied the George W. Truett Chair of Ministry.

Beau Brewer: Wonderful. Can you give specific dates that you served in the Truett Chair of Ministry?

Malcolm McDow: I'm sorry, I cannot. I know that when I retired I was occupying that chair, and that was 2005. But when I was given the chair, I don't remember the date. I apologize for that.

Beau Brewer: No problem. What were some of the responsibilities of occupying the "Chair of Fire" during your occupation?

Malcolm McDow: Actually, maintaining the true spirit of the chair which is the awareness of evangelism in the Southern Baptist Convention. And also, making sure that Southwestern fulfills her mission of evangelism and missions, and to maintain the standard and the status that would be complimentary to the L. R. Scarborough "Chair of Fire."

Beau Brewer: That's a heavy burden. A joy, but a heavy burden. Do you believe—

Malcolm McDow: No, no, it's a privilege.

Beau Brewer: It's a privilege?

Malcolm McDow: If you live it, it's not a burden.

Beau Brewer: Well, that's true. Do you believe that each occupant during the eight-year rotation of the "Chair of Fire," that would be between Dr. Roy Fish, Dr. James Eaves, and yourself, do you believe that you guys provided continuity for the ideas of evangelism at

	Southwestern? Or do you believe that you acted individually and defined your role separately?
Malcolm McDow:	Roy, Jim, and I made a team. Each one brought a different contribution to the table.
Beau Brewer:	Can you talk about those contributions?
Malcolm McDow:	Contribution number one, we both had hearts for evangelism. Number two, all three of us had hearts for evangelistic preaching. Number three, we all had the passion to instill evangelism in our students. Number four, we all had a burning desire to reach the world for Jesus Christ. When you do that, you're New Testament.
Beau Brewer:	Do you feel like there was continuity between the three of you because obviously—
Malcolm McDow:	Absolutely. As I said, we were a team. We were a team. You could not have had three professors who were more a team than the three of us. We were teammates in the battle. We had no conflicts. We had no arguments. We all three had the same passion. We all three had the same desire. We all three had a burning, a burning, passion for evangelism.
Beau Brewer:	That's wonderful.
Malcolm McDow:	We were perfect for each other. Each one of us brought a different aspect of evangelism to the table but it was all welded together into one evangelistic force.
Beau Brewer:	That is wonderful. Can you discuss the "Chair of Fire's" importance in theological education?
Malcolm McDow:	Academic chairs bring status to an institution. This is the major contribution of a chair. Anytime an institution has a chair, it augments the academic standing, standard, and whatever you want to call it, and consequently, when you have a chair and you mention that this is a chair, even to the layperson, it creates more respect for the institution. And really, it creates respect for them as an occupant.

In certain circles, it opens doors for ministry that you may not have otherwise. So therefore, a chair is very significant for education.

Now, a chair is a chair. And the chair is as strong as the person who occupies that chair. The person who does not occupy that chair, if that person is not strong, the chair's not going to be strong. Consequently, a chair within itself is just a chair. But the chair becomes a force when the person who occupies that chair is a force.

Beau Brewer: Just a moment ago, you were talking about the chair's biggest contribution; would you share your personal comments on the biggest contribution of this chair?

Malcolm McDow: In my own ministry?

Beau Brewer: Yes.

Malcolm McDow: I think the biggest contribution is when I was out preaching on state conventions, state evangelism conferences in churches, and Southern Baptist programs, and I was introduced as a person who occupied the L. R. Scarborough "Chair of Fire," it immediately created interest and demanded attention. Consequently, this is what a chair is assigned to do. It's to make awareness and also to give standing to academic education. I cannot begin to tell you how important the chair is when you occupy it and you're on the program and you're introduced as the person who occupies that chair. You've automatically got an audience.

Beau Brewer: Yes sir, and this particular chair is the first of its kind, correct?

Malcolm McDow: That's right.

Beau Brewer: It was the very first of its kind in 1908. There had never been a chair of evangelism, much less a professor of evangelism or a department of evangelism before that time.

Malcolm McDow:	In 1908?
Beau Brewer:	In 1908, yes.
Malcolm McDow:	Well, that's when Southwestern was founded. There were courses in evangelism in previous schools but those courses were more of an afterthought than a real focus upon evangelism. When the Convention in 1906 met and the Evangelism Department was established in 1906, and by the way, B. H. Carroll was the catalyst that got that convention to vote in favor of the Evangelism Department, and W. W. Hamilton became the first Superintendent of Evangelism January 1 of 1907. But the seminary was founded in 1908 in Baylor and moved to Fort Worth in 1910.
	The Scarborough Chair of Evangelism has always been tied to Southwestern Seminary, and it has been an image of the focus of Southwestern Seminary on evangelism and missions. In other words, the L. R. Scarborough Chair mirrors the purpose of Southwestern Seminary.
Beau Brewer:	That is great. Can you articulate your teaching approach to evangelism?
Malcolm McDow:	In what respect?
Beau Brewer:	What textbooks did you use? Obviously you and Dr. Alvin Reid from Southeastern published books on spiritual awakening like *Firefall* and I know you've contributed to other books throughout your time at Southwestern. So what was your approach? Did you focus mainly on personal evangelism or church evangelism or a combination of the two?
Malcolm McDow:	Both.
Beau Brewer:	Both, okay.
Malcolm McDow:	Yes. You're not going to have New Testament evangelism if you're not going to be incorporating the church.
Beau Brewer:	Sure, sure.

Malcolm McDow:	You can't have one or the other. You have to have both. And the church is not the church unless it is evangelizing. And evangelizing is going to grow the church.
Beau Brewer:	You have a very unique philosophy on evangelism. You believe that evangelism is not the action but it is actually the gospel itself.
Malcolm McDow:	That's right. Where did you get that?
Beau Brewer:	Well, I've done a lot of reading, sir. I've read a couple of different dissertations, one with Dr. Keisling and one with Dr. Dickard. So would you explain your philosophy on evangelism?
Malcolm McDow:	All right. Do you have a piece of paper?
Beau Brewer:	I do, right in front of me.
Malcolm McDow:	Okay, write down euaggelion.
Beau Brewer:	Okay.
Malcolm McDow:	E-U-A-G-E, excuse me. E-U-A-G-G-E-L-I-O-N. Now, right under it, let's transliterate.
Beau Brewer:	Okay.
Malcolm McDow:	Right under it, that first E becomes E.
Beau Brewer:	Yes.
Malcolm McDow:	The U, when you transliterate becomes a V. The A—
Beau Brewer:	The A becomes the A.
Malcolm McDow:	When you have a double gamma, the first gamma is an N.
Beau Brewer:	Is an N, that's correct.
Malcolm McDow:	The next is a G.
Beau Brewer:	Okay.
Malcolm McDow:	The next is an E. The next is an L. The next is an I. And the S-M is an ending. Now what did we do?
Beau Brewer:	Transliterated the word from euangelion—
Malcolm McDow:	From euangelion to evangelism.
Beau Brewer:	. . . to evangelism.

Malcolm McDow:	Now what does euangelion mean?
Beau Brewer:	Gospel.
Malcolm McDow:	Okay.
Beau Brewer:	Or good news.
Malcolm McDow:	All right, good news, the gospel. If euangelion means the good news of the gospel and you transliterate euangelion into English, evangelism, then what's evangelism?
Beau Brewer:	Good news, gospel.
Malcolm McDow:	That's right.
Beau Brewer:	That's correct.
Malcolm McDow:	Now, most people define evangelism as witnessing, sharing. Now, what part of speech is "sharing?"
Beau Brewer:	I'm sorry? What parts are we sharing? We're sharing the good news. We're sharing gospel.
Malcolm McDow:	I know, but is it a noun, verb, or adverb?
Beau Brewer:	Oh, well, sharing would be an adverb.
Malcolm McDow:	No, "sharing" would be a verb.
Beau Brewer:	Verb, I'm sorry. Verb, yes.
Malcolm McDow:	All right, can you translate a noun into a verb? Or transliterate a noun into a verb?
Beau Brewer:	Not without changing its meaning.
Malcolm McDow:	That's right. What Greek word is it that is transliterated into sharing? It's the verb *euangelitso*. *Euangelitso* means sharing. What people define, when they define evangelism, is not evangelism. It's the sharing of evangelism. And the sharing of evangelism is the track on which evangelism travels.
Beau Brewer:	That is so good.
Malcolm McDow:	Consequently, evangelism is the gospel. I had finals for twenty-three years as faculty. Every aspect of.... Don't you put this in your dissertation, you'll flunk it. But every aspect of theological education is simply a branch of evangelism. Theology is the

theology of evangelism. Now, the gospel, good news. Church history is the church history of evangelism. And ethics is the ethics of evangelism. You can take it down the line.

Consequently, evangelism is not what you do. It's what you are proclaiming. Evangelizing is what you do in sharing evangelism. You cannot transliterate a noun into a verb. Impossible.

Beau Brewer: That's right, not without changing it. That is incredible.

Malcolm McDow: Prove me wrong.

Beau Brewer: I can't. Because I know you can't change the word.

Malcolm McDow: All right, what do you think now?

Beau Brewer: I think it's a fantastic definition. I wish you'd let me print that in my dissertation.

Malcolm McDow: Well, go ahead, go ahead. Do what you want to do. You do want you want to do.

Beau Brewer: Well, Dr. McDow, I agree with you.

Malcolm McDow: Be sure that you understand that some of your readers are not going to approve it because they don't understand it. They've been so programmed into evangelism as sharing the gospel instead of evangelism is the gospel.

Beau Brewer: Can you talk about some of your favorite classes that you taught?

Malcolm McDow: My favorite classes were my PhD seminars. I loved them.

Beau Brewer: Which particular seminar was your favorite?

Malcolm McDow: I offered two, Evangelism and the Early Church, from the Time of Christ to the Death of Augustine in 430 AD. The second was Evangelism in the Middle Ages and the Reformation, from 430 AD to the death of John Knox on November the twenty-fourth of 1572. If you want to know the time, it was 11:00 p.m.

Beau Brewer:	11:00 p.m., that's a good hour to study history. So you were a church historian, correct?
Malcolm McDow:	I'm sorry, what?
Beau Brewer:	You're a historian.
Malcolm McDow:	Yes, I am. I majored in American history at Baylor. My PhD is in the history of preaching but it's more in history than it is in preaching, though we studied every major preacher in Christian history. As we studied those preachers, we also studied the culture in which they preached.
Beau Brewer:	So, would you talk to me a little bit about the concept and the implementation of the first full-fledged PhD in evangelism that was started in 1984?
Malcolm McDow:	Exactly which direction do you want me to go?
Beau Brewer:	Just give a little bit of the history of it? How did that conversation start between—
Malcolm McDow:	I joined the faculty in 1982. When I came to the faculty, I saw a lot of things to do to really improve the Evangelism Department. One of the things that I saw that we could do was to implement a PhD in evangelism. But if we implemented a PhD in evangelism, I wanted it to be a full-fledged PhD in evangelism. I did not want it to be hybrid.
	I did my research and I found that there were six, there may have been more, but I found six seminaries who offered a doctorate in evangelism. However, in order to get that doctorate in evangelism, they had to cross disciplines to pick up enough seminars to meet the requirements for a PhD in evangelism. Therefore, they were not full-fledged PhDs in evangelism.
	Consequently, I wanted to have a full-fledged PhD in evangelism at Southwestern. I did my homework and after I came up with a plan, I met with Roy Fish and Jim Eaves, two of my companions in the Evangelism Department. We went over the

implementation of a full-fledged evangelism PhD. All three of us became so excited, we had to be roped to pull back to Earth.

At those meetings, we decided how we would approach. My approach was, in order to make it academic, we would approach it from the historical perspective. We would cover the total history of evangelism from the time of Christ up until the modern times, from the historical perspective.

Now, since I had a PhD in a base of church history, Roy Fish had a PhD in church history, we were both qualified to offer PhD seminars in church history. Doctor Eaves had his major in New Testament. Consequently, he was adept at modern pragmatic ... Well, he was apprised of the modern application of evangelism. So we decided that I would offer the PhD seminar in the early church, from the time of Christ to the death of Augustine in 430 AD, and also a PhD seminar on the Middle Ages and the Reformation, from the death of Augustine to the death of John Knox.

Roy Fish would offer a PhD seminar in the history of spiritual awakening, picking up with Knox. Actually, I think he started with the First Great Awakening and I wish he'd gone back and picked up Richard Baxter. But I don't think he did. He may have mentioned it in his seminars, but from my understanding, he started with the First Great Awakening. And he brought it up to modern times. Then Dr. Fish applied all of it for modern ministry.

Beau Brewer: How wonderful. And what did Dr. Eaves teach?

Malcolm McDow: He taught Contemporary Evangelism. In other words, he applied it.

Beau Brewer: Yes, fantastic.

Malcolm McDow: You have the historical background, you need to apply it. Dr. Eaves applied it.

Beau Brewer: Fantastic.

Malcolm McDow:	Southwestern was fortunate to have two professors who had historical backgrounds in Dr. Fish and me.
Beau Brewer:	Well, I'd say so.
Malcolm McDow:	We were academically qualified to offer those seminars.
Beau Brewer:	Yes sir. Can you talk about the chair's impact on Southern Baptist evangelism as a whole through the revivals? You mentioned earlier that you participated in evangelistic preaching and revivals and such. Can you talk a little bit about that impact on Southern Baptist evangelism as a whole?
Malcolm McDow:	The chair?
Beau Brewer:	Yes.
Malcolm McDow:	The impact came from the men who occupied the chair. The chair simply gave support and standing and also credibility to the person who was doing the proclamation. Consequently, I cannot begin to overestimate the importance of the credibility that a chair gives to the person who occupies it.
Beau Brewer:	Dr. McDow, Dr. Carroll, B. H. Carroll, when he implemented the chair at the same time he created the seminary in 1908, he brought L. R. Scarborough from his church in Abilene to Baylor to start teaching in the field of evangelism. We now know that a lot of that was because of the events that took place in 1906, 1907, with the creation of the Department of Evangelism at what was then the Home Mission Board, now the North American Mission Board.
	So there's been an interconnection between our Department of Evangelism and the North American Mission Board for 114 years now. Can you talk a little bit about that connection during your time as the "Chair of Fire?"
Malcolm McDow:	Southwestern and the Board would be 112 years since it was started in 1908.

Beau Brewer:	Yes, I'm sorry. I got my math wrong.
Malcolm McDow:	This is parenthetical. You mentioned the world-wide revival. In the book that I wrote, *Firefall*, I mentioned I have charts of all the major awakenings in Christian history.
Beau Brewer:	Yes sir.
Malcolm McDow:	This is the global revival of 1904 to 1910. You get different dates for that. But it really broke out in Wales under Evan Roberts in October of 1904 when he heard Seth Joshua preach at Emlyn Academy. He was revived and that revival just swept all of Great Britain.
	But it broke out in the United States in Wilkes-Barre, Pennsylvania on November 2, 1904. Out of that revival came the Evangelism Department of the Southern Baptist Convention. Out of that revival came Southwestern Baptist Theological Seminary. Southwestern was birthed in spiritual awakening. The L. R. Scarborough "Chair of Fire" was simply an extension of that spiritual awakening.
Beau Brewer:	That's fantastic. Thank you for that statement. I definitely am going to have to record that in the dissertation. That's fantastic. I wouldn't have put those two together but you're absolutely right.
Malcolm McDow:	I know I am.
Beau Brewer:	Yes sir, you are.
Malcolm McDow:	I'm just kidding.
Beau Brewer:	Not only did you write the book, but you got that one right, absolutely. I hadn't put those two together because there were so many different things going on, the Whitsitt controversies and so forth. But man, that is really, really good.
	Dr. McDow, is there anything further you would like to share about the significance of the chair?
Malcolm McDow:	I consider it a great privilege to occupy that chair because I feel like it gave credibility to what I was

trying to do. It gave academic standing to what I was trying to do. When a professor occupies a chair, the student has greater respect for that professor. Consequently, occupying those chairs, I feel like I had greater academic respect from those students that I would not have had otherwise.

Now, as I said before, a chair is not going to witness to anybody. The person who occupies the chair is going to do the witnessing. But the chair gives importance to that witness.

Beau Brewer: That's incredible. Thank you so much for your time today, Dr. McDow. I pray that you are blessed. You have just blessed me so much.

Malcolm McDow: Well, I haven't gotten started yet. What are your other questions?

Beau Brewer: Well, my goodness. Can you talk about the greatest contribution that Dr. Roy Fish made to the "Chair of Fire?"

Malcolm McDow: Proclamation, preaching. Roy was really a preacher in the classroom teaching evangelism. He taught evangelism like he was preaching. Consequently, Roy was very brilliant. The chair gave him that standing that we discussed, gave him that credibility that we discussed. He already had credibility but the chair simply intensified that credibility.

Beau Brewer: How about Dr. Eaves? What was Dr. Eaves's greatest contribution?

Malcolm McDow: Dr. Eaves was a great preacher, just an outstanding preacher. But he also had a good understanding, an excellent understanding, of the working of a church. He had been pastor of some pretty good churches. He had the understanding of the workings of the local church and he brought that to the classroom. Consequently, occupying that chair simply also gave him credibility.

Beau Brewer: How about yourself? What was your greatest contribution to the chair?

Malcolm McDow: Ah . . .

Beau Brewer: I know. I know nobody likes to talk about them-
                   selves but I'd love to hear what you personally think
                   your greatest contribution is.

Malcolm McDow: Oh, goodness. I don't want to sound like I'm brag-
                   ging. Bragging is the last thing I want to do. But let
                   me just be humbly braggadocious, okay?

Beau Brewer: Okay.

Malcolm McDow: With humility, I consider myself an acceptable
                   preacher. That chair gave me that credibility. I did
                   preach on many, many state conventions. I always
                   preached two, three, and four state conventions and
                   conferences ever year, all across the United States.
                   You don't get on those programs if you can't preach.

Beau Brewer: That's for sure.

Malcolm McDow: In addition to that, I think that the chair, because
                   it gave me credibility, I was able to work with the
                   students. I was able to relate to the students. Now,
                   Beau, my philosophy of education—

Beau Brewer: Please.

Malcolm McDow: The student is not there for the professor. The pro-
                   fessor is there for the student. If it's not for the stu-
                   dent, the professor wouldn't have a job. And the L.
                   R. Scarborough Chair of Evangelism gave me cred-
                   ibility to relate to those students on an academic
                   level. In other words, it gave me credibility.

                   If you asked students who had me, I think the one
                   thing that they would say is, "He was passionate.
                   He believed in evangelism. He was focused on
                   Jesus." I always said many times over, "He cries of
                   Jesus." That was my statement, he cries of Jesus.

Beau Brewer: Dr. McDow, did you take classes at Southwestern?

Malcolm McDow: Yes, I have my basic degree from Southwestern. I
                   had C. E. Autrey.

Beau Brewer: I was going to ask, "Was C. E. Autrey your profes-
                   sor?" Can you—

Malcolm McDow:	He wasn't just my professor, he was my father in evangelism.
Beau Brewer:	Wonderful.
Malcolm McDow:	I knew Dr. Autrey incredibly well. Dr. Autrey taught me evangelism. But when he retired, I was pastor in Memphis, Tennessee, and when he retired, he retired two blocks from my house. And consequently, every Monday, I took him to the pastors' conference, which met at Bellevue Baptist Church. We fellowshipped every week.
	I will never forget the first time he called me. He said, "Malcolm," he had the drawl, "Malcolm, would you like to go out and witness this afternoon?" Well, if Dr. Autrey called you and said would you like to go out witnessing, you dropped everything to go out and witness.
Beau Brewer:	Absolutely.
Malcolm McDow:	Well, he said, "Pick me up about 1:00." I got some great prospects out of the prospect file and picked him up. There was not a single person home. And we left at 1:00 so about 2:45, I was out of names. When I told him I was out of names, he jumped all over me. I mean, he raked me up and down the coals. He said, "You're out of candidates? What do you mean?" Good night, he leveled me to the ground.
	Well, the next time, we went out many, many afternoons to do personal soul-winning, the next time, I took the entire box.
Beau Brewer:	I don't blame you. I can't blame you a bit.
Malcolm McDow:	I was not going to get raked across the coals again. But we had the privilege of meeting a number of people to the Board and I had a revival at my church. In fact, it was going to go through the Sunday night service but I had to cancel the Sunday night service and end the revival with the Sunday morning service because I needed that night to

resign the church to go to the Tennessee Baptist Convention to become the director of evangelism at the Baptist Convention. Because the next week, it was going to be in the *B & R, Baptist & Reflector*, that I was director and I didn't want my church members to find out that I was going without them knowing it. I wanted to make sure that they knew before the *B & R* came out. You understand that?

Beau Brewer: Yes sir.

Malcolm McDow: So he was gracious enough to end that Sunday morning so I could have a moment that night to resign. But another thing about Dr. Autrey, I had Roy Fish in 1976 for revival at my church, and on that Thursday morning of the revival, Dr. And Mrs. Autrey invited us over for breakfast. So Roy and I went over to Dr. Autrey's house and after breakfast, the three of us sat in the den discussing, talking, so forth. The phone rang and the other end of the line was my wife, and my wife said, "You better get home right now."

I hung up and I turned to the men and said, "Gentlemen, I've got more important things to do than to talk to you." I raced home, picked up my wife, rushed her to the hospital, and that afternoon, she gave birth to our second child.

Beau Brewer: Aw, what a day you'll never forget.

Malcolm McDow: That's a day I'll never forget. And I told Roy we added one member to the church.

Beau Brewer: My goodness.

Malcolm McDow: But Dr. Autrey was my father in evangelism. I loved that man. Oh, I loved that man. If Roy Fish were here, he would say that C. E. Autrey was his father in evangelism.

Beau Brewer: Can you talk a little bit about Kenneth Chafin?

Malcolm McDow: Yes, I had Kenneth Chafin—

Beau Brewer: As a professor?

Malcolm McDow: At Southwestern. I had him for church growth.

Beau Brewer: Thank you for this interview.

Appendix 13

Personal Interview with Preston Nix, May 28, 2020

This is a complete and accurate transcript of the oral history interview of Dr. Preston Nix by Beau Brewer over the phone. No spoken words which were recorded were omitted, except for any non-English phrases which could not be understood by the transcriber. This is a transcript of spoken English, which of course follows a different rhythm and rule than written English. In very few cases, words were too unclear to be distinguished. In these cases, [unclear] or [?] was inserted. Both interviewee and interviewer would interject "Uh hmm" or "Uh huh" frequently, but these were not transcribed unless they came at a definite break in the conversation. In some sections of the tape, the microphone was apparently frequently bumped and every occasion of this has not been noted.

...   Three dots indicate an interruption or break in the train of thought within the sentence of the speaker.

....   Four dots indicate what the transcriber believes to be the end of an incomplete sentence.

( )   Words in parentheses are asides made by the speaker.

[ ]   Words in brackets are comments made by the transcriber.

This transcription was made by Rev.com Transcription Services and was completed in May 2020.

Beau Brewer:	This is Beau Brewer. I am a PhD Candidate at Southwestern Baptist Theological Seminary in Fort Worth, Texas. I am on a live telephone interview with Dr. Preston Nix, professor of evangelism at New Orleans Baptist Theological Seminary, and the

	occupant of the Roland Q. Leavell Chair of Evangelism there at that seminary. Today is May 28, 2020. Dr. Nix, thank you for joining me.
Preston Nix:	I'm glad to do so. You're welcome.
Beau Brewer:	Well, I have been researching your career. You have an interesting one, because you are a fellow Southwesterner.
Preston Nix:	Yes, sir.
Beau Brewer:	You studied under the longest occupant of the "Chair of Fire," Dr. Roy Fish.
Preston Nix:	Yes.
Beau Brewer:	You also studied with Malcolm McDow and some others. Researching your academic career, would you please list your degrees, the institutions you received them at, and then give the dates of service to New Orleans Baptist Theological Seminary?
Preston Nix:	Okay. I got my bachelor of arts at the Stephen F. Austin State University in 1978. And then I went to Southwestern and got my master of divinity in 1984. And then I entered the PhD program. My claim to fame at Southwestern Seminary, I was the one who pioneered the brand-new evangelism major at Southwestern Seminary. I was the only one that first year. A New Testament guy, I think, transferred over, and then the next year several guys came in. I think Alvin Reid, Johnny [Hunt], and some others entered, but I pioneered the program, brother, with Dr. Fish, Dr. McDow, and Dr. James Eaves at the time. And then I got my PhD in evangelism in 1992.
Beau Brewer:	What year did you begin teaching at New Orleans Baptist Theological Seminary?
Preston Nix:	August of 2005. I've been here coming up fifteen years.
Beau Brewer:	Fifteen years.

Preston Nix:	I was the new faculty member who arrived three weeks before Hurricane Katrina and then lost everything I owned, thirty years of sermon notes. I've been in local church ministry for thirty years, and I had an extensive library. It all turned to mush in the flooding that happened after Hurricane Katrina. So I had a very interesting initiation to the Gulf Coast, New Orleans, and being a professor at New Orleans Seminary. My first classes, I was technologically challenged, but my classes went online. So I didn't see students for a year . . .
Beau Brewer:	Oh, goodness.
Preston Nix:	. . . face-to-face hardly. It was a crazy time, brother.
Beau Brewer:	Yes, it sounds like it. Boy, talking about shaking things up. How long have you been the Roland Q. Leavell Chair of Evangelism?
Preston Nix:	I was installed in that chair in August 1, 2008.
Beau Brewer:	2008.
Preston Nix:	I've been in it thirteen years.
Beau Brewer:	Thirteen. Oh, my goodness, thirteen of fifteen, so that's excellent. And before you, Dr. Charles Kelley or Chuck Kelley was the—
Preston Nix:	Dr. Kelley, yes. Dr. Kelley is so kind and gracious. He brought me on, and I had fulfilled all the roles and teaching that he did before he became president. I became the director of the Leavell Center for Evangelism and Church Health, and I'm still there at this time that he established when he was a professor, evangelism professor here. He put me in the chair, Roland Q. Leavell Chair of Evangelism, that he was in. I also happened to be chairman of our largest division here in the seminary, the Pastoral Ministries Division. I wear several hats. I'm also the director of our Supervised Ministry Program.
Beau Brewer:	My goodness. You are a busy man.

Preston Nix:	I stay pretty busy, but I've been busy since I was a little boy. Man, that's the way I live life. Man, I live life in the fast lane. That's what I do. Also, they find a guy that's a good workhorse and they work him. We wear several hats. The reason I'm sharing that, one, is not to impress you with anything, but to let you know that Dr. Kelley was so gracious to allow me to do the things that he did while he was [the Roland Q. Leavell Chair of Evangelism and the director of the Leavell Center for Evangelism and Church Health.] His staff is to supervise the ministry program, which, Supervised One is personal evangelism, where you partner with a local church or ministry, other ministry, and you have supervision to share your faith during that semester. And then Supervised Two is what we would call "field ed" or "applied ministry" in the local church or local ministry, church ministries, or even parachurch ministries, where they get their field education requirements fulfilled.
Beau Brewer:	Fantastic. Well, I think I probably know what your philosophy is, but would you give me your best stab at a philosophy of evangelism?
Preston Nix:	Well, probably. How much do you want?
Beau Brewer:	Oh go as long as you want. Just give—
Preston Nix:	I've got about twelve tenets. If you want them, brother, I'll be happy to give them to you.
Beau Brewer:	If you want to give me all twelve, that's fine. I just would like to hear your philosophy of evangelism.
Preston Nix:	Okay. Well, I have the basic foundation of evangelism is found in the New Testament, and that is where you find the message, the motivation, and the methods for personal evangelism. I'm also a preaching professor for the second part, [part-time] professor of evangelism and evangelistic preaching. I think I'm the only one in the Convention that has that designation in the preaching part, because I

basically double majored at Southwestern because they hadn't developed all of the PhD seminars in evangelism. That was so new. I took the same amount in evangelism and preaching. So preaching and reaching, brother, that's what I'm about.

Beau Brewer: Yes, I love it.

Preston Nix: I have the alliteration as well, because being a preaching professor and I think along those lines. So the basis foundation evangelism course this is very basic, but the reality is some try to make evangelism something other than what the New Testament has it. So you drive your message, your motivation, your methods. Number two, the message is the gospel. 1 Corinthians 15, the life, death, and resurrection of Christ, his incarnation, his crucifixion, his resurrection. If you don't share those three aspects, you are not sharing the complete gospel. Yeah, I can share the gospel. I share it. I can state what it is in those three words: incarnation, crucifixion, resurrection of life, death resurrection. But if you press me, I can get it into one word. The gospel is Jesus.

Number three. The motivation is the Great Commission. There are many different motivations, but the primary motivation for sharing the gospel is obedience for the Great Commission, which is not a suggestion, but a command of Christ. The Great Commission provides the marching orders for the church. The Great Commission is not just in Matthew's gospel. There are five of them: Matthew, Mark, Luke, John, and Acts. Motivation: obedience to the Great Commission. Then methods. The two primary methods I see in the New Testament are public proclamation and personal witness. Preaching, publicly preaching, sharing personally. That comes, of course, from the truth and God's word about the gospel and Romans 10:17: "Faith cometh by hearing and hearing by the word."

All right. Number five. The authority for evangelism comes directly from Christ, stated in the most famous or most well-known of the Great Commission passages, Matthew 28. The Great Commission does not begin with "go." It begins with "all authority has been given me in heaven on Earth," so the authority we have to share the gospel is directly from Christ. All right?

Beau Brewer: Yes.

Preston Nix: Number six. The power for life-change, for regeneration conversion, comes from the Holy Spirit and the word of God. We are regenerated, changed, transformed by the Holy Spirit and the truth of the word. All right?

Beau Brewer: Yes, sir.

Preston Nix: Maybe you're recording this. You may be jotting it down. Tell me if I need to slow down.

Beau Brewer: No, I'm recording and jotting. Don't worry. I got it.

Preston Nix: I probably don't need to speed up. I talk fast, man.

Beau Brewer: No, it's fine. Keep going.

Preston Nix: Okay. Number seven. I would say the authority comes from Christ. This is very Trinitarian. The authority comes from Christ for evangelism, for power, for life change because of the Holy Spirit, and the Father is in pursuit of all humanity. It is his will, I believe, according to the word of God, that all people be saved. Of course, we know all are not going to be saved. Paul said, "I become all things to all men, that by all means save some." 1 Timothy 2:4, "This is acceptable in the sight of God our Savior because of all men to be saved and to come to the knowledge of truth." 2 Peter 3:9, "The Lord is not slow about his promise." Promised a second coming. "Some count slowness as face toward him not wishing for any to perish, but for all to come to repentance." That Greek word "all" in both of those passages means exactly that, all. Romans 10:13,

"Whosoever should call on the name of the Lord shall be saved." John 3:16, "For God so loved the world he gave his only begotten son. That whosoever believes in him should not perish but have eternal life." So the Father's in pursuit of all humanity that I believe can be saved if they will repent and trust in Christ. There's my Trinitarian part in the middle there. Authority from Christ, power from the Holy Spirit, and the word of the Father in pursuit of us.

Number eight. The local church is the primary human instrument for the fulfillment of the Great Commission, and it should be the focus of our ministry. It is the purpose from the functional standpoint of the church. We know, ultimately, we ought to give glory to God. That is what we're all about and everything, but the purpose of our church is to reach people with the gospel.

Beau Brewer: Yes, sir.

Preston Nix: Number nine. Evangelism should be characterized by intentionality. You can't just say [that] hopefully it will happen, it's random, or haphazard. One of my favorite intentional verses is John 4:4, when the word says that Jesus had to pass through Samaria. Of course, any self-respecting Jew wouldn't even go through Samaria, but he had the pass through it. I love the King James version, [which] said, "He must needs to go through Samaria." Why did he have to? Why did he needs to go? Because there was a woman in Sychar, a woman at the well. They need to hear the gospel. When she got saved, then she told everybody else about it. And then every other [unclear] are wide at the harvest. There was a great harvest, because of her salvation. And then John 1:41 is another intentional verse that says Andrew found first his own brother. He was very intentional. When he found the Messiah, he went and got his brother. So intentionality.

Number ten. Evangelists should be characterized by urgency and passion. John 9:4, before the healing of the blind man, Jesus said, "We must work the works of him who sent me while it is day and night cometh when no man can work." Luke 12:20, "This very night your soul is required of you." Urgency, and we ought to be ready to attend. 2 Corinthians 6:2, "Now is the time. Behold today. Now is the time today as an acceptable time to hold today as the day of salvation." Therefore, evangelism should be characterized by urgency and passion. All right, I got two more, brother.

Beau Brewer: Come on. I'm with you.

Preston Nix: Okay. Number eleven. Conversion, salvation, regeneration follows repentance and faith. That is an important distinction in the theological debate we're having today. I don't believe regeneration results in repentance and faith. Repentance according to the word of God, repentance in faith, results in conversion. So conversion, salvation, regeneration follows repentance and faith, and you must repent, believe, receive. John 1:12. Right?

Beau Brewer: Yes, sir.

Preston Nix: Number twelve. Gospel proclamation, personal witness, public preaching of the gospel is not complete unless an opportunity to respond is given.

Beau Brewer: Oh, good one.

Preston Nix: As I heard Dr. Fish say many times, the gospel by its very nature demands a response.

Beau Brewer: Yes, sir. It does.

Preston Nix: I believe in decisional preaching, and that's what I do. That's my dozen philosophy evangelism, brother.

Beau Brewer: Oh. Sir, I couldn't have said it better. That's great. You could preach that all day long.

Preston Nix: Thank you, man.

Beau Brewer:	I may keep you on the phone all day long. That's great. That got my blood going.
Preston Nix:	Well, thank you, brother. Listen, apparently, we have a lot of cards here, man. We believe the word and what it says about witness, and we share. What you don't know about is I was a long-haired hippie Jesus freak. What you have is a guy who's, I'm now sixty-four. That was almost fifty years ago now, forty-five to fifty years ago, the Jesus movement. What I say is I've gained a lot of weight, and I've lost a whole lot of hair, but I'm still a Jesus freak at heart.
Beau Brewer:	I hear you. Well, I got saved at twenty-four, and I've never gotten over it.
	Yes, sir. My sweet pastor, the one that led me to the Lord, Johnny Tims, he put me under his wing. Literally, the day after I came to Christ, that Monday morning, took me out witnessing. Took me to the other side of the tracks.
Preston Nix:	That's good.
Beau Brewer:	He took me to three houses. On the third house, he said, "It's your turn. Share what you know." I go, "I've never even read the Bible." Really hadn't. Hadn't done anything. He goes, "Well, share what you know. If you know enough to be saved, you know enough to share the gospel." And so I did. It was amazing, and I've never gotten over it.
Preston Nix:	Well, amen. That's good. I like your pastor, man. Where'd you grow up? Where is this?
Beau Brewer:	Well, I grew up in West Texas in Sweetwater, Texas. Of course, then I went to college at Hardin-Simmons, and then I transferred to a small college in Oklahoma, the University of Science and Arts of Oklahoma in Chickasha, Oklahoma. That's where I met Johnny Tims. He was the pastor then of the First Baptist Church of Chickasha, Oklahoma. Really sweet longstanding history. One of the

	interesting things is that was actually one of Dr. Criswell's churches before he went to First Dallas.
Preston Nix:	Yeah, man. That is great, brother. Well, we have a couple of little connections. My wife is from West Texas.
Beau Brewer:	Okay.
Preston Nix:	I'm from central Texas. I'm from a little town of Waco you probably heard of.
Beau Brewer:	I have.
Preston Nix:	Before Chip and Joanna Gaines put it on the map it was on the map by the Branch Davidians back many years ago. But people ask me if I knew Chip and Joanna Gaines, because they weren't born until after I left there. But anyways . . . Very literally, I'm telling you the truth. Also, I pastored in Oklahoma for many years, so I'm aware of the ministries that happened in Oklahoma. I was at the Eastland Baptist Church in Tulsa, Oklahoma, for eleven years.
Beau Brewer:	Yes.
Preston Nix:	Both my daughters were born in Oklahoma, so they're little Okies.
Beau Brewer:	Well, I love that. I have family in Oklahoma. Of course, my wife is from Oklahoma, so we've got deep roots there. Yes.
Preston Nix:	Yes, sir, brother.
Beau Brewer:	I know you've already mentioned some of them. You occupied the Leavell . . . What is it? The Leavell Center—
Preston Nix:	Director of Leavell Center for Evangelism and Church Health, yeah. That's not necessarily you do that because you're in the chair, but I think that's who's been in that chair has been the director here.
Beau Brewer:	Gotcha.
Preston Nix:	We do demographic studies, have in the past, and psychographic studies and all for the local church

and for students who need them for strategies for different classes, Church Evangelism, Discipleship Strategy class, and Church Revitalization. We've been doing that. We have conferences. We've had different conferences on different aspects of church health, church growth, and evangelism, sometimes evangelism training. We also do events. Plan events in the community outreach. One we did for the inauguration of our new president, Dr. James K. Dew. I had an outreach to the community for part of his inauguration, which he asked us to minister to the city. So I do that. But usually the . . . I'm looking at your interview questions here, so I think we're on number three, the responsibilities.

Beau Brewer: Good. Yes. We are.

Preston Nix: Roland, the chair, as I understand it, has been also like the chair of the Evangelism Department. We really don't have departments. We have divisions. Evangelism is a part of the Pastoral Ministry Division, but we do meet by disciplines and in many places we call departments. So I am really the department head or the leader in the evangelism area. I just happened to be for the Pastoral Ministry Division. Also, that's not directly connected with the chair, but because of Dr. Kelley, and he fulfilled these roles, then that's what's happened that I've done. I'm also leading supervisor. Now, a couple of other guys have actually had Supervised Ministry through the last fifteen years. I had it for the first few years. Then another guy came in as the evangelism professor. And then after that, another one, but it's come back to me now. That's not one that is tied to the chair, but that's normally a guy in that chair does that.

Anyway, your question, "What are the responsibilities?" I'm giving you some of them. Each occupant does define that role somewhat, but the one thing that has been consistent is that person has been

the chair of the department, although it's not official title. It's led by guys that are the evangelism
professor.

Beau Brewer: Well, great. I'm just curious, how many evangelism
professors do you guys have at New Orleans?

Preston Nix: We have four. One's about to retire. Our graduate
dean actually is an evangelism-preaching professor.
We have another evangelism professor in leadership. We just brought on a new evangelism professor that will start in March, and myself. We actually
have five presently, but our research professor,
who's the assistant director of the Leavell Center
for Evangelism and Church Health, Dr. Bill Day,
he is retiring. Actually, he was retired as a research
professor in this past year, but he will be leaving
us at the end of July. So we've got five today, but in
essence, four. The one is brand new. We have four
evangelism professors.

Beau Brewer: Okay. Well, can you talk about the connections
between the Roland Q. Leavell Chair and the L. R.
Scarborough Chair of Evangelism, the "Chair of
Fire?" Do you know of any connections?

Preston Nix: Well, I can give you a couple. I don't know if we call
it connections or parallel aspects of them. I thought
it's interesting that both of the chairs are occupied,
I mean, were established by presidents of both of
the seminaries. Scarborough being president, and
then he was in the chair. Dr. Leavell was never in
the chair, but it was established right after he retired
because of his health. I think, yeah, he was here
through '58. I think it was established in '59. Maybe
Dr. Kelley has shared that with you.

Beau Brewer: Yes. It was.

Preston Nix: So both came forth from the evangelistic hearts
of the presidents of the seminaries, and both of
them wrote books that were used as evangelism
textbooks in both of the schools. And then further

out from the individual schools, *With Christ after the Lost*, of course, with Dr. Scarborough and Dr. Leavell's book. I don't know if you know this book, *Evangelism: Christ's Imperative Commission*.

Beau Brewer: No, I haven't. I hadn't done that one, but I'm writing it down.

Preston Nix: It is a great book. It's been revised, and it's been used for many years. It's a great, wonderful book. It's an evangelism survey book, one of the first surveys. Dr. Scarborough's book, *With Christ after the Lost*, was used for so many years, and then *Evangelism: Christ's Imperative Commission* by Dr. Leavell. So both our presidents that the chairs were established with presidents, both were pastors who had seen success in their churches in evangelism. Of course, Dr. Leavell was at the domestic ministry for Home Mission work, I guess it was, by that time. Both wrote books that became textbooks for evangelists. Those are some of the connections I see. I don't know if there's a direct connection of the actual chair itself, but the purpose of the chair, who it was established for, and both writers, I think those are significant.

Beau Brewer: Wow. Well, how has the Roland Q. Leavell Chair impacted your campus?

Preston Nix: Well the chair, the guy in the chair has been the leader or the head of the evangelism. Whatever his passion and whatever his direction he gave in [the] evangelism area certainly has impacted the school. Of course, Dr. Kelley, he has such an incredible and left such an incredible imprint, had impact here, because of his ministry. He was an evangelist. Highly unusual to have a president who's a full-time vocational evangelist before he became the president of the seminary. That's highly unusual. Also, he established Supervised Ministry One, which was where you do not just take a course and learn about evangelism. You have to do it. For ten of the sixteen weeks, you have to be out with a team. Originally, and for many years, it was what you did in New Orleans, but then after Katrina especially, we became a lot more of a commuter campus and people were scattered. So people are doing their evangelism with their local churches, but they have to have a team. Again, at least one other person, ideally two others. They go out in their church community.

But still, much of the evangelism through the classes on campus are done in New Orleans. I take a group out. I've been doing this for most of the time I've been here on Thursday afternoons at 2:30. We go into the community and share the gospel door-to-door. We've covered much of the areas here in the city where we live where the seminary is located in the last fifteen years. Maybe a little less than fifteen, because we were out for a year with Katrina. We've been doing that. Of course, they say door-to-door. This distance side door-to-door evangelism doesn't work. I agree it doesn't work if you don't work it.

Beau Brewer: That's right.

Preston Nix: But when you work it, it's amazing how much it works. We have seen many people come to faith in Christ. Also, we don't do it out of the seminary directly. It is seminary-led and seminary-motivated, but we partner with a local church. Sometimes even the pastor or some of his members have gone with us, but most of the time it's myself. We've had a couple of other professionals through the years and other seminary students. We always tie it to the local church and say we're with Gentilly Baptist Church or we're with Edgewater Baptist Church or we're with whatever the church is, Franklin Avenue Baptist church. And then we give the follow-up information to the church, and then they follow up so we have a holistic ministry there of evangelism through the locals. When we're dead and gone, the seminary might not always be around, but the church is always going to be there . . .

Beau Brewer: We pray so.

Preston Nix: . . . until it's raptured out of here. Anyway, we base our personal evangelism. That's how there's been an influence through the chair instead of a person and through the function of that person and his responsibilities in being, what we call, the point man in evangelism for the campus.

Beau Brewer: Fantastic. Well, that is another commonality, I would say between our chairs, because of course, B. H. Carroll, the father of the "Chair of Fire," the creator of that chair, wanted the chair's occupant to infuse this campus with an evangelistic fervor that did not waiver. And so that has been one of the primary roles and responsibilities of the "Chair of Fire" at Southwestern Seminary. It sounds to me that is a similar . . .

Preston Nix: Very similar to here, yes.

Beau Brewer: . . . characteristic of the Roland Q. Leavell Chair.

Preston Nix: Yes, sir.

Beau Brewer: How has the Roland Q. Leavell Chair of Evangelism impacted Southern Baptist evangelism through theological education?

Preston Nix: Well again, as you'd shared with who we were talking at the beginning, the equipping of the students here. Everybody in every degree has to take, as far as a master's, has to take Supervisor One, which is personal evangelism. They are trying to share their faith in whatever ministry context, ministry calling that each one has. It impacts every student that comes through here. They have to share. They have to learn how to share their faith, and they have to do it practically and have to report on it. Can you believe that? We are terrible professors. We make them do what we teach them to do.

They are responsible. They're supervised in it, and they're accountable. They have to share the gospel of the lost people. So you cannot really come through this seminary without having the opportunity to share your faith, or you're required to share your faith. So as far as the equipping training and then the sending out of students, it certainly has had that effect on the summit convention. Also, this is more of a personal, not so much personal, but more specific, in the last several years, I've been the point person with Crossover and NAMB with the seminaries. Then we started passing it off, as far as coordinating all the seminaries and their involvement in the different areas, and generally it was the seminary closest to that location, whatever city where the convention was held. But I have been the guy that's been the point man for that from almost the very beginning and have continued to serve in that capacity. It's not so much connected to the chair, but it's because of my position. I think I may be the most senior full-time trustee elected evangelism faculty member of the six seminaries. I'm not absolutely certain about that, but I think so.

Anyway, that's another thing that I've done and been a part of. At one time it was Crossover shifting going to change and had to be in New Orleans. So I was actually hired. It wasn't paid, but I was hired to be the liaison between NAMB and the local association, the New Orleans Association. We saw a great harvest. Over one thousand people came to faith in Christ during that Crossover. And then Crossover came back to what it was supposed to be. Anyway . . .

Beau Brewer:	Well, that is excellent. I'm assuming you served with Dr. Fish during Crossover as well.
Preston Nix:	Sure. I was at the very first Crossover in 1989 in Las Vegas. Have not been at every one since then, but since . . . I'm trying to think of the year that we did

a partnership. It's been several years ago, over a decade ago that we started partnership with NAMB, where we would have seminary students come in with the full-time evangelists and others in the local area that would come in. It used to be just the Saturday before, and then it turned into the week before. We would partner with local churches. Go out and basically you got evangelism thrust into the community.

Beau Brewer: I believe that was in 2010 when that particular thrust began. Well—

Preston Nix: Yeah. That's what I'm saying. It's been about a decade that we were a part of it. I was not leading the class that first year, but following that, then I've led the class for New Orleans and then the point person with NAMB during those last ten years. But again, we started passing it around the different seminaries to do basically the organization of where are you going to stay and how the classes are going to work and all that working with the churches.

Beau Brewer: Absolutely. Can you list the occupants of the chair? Do you know who has occupied the chair before you?

Preston Nix: No, I'm sorry. I just know I'm here now and have been since 2008. Dr. Kelley was many years before that. There are some . . . . No, wait a minute. I might know. Dr. Kelley had given me some of that information. Hang on. I will tell you.

Beau Brewer: Sure.

Preston Nix: Sorry. I forgot. Dr. Bob Hamblin was, I think, the first occupant.

Beau Brewer: Yes.

Preston Nix: They then went to the whole mission board. And then following that was a man named C. C. Randall, a well-known and respected pastor and then became evangelism professor. I think that's right. I think that's it. Dr. Hamblin, Dr. Randall, Dr. Kelley, Dr. Nix. I think that's it.

Beau Brewer: Oh, so there's only been four of you.

Preston Nix: There's four as far as I know. Those are the only ones I'm aware of, because Dr. Hamblin was the first in the chair, Dr. Kelley said, and following him was Dr. Randall. I'm pretty certain that Dr. Kelley . . . . There may have been someone between Randall and Kelley, but I don't know if there was. Then Kelley had it for all the years he was evangelism professor and president, and then he handed it to me in 2008.

Beau Brewer: Well, excellent. Well, can you offer anything further that you think that I should know about the Roland Q. Leavell Chair, or about evangelism and theological education that I haven't asked?

Preston Nix: Well, here's the thing. I just hope that we don't lose it, what we've gotten, what we've gained, what the heritage we have, especially with the "Chair of Fire" and the Roland Q. Leavell Chair, L. R. Scarborough Chair and the Roland Q. Leavell Chair of Evangelism. The reality is we have lost the fervor. What I've said, it's a real simple statement. I said, what's happened with us at Southern Baptist, we've lost our concern for the lost.

Beau Brewer: Yes.

Preston Nix: When at one time, we were the cutting edge. We were known as the evangelistic denomination, and I've worked with groups with Luis Palau and Franklin Graham and other groups like that. That was a few years ago. We were still known among other denominations as very evangelistic, but I could let them know we weren't quite as evangelistic as we once were. So here's the thing. I was just saying, I don't mean to be cliche-ist or cute here, but the "Chair of Fire," we need to catch fire again, brother. I'm telling you. We have lost the fire, the zeal that established who we are. We really, for the most part, Dr. Kelley's alluded to this, I think in his book, *Fuel the Fire*, and before that, *How Did They Do It?: History of Southern Baptist Evangelism*. We had a Great Commission hermeneutic even. We believe that everything should be understood that God is in pursuit of us, and we ought to be in pursuit of others. He's given it to us, and that's plan A. He doesn't have a plan B, apparently. It's the church. It's us. Basically, we're no longer doing that.

We've tried to soften the gospel and compromise a little bit to be acceptable. Here's the thing. The gospel is never going to be popular and acceptable. It's always going to have an offense, but we don't need to be the offense. The gospel is always going to be the offense. The rub is the exclusivity of Christ like it was in the Roman Empire in the first century, and it is today in the twenty-first century. But I better stop, or I'll just get to preaching, brother, and I give you an invitation here in a minute.

Beau Brewer: Hey, that would be great. Give me one.

Preston Nix: That's one of our struggles. I just have watched it, the fire school. I've seen it in my lifetime. I've lived long. I'm not real old, but I got a lot of miles on me. But having tasted revival and awakening in the Jesus movement, which Dr. Fish used to call the "mild awakening," but it was the last national awakening that we experienced, like I said, forty-five, fifty years ago. I got to taste it, and I saw the evangelist zeal of all of us lon- haired kids who got saved. The two main things about the Jesus movement was we wanted to know the word of God, and we wanted to share the gospel with our friends and wanted them to know Jesus. That was where the hallmarks.... and I just watched that change, things that NAMB had changed. We don't quite have the advantage of structure nor the program approach to help us. I'm not all for thinking programs are what's going to save us, but the way that the Home Mission Board, Domestic Mission Board before that, NAMB was set up, we had a greater focus and we were producing more literature and training materials and helps. We just we don't have that. It's almost nobody's business anymore. It went to Lifeway for a while. Who's producing the materials?

We relegated to East Church, but the reality is we, as Southern Baptists, have been a people who've rallied together. And whether it was *EE, CWT, Faith Evangelism, Share Jesus Without Fear, 3 Circles,* or what have you, we've had something that's been a focus for us. We no longer have that hardly anymore. I even alluded the fact that Crossover is about to change its focus for a while, and we helped to pull that back. That's a long story, involved more than you want to know, and not anything germane to your interview. But nonetheless . . . But anyway, brother, I'm talking more on that I should. I'm just telling you. We are not who we were and where we need to be. I've said this.

We have a degree of evangelistic church growth, and it's probably one of the smallest. Hardly anybody is in that degree program anymore. When evangelism used to be at the forefront, it's [now] relegated to second class. I said, we, as evangelism professors and the students that are very evangelistic are, if they were an archaic person, like a full-time evangelist, hardly we hear of those anymore. We are a minority today.

Beau Brewer: Yes, we are.

Preston Nix: Evangelists, evangelistic guys, door-to-door guys, those kinds of fellows, and people say, "What's your methodology?" No, it's not the methodology. It's the fact that evangelism ought to be at the forefront of our ministries, and it no longer is.

Beau Brewer: That's right.

Preston Nix:	That's just reality where we are. Now, for some churches and some ministers, it is, but overall it is no longer what it once was. Anyway, we need to get back to evangelism and certainly we need a revival and awakening in our day. A lot of times those go together and they certainly did. There's a Jesus movement in history, the First Great Awakening, Second Great Awakening. The evangelistic fervor that came out of the movements of the spirit of God, we need that again. I'm praying for it to happen. I fast and pray for revival, and I try to be faithful to equip others and share my faith and try to keep the fires burning, brother.
Beau Brewer:	That's all we can do. Right?
Preston Nix:	What we got to do, man.
Beau Brewer:	Well, I'm praying. I'm praying that this—
Preston Nix:	I feel like a boy who's crying in the wilderness, but God used John the Baptist. So maybe he'll use us, too, to make a difference.
Beau Brewer:	I pray he does.
Preston Nix:	[crosstalk] our focus was on the gospel.
Beau Brewer:	I pray he does. I'm praying that this dissertation will spark the fires of at least some scholars and some future scholars as they discover who these guys were that carried this flame of evangelism.
Preston Nix:	That's right. Yeah, amen.
Beau Brewer:	Well, thank you so much, Dr. Nix. I pray that you have a blessed day, and thank you for your time.
Preston Nix:	You're very welcome. By the way, good to meet you by phone, and maybe we'll face-to-face. I'm just glad I got to pioneer what you're doing, brother. It is a blessing for me to visit with a student presently who I got to pioneer that back in the mid eighties.
Beau Brewer:	Excellent. Well, thank you so much.
Preston Nix:	It's neat seeing that be with you in that line, my friend.

Beau Brewer:	Yes. I love it. Thank you so much for sharing so much of your story with me.
Preston Nix:	Well, probably more than you wanted, more than you needed, but hopefully it was encouragement to you at some level.
Beau Brewer:	Yes, sir.
Preston Nix:	The biggest thing is helping you with your dissertation research we can pump out what you need, man, that God might use.
Beau Brewer:	Yes, sir.
Preston Nix:	Okay, brother.
Beau Brewer:	Well, you have a blessed day.
Preston Nix:	Well, you, too, Beau. Bye bye now.
Beau Brewer:	All right. Talk to you soon. Bye bye.

APPENDIX 14

PERSONAL INTERVIEW WITH EDSEL D. PATE, MAY 18, 2020

THIS IS A COMPLETE and accurate transcript of the oral history interview of Dr. Edsel "Eddie" Pate by Beau Brewer over the phone. No spoken words which were recorded were omitted, except for any non-English phrases which could not be understood by the transcriber. This is a transcript of spoken English, which of course follows a different rhythm and rule than written English. In very few cases, words were too unclear to be distinguished. In these cases, [unclear] or [?] was inserted. Both interviewee and interviewer would interject "Uh hmm" or "Uh huh" frequently, but these were not transcribed unless they came at a definite break in the conversation. In some sections of the tape, the microphone was apparently frequently bumped and every occasion of this has not been noted.

. . .   Three dots indicate an interruption or break in the train of thought within the sentence of the speaker.

. . . .   Four dots indicate what the transcriber believes to be the end of an incomplete sentence.

( )   Words in parentheses are asides made by the speaker.

[ ]   Words in brackets are comments made by the transcriber.

This transcription was made by Rev.com Transcription Services and was completed in May 2020.

Beau Brewer:	This is Beau Brewer. I am a PhD student at Southwestern Baptist Theological Seminary in Fort Worth. I am live on a telephone recording with Dr. Edsel D. Pate, a professor of evangelism at Gateway Seminary in Anaheim, California.

Edsel D. Pate:	We're actually in Ontario, Beau. Ontario, California.
Beau Brewer:	Ontario, California. There I go, I get the wrong city altogether. Well go to Gateway Seminary in Ontario, not in Anaheim. Well, thank you for being with me, Dr. Pate. So today we are going to be discussing Gateway Seminary and the connections between our Departments of Evangelism. Between your Department of Evangelism there at Gateway and the Department of Evangelism and the "Chair of Fire" at Southwestern Seminary. And see if we can draw any conclusions or connections. So researching your academic career, Dr. Pate, you presently serve Gateway Seminary. Would you give the dates of that service?
Edsel D. Pate:	I have been . . . Yeah, let me . . . It's going to take a bit, but I can give you that. I have been at Gateway in one way or another from 2005 until now.
Beau Brewer:	So that's fifteen years.
Edsel D. Pate:	That's about fifteen years. Now in one way or another, I've only been the evangelism professor about the last four years. I had been their director of the School of Missions and the campus director in Orange County previous to that as well.
Beau Brewer:	So who served in your position before you did?
Edsel D. Pate:	Well, I have taught evangelism since about them, but we really didn't have a standalone evangelism prof, other than a man named Bill Wagner. And that was up in northern California before Golden Gate became Gateway and moved down to Ontario or Southern California about four years ago.
Beau Brewer:	Okay. Real quick. Would you give your credentials, give your academic credentials?
Edsel D. Pate:	I got a BA from California Baptist College, MDiv from Southwestern, and DMin from Southwestern. And the DMin back in '89? My MDiv was 1984, I think.

Beau Brewer:	So you are a Southwestern and you sat under, probably, Dr. Fish and—
Edsel D. Pate:	Dr. Fish. Yes.
Beau Brewer:	Okay. Well, that's wonderful. That's a great guy to sit under. I sat under him in my MDiv as well.
Edsel D. Pate:	That's it, really. Right on.
Beau Brewer:	There you go. So would you articulate your philosophy of evangelism?
Edsel D. Pate:	Wow. I mean, that's a nice question. I don't know that I have pinned that. So just a verbal, as far as just teaching and how I view evangelism . . . . Probably the closest thing I've got to that actually, Beau, is a mind map that puts the local church in the center. So it's not just a personal thing. It's a local church thing. I mean, we do do standalone evangelism, but the church is a big part of that. It's every-member evangelism. It's the gift of evangelism, but it's also carrying out the Great Commission one by one. And that's all of our responsibility. Believers ought to be ready at all times to give an account for the hope that's in them.

Yeah, so that's pretty much how I teach it. With being equipped individually to share Christ. But also connecting the . . . I don't make a big distinction between evangelism and discipleship. I think those are two parts of the same hand, but the church is a big part of that as well. I don't, in other words on the negative side, I don't like just, "Hey, let's share Christ. And then just hope that they find their way somewhere." I mean, I want the local church to be a piece of that. So take that for what it is. I don't know if that's a really clear, articulated philosophy of evangelism, but that's kind of where I had my class. |
| Beau Brewer: | So before we started recording, you did mention that you have seen a plaque. Would you tell me as much or as little . . . ? |

Edsel D. Pate:	Well, even as we were talking, I just did a quick search for "Westmoreland Chair of Evangelism." So it looks like . . . I don't know when that began, but I'm seeing if you just Google that. So that is something that exists at Gateway, but like I said, I've been there about fifteen years, Beau, and I don't know that I have reference to that chair since I've been there. And I'm looking at an old *Baptist Press* article from 1997. And in that article, it references the E. Hermond Westmoreland Chair of Evangelism. So whether that's something that played out . . .
	Like I said, I came on about 2005. I was a campus director. I had come from Liberty where I taught missions at Liberty University for a year. And then before that, we were with the International Mission Board, eleven years. And I came originally as the campus director and then became the school admissions guy at Gateway, probably about 2007 or eight. So, yeah. Anyway, that's a weird truth, but I'm telling you I've seen the plaque and wondered. But don't know that there's any active application of the E. Hermond Westmoreland Chair of Evangelism at Gateway. So yeah, your guess is good as mine.
Beau Brewer:	Well. I'm going to go and research that. I sure am.
Edsel D. Pate:	Look it up.
Beau Brewer:	You said the *Baptist Press* of '19?
Edsel D. Pate:	Yeah, it's . . . I just Googled the thing and it came up in 1997, a *Baptist Press* article. But I don't know if there's anything in our, in our catalog or not.
Beau Brewer:	I don't know either. But I'm going to check that one out. Well, thank you for that little tidbit. Do you know if there's any connection that exists between Gateway Seminary's Department of Evangelism and the "Chair of Fire" other than your two degrees?
Edsel D. Pate:	There's no formal connection other than we partner occasionally with the Association of Evangelism

Profs. Tom Johnston at Midwestern kind of leads that. And other than just having a connection through that organization, we don't, as far as I know, have any formal connection with the "Chair of Fire" there at Southwestern.

Beau Brewer: Okay. Well, then, can you discuss the "Chair of Fire's" importance in theological education?

Edsel D. Pate: I can't. No.

Beau Brewer: That's okay.

Edsel D. Pate: I know it sounds bad. I can't.

Beau Brewer: No, it's fine. Can you give any significance as to how the "Chair of Fire" has impacted Southern Baptist Evangelism?

Edsel D. Pate: I mean, other than personally, I surely don't know, Beau. The impact that Southwestern has always had in evangelism and the history that you've mentioned briefly, that's kind of . . . . If you're trying to connect dots, I mean, I would say that's where it gets pretty fun. If you're connecting the dots. And if I'm a spiritual child of Roy Fish. And if Roy is from Dr. Scarborough, then in that sense, all of us . . . . I mean, I'd say at Gateway . . . And I mention kind of in jest, but I am what keeps them from having a real evangelism prof. I mean, I think I was the missions guy, Beau. And I've also been a pastor. So I left Gateway full-time, eight years ago, to go back and pastor the church that I left before I went to Jordan and Sudan. I am back as a full trustee-elected faculty member. And all I'm teaching pretty much is evangelism, but I think that the dotted lines are pretty strong.

If Roy is my mentor or father in evangelism, for me as a pastor, and a missionary, and as a prof at Gateway, and the students that that I'm putting into . . . . So then if Scarborough is our great granddaddy and Roy is our dad, I mean there's a pretty strong connection between what's happening at

	Gateway in evangelism, and what I got when Roy Fish came into the room singing hymns. And we all had to learn how to witness and do *CWT* back in the day. So that's all I can say regarding the connection of . . . . For me personally, and then to my students now at Gateway from Southwestern.
Beau Brewer:	No, that's good. That's good.
Edsel D. Pate:	That's true. So whether it's good or not. Like I said, it's all they got. But I mean, I was inspired every day, and humbled, and weeping really before the Lord through Dr. Fish's passion, and just what he brought in that. I mean, that's one of those classes you never forgot. And yeah, hopefully I'm passing some of that on out here.
Beau Brewer:	So you did mention that you do teach evangelism classes. So I'm assuming you do a personal evangelism class and then you probably do something along the lines of Church Evangelism.
Edsel D. Pate:	We have one required evangelism class and that's it. So it's just basic evangelism. I have about . . . I mean, the emphasis in that class is really personal evangelism. So that's eight evangelism verbatims in the semester. And that could either be a six- or an eight-session semester, or a fifteen-session. But they're required to do eight evangelism verbatims. In that I probably have about a quarter of that class is church evangelism, because that's the only chance I've got. For us, I mean, electives are pretty much few and far between. And we've got . . . You guys probably do too. But we've got a couple of degrees where evangelism is an option. So there's some people that could get out of Gateway without having that. We're not happy about it, me and the other guys in our department. But yeah. I mean, I have an elective that is rarely taught, that's sort of a church-growth elective. This summer, I'm doing an apologetic evangelism class with J. Warner Wallace. And that'll be fun.

Beau Brewer:	Oh wow. That will be fun.
Edsel D. Pate:	And he's a Gateway grad. Golden Gate grad, believe it or not. Back [when] we had a Brea campus as well.
Beau Brewer:	Wonderful. Since you are kind of the head of your Department of Evangelism there, do you have a specific emphasis that you emphasized most on the campus in terms of working with faculty, working with the administration, working with students? Is there anything you're trying to constantly infuse?
Edsel D. Pate:	Well, I think our president, Jeff Iorg, is also pushing that as well. So he's written a book called *Unscripted*. That's kind of a personal evangelism book. So Jeff pushes that. I mean, we push it as much as we can. We have other classes where they'll use the three circles and try and nudge people toward evangelism in those. But yeah, I mean, that's . . . I do what I can, but I'm limited. And I'm limited in a lot of ways. Pretty much our department only teaches three classes, my whole curriculum really, that are required. And that's Intercultural Communication, Missions, and Evangelism.
Beau Brewer:	And all three of those are required.
Edsel D. Pate:	Those are all required for an MDiv. Only a couple of them, or for an MTS for some of our other degrees.
Beau Brewer:	Wow. Okay. So anything else you'd like to share?
Edsel D. Pate:	I mean,
Beau Brewer:	I'll tell you, I'm thrilled about this Westmoreland Chair of Evangelism. That's what's exciting for me because I was unaware that there was even a chair there.
Edsel D. Pate:	Yeah. And I'm sorry. And you'll probably find out that where you dig that I'm just a complete idiot. [crosstalk]
Beau Brewer:	No. No, Dr. Pate.

Edsel D. Pate:	It's just the weirdest thing though. I pass a plaque and numerous times, I've looked at it and thought, "Well, that's interesting. I never knew we had that." And again, I've been associated with the school fifteen years. And I don't know that we have applied that title to anyone. Maybe Bill Wagner. So if you check that out, Bill Wagner was in Mill Valley at Golden Gate Seminary. And I'm guessing he probably retired ten or twelve years ago, maybe longer. And I've pretty much taught evangelism since then, but I was teaching it in Brea before. But yeah, check that out. If you find out something, let me know. Right. And I'll know what the plaque means next time I'm allowed on campus, when COVID allows us to walk back into the classrooms. Right?
Beau Brewer:	Isn't that the truth?
Edsel D. Pate:	I know it.
Beau Brewer:	Absolutely. Well, Dr. Pate, thank you so much for your time. I pray that you don't feel like this has been a waste of your time.
Edsel D. Pate:	Oh no, man. Thanks for what you're doing, I'll print this release out and get it to you too in just a bit though.
Beau Brewer:	Please do. Thank you so much.
Edsel D. Pate:	All right.
Beau Brewer:	God bless have a great day, sir.
Edsel D. Pate:	You too, thanks. Bye bye.
Beau Brewer:	Goodbye.

Appendix 15

Personal Interview with
L. Paige Patterson, May 12, 2020

This is a complete and accurate transcript of the oral history interview of Dr. L. Paige Patterson by Beau Brewer over the phone. No spoken words which were recorded were omitted, except for any non-English phrases which could not be understood by the transcriber. This is a transcript of spoken English, which of course follows a different rhythm and rule than written English. In very few cases, words were too unclear to be distinguished. In these cases, [unclear] or [?] was inserted. Both interviewee and interviewer would interject "Uh hmm" or "Uh huh" frequently, but these were not transcribed unless they came at a definite break in the conversation. In some sections of the tape, the microphone was apparently frequently bumped and every occasion of this has not been noted.

. . .   Three dots indicate an interruption or break in the train of thought within the sentence of the speaker.

. . . .   Four dots indicate what the transcriber believes to be the end of an incomplete sentence.

( )   Words in parentheses are asides made by the speaker.

[ ]   Words in brackets are comments made by the transcriber.

This transcription was made by Rev.com Transcription Services and was completed in May 2020.

Beau Brewer:	This is Beau Brewer. I'm a PhD candidate at Southwestern Baptist Theological Seminary in Fort Worth, Texas. I am live with Dr. L. Paige Patterson, the eighth occupant of the illustrious "Chair of

Fire." We are on a telephone recording. This is May
12, 2020.

Dr. Patterson, thank you for joining me.

Paige Patterson: No, thank you, Beau. It's a delight to be with you.

Beau Brewer: Well, we're going to be discussing the "Chair of
Fire" at Southwestern Baptist Theological Semi-
nary, otherwise known as the L. R. Scarborough
Chair of Evangelism. I selected you because you
are pertinent in many, many ways, not only with
your occupancy of the "Chair of Fire" but also the
assistance and probably the mastermind thought
and plan of the Bailey Smith Chair of Evangelism
at Southeastern Baptist Theological Seminary in
Wake Forest.

We're going to dive in in just a moment but first I
would like for you to articulate your philosophy of
evangelism.

Paige Patterson: Well, Beau, my philosophy if evangelism is that
evangelism is like breathing. It's the thing that you
do if you're alive. If we're determined to follow
Christ, he said, "Follow me and I'll make you fishers of men." That statement, "I'm going to make you
fishers of men," defines what our responsibility is.
No matter what area of God's work we happen to
be in, it doesn't matter whether a man is a pastor
or whether he is a minister of children's work or a
pastoral counselor or whatever, evangelism is like
breathing. It's just what he does. He is a fisher of
men. By definition.

That's the way I see it. I see it in academic discipline
as basically broken down into two phases, personal
evangelism and church evangelism. I was always
a little bit irritated in the seminary world because
we could basically only teach one- or three-hour
course required for evangelism where I was at
Criswell College for those sixteen years or seventeen years. I actually set it up where they had to

have two courses of evangelism, one was personal evangelism and the other was in church evangelism, because I said, "Not only are you responsible for doing this individually but you got to build a church program that reflects evangelism."

To me, it was a matter that is a question of following Christ and is just as necessary to the spiritual life of an individual as breathing is to his physical life.

Beau Brewer: Amen. Amen. Researching your academic career, you have presided over three Baptist institutions. Is that correct? As president?

Paige Patterson: Yes. That's true. It's unfortunate for the people who were there but it happened.

Beau Brewer: Well, could you give me the dates of service at each of these institutions leading up to your service at Southwestern Seminary?

Paige Patterson: Yeah. Well, I can make a stab at it. That's about the best I can do without having it written down in front of me. Let's see, I was at the Criswell College, which when I went there was the Criswell Bible Institute. We changed the name of it to Criswell Center for Biblical Studies and then went ahead and changed it to Criswell College and that stuck. I was there from 1975 until 19 . . . Let's see. About 1992 I guess.

Beau Brewer: Oh, wow. Then your time at Southeastern Baptist Theological Seminary?

Paige Patterson: Was immediately following that from 1992 until 2003. Or 2002. I'm not sure. It was eleven years there.

Beau Brewer: Okay. Then from Southeastern you came to Southwestern?

Paige Patterson: Yes.

Beau Brewer: Okay. That was in 2003, correct?

Paige Patterson: Either '02 or '03. I can't remember for sure which.

Beau Brewer:	Okay.
Paige Patterson:	But through 2019.
Beau Brewer:	Okay. Then can you give me the dates of your service in the "Chair of Fire?"
Paige Patterson:	No, I really can't.
Beau Brewer:	Okay.
Paige Patterson:	To be honest with you. Let me tell you what happened. Hopefully, you can piece it together there. I can actually get it pieced together but I'd have to consult my wife, who is my basic caretaker on such things as dates.

Anyway, what happened was the Chariot of Fire, of course, the "Chair of Fire" already existed when I came, but when it was left open. Dr. Blaising suggested that I step into that as president of the institution.

I did not want to do that. I felt that it was a certain amount of chutzpah involved in doing that. I really wanted to use that more for some special person that we would choose, that it might be the elixir of life for what he was doing.

I hesitated about it but finally Dr. Blaising suggested, first of all, that evangelism needed a strong rebirth in [the] Southern Baptist Convention. He said that nobody had been more identified with it in positions like leaders of schools than I had and so that ought to at least do it for a little while.

Basically, what I agreed to do was I agreed to accept the position for a while. I had no intention of staying there permanently and, of course, did not but I did accept it for a short time.

Then when the opportunity came along to bring its present occupant into that chair, well, that's exactly what I wanted to do and so I gave up the chair at that point. As much as I loved and appreciated it, I gave it up because I wanted your professor to have it.

Beau Brewer: You realize that your occupancy of the "Chair of Fire" made you the third president to occupy that chair.

Paige Patterson: Yes. I am aware of that. I don't think I knew it completely at the time because I didn't know about the second one at the time but Dr. Blaising did make me aware of that too.

Beau Brewer: Do you feel like being in the president's seat . . . . I know this isn't one of the questions that I had planned to ask but do you feel as though being in the president's seat and occupying the "Chair of Fire" gave the "Chair of Fire" an advantage?

Paige Patterson: I think it was a John plus-minus.

Beau Brewer: Okay.

Paige Patterson: To quote Dr. Criswell, who often said "John plus-minus." By then, of course, he meant that, yes, it definitely did give some status to the chair that otherwise it might not have for the president of the institution. To be in that chair stated that my ultimate interest after all was said and done was always in evangelism. That was good and that was helpful.

It was a minus in that, of course, by definition the president of the institution has to be mindful of everything else going on in the institution and has to be an advocate for all of it so, therefore, it, by definition, truncates a little bit what he might be able to do. That's the reason why I feel like Dr. Queen has been a far better representative as the director of chair because he has been able to just devote his time to that.

Beau Brewer: He has done a splendid job. What are some of the responsibilities of occupying the "Chair of Fire?" Do you believe that each occupant defines the role of this chair?

Paige Patterson: Yeah. Well, of course, like everything else in the church of the Lord Jesus Christ, the advocate to some degree defines it by the talents and abilities that he happens to bring to it. He develops it after whatever God's gifts to him may be. That's certainly true. I do think there are some things that cross all lines there.

First responsibility that I believe he has to do with the spirit of evangelism on the campus. There's another question a little bit later on where we talk about the origins of the chair, but let me just say at this point even that, of course, what B. H. Carroll had in mind when he brought Lee Scarborough to be the director of the "Chair of Fire," he had in mind that the whole developing western part of the United States was, of course, pagan country. Right? It was Christians there, wonderful believers as part of it but it was there to be evangelized, there to be won for Christ.

What Carroll had in his gunsight, so to speak, was he had a tremendous number of lost men moving around on the frontier of the United States and how to get the gospel to them was his concern. He believed that seminary needed to be imbued by that spirit.

He also felt that was true, of course, for the whole world, and so what he was trying to do was to create a spirit of evangelism in all of his men. He realized not everybody would major in evangelism. He knew most would not but he knew that if someone on campus had that as his major concern and his driving impetus that that would tend to repeat itself in the lives of the students as they became graduates and representatives of the institution out in the churches.

The second thing I think that the holder of the chair would be responsible for; I think he would be responsible for not only creating a spirit of evangelism but also teaching the essential element involved in becoming an evangelist. The Bible says, "Do the work of an evangelist." Fine, I want to do that, but how? How do I do it? What does it mean to do the work of an evangelist? Well, that above all else is the responsibility of the leader of the chair of evangelism. He is responsible for teaching how that's to be done.

Now, realistically, it doesn't begin with students. Realistically, it begins with professors. A professor is, by definition, a person who does not witness very well. That's a shame but it must be very honest and truthful. There's a man who has spent his life studying systematic theology or here's a man who spent his life delving into ecclesiology or here's a man who has spent his life in some other discipline and he's been in the library for untold ageless hours working on dissertation, maybe writing books, articles in his field, and he goes and he sees this class and he meets this class and he talks to them but he's not in a church situation on a regular basis. Hopefully he is, but realistically some are not.

As a result of that, he does not have a concourse with people that he probably ought to have and sometimes they just have to be made acquainted with the people to whom they ultimately minister.

I think it starts with faculty and it goes to the student body and even to those people who are on staff of the institution that it is his responsibility to seek to it that they learn a way of witnessing and a way of sharing their faith.

A third responsibility that he has is through the classroom. He has to superintend all of the classroom responsibilities. That includes the teaching of evangelism, but it also includes such things as supervision of graduate students and doing dissertations, for example, and you have experienced that firsthand yourself.

Beau Brewer: Yes, sir.

Paige Patterson: That's one of the things that Dr. Queen has proven to be so stupendously helpful, and he is supervising dissertations and also other research projects that have been very helpful. He is responsible for tying into the school things like [the] Billy Graham School approach that involves our students and others in being involved with the phones and actually receiving calls from people who have witnessed something that has come about in the Graham association that has led them to seek the Lord. He is responsible for doing that kind of thing.

All of that, it seems to me, he is responsible for doing, plus, hopefully, he is an author of some literature along the line of evangelism himself.

Beau Brewer: Yes. Did you or have you published anything in the field of evangelism?

Paige Patterson: Yes, I have. I have a couple of articles that are part of books. Lewis Drummond, my predecessor in the presidency at Southeastern Seminary, published a book and he asked me to do the . . . I think it was the lead chapter in it. I'm not sure. I think it was.

He specifically wanted me to deal with whether it was more important to do spontaneous evangelism or whether it was more important to do heavily crafted friendship evangelism over a period of time.

In that article, I simply raised the question if you have been asked to build an NBA, a National Basketball Association, franchise and you want to be the big one or you would like to win the national basketball championship, what kind of a player do you want to draft? Do you want to draft a tall center or forward who is able to slam dunk a ball easily? Do you want somebody who is a smaller man with a degree of versatility who can set up a three-point man and hit a three-point shot? Which one do you want?

Well, obviously, any coach that's worth his hire is going to tell you it's not one or the other. It's both-and. That's been one of the difficulties in evangelistic development in local churches is that people don't understand you got to do both; friendship evangelism is always in order but so much spontaneous evangelism also be. That's one article that I've written.

I've also written an article on the theology of evangelism. I have to go back and see where they are.

Beau Brewer:	That was Schofield, *The Gospel for the New Millennium,* correct?
Paige Patterson:	Yes. I think so. That's exactly correct.
Beau Brewer:	A terrific article on the theology of evangelism. You're not the first occupant of the "Chair of Fire" to write on a theology of evangelism. I believe Autrey—
Paige Patterson:	Oh, no.
Beau Brewer:	I believe Autrey was the first to actually publish a work.
Paige Patterson:	Yeah. I'm sure that's true. They did a fine job of it. All I needed to do was just kind of restate it for contemporary audience.
Beau Brewer:	That was actually one of the classes that you taught while you were the occupant of the chair, was A Theology of Evangelism. Correct?
Paige Patterson:	Yes. That's the main course I taught on campus. The reason for that was at that particular point in time we really didn't have anybody that was focusing on that area, so I figured, well, okay, we've got people that do know how to teach General Evangelism and Personal Evangelism, and I'll just focus on this area of theology evangelism, which did combine what I had my degree in since I did my PhD, of course, in theology.

Beau Brewer: Well, while we're talking about theological educa-
                      tion can you discuss your views of the "Chair of
                      Fire's" importance in theological education?

Paige Patterson: Yes. Of course. This goes back to Carroll's insight
                      on it. To me, B. H. Carroll was bigger than life. I
                      know that he wasn't perfect and nobody is but the
                      Lord Jesus. You know, Carroll was a remarkable
                      man who, though not having as much formal edu-
                      cation as some people would have deemed neces-
                      sary for a seminary president, he made up for it by
                      the fact that he was very farsighted. He could see
                      some things coming.

                      As he looked at general seminary curricula he dis-
                      covered that . . . No evangelism curriculum that I'm
                      aware of and I think he was aware of there was no
                      emphasis on evangelism. It was sort of expected in
                      some cases but while it was expected there was no
                      teaching of it. It wasn't considered in a sense a dis-
                      cipline on the par with ecclesiology or a discipline
                      like even missions.

                      Carroll thought, "Well, but it should be because
                      there's nothing more important that we do." It is
                      important to expound the word. Carroll demon-
                      strated that in his own works. It is important to
                      know how to pastor a church. He certainly had
                      done that and had been foremost in his mind but
                      he also realized that if evangelism is really the most
                      important thing we do, if it's true, that Jesus loved
                      the church and gave himself for it, that he can seek
                      and to save that which was lost. He defined his own
                      mission that way as coming to seek and save that
                      which was lost, then it had to be the case that atten-
                      tion should be given to it in class.

                      He had the idea that Lee Scarborough, who had
                      been, of course, at the First Baptist Church in
                      Abilene, Texas, during those days and had a very
                      wonderful ministry there, very effective evangelist
                      ministry and that would be the perfect way, not

only to interest Scarborough but also the way to most skillfully use Lee Scarborough.

That's what he came up with and I do share that conviction totally and completely that it does need to be a discipline.

Beau Brewer: During your tenure as the president and I am going to assume you weren't the occupant yet but you did assist Dr. Fish and Dr. McDow and Dr. Eaves in the creation of Southwestern Seminary's PhD in evangelism.

Paige Patterson: Well, you know, that's an interesting story. I think they had already done it. I think I'd love to take credit for it but I believe they had already established PhD work in evangelism.

Beau Brewer: Okay.

Paige Patterson: You'll have check that.

Beau Brewer: I'll check that detail.

Paige Patterson: I'm just pretty sure they had.

Beau Brewer: Okay.

Paige Patterson: Thank you for the compliment. In fairness, I would have to say they were ahead of me on that.

Beau Brewer: Okay. How is the "Chair of Fire" impacted Southern Baptist evangelism through revivals?

Paige Patterson: There's no doubt that it had considerable effect just because it created pastors that had evangelism on their docket. People like my father, who was a PhD graduate, ThD graduate, actually in theology under W. T. Connor, but Dad, of course, was very much impressed by Lee Scarborough. He never actually had a class from him, but he was nevertheless profoundly impressed, as were all students who came to Southwestern.

It led him, for example, to schedule three revivals every year in the churches that he pastored. For example, during the years at First Baptist Beaumont when dad was there for fourteen years and during that fourteen-year period there were three revivals every year. One would always use a vocational evangelist, one would use a notable pastor who was a strong preacher, and the third one would make use of somebody who was perhaps a missionary or some other area like that, professor of evangelism or whatever, and those would come to the church and we would have great revival meetings, which we saw a tremendous number of people come to Christ.

I was personally very much influenced by many of those people. That was where I met Angel Martinez, the Hispanic evangelist from San Antonio, who cut such a swath in those days. He was very influential in my life. I met John Edmond Haggai, who was widely used in those days . . . the fact that I can sit here and enumerate more and more evangelists . . . and pastor Wayne Ward, a professor at Southern Seminary, who happened to be a particularly great expositor of scripture but also a great personal evangelist. Wayne Ward came to our church during that time and preached a revival that I'll never forget. It was Wayne Ward, a professor of theology at Southern Seminary who taught me an enormous amount about doing personal evangelism.

That would be a concrete example of what happened a thousand times all over the nation as a direct result of the emphasis in Southwestern put on evangelism.

Beau Brewer: What do you believe was C. E. Autrey's influence on revivals as the chair?

Paige Patterson: Oh, say it one more time. I'm missing one word.

Beau Brewer: What do you believe was C. E. Autrey's, Dr. Autrey's impact on Southern Baptist evangelism?

Paige Patterson: Well, periodically, of course, over the years it was pretty profound. In the sense that, first of all, you had the influence of C. E. Matthews and others who C. E. Autrey and others who were very much involved in the general revival movement that was spawned there. That took various forms, such as the Baylor revivals that came out of Baylor in the late forties and early fifties.

All that was influenced by Southwestern but it also took other forms, and two of them I would like specifically to mention that might not be mentioned to you. One of the places where you can really see this is in the New Life Movement in Japan.

Beau Brewer: Okay. That was the mid-sixties, correct?

Paige Patterson: Yes. That involved a graduate of the MDiv program, Dub Jackson, who just died just a few months ago, just two or three months ago, and he was a P-38 pilot in World War II and he inflicted so much damage on Japan and killed so many people that he could not get it out of his head. Of course, he had studied in the "Chair of Fire," and while he was here at seminary and he just could not get it out of his head that he was responsible to go back and repair some of this damage he had done to the people who he would win to Christ.

He had Japan on his heart. Dub is a great example in other ways too. He never became all that proficient in the language. He got along fine but he was not what anybody would call a great connoisseur of the Japanese language. As the people would often say to him, "We sometimes didn't know exactly what you were saying, but it was always apparent how much you loved us." I heard more than one say that to him.

He came directly out of the emphasis at Southwestern on evangelism and went to Japan and, of course, as a result of that, he got my father involved in the Japanese New Life Movement because at that time foreign mission work, as it was known, international mission work today, foreign mission work did not accept the importance of partnership evangelism. That is involvement of churches here overseas.

Dr. Baker James Cauthen, who was the head of the International Mission Board at that time, foreign mission board, he did not think anybody but a trained missionary should be involved in mission work. He didn't want the churches to get involved in it.

It was while my dad was serving as a member of that foreign mission board that Dub Jackson came up with this idea and that was also executive secretary of the Baptist General Convention of Texas at that time.

When Dr. Baker James Cauthen refused to have anything to do with it, with the International Mission Board, at first, Dub said to my father, "Dr. Patterson, I don't guess there's any chance that you would be willing to undertake the thing from Texas?" My dad said, "As a matter of fact, there's every chance in the world I'll do it."

He took the Texas Baptist Convention that's from Texas and he became deeply involved in the New Life Movement, and so together with Texas Baptist and eventually the International Mission Board even came onboard and helped us but those were all Texas Baptist pastors out of all of them that were involved in that crusade, which led more than thirty thousand people to Christ altogether and established all kinds of churches all over Japan. That was a movement that grew directly out of the school of evangelism at Southwestern Seminary.

Beau Brewer: Wow. Wow. That is incredible.

Paige Patterson: Yes. No question. That's where it came from. On that, by the way, you want to look at Dub's book if you haven't looked at it already.

Beau Brewer:	I have.
Paige Patterson:	Okay. Good.
Beau Brewer:	Yes, sir.
Paige Patterson:	The second one came about in the same way while we were at . . . . My father was pastor of First Baptist Church in Beaumont, Texas. While he was there he hired a man by the name of . . . I'll tell you in just a second. I'm an old man. Elmin K. Howell. He hired Elmin Howell as an activities director at First Beaumont. We had a really fast-growing church. We had to get a lot of staff. Elmin came on. We loved Elmin.
	Elmin developed interests in the River Ministry, as it was called. That is the ministry for Hispanic development. At that time, there were a number of Hispanic churches in the Texas Baptist Convention, but nowhere close to how many there needed to be because the Spanish population of the state of Texas, especially developing along the river, along the Rio Grande, was humongous, and nobody was doing anything about it.
	Dad became executive secretary and, once again, acting on the impulse from Dr. Carroll and Lee Scarborough, he called Elmin Howell to become the leader of the River Ministry, sponsored by the Baptist General Convention of Texas, which led to the organization of hundreds of churches on either side of the Rio Grande River.
Beau Brewer:	Do you happen to know the dates of that or around what time the River Ministry might have been done?
Paige Patterson:	Let's see. It would be . . . Hang on just one second and I'll figure it out. It would have been in the late sixties and early seventies that it really got going.
Beau Brewer:	Okay.
Paige Patterson:	About 1965, right along there.
Beau Brewer:	Okay.

Paige Patterson: It's pretty well documented in the BGCT annals and so there will be lots of information about it there. That was a direct impact of Lee Scarborough and Carroll and their view of revival evangelism.

Beau Brewer: That's fantastic. I'm like a shark on a blood trail right now. Yes, sir. Talk to me a little bit about Dr. Fish. Of course, Dr. Fish would have been . . . . Well, he would have been your professor had you gone to Southwestern like you had originally planned.

Paige Patterson: Yes. Then as such it's a stark reminder that one's impact does not always have to be in being one's direct professor. Sometimes your impact can be much greater. Roy Fish, when he was called to be the professor of evangelism at Southwestern Seminary, nobody knew that much about him.

He was a pastor in a mission-developing area but he was not that well known. Everybody was a little bit shocked, I think, that he was the choice, because there were other men who were far better known. But two or three things developed with Roy Fish that were most remarkable.

The first thing that developed with him was [that] the general piety of the man was second to none. You know, you could work hard to find something wrong with him. All men are sinners and Roy Fish was no exception to that, but it's a lot easier to talk about it in general terms than specific terms. You've got to try and find what he actually done wrong, it's pretty hard to do. He wasn't boastful about it. He was very humble and very self-deprecating in all his ways. You just came away from a meeting with Roy Fish feeling as though you had just met with one of the twelve disciples of our Lord.

Beau Brewer: Yes.

Paige Patterson: That was the impact he not only had on the seminary but he began to have, that as time went along more and more on people all over the Southern

Baptist Convention. So much so that, of course, evangelism became identified with Roy Fish.

If anybody thought evangelism, especially if you thought of evangelism in the seminary, there were some other fine guys like Louis Drummond at Southern, who was well known and so forth. But everybody . . . . The first thought that would come to everybody's mind would be Roy Fish.

No doubt about the fact that, again . . . . You know, oftentimes evangelists were looked about or looked at as being kind of boastful guys or whatever. Roy was just the opposite of all of that. He was the epitome of humility and yet his impact was profound on Southern Baptists in general.

There was a second thing that was true of Roy that ended up being very profound in its influence and that was he became a historian of revival movements.

Beau Brewer: Yes.

Paige Patterson: Nobody I don't think ever among Southern Baptists was a student of the history of revivalism like Roy Fish was. Well, you already know what happened in the Great Welsh Revival, and you all know who Christmas Evans [was] and you want to know questions like that, there was only one place to come and that was come to Roy Fish. He knew what happened and what had happened and he knew what the excesses were. He never denied those, that there were excesses in almost [every] revival movement.

In fact, he openly talked that there were excesses that had to be overcome at every revival movement, but he said you don't throw out the movement because there are some excesses. You look at what the movement has done overall. It makes a big difference. That was the second thing that was true of him.

The third thing that was true of him is that Roy Fish genuinely loved it when he saw people saved. Now you didn't hear a lot of talk out there about so-and so-loves to witness, loves to talk to people about Jesus and that may be true.

With Roy, he was not very far from an eyeful of tears whenever somebody would come to the Lord. It didn't matter. Might be a boy, might be a nine-year-old boy, might be a ninety-year-old man. When a person came to Christ to Roy Fish it was a miracle. It was every bit as much of a miracle as if he had never walked and was invited to walk and did so. That spirit of the miraculous was quite remarkable.

Beau Brewer: That's beautiful. Yes. I agree. I had Dr. Fish during my MDiv. He had already retired, of course, but he was still teaching adjunctively as the distinguished emeritus professor of evangelism. I had Jesus and Personal Evangelism with him and I'm sorry the second class fails me but I remember distinctly, one prayer time at the beginning of every class and he would just bring a list of people that he was witnessing to continuously and then, secondly, just his . . . I wouldn't say it was an obsession in a bad way but his obsession with the teachings of Christ through the woman at the well. I think he wept and he brought tears to everybody's eyes when he would tell that one and teach about Jesus and the woman at the well. Goodness. It was a remarkable lecture.

Paige Patterson: And when you consider that there is a sense in which evangelism caught, not taught . . .

Beau Brewer: Absolutely.

Paige Patterson: . . . that becomes more important than ever before.

Beau Brewer: Absolutely. Finally, yourself, how do you feel like your time in the chair impacted so in Baptist evangelism through revivals?

Paige Patterson: My particular contribution?

Beau Brewer: Yes, sir.

Paige Patterson: Well, one can only hope, I tried to do my part. I feel like if we asked specifics on where I might have been somewhat blessed of God. At Southeastern Seminary when I was there a man spoke to me one day, his name was John Kuespert. He was an associational missionary in New Hampshire.

He asked to come see me and he came and sat down in my office and he said, "Could I talk to you into being willing to use your students and professors to sponsor a church or two in New Hampshire? We desperately need to plant more churches in New Hampshire."

Well, New Hampshire rang a bell to me because of the New Hampshire Confession of Faith. I thought, "Well, yeah. Good night, we've been greatly blessed by New Hampshire in Southern Baptist Convention, we never paid our debt there and now they need churches." I said, "Well, how many churches are you talking about?" He said, "Is there any possibility you could do two or three?"

Well, now I'm sitting there thinking about L. R. Scarborough. You have to remember that the first book that my father ever had me read once I surrendered to preach, he had me read L. R. Scarborough's *With Christ after the Lost*.

You have to remember that's where I'm coming from. I said to Kuespert, "No. I wouldn't consider that." He said, "Oh, my goodness! You had me so hopeful. Why would you not consider it?" I said, "Well, you're not thinking big enough." I said, "Ask me if I'm willing to plant fifty churches."

Beau Brewer: Oh, praise the Lord.

Paige Patterson: Kuespert just about fainted. He said, "Okay, are you willing to plant fifty churches?" I said, "Yes. If you ask me to come do that, we'll do that." That began the massive church-planting movement, which eventually included most of New England but definitely New Hampshire and Maine.

We didn't make fifty. I'd love to tell you did. We only made forty-two, but we planted forty-two new churches in just a few years' time. You've seen Southeastern Seminary students who graduated and they went up there and started churches, and planted those churches, and saw them grow and it's still going on, still going on now. Mark Ballard went up and planted a church and developed that church there and now is the president of a college that they've started, Northeast Baptist University they're called. Northeast Baptist College. He is the president of that and developing church-planters of his own for New England.

All that came directly out, again, it's not very tangentially related, it's pretty directly related to what Lee Scarborough's influence in my life and others. That would be typical of what we did there. That's not the only case of it but there's several there.

While I was at the Criswell College, we had come to a similar church-planting assignment in Brazil. Eventually, established thirty churches in Brazil. When I came to Southwestern I was looking for a similar opportunity and nothing presented itself immediately because I was rather particular about some unusual things and I didn't want to be bothered with other people who didn't have our same commitment. Could have been considered a little snooty on that but I just don't want to do that.

One day when I wasn't much thinking about anything, I got a call from Tom Eliff, and he was at that time the president of the International Mission Board, and he said, "Paige, we've got this new church-planting movement going among unreached people groups and we're asking churches to take unreached people groups," and he said, "It just occurred to me the other day that if I could get a seminary to take an unreached people group that it would be ideal and it would be a kind of an example to our churches."

He said, "I just thought about you and I'm calling you to see, would Southwestern take an unreached people group?" I said, "No." Tom went blank for a few seconds. He said, "Excuse me. You've never said no to me before." He said, "I'm not sure how to take it."

Beau Brewer: I'm not either.

Paige Patterson: He said, "Why did you say no?" I said, "Because you won't do what I want you to do." He said, "Well, how do you know? Why don't you try me out? What is it that you want?" I said, "Well, I want you to give me an unreached people group of at least a million people. I want them to be in impossible-to-reach places where you can't get there from here. I want there to be no known Christians in the group at all. I want you to promise me that you will not put a missionary from the International Mission Board there."

There was a long pause. He said, "All right, Paige." First of all, he says, "I'm curious about one thing. Do you just not like our missionaries?" I said, "Oh, no, Tom. I love your missionaries. I do all I can to support them. I'm a faithfull giver to the Lottie Moon Christmas Offering and all that." I said, "I want to do that." I said, "Let me just say to you that you all got so many layers of bureaucracy that I don't want to fool with all that. I want to be free just to take off in a pioneer-type situation and do what has to be done." I said, "The day will come when I will be happy to have your missionaries but you've got to promise me that you won't do that until I give you the word."

He said, "Let me get back to you." Two or three weeks went by and he called me again and he said, "Okay. I got your group." I said, "What is it?" He said, "It's the Antandroy people of Southern Madagascar." He said, "There are almost exactly a million of them." He said, "There is no known Christian in the group at all." He said, "They are difficult to get to. They're called 'the people of the thorn' because you can't go any place without getting into thorns." He said, "They're just very difficult." He said, "Oddly enough, I'm going to make the deal with you, I will not put a missionary there like you said." I said, "Fine. We'll take them."

I don't know that you were there but I went to the student body with it about three weeks later and I put a map of Madagascar up on the screen and told them about the Antandroy people. I said, "We're going to take those people from Christ and we're going to go there and it all depends on us. If we fail then they fail to know Christ. It's up to us. We've got to do it."

I said, "I want every physically able–bodied man in the house who is willing to do that, stand up if you're willing to go to Madagascar, if God gives you an opportunity to go, you're willing to go. Stand up." We had about thirty-five, forty stand up. I said, "I'm waiting for the rest of you." I just waited until finally I had every man in there standing.

Beau Brewer: I do remember that, sir. I was one of the first ones standing, but I worked in Dr. Eitel's office when I was employed by the seminary. I was semi-privy to some of the behind-the-scene conversations between your office and his at the time and so, of course, it was very exciting times for the seminary. It was incredible because, as you said, you were the "Chair of Fire" at the time and you were using both roles, the chair and the influence of the office of the president, to push in such a mighty way.

Of course, you also did some localized evangelism there around the campus. Would you talk a little bit about no soul left behind and reaching the seminary hill mile and those campaigns?

Paige Patterson: Yes. We did thos, too. We, of course, came up with a slogan that everybody within a mile of the seminary would have an evangelistic opportunity and set out to do that. Took us a couple of years to actually get that done but we set out to see to it that the gospel was presented in every home.

That really got to be a lot of fun because I had some theological professors that I'm ashamed to admit to you never witnessed to anybody and they got into it and one of them, I won't give you his name because I don't want to . . . you may have had him. I couldn't find him. He was a guy that never witnessed. Everybody knew he didn't.

I couldn't find the guy anywhere. I was looking for him for over a week and I couldn't find him. I said, "Will somebody please tell me where this man is?" Some of the faculty members knew, they said, "Well, sir. He's led a man to the Lord over here just a couple blocks from school. He has ended up discipling him and he's there all the time on the front porch out there sitting there and discipling that man. He's got a whole group of people now that he's in the process of bringing to the Lord." I was an Old Testament professor. I thought that was remarkable.

We had a lot of experiences like that in that experience and we also got involved. One of the most interesting things we did was, there is an association out west of town out here called the Cross Timbers Association. You may be familiar with it.

Beau Brewer: Yes, sir.

Paige Patterson: It refers to a formation of trees that grow down to there and those churches and me were having a meeting and they were saying to us that there was so many churches out here that were not baptizing anybody in a year. You know? It occurred to me, well, look, those churches want to baptize people. How about letting me send a student out to each of those churches and the Cross Timbers Association and let's enter into an agreement that we're going to have an emphasis on witnessing in the area with our students going out and one of your people with one of my students and we'll put them out there witnessing and see if we can't win some people for Christ.

Well, they ended up having me preach for them and that kind of thing but they did that, they got into a witnessing program and we started a witnessing program out at Cross Timbers and saw a number of those churches that had baptized next to nobody, in some cases, nobody, for years actually reach people for Christ and have baptisms.

Beau Brewer: It was exciting times. Yes, sir. Not to take too much more of your time, but I would like to back up just a little bit to your time as president of Southeastern Baptist Theological Seminary in Wake Forest, North Carolina.

As I believe I have read, you were instrumental in the creation and the funding and the fundraising of the Bailey Smith Chair of Evangelism. Were you not?

Paige Patterson: Yes. That's true.

Beau Brewer: Okay. Would you tell me a little bit about this decision and the event that led up to the inauguration of this chair? Can you give me some of the dates of its inauguration and just who you selected and how they were selected and what are their tenets?

Paige Patterson: Let me plead Fifth Amendment on the dates. What I'll have to do is I've got it all but I just didn't happen to have it out here in front of me. I'll have to call you back on that.

Beau Brewer: That'll be fine.

Paige Patterson: I'll do so and I'll send it to you in email or something.

Beau Brewer: That would be wonderful.

Paige Patterson: I'll get that back to you. Here's what happened on it. This was another one of my crazy deals that I did. Keith Eitel, who you know, of course . . .

Beau Brewer: Yes, sir.

Paige Patterson: . . . was there and he had the idea of starting what became known as the Two Plus Two program. You're familiar with that.

Beau Brewer: I am familiar with that.

Paige Patterson: I told Keith, I said, "Well, you know, go see the foreign mission board, the International Mission Board, and see if they'll cooperate with you." He went to see them and they said, "No, we're not going to do that. That's crazy." He came back and he told me, "They won't do it. They said it's crazy." I said, "Well, okay. We'll do it on our own." You know?

We started doing it on our own. Then they had second thoughts about it and they called us back and they said, "Yup. We'll work with you on that." We started working with them and we put these kids out all over the world doing what would be their third and last year of the MDiv program but, of course, now they had four years and two years out on the field.

Toward the end of that first year on the field, I realized that we had a significant problem out there. Here was the problem: the problem was that these kids were isolated, I liked that, they were all by their lonesome in most cases, and they were up against it and they were very, very young, too. Some did great and I'm certainly grateful for that, but there were also some that were having a hard time. I knew that.

Bailey and I had a mutual friend. His name was Richard Headrick. By the way, it wouldn't be a bad idea to schedule a telephone call and talk to Richard. First of all, you'd get a big kick out of him. He is funny as he can be. Second, he would love to tell you about the story from his angle.

I was with Richard one night for supper. Richard is a wealthy man. He has Headrick Sign Company. They do billboards and signs all over the South. He's out of Mississippi. He looks like a total gun runner to South America. That's only because he was. He was a gun runner and a drug runner. Funny guy in a way because he grew up in a Christian home and so consequently his father had a very strong influence on him and Richard didn't drink and he didn't do drugs himself but boy's big time into it. Matter of fact, he lived through three airplane crashes. How many people do you know that ever lived through one airplane crash?

Beau Brewer: Not many.

Paige Patterson: He lived through three. He's living there and he is cognizant of the fact that he's lost as he can be but God must have some reason to keep him alive because he's lived through three airplane crashes and all kinds of gun wars and everything else in South America.

In short, he's my kind of guy. I hate to admit it, but he is. He's a man's man. We hit it off. Bailey introduced me to him because Bailey was the one that was preaching the night that Richard got saved. Richard had come to the Lord. He was rough as a cop but he had come to the Lord.

I said to Richard, I said, "Richard, I have an assignment for you." He said, "Well, what's that?" I said, "I want you to come on staff at the seminary, you and your wife, and at your expense, because I don't have any money for it, I want you to travel. Every year, I want you to go and visit every one of our kids that is a missionary in the Two Plus Two program."

I said, "Here's what I want you and your wife to do. I want you to go see them and I want you to go into the hardest places in the world, which is where they are. You're going to go into places that the State Department tells America not to go. You're going there and you're going to take them to a hotel or someplace nice to eat because most of them haven't had a good meal since they got there.

You're going to visit with them and stay with them for about a week and see what they're doing and then when you come back you're going to write me a report. I want a report on every one of them." His reports are amazing things to be seen. Truth of the matter is they ought to be in your dissertation. Totally unique. I have a couple of Richard's reports.

Beau Brewer: Do you have permission to share?

Paige Patterson: Huh?

Beau Brewer: Do you have permission to share those reports?

Paige Patterson: Yeah. I think I can get it, anyway. I think he'd let us. He's a pretty open guy. We can try, that's for sure. He would tell me . . . . He was better at this than I ever dreamed he would be. Nobody ever had any idea he'd do what he did. Truth of the matter is he could go anyplace in the world. He looked like such a bum. He looked like a . . . First of all, she was beautiful. She was gorgeous. He looked like a total bum. He could walk through security lines anywhere. I think he could have walked through carrying a weapon, carrying an AK-47, and they would have said "fine." I think they just looked at him and thought, "He's one of us."

He'd go through the security line and get in there. He'd look at those kids and they would come back and he would write me and he would say one of three things. He would say, one, "This kid has it made. He knows exactly what he's doing. He's doing X, Y, Z. He has it figured out. He's going to do fine. The work here, he can adjust to anything."

Or he would come back and he would write, "You need to look into this guy a little bit. We've got to put some extra help with him. He can make it but he's going to have to have a little extra help along the way. He's going to have to have some encouragement because he's really discouraged."

Or, in a few cases, he would write me and tell me, "This person is not going to make it." I want to tell you, he was unbelievably accurate. Everyone he said wouldn't make it, didn't make it. Everybody else did. He was so accurate in his judgment about his kids and he loved them so much and did so much to help.

Well, that came about as a result of combining the mission program, the Two Plus Two program, with intense evangelism and, again, can relate in some ways to Lee Scarborough, and the development of the "Chair of Fire." That was our major program of overseas evangelism at Southeastern.

Beau Brewer:	Who did you select to be the first Bailey Smith Chair of Evangelism?
Paige Patterson:	Oh, yeah. Sorry. I was going to tell you about that.
Beau Brewer:	It's okay.
Paige Patterson:	That's where I was going with it and forgot.
Beau Brewer:	That's okay.
Paige Patterson:	He becomes involved in that. Then one day I was sitting and made a deal with him and I said, "You know what? You came to Christ under Bailey Smith," and he said, "Yes, I did." He may tell you a funny story about that. I don't know. I hope he does. It's hysterical.

He came to the Lord under Bailey Smith. I said to him, I said, "You know, all these years of Bailey Smith doing this winning people to the Lord, like you, nobody has ever said anything to Bailey to thank him for it and to recognize the gravity of what he has done." I said, "I'm going to tell you what I want you to do." I said, "I need a million-dollar gift to the Southeastern Seminary and we're going to establish the Bailey Smith Chair of Evangelism."

My pattern, of course, you guessed it—

Beau Brewer: Was the "Chair of Fire."

Paige Patterson: Of course. He said, "You want me to give a million dollars?" I said, "Yup. That's what it takes to endow a chair." I said, "I know you can do it. I want you to pray about it and see what God says." He says, "Well, Paige, we've been through a down-time financially and there's just no way I can do it." I said, "Well, fine. I understand that. Can't help down times," I said, "You just pray about it."

He went home and he prayed about it and in a couple of weeks he called me back and said, "All right. You've got your million dollars." He endowed the Bailey Smith chair out of appreciation for Bailey bringing him to the Lord. That became the Bailey Smith Chair of Evangelism there.

Beau Brewer: Who was installed as the inaugural occupant?

Paige Patterson: You know, I'll have to go back and look, but I'm pretty sure I'm right about who it is and it's a sad story from there on but I'm pretty sure that the first occupant of that chair was a young man who did his training here under Roy Fish and who was a great personal soul winner but, unfortunately, had a moral lapse and was involved in multiple affairs and so he, of course, is no longer teaching at all.

Beau Brewer: I know who you're talking about, Dr. Alvin Reid.

Paige Patterson: Alvin Reid.

Beau Brewer:	I'm sorry to hear that. Yes. I agree. He was a very gifted personal evangelist.
Paige Patterson:	He was.
Beau Brewer:	He was a very gifted professor too.
Paige Patterson:	Yes.
Beau Brewer:	Very sad indeed. In fact, he was Dr. Matt Queen's supervisor, I believe.
Paige Patterson:	Yes, he was.
Beau Brewer:	Yes. That is tragic. Well, Dr. Patterson, thank you so very much for spending an hour and fifteen minutes with me and really talking to me about some of this and to give me about three or four really good leads on some information that I need to research.
Paige Patterson:	Well, I'm just grateful you're doing it. That's good. I will check these dates on two or three of these things that you mentioned and try to get those to you.
Beau Brewer:	Wonderful. If I can, I will email you in a few minutes and request Mr. Headrick's personal information, if you have it. Even an email would be just fine.
Paige Patterson:	I do. He is fighting cancer now.
Beau Brewer:	Oh, okay.
Paige Patterson:	He's my age. He's seventy-seven. Where I'm going to give you to call him, he's down at his place in Florida right now and he would be super glad to talk to you. I'll run interference for you there and tell him what's going on.
Beau Brewer:	That would be wonderful.
Paige Patterson:	He'll be happy to talk with you. Like I say, you will be entertained and blessed.
Beau Brewer:	I can't wait. I would love to talk more about those files and his reports to you if you can find me a couple of really great ones. That'd be terrific.
Paige Patterson:	I'll be happy to do that.

Beau Brewer: Thank you so much, Dr. Patterson. I pray you have a blessed day.

Paige Patterson: Thank you, Beau. Have a good one yourself.

Beau Brewer: All right. Thank you. Have a good day, sir. Bye bye.

Paige Patterson: Bye bye.

APPENDIX 16

EMAIL CORRESPONDENCE WITH REBEKAH PHILLIPS, JUNE 16–17, 2020

From: Beau Brewer
Sent: Friday, May 22, 2020, 2:02 p.m.
To: library@nobts.edu
Subject: Dissertation Research Questions

To whom it may concern:

My name is Beau Brewer. I am presently doing research for my dissertation at Southwestern Seminary and would appreciate some help. I am searching for a listing of every occupant of the Roland Q. Leavell Chair of Evangelism at New Orleans Baptist Theological Seminary. Presently, Dr. Preston Nix occupies this chair, but I am looking for a roster with dates served in the chair. Do you have any such list, possibly in your library archives? Thank you for your time and consideration.

In Christ,

Beau K. Brewer

From: Rebekah Phillips
Sent: Tuesday, June 16, 2020, 3:58 p.m.
To: Brewer, Beau
Subject: Dissertation Research Questions

Beau,

Thank you for your patience. I'm sorry it's taken me so long to get this information to you. I looked through our archived catalogs and campus directories to see who was listed as the Roland Q. Leavell Chair of Evangelism each year. Below is what I found.

1965/66 school year
B. Gray Allison is listed as the "Professor of Evangelism" in the campus bulletin (catalog), but there is no mention of the "Roland Q. Leavell Chair." I think you already have this information but wanted to mention it again—An 8/12/66 *Baptist Press* article (attached) mentions that he was the first person to occupy the Roland Q. Leavell Chair of Evangelism, and that he had the position until he resigned earlier in the 1966 year to take a position at the Home Mission Board.

1966/67 school year–1973/74 school year
Eugene N. Patterson is listed as the "Professor of Evangelism" in the campus bulletin (catalog) but there is no mention of the "Roland Q. Leavell Chair." The same 8/12/66 *Baptist Press* article explains that he is the second person to occupy the chair and he began the position on 9/1/66.

1974/75 school year–1979/80 school year
None—No one is listed as professor of evangelism in campus catalogs.

1980/81 school year–1982/83 school year
Robert L. Hamblin is listed as the "Associate Professor of Evangelism" but there is no mention of the Roland Q. Leavell Chair.

1983/84 school year–1987/88 school year
C. Cecil Randall is listed as the Roland Q. Leavell Chair of Evangelism.

1988/89 school year
None—No one is listed as the professor of evangelism or as occupying the chair.

1989/90 school year–1995/96 school year
Charles S. Kelley is listed as occupying the Roland Q. Leavell Chair of Evangelism.

1996/97 school year–1999/2000 school year
Charles L. Register is listed as occupying the Roland Q. Leavell Chair of Evangelism.

2000/01 school year–2002/03 school year
James Cogdill is listed as occupying the Roland Q. Leavell Chair of Evangelism.

2003/04 school year
None—No one is listed as the professor of evangelism or as occupying the chair.

2004/05 school year–2006/07 school year
David Meacham is listed as occupying the Roland Q. Leavell Chair of Evangelism. *****The library is missing a copy of the 2005 catalog, so I can't verify that Meacham was the chair during that year, but since he's listed the year prior and the year after, I think it's a safe assumption.

2007/08 school year
None—No one is listed as the professor of evangelism or as occupying the chair.

We do not have any catalogs or directories after the 2007 school year, which makes me wonder if this is the year that both began to be published online and not in print. I hope this is helpful!

Rebekah Phillips, MLIS
Circulation Librarian
John T. Christian Library
New Orleans Baptist Theological Seminary

From: Rebekah Phillips
Sent: Wednesday, June 17, 2020, 3:32 p.m.
To: Brewer, Beau
Subject: Dissertation Research Questions

Beau,

My coworker Kyara St. Amant reminded me that we have additional archived catalogs so I was able to find more info today! Please update your list with the info below:

2004/05 school year–2007/08 school year
David Meacham is listed as occupying the Roland Q. Leavell Chair of Evangelism. *****I previously stated that we were missing our 2005 catalog copy and that no one was listed for the 2007 school year (in the pictorial directory) but I found our 2005 and 2007 onward catalog copies. David Meacham is listed in both the 2005/06 and 2007/08 catalogs as the Leavell Chair of Evangelism.

2008/09 school year
None—No one is listed as the professor of evangelism or as occupying the chair.

2009/10–present
Preston Nix is listed as occupying the Roland Q. Leavell Chair of Evangelism.

Rebekah Phillips, MLIS
Circulation Librarian
John T. Christian Library
New Orleans Baptist Theological Seminary

From: Brewer, Beau
Sent: Wednesday, June 24, 2020, 10:40 a.m.
To: Rebekah Phillips
Subject: Dissertation Research Questions

Ms. Phillips,

I am hoping that you can track down a couple more professors for me with ease.

- Who held the Max and Bonnie Thornhill Chair of Evangelism from 1993–2001, when Will McRaney was installed into the chair?
- Who held the Thomas Gurney Chair of Evangelism and Church Health from 1997–2007?

These are important details to the overall final product of my research. Please try and get this back to me ASAP as I am trying to complete my dissertation in the next few days.

Thank you for your assistance. Please confirm that you have received this email and if you have any further questions, please do not hesitate to contact me.

With Christ, after the Lost,

Beau K. Brewer

From: Phillips, Rebekah
Sent: Wednesday, June 24, 2020, 3:08 p.m.
To: Beau Brewer
Subject: Dissertation Research Questions

Beau,

It's no trouble at all! I'm glad someone is doing the research and happy to be a small part of it. Below is what I found; let me know if there's anything else I can help with.

Bekah

Max and Bonnie Thornhill Chair of Evangelism
93/94 school year
none listed
94/95 to 97/98 school year
Robert L. Hamblin
98/99 school year
none listed

99/00 to at least the 01/02 school year (I did not check past this year)
Will McRaney (sometimes listed as Will H. McRaney Jr. or Will H. McRaney)

Thomas Gurney Chair of Evangelism and Church Health
97/98 school year
none listed
98/99 to 99/00 school year
Randall C. Millwood
00/01 school year
none listed
01/02 to at least the 07/08 school year (I did not check past this year)
William H. Day Jr.

Rebekah Phillips, MLIS
Circulation Librarian
John T. Christian Library
New Orleans Baptist Theological Seminary

APPENDIX 17

EMAIL CORRESPONDENCE WITH BRENT S. RAY, MAY 13, 2020

From: Beau Brewer
Sent: Wednesday, May 13, 2020, 1:05 p.m.
To: Ray, Brent
Subject: RTN Information for Dissertation

Dr. Ray,

The Spring Break Revival program is still called "Revive This Nation," correct? Just double-checking my facts. Thank you.
Blessings,
Beau K. Brewer

From: Brent Ray
Sent: Wednesday, May 13, 2020, 4:14 p.m.
To: Brewer, Beau
Subject: RTN Information for Dissertation

Beau—As of this fall it is "*Reach* This Nation" and no longer "Revive" in order to broaden the focus from conducting spring revival services to carrying out all forms of evangelism and church revitalization efforts. This change in nomenclature also gives us the opportunity to engage SWBTS women in RTN ministry, given that the focus is broader than just preaching.

Brent S. Ray
Director | World Missions Center
Adjunct Professor of Missions | Roy Fish School of Evangelism & Missions

APPENDIX 18

EMAIL RESPONSES FROM
GEORGE G. ROBINSON IV, MAY 18, 2020

1. Researching your academic career, please list your degrees, institutions, and years of service to Southeastern Seminary. Give me the specific date that you were installed as the occupant of the Bailey Smith Chair of Evangelism.

   - See https://www.sebts.edu/academics/faculty/Robinson,-G.,-CV_2020.pdf 2

2. Would you please articulate your philosophy of Evangelism?

   - I am convinced that the gospel is the only hope for sinful humanity to be reconciled to our Holy God. God initiated the rescue plan, making a promise in the garden in Genesis 3:15 that would not only reconcile humanity, but restore all of creation. That promise made by God was kept and the rescue plan brought to its climax in the God-man, Jesus Christ. He came to rescue sinners, and through his sacrificial and atoning death, did all that was necessary to make the only way to be reconciled to the Father. He commissioned all who follow him in repentance and faith to be fishers of men (Matt 4:19). This means that a verbal proclamation of the gospel of Jesus is indispensable to the fulfillment of the mission of God. As new creations in Christ, all believers are to live as ambassadors for Christ, having been entrusted with the ministry of reconciliation (2 Cor 5:17–21). And God has given the church the gift of the evangelist, who not only personally proclaims that message, but is to equip the church for the work of the ministry (Eph 4:11–16). Therefore, my philosophy of evangelism is that God has uniquely gifted some to serve the church so that all may joyfully participate in the sacred task of bearing witness to Christ among our neighbors and the nations until Jesus returns and makes all things new.

3. What are some of the responsibilities of occupying the Bailey Smith Chair of Evangelism, or do you believe that each occupant defines the role of the chair?

- The original anticipated impact of the Bailey Smith Chair of Evangelism was that "Three thousand God-called men" would be trained in ten years. The initial hope was that "in just one year these three thousand could share the gospel with at least three hundred thousand lost souls." Since the inception of the chair in September of 1994, far more than three thousand men (and women) have been equipped through evangelism training and events led by its occupants. Each semester, as many as 250 Southeastern Baptist Theological Seminary students have been equipped and required to share the gospel through personal evangelism with a minimum of ten people who are far from God. Conservatively speaking, in the roughly fifty semesters since the chair's endowment, some ten thousand students have gone through that one-semester training, sharing the gospel with more than a hundred thousand people during the single semester of training. Those students are now serving churches and on the mission field the world over multiplying the number impacted exponentially. Given the fact that "the mission of Southeastern Seminary is to glorify the Lord Jesus Christ by equipping students to serve the church and fulfill the Great Commission," countless church members have been equipped and mobilized to evangelize, having never set foot on our campus or met the professors who have occupied this prestigious chair. Add to that the countless evangelistic/revival services led by those influenced, and there is no doubt that Dr. Smith's vision was met and surpassed even prior to his entering the presence of Jesus in January of 2019.

- During the 1994 service in which Smith preached, he passionately spoke on the importance of the Christian call to share the gospel to everyone, no matter their background, emphasizing the heartbeat of the Great Commission focus of SEBTS. Noting Jesus' love for all people, Smith said, "There is only one kind of person in the world: those for whom Jesus shed his precious blood—red, yellow, black, white, rich, poor, illiterate and educated," said Smith, who was quoted in a 1994 *Baptist Press* article reporting on the dedication service. I am convinced that the chair named in Dr. Smith's honor has and continues to cultivate passion for all kinds of people everywhere.

4. Can you discuss any connection between the Bailey Smith Chair of Evangelism at Southeastern Seminary and the L. R. Scarborough Chair of Evangelism, the "Chair of Fire," at Southwestern Seminary?

   - As for the historical connection, there is no doubt that Bailey Smith was influenced by the evangelistic fervor he encountered in his training at SWBTS working toward his BD degree since Dr. Fish had recently joined faculty in 1965.

   - Dr. Scarborough's legacy as the first to occupy an academic chair in an SBC seminary coupled with his impassioned evangelistic zeal has had an inestimable influence on the development of Southern Baptists' focus on evangelism and missions.

   - Though I'm not privy to any details linking the two chairs beyond the influence of Scarborough to Fish to Smith, I do know that Dr. Matt Queen, the current occupant of the "Chair of Fire," and I, the current occupant of the Bailey Smith Chair, studied together at SEBTS in the late nineties, both being influenced by the then-occupant, Dr. Alvin Reid. Though Dr. Queen and I serve in different locations; it has been evident through the years that our mutual passion to equip students and churches to reach the lost is grounded in that influence from our seminary days together.

5. Can you briefly articulate the impact of Richard Headrick on the Bailey Smith Chair of Evangelism?

- This is an interesting question because I occupied the Richard and Gina Headrick Chair of World Missions at SEBTS from 2011 until 2019, when I moved into the Bailey Smith Chair of Evangelism. Richard Headrick had a profound influence on me dating back to my days as a student at SEBTS when he helped fund our Two Plus Two International Church Planting student expenses. He and Gina even visited my wife and me when we were serving with the IMB in South Asia. We have remained in touch through the years in various ways. Richard led a weekend evangelistic/missions-focused service at a church where I was associate pastor in Georgia in 2002. Then he partnered financially with my evangelism/missions ministry with e3 Partners Ministries. And most recently, I have participated with his Hell-fighters Biker Ministry, leading evangelism training and outreach in both Sturgis (2018) and Daytona (2020). In early March I sat with Richard and Gina at Daytona Bike Week at their Hell-fighters tent discussing evangelism training and the hope of the gospel. In God's providence, I was able to share the gospel with a biker that day and lead him in a prayer of repentance and faith in Jesus. Richard and I prayed over the young man and I continued to follow up with him and offer help with his early discipleship.

- As far as the Headricks' relationship to the Bailey Smith Chair of Evangelism, I'm not sure. I do know that Richard was deeply influenced by Bailey's passion for evangelism. And I believe, though I'm not positive, he mentioned serving on Dr. Smith's board at one time. Regardless, Richard Headrick is certainly another person whose path was shaped and evangelism refined through his relationship with Dr. Smith.

6. How has the Bailey Smith Chair of Evangelism impacted Southern Baptist Evangelism through theological education?

- Alvin Reid—you will have to look at Dr. Reid's books for the answer to this question. One that you may find helpful was edited by your doctoral mentor, Dr. Matt Queen. I contributed a chapter in that book that provided some idea of Dr. Reid's influence on my ministry.

- Yourself—since I'm relatively new to the chair, I'm not sure I could answer this with much detail yet. I can say that looking back over the past twenty-nine years of walking with the Lord and engaging in evangelism, both personally and in church services and youth camps, that I have grown in my broad SBC impact most directly through helping develop evangelistic resources such as "The Story" (see www.yourpartinthestory.com) and related resources. I serve as a consultant with Spread Truth Ministries on the development of their evangelism/disciple-making resources, many of which have been adopted/used widely in SBC churches. I would have to say that the depth of impact is rooted in my investment in equipping, coaching, and mentoring my students at SEBTS. Their accomplishments in evangelism dot the landscape of the SBC (Josh Reed as the senior consultant for evangelism at the Baptist State Convention of NC, Jon Reed who is a vocational evangelist in Georgia, and numerous missionaries serving with NAMB, IMB around the world).

7. Please give me any information about the creation and endowment of the Bailey Smith Chair of Evangelism at Southeastern Baptist Theological Seminary in Wake Forest, North Carolina. Would you tell me about this decision and this event? What is the date of its inauguration? Who was the selected as the inaugural occupant of this chair? What are the tenets of this academic chair?

  - I will gladly put you in touch with Jonathan Six (jsix@sebts.edu) who can give you much of this information from his office records. I do know that the primary donor for the chair asked to remain anonymous. The stated objectives for the chair when initially proposed were as follows:

    - To underwrite the salary of a professor for the Bailey Smith Chair of Evangelism
    - To provide administrative support
    - To provide funds for research in the essential area of evangelism

- To provide the necessary resources for the professor to participate in evangelism conferences and crusades at the local, national, and international levels

- To provide financial resources for evangelism conferences and workshops on the campus of Southeastern Seminary

- The Bailey Smith Chair of Evangelism was dedicated in the September 6, 1994, chapel service at Southeastern Seminary with Dr. Bailey Smith preaching the service and his son, Steve Smith (a student at the time), giving the invocation. To my knowledge, Dr. Alvin Reid was the first to be installed into the chair after he joined faculty in 1995.

8. Any further information that you would add to this interview with regard to the Bailey Smith Chair of Evangelism and the "Chair of Fire."

- My own spiritual journey features several encounters with Dr. Bailey Smith. The first was when he preached a Starlight Crusade revival service at the church I eventually came to faith at Hebron Baptist Church in Dacula, GA. The second encounter came years later, when my dear friend and vocational evangelist, Jon Reed, was serving as interim pastor at First Baptist Church of Buford, GA. Jon invited Dr. Smith to preach at their tent revival and I was able to spend the evening with him both before and after the service. On both occasions Dr. Smith left a deep impression on me of his love for the gospel and for the lost. I hope that when I preach, train, or interact with people in my ministry that they will be able to say the same of me.

Appendix 19

Personal Interview With
Sandy L. Smith, May 28, 2020

This is a complete and accurate transcript of the oral history interview of Sandy L. Smith by Beau Brewer over the phone. No spoken words which were recorded were omitted, except for any non-English phrases which could not be understood by the transcriber. This is a transcript of spoken English, which of course follows a different rhythm and rule than written English. In very few cases, words were too unclear to be distinguished. In these cases, [unclear] or [?] was inserted. Both interviewee and interviewer would interject "Uh hmm" or "Uh huh" frequently, but these were not transcribed unless they came at a definite break in the conversation. In some sections of the tape, the microphone was apparently frequently bumped and every occasion of this has not been noted.

. . . Three dots indicate an interruption or break in the train of thought within the sentence of the speaker.

. . . . Four dots indicate what the transcriber believes to be the end of an incomplete sentence.

( ) Words in parentheses are asides made by the speaker.

[ ] Words in brackets are comments made by the transcriber.

This transcription was made by Rev.com Transcription Services and was completed in May 2020.

Beau Brewer:	This is Beau Brewer. I am a PhD candidate at Southwestern Baptist Theological Seminary in Fort Worth, Texas. I'm in a live telephone interview with Mrs. Sandy Smith, the wife of Dr. Bailey Smith, whom the chair of evangelism at Southeastern

Baptist Theological Seminary in Wake Forest, North Carolina, is named after.

Mrs. Smith joins us from her home. And today is May 28, 2020. And, Mrs. Smith, thank you for joining me today.

Sandy Smith: You are so welcome. I am looking forward to it.

Beau Brewer: Well, I hope so. So, can you talk about your husband's evangelism? What was his career like?

Sandy Smith: Well, Bailey pastored for, I think, maybe thirty or forty years before he ever went into evangelism, and he was always very intentional about bringing people to the Lord. And that was just such an important thing to him from the beginning of his ministry. But, he had, I think, his philosophy would have been, everyone is lost until we know by their explanation that they are not. And never assume that somebody is saved. And so I think with that in mind, that is why he spent hours and hours and hours, all day, every Saturday and days of the week, while he was a pastor, to go to people's homes and talk to them about Jesus.

From the very beginning of our marriage, he would spend all day Saturdays and many other days, much of the day, just going visiting. And the purpose of that was to find people that did not know Jesus. So, he was pretty single-minded about that for his entire ministry. And it became evident I think, I cannot remember exactly when, maybe 1985. He was really struggling about whether or not to leave the First Southern Baptist Church in Del City, Oklahoma, which was the second largest, at that time, Southern Baptist church in the Convention and the largest church of any kind in Oklahoma. And we loved being there. We loved the people. The ministry was flourishing, and John Bisagno had started something that we continued every summer, which was called Starlight Crusade.

And the Starlight Crusades were just that. They would just bring people to Jesus. And they just loved those, the whole church, the whole city just loved those. People would come and fill up the football stadium and Bailey would preach his heart out. And I think one summer we had around two thousand people come to the Lord during the Starlight. We continued it for an extra week. So, in those three weeks we had, I think, close to two thousand people who came to the Lord.

Beau Brewer: Praise the Lord.

Sandy Smith: Oh, it was wonderful.

Beau Brewer: No kidding.

Sandy Smith: The Starlight Crusades, I think, were very instrumental in helping Bailey make the decision to go into evangelism. Because, even though we loved where we were, there was nothing that we did not love about it. He just felt so called to evangelism. And it was very difficult, I will just say selfishly from my side, my mother, who was just an absolutely incredible mother, passed away, and in 1985 Bailey resigned our church two weeks later. That was really difficult for me.

Beau Brewer: Oh, I bet.

Sandy Smith: Because, when you are not the pastor's wife, in some senses, you lose your ministry. You are not doing the same things that you used to. And even though the pastor that came after Bailey is my brother and Tom Eliff, and he had a wonderful ministry there, but it is still different. As the pastor's wife, you are not . . . it is just different situation.

And so when we finally moved from there to Atlanta, because this was better for an evangelist to live by a major airport, when we moved here, it was really lonely for me. And Bailey would be gone on the weekends. I had a child still at home and I was not going to leave him all the time. And it took a few years. I cannot remember exactly when we started our women's ministry, but God gave us a wonderful opportunity to minister to women for many, many years, all over the Southeast and down the East Coast. And it was a blessing for me, but Bailey was in his element.

He was doing exactly what God had called him to do. And there could be no doubt of that. So, it was absolutely the best choice that he could have met.

Beau Brewer: Well, Mrs. Smith, what was the name of your women's ministry?

Sandy Smith: Balancing the Demands of Life.

Beau Brewer: Balancing the Demands of Life. And I'm assuming you led that ministry?

Sandy Smith: Yes, I did. And I had someone to help me with the leg work and the organization part, but we were very much in agreement that we were not going to do fluffy things. This was a time of fellowship, a time for women to examine their hearts. A time where they could bear their hearts and be heard. And we purposed that we would not allow that our retreats to become larger than the size of twelve hundred. Now, I think we had a retreat once that was sixteen hundred because we couldn't come back and do it the next week. But, most of the times, even though in the place where we started here at Georgia at Telway Gardens, we had back-to-back retreats for many years.

Beau Brewer: How wonderful. And so this is a ministry you help for a number of years, correct?

Sandy Smith: Yes.

Beau Brewer: Are you still participating in this ministry or have you handed it off to someone else?

Sandy Smith: I am not participating in it. And there came a time, which I struggled with it for two or three years before that, because I did not want to stop those retreats, but I went to this retreat, the first retreat of the year, and I am sorry, I cannot tell you what year it was. And with this still in the back of my mind, but with no intention to calling them to a close. And I knew once I got there, I knew this was the time. And so I said, "I hope that this will, and I pray that this will not be the end of the retreats, but that you have learned and have grown in so many ways throughout all these years that you will have your own retreats and carry the ministry on through your own churches."

I think the fact that we were focused on Christian fellowship. We only had one and all those years in a church and that was in Virginia. We always tried to get the women out of town, so they wouldn't go home at night, so they could just be away with their friends and share their hearts. And we laughed a lot. We had excellent speakers, excellent speakers. And we always focused on several topics. Basically, the same topics for every year we ever had. We had on Bible study and prayer. We had seminars on marriage. We had seminars on raising your children.

Beau Brewer:	I'm assuming that your husband was, was a behind the scenes support and stay to this ministry for you?
Sandy Smith:	Yes, absolutely. And we remained a part of the base of his ministry.
Beau Brewer:	Oh, sure.
Sandy Smith:	So we were not a separate entity. We were a part of the ministry.
Beau Brewer:	Sure. I think that partnership is neat. I'm trying to establish that for you. So, can you talk about . . . did your husband have a favorite sermon and a favorite passage that he used?
Sandy Smith:	I would say that Bailey's . . . how do you say that? Do you call it the sugar stick?
Beau Brewer:	Yes.

Sandy Smith: I think the message that got more results through the years for salvations was "Wheat and Tares." And that was a message that he preached every crusade. And it is one that he developed while he was bridging the Starlight Crusades in Oklahoma, where we preached as pastor. And through the years, I cannot even tell you how many thousands of people came to the Lord through that sermon. And so that was really, I would say, it was everybody's favorite.

Beau Brewer: Well, how many years did he actually preach as an itinerant evangelist?

Sandy Smith: I am thinking that he started in 1982 or '83. I'm not quite sure. Oh, I think, yeah, at least '82. And for a while we still lived in Oklahoma City for a few years and then we moved to Atlanta. So he began in '82 and he did not stop. I mean, when we were in Houston at MD Anderson, Bailey continued to preach. He preached in several churches there in Houston, and then he had some, that first year, he was able to do some preaching around where we lived but he did not stop preaching until he was to his deathbed.

Beau Brewer: Yes, ma'am, I am looking at my bookshelf and I have two books that he wrote. *Real Evangelism*, which I read my second semester of my MDiv, and boy did that book just turn the pilot light on in my soul; the book just really impacted me. And then a second book, and I believe it follows *Real Evangelism*, was *Real Christianity*. I'm sure you're familiar with them.

Sandy Smith: Yes, of course.

Beau Brewer: Those books have been used in so many classrooms around the way. And I am not going to put words in your mouth, but I can presume that that is a lot of the reason why he lent his name to Southeastern Seminary for this specific chair of evangelism,

	because it is clear from those two books that he believed heavily in theological education.
Sandy Smith:	Absolutely. He did. He did. And I'm going to suggest, I'm going to skip down to the importance of evangelism . . .
Beau Brewer:	Sure, please.
Sandy Smith:	. . . being taught in seminary. And I think that Bailey would tell you clearly that you can be an excellent communicator and a skilled musician, but unless that person is filled with the spirit of God, his music or his preaching won't reach the hearts of people and it won't make any difference. And the reason I think is that we cannot . . . evangelism is the heart of God. And if we refuse to obey in that area of our lives, then we can't expect the glory of God to fill us and flow through us and call attention to him.
	So, I think if someone refuses to be very intentional about evangelism, then it will affect every other part of this ministry.
Beau Brewer:	I could not agree more. And I couldn't have said that better. Now, can you talk to me a little bit about when Dr. Paige Patterson, who was then-president of Southeastern Baptist Theological Seminary, about when he approached, obviously Dr. Bailey Smith and yourself about the creation and founding and establishment of this particular chair?
Sandy Smith:	Yes. We were friends with the Pattersons from the early days, right after we . . . we did not go to the same seminary, but we became friends with them quickly after that. And one reason we became close to them was because Dr. Patterson came to Oklahoma and spoke with Bailey probably in '78 or '79, maybe in '78, and about what would become the resurgence of our denomination coming back to the biblical principles. And we became such good friends, we believed very much the same things.

And we had such respect for them that when Dr. Patterson approached Bailey, who . . . Dr. Patterson is a few years younger than both of us, but when he approached Bailey about this chair of evangelism by, and he was thrilled to death, because it was such a passion of his. And so I do not know exactly how that conversation went, but I do know that Bailey has a dear friend who was named Randy Bates.

And he spoke with Randy about funding that chair and it was a great day when we went to Southeastern. And it was inaugurated or initiated, it was a great day. And it was a thrill for Bailey because it became even more obvious to him that he was respected for his concentration and his single-mindedness toward evangelism. As far as I know, he did not, I am pretty sure that he did not choose the person who would fill that chair, but I am quite sure that Dr. Patterson talked, spoke together about what it should be, what should be taught, how it should go. And that was an exciting time. A really exciting time.

Beau Brewer: I bet. I bet. I mean, that is a very significant thing. Just, to give you an idea how significant it is, there are only six chairs of evangelism and six Southern Baptist Seminaries. So, you were married to one of six precious names that have been, I mean, that is a tremendous honor.

Sandy Smith: In my book, he was number one.

Beau Brewer: Oh, of course. Yes ma'am, of course. I just mean to say that is saying a lot about the person whom the chair is named after, because it will forever be known as the Bailey Smith Chair of Evangelism at Southeastern Baptist Theological Seminary. And that's a tremendous honor.

Sandy Smith: Yes it is.

Beau Brewer: Well, is there anything else you would like to share? Did you attend Southwestern as well?

Sandy Smith: I just wanted to also say that we have both felt like having an evangelism focus in our seminaries was vitally important for our seminary students, because the earlier we get that passion and the tools we need to help engage other people with the gospel, then the more natural the desire is to evangelize wherever they are and wherever we are, it is vital. I think it is very vital. And I think that if we didn't have a school of evangelism, something would be missing in our seminaries and it would be missing in Southern Baptist churches.

Beau Brewer: Yes, it would.

Sandy Smith: Dr. Queen, he is such an example, such a stellar example of single-minded focus on evangelism. Dr. Patterson was certainly that also, and Dr. Fish was a dear, sweet friend that we so highly respected, even though he was older than we are, how could you not respect Roy Fish?

Beau Brewer: Oh, my goodness.

Sandy Smith: Such a Godly man.

Beau Brewer: Yes Ma'am.

Appendix 20

List of Southern Baptist Seminary Chairs of Evangelism and Their Occupants

1. **L. R. Scarborough Chair of Evangelism "Chair of Fire" (Established 1908)**

   Southwestern Baptist Theological Seminary, Fort Worth, Texas

   - Lee Rutland Scarborough (1908–42)
   - Eldred Douglas Head (1942–50)
   - Cassius Elijah Autrey (1955–60)
   - Kenneth Chafin (1960–65)
   - Roy J. Fish (1965–2006)
   - James Eaves (1973–1990)
   - Malcolm McDow (1982–2005)
   - L. Paige Patterson (2006–14)
   - Matt Queen (2014–)

2. **Roland Q. Leavell Chair of Evangelism (Established 1959)**

   New Orleans Baptist Theological Seminary, New Orleans, Louisiana

   - B. Gray Allison (1959–66)
   - Eugene N. Patterson (1966–74)
   - Clarence Cecil Randall (1982–88)
   - Charles Kelley Jr. (1989–96)

- Charles L. Register (1996–2000)
- James Cogdill (2000–2003)
- David Meacham (2004–07)
- Preston L. Nix (2008–)

3. **Billy Graham Chair or Evangelism (Established 1965)**

   Southern Baptist Theological Seminary, Louisville, Kentucky

   - Kenneth Chafin (1965–1969)
   - Howard Gordon Clinard (1970–1972)
   - Lewis Drummond (1972–1988)
   - David D'Amico (1989–1996)
   - Timothy Beougher (1996–)

4. **E. Hermond Westmoreland Chair of Evangelism (Established 1966)**

   Gateway Seminary, Ontario, California

   - G. William Schweer (1978–1996)
   - William Lyle Wagner (1996–2006)
   - Unoccupied (2006–)

5. **Bailey Smith Chair of Evangelism (Established 1994)**

   Southeastern Baptist Theological Seminary, Wake Forest, North Carolina

   - Alvin Reid (1994–2018)
   - George G. Robinson IV (2019–)

6. **Gary Taylor Chair of Missions and Evangelism (Established 2012)**

   Midwestern Baptist Theological Seminary, Kansas City, Missouri

   - Robin D. Hadaway (2012–)

Appendix 21

PIONEER PENETRATION/SPRING EVANGELISM PRACTICUM TOTALS, 1965–2008

YEARLY TOTALS

1965

Students Participating	38
Candidates for Baptism	81
Transfers of Letter	23
Statement of Faith	6
Rededications	247
Christian Service Commitment	7
Other Decisions	8

1966

Students Participating	63
Churches Served	56
Professions of Faith	215
Transfers of Letter	45
Rededications	369
Christian Service Commitment	6
Churches or Missions Begun	4
Evangelistic Visits	2,560

1967

Students Participating	88
Churches Served	67
Professions of Faith	304

Transfers of Letter	80
Christian Service Commitment	25
Rededications	727

1968

Students Participating	70
Churches Served	61
Professions of Faith	241
Transfers of Letter	48
Rededications	306
Christian Service Commitment	11

1969

Students Participating	60
Churches Served	47
Professions of Faith	204
Private Professions of Faith	40
Candidates for Baptism	138
Transfers of Letter	28
Statement of Faith	5
Christian Service Commitment	14
Rededications	275
Other Decisions	51
Visits Made	1,617

1970

Students Participating	78
Churches Served	60
Professions of Faith	380
Private Professions of Faith	47
Candidates for Baptism	248
Transfers of Letter	42
Statement of Faith	5
Rededications	517
Christian Service Commitment	14
Other Decisions	97
Visits Made	1,850

1971

Students Participating	115
Churches Served	80
Professions of Faith	565
Transfers of Letter	100
Christian Service Commitment	13
Rededications	955
Candidates for Baptism	383

1972

Students Participating	108
Churches Served	68
Professions of Faith	360
Transfers of Letter	53
Candidates for Baptism	150
Rededications	446
Christian Service Commitment	4

1973

Students Participating	112
Churches Served	96
Professions of Faith	627
Transfers of Letter	101
Rededications	899
Christian Service Commitment	13

1974

Students Participating	97
Churches Served	64
Professions of Faith	338
Candidates for Baptism	153
Transfers of Letter	28
Rededications	615
Christian Service Commitment	22

1975

Students Participating	108
Churches Served	65
Professions of Faith	327

Candidates for Baptism	129
Transfers of Letter	54
Rededications	475
Christian Service Commitment	21
Other Decisions	47
Telephone Surveys	550
Visits Made	2,012

1976

Students Participating	134
Churches Served	90
Professions of Faith	420
Candidates for Baptism	181
Transfers of Letter	62
Rededications	801
Christian Service Commitment	20

1977

Students Participating	120
Churches Served	80
Professions of Faith	332
Candidates for Baptism	130
Transfers of Letter	31
Rededications	375
Christian Service Commitment	10

1978

Students Participating	130
Churches Served	100
Professions of Faith	309
Candidates for Baptism	137
Transfers of Letter	64
Rededications	521
Christian Service Commitment	10
Visits Made	3,526

1979

Students Participating	144
Professions of Faith	105

Candidates for Baptism	75
Transfers of Letter	23
Rededications	271
Christian Service Commitment	2
Other Decisions	24

1980

Students Participating	120
Churches Served	84
Professions of Faith	297
Candidates for Baptism	174
Transfers of Letter	33
Christian Service Commitment	8
Rededications	603
Other Decisions	49

1981

Students Participating	128
Churches Served	72
Professions of Faith	198
Candidates for Baptism	112
Transfers of Letter	35
Rededications	443
Christian Service Commitment	7
Other Decisions	45
Visits Made	3,465
Total Expenditures	$18,000

1982

Students Participating	246
Churches Served	148
Professions of Faith	425
Candidates for Baptism	233
Transfers of Letter	62
Christian Service Commitment	14
Rededications	606
Other Decisions	20

1983

Students Participating	184
Churches Served	134
Professions of Faith	326
Candidates for Baptism	175
Transfers of Letter	42
Christian Service Commitment	11
Rededications	614
Other Decisions	104
Evangelistic Visits	3,202
Tracts Distributed	6,253

1984

Students Participating	206
Churches Served	164
Professions of Faith	356
Candidates for Baptism	187
Transfers of Letter	86
Rededications	905
Christian Service Commitment	14
Other Decisions	183
Evangelistic Visits	4,582
Tracts Distributed	5,227
Individuals Witnessed To	1,679

1985

Students Participating	240
Churches Served	191
States Served	23
Professions of Faith	436
Candidates for Baptism	293
Transfers of Letter	94
Rededications	1,168
Christian Service Commitment	28
Other Decisions	113
Evangelistic Visits	6,028
Tracts Distributed	15,189
Individuals Witnessed To	2,667

1986

Students Participating	205
Churches Served	138
States Served (2 in Canada)	28
Public Professions of Faith	245
Personally Led to Christ	55
Other Decisions	409
Sermons Preached	901
Training Sessions	128
Evangelistic Visits	7,056
Tracts Distributed	5,306
Estimated Persons in Services	21,731
Total Expenditures	$29,245.72

1987

Students Participating	194
Churches Served	150
States Served	27
Public Professions of Faith	263
Non-public Professions of Faith	78
Rededications	766
Other Decisions	311
Evangelistic Visits	5,178
Tracts Distributed	4,654
Sermons Preached	1,173
Training Sessions	167
Estimated Persons in Services	42,381
Total Expenditures	$33,031.79

1988

Students Participating	205
Churches Served	194
States Served	30
Professions of Faith	118
Witness Training Professions of Faith	35
Public Professions of Faith	1,642
Sermons Preached	1,359
Evangelistic Visits	3,721
Estimated Persons in Services.	19,797

1989

Students Participating	228
Churches Served	220
States Served	35
Canadian Provinces Served	4
Public Professions of Faith	307
Witness Training Professions of Faith	78
Professions of Faith from Visits	244
Sermons Preached	1,587
Evangelistic Visits	4,572
Rededications	999
Transfers of Letter	97
Other Decisions	737
Total Expenditures	$56,623.32

1990

Students Participating	164
Faculty/Staff Participating	4
Churches Served	197
States Served	32
Canadian Provinces Served	2
Other Countries Served	2
Public Professions of Faith	279
Witness Training Professions of Faith	77
Visitation Professions of Faith	183
Rededications	833
Transfers of Letter	64
Other Decisions Public	317
Other Decisions Private	383
Sermons Preached	1,085
Witness Training Sessions	50
Persons Trained in Above	414
Evangelistic Visits	2,115

1991

Students Participating	260
Sermons Preached	880
Churches Served	138
Individuals Witnessed To	1,276

Professions of Faith in Church	154
Private Professions of Faith	187
Rededications	594
Transfers of Letter	29
Other Decisions	256
Professions of Faith (Non-Church)	40
Professions of Faith from Visits	61
Witness Training Sessions	32
Stewardship Training Sessions	3

1992

Students Participating	141
States Served	25
Countries Served	3
Churches Served	165
Sermons Preached	991
Witness Training Sessions	28
Persons Trained in Above	287
Public Professions of Faith	227
Witness Training Professions of Faith	21
Professions of Faith from Visits	53
Rededications	530
Transfers of Letter	39
Other Decisions Public	201
Other Decisions Private	300
Evangelistic Visits	1,111

1993

Students Participating	116
States Served	28
Countries Served	3
Churches Served	132
Sermons Preached	705
Witness Training Sessions	16
Persons Trained in Above	133
Public Professions of Faith	166
Witness Training Professions of Faith	25
Visits Professions of Faith	82
Rededications	452

Transfers of Letter	17
Other Decisions Public	149
Other Decisions Private	126
Evangelistic Visits	939

1994

Students Participating	107
States Served	26
Countries Served	4
(Canada, England, Puerto Rico, & American Samoa)	
Churches Served	120
Sermons Preached	762
Witness Training Sessions Led	21
Persons Trained in Above	158
Public Professions of Faith	89
Witness Training Professions of Faith	22
Visits Professions of Faith	48
Rededications Made Publicly	278
Transfers by Letter	25
Other Decisions Public	187
Other Decisions Private	130
Evangelistic Visits	520

1995

Students Participating	95
States Served	25
Other Areas Served	2
(District of Columbia and Canada)	
Churches Served	104
Sermons Preached	638
Witness Training Sessions Led	26
Persons Trained in Witness Training Sessions	201
Public Professions of Faith in Services	203
Professions of Faith as a result of Witness Training	20
Professions of Faith as a result of Personal Visitation	32
Rededications Made Publicly	281
Transfers by Letter	20
Other Decisions Made Publicly	88
Other Decisions Made Privately	160

Personal Witnessing Visits Made   835

1996

Students Participating	82
States Served (Plus Canada)	25
Churches Served	87
Sermons Preached	551
Witness Training Sessions Led	17
Persons Trained in Above	79
Public Professions of Faith in Services	80
Professions of Faith as a result of Witness Training	12
Professions of Faith as a result of Personal Visitation	39
Rededications Made Publicly	109
Transfers by Letter	17
Other Decisions Made Publicly	138
Other Decisions Made Privately	117
Personal Witnessing Visits Made	890

1997

Students Participating	98
States Served (plus Mexico)	28
Churches Served	113
Sermons Preached	701
Witness Training Sessions Led	15
Persons Trained in Above	207
Public Professions of Faith in Services	152
Professions of Faith as a result of Witness Training	49
Professions of Faith as a result of Personal Visitation	94
Total Professions of Faith	295
Rededications Made Publicly	206
Transfers by Letter	31
Other Decisions Made Publicly	127
Other Decisions Made Privately	182
Total Decisions	841
Personal Witnessing Visits Made	809

1998

Students Participating	94
States Served	30

Churches Served	100
Sermons Preached	588
Witness Training Sessions Led	21
Persons Trained in Above	220
Public Professions of Faith in Service	131
Professions of Faith as a Result of Witness Training	32
Professions of Faith as a Result of Personal Visitation	58
Rededications Made Publicly	425
Transfers by Letter	27
Other Decisions Made Publicly	174
Other Decisions Made Privately	108
Total Decisions	955
Personal Witnessing Visits Made	826

1999

Students Participating	88
States Served + Caribbean	26
Churches Served	109
Sermons Preached	646
Witness Training Sessions Led	20
Persons Trained in Above	128
Public Professions of Faith in Service	164
Professions of Faith as a Result of Witness Training	4
Professions of Faith as a Result of Personal Visitation	50
Rededications Made Publicly	476
Transfers by Letter	10
Other Decisions Made Publicly	112
Other Decisions Made Privately	111
Total Decisions	927
Personal Witnessing Visits Made	1,111

2000

Students Participating	83
States Served	25
Churches Served	117
Sermons Preached	468
Witness Training Sessions Led	16
Persons Trained in Above	200
Public Professions of Faith in Service	117

Professions of Faith as a Result of Witness Training	13
Professions of Faith as a Result of Personal Visitation	131
Rededications Made Publicly	347
Transfers by Letter	18
Other Decisions Made Publicly	125
Other Decisions Made Privately	140
Total Decisions	891
Personal Witnessing Visits Made	739

2001

Students Participating	86
States Served	26
Churches Served	88
Sermons Preached	446
Witness Training Sessions Led	4
Persons Trained in Above	49
Public Professions of Faith in Service	79
Professions of Faith as a Result of Witness Training	9
Professions of Faith as a Result of Personal Visitation	35
Total Professions of Faith	123
Rededications Made Publicly	342
Transfers by Letter	24
Other Decisions Made Publicly	47
Other Decisions Made Privately	82
Total Decisions	618
Personal Witnessing Visits Made	400

2002

Students Participating	96
States Served	25
Churches Served	106
Sermons Preached	549
Personal Witnessing Visits Made	631
Witness Training Sessions Led	13
Persons Trained in Above	83
Public Professions of Faith in Services.	95
Professions of Faith as a Result of Witness Training	11
Professions of Faith as a Result of Personal Visitation	33
Total Professions of Faith	139

Rededications Made Publicly	354
Transfers of Church Membership	17
Other Decisions Made Publicly	85
Other Decisions Made Privately	132
Total Other Decisions	588
Total Decisions	727

2003

Students Participating	97
States Served	30
Churches Served	97
Sermons Preached	501
Personal Witnessing Visits Made	1908
Witness Training Sessions Led	14
Persons Trained in Above	137
Public Professions of Faith in Services	102
Professions of Faith as a Result of Witness Training	7
Professions of Faith as a Result of Personal Visitation	15
Total Professions of Faith	124
Rededications Made Publicly	283
Transfers of Church Membership	14
Other Decisions Made Publicly	174
Other Decisions Made Privately	117
Total Other Decisions	588
Total Decisions	712

2004

Students Participating	97
States Served	29
Churches Served	97
Sermons Preached	517
Personal Witnessing Visits Made	702
Professions of Faith	91
Other Decisions	543
Total Decisions	634

2005

Students Participating	117
States Served	28

Churches Served	117
Sermons Preached	583
Personal Witnessing Visits Made	953
Professions of Faith	151
Other Decisions	363
Total Decisions	514

2006

Students Participating	112
States Served	24
Churches Served	112
Sermons Preached	558
Personal Witnessing Visits Made	806
Professions of Faith	118
Other Decisions	304
Total Decisions	422

2007

Students Participating	98
States Served	29
Churches Served	98
Sermons Preached	498
Personal Witnessing Visits Made	764
Professions of Faith	83
Other Decisions	201
Total Decisions	284

2008

Students Participating	68
States Served	25
Churches Served	68
Sermons Preached	336
Personal Witnessing Visits Made	499
Professions of Faith	57
Other Decisions	163
Total Decisions	220

PIONEER PENETRATION/SPRING EVANGELISM PRACTICUM

OVERALL TOTALS, 1965–2008

(No available records for 1959–1964)

Students Participating	5,523
Churches Served	4,839
(not including 1965, 1979)	
Professions of Faith	13,898

BIBLIOGRAPHY

WORKS BY SCARBOROUGH

Scarborough, L. R. *After the Resurrection, What?* Grand Rapids: Zondervan, 1942.

————. *A Blaze of Evangelism across the Equator.* Nashville: Broadman, 1937.

————. *Christ's Militant Kingdom: A Study in the Trail Triumphant.* New York: George H. Doran Co., 1924.

————. "The Doctrine of Evangelism." *Southwestern Journal of Theology* o.s. 4 (October 1920) 5–8.

————. *Endued to Win.* Nashville: Sunday School Board of the Southern Baptist Convention, 1922.

————. "Evangelism in Baptist Schools," 1918. Manuscript. The L. R. Scarborough Collection, Files 415–45. J. T. and Zelma Luther Archives, A. Webb Roberts Library, Southwestern Baptist Theological Seminary.

————. "Evangelism in Baptist Schools." *Southwestern Journal of Theology* o.s. 2 (July 1918) 3–8.

————. "The Evolution of a Cowboy, or The Story of My Life." Typed manuscript. The L. R. Scarborough Collection, A. Webb Roberts Library, Southwestern Baptist Theological Seminary, Fort Worth, Texas.

————. *Gospel Messages.* Nashville: Sunday School Board of the Southern Baptist Convention, 1922.

————. *Holy Places and Precious Promises.* New York: George H. Doran Co., 1924.

————. *How Jesus Won Men.* New York: George H. Doran Co., 1926.

————. Letter to Carroll on Accepting Position at Southwestern Baptist Theological Seminary, February 24, 1908. Typed manuscript. The L. R. Scarborough Collection, File 279. A. Webb Roberts Library, Southwestern Baptist Theological Seminary.

————. *L. R. Scarborough Collection.* J. T. and Zelma Luther Rare Books and Special Collections, A. Webb Roberts Library, Southwestern Baptist Theological Seminary.

————. *Marvels of Divine Leadership, or The Story of the Southern Baptist 75 Million Campaign.* Nashville: Sunday School Board of the Southern Baptist Convention, 1920.

————. *A Modern School of the Prophets: A History of the Southwestern Baptist Theological Seminary, a Product of Prayer and Faith, Its First Thirty Years, 1907–1937.* Nashville: Broadman, 1939.

————. *My Conception of the Gospel Ministry*. Nashville: Sunday School Board of the Southern Baptist Convention, 1935.

————. "The Need of Indoctrination." *Southwestern Journal of Theology* o.s. 4 (April 1920) 3–6.

————. "The Need of Training in Evangelism." Typed lecture notes. The L. R. Scarborough Collection Archives, A. Webb Roberts Library, Southwestern Baptist Theological Seminary.

————. "Our Summer Evangelism," May 24, 1925. Typed manuscript. The L. R. Scarborough Collection, J. T. and Zelma Luther Rare Book Archives, A. Webb Roberts Libraries, Southwestern Baptist Theological Seminary.

————. *Phephraekhrissasana*. Bangkok: Ronghim Thai phathaya Phranakhon, 1963.

————. *Prepare to Meet God*. New York: George H. Doran Co., 1922.

————. "The Primal Test of Theological Education: The Inaugural Address of President Scarborough," *Bulletin of Southwestern Baptist Theological Seminary*, May 1915. Typed manuscript. The L. R. Scarborough Collection, File 110. J. T. and Zelma Luther Archives, A. Webb Roberts Library, Southwestern Baptist Theological Seminary.

————. *Products of Pentecost*. New York: Fleming H. Revell, 1934.

————. *Recruits for World Conquests*. New York: Fleming H. Revell, 1914.

————. *A Search for Souls: A Study in the Finest of Fine Arts—Winning the Lost to Christ*. Nashville: Sunday School Board of the Southern Baptist Convention, 1925.

————. "A Serious Educational Matter." *Southwestern Journal of Theology* o.s. 5 (October 1921) 88–90.

————. "Summer Evangelism." *Southwestern Journal of Theology* o.s. 8 (July 1924) 3–6.

————. *The Tears of Jesus*. New York: George H. Doran Co., 1922.

————. *Ten Spiritual Ships*. Nashville: Sunday School Board of the Southern Baptist Convention, 1927.

————. "What the Southwestern Baptist Theological Seminary Can Do." *The Baptist Standard*, January 19, 1925. The L. R. Scarborough Collection, File 54. J. T. and Zelma Luther Archives, A. Webb Roberts Library, Southwestern Baptist Theological Seminary.

————. *With Christ, after the Lost: A Search for Souls*. Nashville: Sunday School Board of the Southern Baptist Convention, 1919.

————. *With Christ after the Lost: A Search for Souls*. Rev. and expanded by E. D. Head. Nashville: Broadman, 1953.

ARTICLES AND CORRESPONDENCE

"3 Southwestern Profs Are Joint Book Authors." *Baptist Press*, September 29, 1963, 3. http://media.sbhla.org.s3.amazonaws.com/1796,29-Sep-1963.pdf.

"Annual Catalogue 1913–1914." *Southwestern Baptist Theological Seminary*, 1913–14.

Autrey, C. E. Personal Biographical Notes. Held by the family of C. E. Autrey.

"Autrey Resigns 'Chair of Fire.'" *Southwestern News*, December 1959, 3.

"B. Allison 1924–2019 Obituary." *The Commercial Appeal*, February 17, 2019. https://www.legacy.com/obituaries/commercialappeal/obituary.aspx?n=b-gray-allison&pid=191576360.

Baker, Shannon. "New Orleans Trustees add Jim Cogdill, Archaeologist, Church Historian, to Faculty." *Baptist Press*, June 9, 2020. https://www.bpnews.net/5961/new-orleans-trustees-add-jim-cogdill-archaeologist-church-historian-to-faculty.

———. "Nevada Exec David Meacham Among 4 New Faculty Members at NOBTS." *Baptist Press*, October 23, 2001. https://www.baptistpress.com/resource-library/news/nevada-exec-david-meacham-among-4-new-faculty-members-at-nobts/.

Carroll, B. H. "An Address on Evangelism," May 14, 1906. B. H. Carroll Collection, J. T. and Zelma Luther Archives, A. Webb Roberts Library, Southwestern Baptist Theological Seminary. http://digitalarchive.swbts.edu/digital/collection/p16969coll10/id/147.

———. "The Chair of Fire," July 2, 1908. Address Presented at the Sixtieth Annual Session of the Baptist General Convention of Texas, Waco, TX, July 2, 1908. Typed manuscript. The L. R. Scarborough Collection, File 58. A. Webb Roberts Library, Southwestern Baptist Theological Seminary.

———. Initial Letter of Invitation to Scarborough, November 1, 1906. Typed manuscript. The L. R. Scarborough Collection, File 58. A. Webb Roberts Library, Southwestern Baptist Theological Seminary.

———. Letter to Scarborough Concerning L. R. Scarborough Appointment to SWBTS Faculty, January 11, 1908. Typed manuscript. The L. R. Scarborough Collection, File 60. J. T. and Zelma Luther Archives, A. Webb Roberts Library, Southwestern Baptist Theological Seminary.

———. Letter to Scarborough Discussing Work at Baylor Theological Seminary, the Forerunner to SWBTS, November 1, 1906. Typed manuscript. The Le. R. Scarborough Collection, File 58. A. Webb Roberts Library, Southwestern Baptist Theological Seminary.

———. Letter to Scarborough on Offering Chair of Evangelism, January 11, 1908. The L. R. Scarborough Collection, File 58. A. Webb Roberts Library, Southwestern Baptist Theological Seminary.

———. "Report on Baylor Theological Seminary," November 1, 1906. Report Presented at the Fifty-Eighth Annual Session of the Baptist General Convention of Texas, Waco, TX, November 8–12, 1906. Typed manuscript. The L. R. Scarborough Collection, File 58. A. Webb Roberts Library, Southwestern Baptist Theological Seminary.

———. "Southwestern Baptist Theological Seminary, Article Three." *The Baptist Standard* (April 2, 1908) 1.

"Catalogue of Princeton Theological Seminary 1947–1948." Princeton: Princeton Theological Seminary, 1947. 11.

"Celebrating 100 Years of Southwestern Baptist Theological Seminary." *Southwestern News: Centennial Edition*, Spring 2008.

"'Chair of Fire' Revived With Full-Time Professor: New Evangelism Professor Outlines Plan of Teaching." *Southwestern News* 13.8 (October 1955) 8.

"Clarence Cecil Randall (1923–1992)." *Geni.com*. https://www.geni.com/people/Clarence-Cecil-Randall/6000000003537264187.

Crawford, Dan R. "History of the Spring Evangelism Practicum." Personal notes. Appendix 4.

Culpepper, Hugo H. "The Legacy of William Owen Carver." *International Bulletin of Missionary Research* 5.3 (July 1981) 119.

Culpepper, R. Alan. "Reflections on Baptist Theological Education in the Twentieth Century." *Baptist History and Heritage* 35.3 (Summer/Fall 2000) 25.

Dilday, Russell. "The President's Report: The First Five Years 1978–1983," 1983. A. Webb Roberts Library, Southwestern Baptist Theological Seminary.

"Dr. G. William Schweer." *PastorOB.com.* http://pastorob.com/dr_schweer.htm.

"Dr. Howard Gordon Clinard." *Find A Grave.* https://www.findagrave.com/memorial/60060905/howard-gordon-clinard.

"Dr. James Paul Cogdill Jr. April 27, 1955–March 17, 2011." *Bailey Funeral Home,* March 17, 2011. https://www.baileyfh.com/obituaries/DrJamesPaul-CogdillJr-867/.

"Elected Faculty," in *Southeastern Baptist Theological Seminary Academic Catalog 2013–2014.* Wake Foresst, NC: Southeasten Baptist Theological Seminary, 2013. 30–35. http://www.collegeatsoutheastern.com/files/catalog.pdf.

"E. N. Patterson Named Grand Canyon President." *Baptist Press,* June 25, 1959, 1. https://www.sbhla.org.s3.amazonaws.com/1309,25-June-1959.pdf.

"Evangelism Dept. Enters New Witnessing Program." *Southwestern News,* December 1978, 2.

"Faculty Retirements: Roy Fish—41 Years." *Southwestern News,* Fall 2006. 43.

"'Field' Revivals Set for Spring." *Southwestern News* 28.7 (March 1970) 2.

"First Annual Catalogue 1908–1909." *Southwestern Baptist Theological Seminary.* Waco, TX: Southwestern Baptist Theological Seminary, March 14, 1908.

"Fish Is Truett Prof." *Southwestern News,* 1981, 3.

Fish, Steve. "A Profile of Roy Fish." In *Evangelism for a Changing World: Essays in Honor of Roy Fish,* edited by Timothy Beougher and Alvin Reid, 294. Eugene, OR: Wipf & Stock, 1995.

"Fish, Tidwell, Walker, Huey, Tolar Begin Teaching." *Southwestern News,* September 1965, 2.

Foreman, A. D. "The Evangelistic Thrust of L. R. Scarborough." *Southwestern Journal of Theology* 7.1 (Fall 1964) 58.

"Funeral Services for E. D. Head Conducted in Truett Auditorium." *Southwestern News,* May 1964.

"Golden Gate Prof to Be SBC 2nd V. P. Nominee." *Baptist Press,* June 06, 1997. http://dev.bpnews.net/3499/golden-gate-prof-to-be-sbc-2nd-vp-nominee/.

"Gordon Clinard Elected Seminary Evangelism Head." *Baptist Press,* August 18, 1970, 2–3. http://media.sbhla.org.s3.amazonaws.com/3041,18-Aug-1970.pdf.

"Graduate Catalog 2019–2020." New Orleans: New Orleans Baptist Theological Seminary, 2019.

Green, Nancy. "George William Schweer, 'Bill.'" *Daily Republic,* May 25, 2018. https://www.dailyrepublic.com/all-dr-news/obituaries/george-william-schweer-bill/comment-page-1/.

Guffin, R. L. *Here We Raise Our Ebenezer: Frontier Settlers and Itinerant Preachers (1818–1831).* Tuscaloosa, AL, 2008. https://anyflip.com/zcvk/pjty.

Head, Eldred Douglas. "Ghost or God?" Pamphlet. n.d.

Hooker, Mike. "Writers Honor Roy Fish with New Book." *Southwestern News,* Summer 1995, 13.

Jameson, Norman. "Chuck Register to be New Executive Leader." Biblical Recorder, December 12, 2008. https:brnow.org/news/chuck-register-to-be-new-executive-leader/.

Kasdorf, Hans. "The Legacy of Gustav Warneck." *Occasional Bulletin of Missionary Research* 4.3 (July 1980) 102.

"Leukemia Claims Kenneth Chafin, Former Seminary Prof & Pastor." *Baptist Press,* January 5, 2001. http://www.bpnews.net/10090/leukemia-claims-kenneth-chafin-former-seminary-prof- and-pastor.

"Lewis Urges Seminarians to Consider US Missions." *Baptist Press,* March 1, 1994, 8. http://media.sbhla.org.s3.amazonaws.com/7727,01-Mar-1994.pdf.

Little, Robyn. "Seminarians' Spring Ministries Span Revivals to Inner-city Needs." *Baptist Press,* April 1, 1999. https://www.baptistpress.com/resource-library/news/seminarians-spring-ministries-span-revivals-to-inner-city-needs/.

"L. R. Scarborough Chair of Evangelism." *Southwestern News,* Winter 2007, 39.

"Malcolm McDow." *Southwestern News,* April 1982.

"MBTS, MBC Launch Chair." *The Pathway,* March 15, 2012. https://mbcpathway.com/2012/05/15/mbts-mbc-launch-chair/.

Moore, Debbie. "First Class from Angola Prison Earn New Orleans Seminary Degrees." *Baptist Press,* December 29, 1997. https://www.baptistpress.com/resource-library/news/first-class-from-angola-prison-earn-new-orleans-seminary-degrees/.

———. "NOBTS Trustees Focus on Prayer for Revival." *Baptist Press,* November 5, 1996, 7. https://www.media.sbhla.org.s3.amazonaws.com/05-nov-1996.pdf.

Mullins, Edgar Y. "Edgar Y. Mullins to Charles S. Gardner," May 4, 1907. Letterpress Copy Book 31, 1906–08. The Edgar Y. Mullins Collection, Archives and Special Collections, James P. Boyce Centennial Library, Southern Baptist Theological Seminary.

Myers, Gary D. "New Orleans Seminary Celebrates One Hundred Years." *SBC Life,* April 20, 2018. https://www.baptistpress.com/resource-library/sbc-life-articles/new-orleans-seminary-celebrates-one-hundred-years/.

———. "NOBTS President Chuck Kelley Announces Retirement; Will Serve Through July 2019." *NOBTS,* October 2, 2018. http://www.nobts.edu/news/articles/2018/Kelley10-02.html.

Naylor, Robert E. "Southwestern and Evangelism." *Southwestern Journal of Theology* 19.1 (Fall 1976) 89.

Nettles, Thomas J. "L. R. Scarborough: Public Figure." *Southwestern Journal of Theology* 25.2 (Spring 1983) 35.

"New MBTS Chair Named for Taylor." *The Pathway,* July 12, 2012. https://mbcpathway.com/2012/07/12/new-mbts-chair-named-for-taylor/.

"New Orleans Trustees Elect Two Profs, Name Two Emeriti." *Baptist Press,* February 8, 1983, 30.

Nunnelley, William. "Dr. Lewis A. Drummond, Retired Beeson Professor, Dies at 77." *Samford News,* January 6, 2004. https://www.samford.edu/news/2004/Dr-Lewis-A-Drummond-Retired-Beeson-Professor-Dies-at-77.

"Obituary: James Franklin Eaves." *Dignity Memorial,* December 14, 2015. https://www.dignitymemorial.com/obituaries/fort-worth-tx/james-eaves-6717258/.

"Our Professors: Lewis Drummond." *Southern Baptist Theological Seminary Archives & Special Collections.* https://archives.sbts.edu/the-history-of-the-sbts/our-professors/lewis-drummond/.

"Our Reviewers." *Missiology: An International Review* 30.1 (January 2002) 2. https://journals.sagepub.com/doi/10.1177/009182960203000107.

Patterson, L. Paige, and Duke K. McCall. "Billy Graham e a Pregação Evangelística," *Pregação & Pregadores* 2.4 (December 2012) 5–10.

———. "The Evangelist." *Crusade Newsletter*, Winter 1981.

———. "Miracle at Love Field." *Arkansas Baptist*, February 12, 1971.

———. "Patterson vs. McCall on the Southern Baptist Controversy." *Fundamentalist Journal* 4.5 (May 1985) 17.

———. "Review of *Effective Evangelistic Churches.*" *Faith and Mission* 13 (Spring 1996) 124–26.

———. "Review of *With Christ after the Lost* by L. R. Scarborough." *Southwestern Journal of Theology* (Fall 2008) 96–99.

———. "The Ultimate Hunt." *The Christian Sportsman*, Winter 2007, 10–11.

———. "Why Southern Baptists Declined and What to Do, Part 1." *Theological Matters Blog of Southwestern Baptist Theological Seminary*, June 4, 2014.

———. "Why Southern Baptists Declined and What to Do, Part 2." *Theological Matters Blog of Southwestern Baptist Theological Seminary*, June 6, 2014.

"Patterson Named Professor at New Orleans Seminary." *Baptist Press,* August 12, 1966, 2.

"Resources by Robin D. Hadaway." *For The Church*, November 14, 2014.

"Rev. Raymond Gary Taylor." *Baue Funeral Homes Obituaries*, May 29, 2012. https://www.baue.com/obit/rev-raymond-gary-taylor/.

"Roberts Resigns as MBTS President." *The Pathway*, February 10, 2012. https://mbcpathway.com/2012/02/10/roberts-resigns-as-mbts-president/.

"Robin D. Hadaway." *Midwestern Baptist Theological Seminary: About the Faculty.* https://www.mbts.edu/about/faculty/robin-d-hadaway/.

"Roy Fish & Malcolm McDow: 'Fishers of Men.'" *Baptist Press*, June 06, 2003. https://www.baptistpress.com/resource-library/news/roy-fish-malcolm-mcdow-fishers-of-men/.

"SBC Digest: Alvin Reid Resigns at Southeastern; Connect316 leader resigns over 'reprehensible' Facebook post; Karen Prior hit by bus in Nashville." *Baptist Press,* May 24, 2018. http://www.bpnews.net/50959/sbc-digest-alvin-reid-resigns-at-southeaster-connect316-leader-resigns-over-reprehensible-facebook-post-karen-prior-hit-by-bus-in-nashville/.

"School of Evangelism and Missions, Division of Evangelism." *Southwestern Baptist Theological Seminary Official Catalog 2006–2007*, 238. http://catalog.swbts.edu/catalog/assets/File/archives/2006-2007catalog.pdf.

Segler, Franklin M. "B. H. Carroll: Model for Ministers," Southwestern Journal of Theology. 25.2 (Spring 1983) 4–23.

Sibley, Alex. "L. R. Scarborough." *Southwestern Seminary Legacy Series*, June 20, 2019. https://swbts.edu/news/swbts-legacy-l-r-scarborough/.

"Southeastern's History: Drummond Presidency, 1988–1992." *Southeastern's History: Archived Catalog.* http://catalog.sebts.edu/content.php?catoid=5&navoid=143.

South Main Baptist Church. "Our History." *About South Main Baptist Church.* https://www.smbc.org/about/our-history.

Toalston, Art. "Gray Allison, Theology Leader in SBC Resurgence, Dies." *Baptist Press*, February 15, 2019. http://www.bpnews.net/52426/gray-allison-theology-leader-in-sbc-resurgence-dies.

"To God Be the Glory: Tokyo Baptist Church Dedication, November 1-8, 1959." Tokyo: Tokyo Baptist Church, 1959.

Tomlin, Gregory. "Eight SWBTS Professors to Be Installed in Academic Chairs." *Southwestern Seminary,* October 11, 2005.

———. "Paige Patterson Elected as President of Southwestern." *Baptist Press,* June 24, 2003. http://m.bpnews.net/16174/paige-patterson-elected-as-president-of-south western.

Trevillian, James. "Crossover Report Emphasizes Evangelism." *Baptist New Mexican,* June 21, 2019. https://gobnm.com/sbc_news/sbc_annual_meeting/crossover-report-emphasizes-evangelism/article_d7251a58-93a3-11e9-b2a4-6f5f86c9680d. html.

"Trustees Elect Eaves and Debord to Faculty." *Southwestern News,* December 1964, 3.

Walker, Ken. "Christians Urged to Prepare for Steady Waves of Change." *Baptist Press,* October 4, 1995, 4. http://media.sbhla.org.s3.amazonaws.com/8057,04-Oct-1995. pdf.

Warner, Greg. "Seminary Trustees to Confront President over Audit, Management Issues." *Word and Way,* February 7, 2012. https://wordandway.org/2012/02/07/seminary-trustees-to-confront-president-over-audit-management-issues/.

White, Jeannette. "Evangelism Class is Southwestern's 'Chair of Fire.'" *Southwestern News,* May 1949, 3.

Wyatt, Mark A. "Golden Gate Trustees Approve Intercultural Studies School." *Baptist Press,* April 18, 1996, 7. http://media.sbhla.org.s3.amazonaws.com/18-APR-1996. PDF.

Zygiel, Linda Joyce. "NOBTS Completes Interims Pilot; Opens Church-Oriented Internet Site." *Baptist Press,* April 15, 1998, 1. https://www.baptistpress.com/resource-library/news/nobts-completes-interims-pilot-opens-church-oriented-internet-site/.

BOOKS

Autrey, C. E. *Basic Evangelism.* Grand Rapids: Zondervan, 1959.

———. *Evangelistic Sermons.* Grand Rapids: Zondervan, 1962.

———. *Evangelism in the Acts.* Grand Rapids: Zondervan, 1964.

———. *Renewals before Pentecost: How God's Spirit Revitalized His People in Old Testament Times.* Nashville: Broadman, 1960.

———. *Revivals of the Old Testament.* Grand Rapids: Zondervan, 1960.

———. *The Theology of Evangelism.* Nashville: Broadman, 1966.

———. *You Can Win Souls.* Nashville: Broadman, 1961.

Autrey, C. E., Jack Stanton, and Kenneth Chafin. *We Are Witnesses.* Nashville: Home Mission Board, 1968.

Avant, John, Malcolm McDow, and Alvin Reid, eds. *Revival!: The Story of the Current Awakening in Brownwood, Fort Worth, Wheaton, and Beyond.* Nashville: Broadman & Holman, 1996.

Baker, Robert A. *The Southern Baptist Convention and Its People, 1607–1972.* Nashville: Broadman, 1974.

———. *Tell the Generations Following: A History of Southwestern Baptist Theological Seminary 1908–1983.* Nashville: Broadman, 1983.

Barnes, William Wright. *The Southern Baptist Convention: 1845–1953.* Nashville: Broadman, 1954.

Beougher, Timothy K., and Alvin L. Reid, eds. *Evangelism for a Changing World: Essays in Honor of Roy Fish*. Eugene, OR: Wipf & Stock, 1995.

Bosch, David J. *Transforming Mission: Paradigm Shifts in Theology of Mission*. Maryknoll, NY: Orbis, 1991.

Carroll, B. H. *Christ's Marching Orders*. Edited by J. B. Cranfill. Dallas: Helms, 1941.

———. *An Interpretation of the English Bible, Vol. 12: The Acts*. Edited by J. B. Cranfill. Nashville: Broadman, 1947.

———. *An Interpretation of the English Bible, Vol. 15: Colossians, Ephesians, and Hebrews*. Edited by J. B. Cranfill. Nashville: Broadman, 1947.

———. *Sermons and Life Sketch of B. H. Carroll*. Edited by J. B. Cranfill. Dallas: Evangel, 1957.

Carroll, J. M. *B. H. Carroll: Colossus of Baptist History*. Edited by J. W. Crowder. Fort Worth, 1946.

———. *The Trail of Blood: The History of Baptist Churches from the Time of Christ, Their Founder, to the Present Day*. Lexington, KY: Ashland Avenue Baptist Church, 1931.

Carson, Glenn Thomas. *Calling Out the Called: The Life and Work of Lee Rutland Scarborough*. Austin, TX: Eakin, 1996.

Chafin, Kenneth L. *The Communicator's Commentary: 1, 2 Corinthians*. Waco, TX: Word, 1985.

———. *The Communicator's Commentary: 1, 2 Samuel, Old Testament*. Waco, TX: Word, 1989.

———. *Evangelism 123*. Nashville: Southern Baptist Convention. Seminary Extension Department, 1969.

———. *Help! I'm a Layman*. Waco, TX: Word, 1966.

———. *How to Know When You've Got It Made: Shaping a Successful Life*. Waco, TX: Word, 1981.

———. *Is There a Family in the House?: A Realistic and Hopeful Look at Marriage and the Family Today*. Waco, TX: Word, 1978.

———. *The Preacher's Commentary: 1, 2 Samuel*. Nashville: Thomas Nelson, 1993.

———. *Speaking in His Name*. Nashville: Sunday School Board, 1970.

———. *The Reluctant Witness*. Nashville: Broadman, 1974.

———. *A Rhythm for My Life*. Vancouver, Sanada: Greystone, 2003.

———. *Tell All the Little Children: Clear, Thorough Guidance for Leading Children toward Personal Faith in Jesus Christ*. Nashville: Broadman, 1974.

Cox, Norman Wade, ed. "B. H. Carroll." In *Encyclopedia of Southern Baptists*, 233. Nashville: Broadman, 1958.

———, ed. "Scarborough." In *Encyclopedia of Southern Baptists*, 1186–87. Nashville: Broadman, 1958.

———, ed. "Whitsitt Controversy." In *Encyclopedia of Southern Baptists*, 1496. Nashville: Broadman, 1958.

Crawford, Dan R., ed. *Before Revival Begins: The Preacher's Preparation for a Revival Meeting*. Fort Worth: Scripta, 1996.

Dana, H. E. *Lee Rutland Scarborough: A Life of Service*. Nashville: Broadman, 1942.

Drummond, Lewis A. *The Awakening That Must Come*. Nashville: Broadman, 1978.

———. *The Canvas Cathedral: A Complete History of Evangelism from the Apostle Paul to Billy Graham*. Nashville: Nelson, 2003.

———. *Evangelism: The Counter Revolution*. London: Marshall, Morgan, and Scott, 1972.

———. *Charles G. Finney: The Birth of Modern Evangelism*. London: Hodder & Stoughton, 1982.gan, and Scott, 1972.

———. *Eight Keys to Biblical Revival: The Saga of Scriptural Spiritual Awakenings, How They Shaped the Great Revivals of the Past, and Their Powerful Implications for Today's Church*. Minneapolis: Bethany House, 1994.

———. *The Evangelist: The Worldwide Impact of Billy Graham*. Nashville: Word, 2001.

———, ed. *Here They Stand: Sermons from Eastern Europe*. Valley Forge, PA: Judson, 1976.

———. *Leading Your Church in Evangelism*. Nashville: Broadman, 1975.

———. *The Life and Ministry of Charles G. Finney*. Minneapolis: Bethany House, 1984.

———. *Life Can Be Real*. London: Lakeland, 1973.

———. *Miss Bertha: Woman of Revival*. Nashville: Broadman & Holman, 1996.

———. *The People of God in Ministry*. Washington, DC: Baptist World Alliance, 1985.

———. *Reaching Generation Next: Effective Evangelism in Today's Culture*. Grand Rapids: Baker, 2002.

———. *The Revived Life*. Nashville: Broadman, 1982.

———. *Ripe for Harvest: The Role of Spiritual Awakening in Church Growth*. Nashville: Broadman & Holman, 2001.

———. *Spiritual Awakening: God's Divine Work*. Atlanta: Home Mission Board, 1985.

———. *Spurgeon: Prince of Preachers*. Grand Rapids: Kregel, 1992.

———, ed. *What the Bible Says*. Nashville: Abingdon, 1975.

———. *Witnessing for God to Men*. Nashville: Convention, 1980.

———. *The Word of the Cross: A Contemporary Theology of Evangelism*. Nashville: Broadman, 1989.

Drummond, Lewis A., and Betty Drummond. *The Spiritual Woman: Ten Principles of Spirituality and Women Who Have Lived Them*. Grand Rapids: Kregel, 1999.

———. *Women of Awakenings: The Historical Contribution of Women to Revival Movements*. Grand Rapids: Kregel, 1997.

Drummond, Lewis A., and Paul R. Baxter. *How to Respond to a Skeptic*. Chicago: Moody, 1986.

Eternal Life. Alpharetta, GA: North American Mission Board, 2012.

Fish, Roy J. *Coming to Jesus: Giving a Good Invitation*. North Charleston, SC: CreateSpace, 2015.

———. *Dare to Share*. Nashville: Convention, 1982.

———. *Every Member Evangelism for Today*. New York: Harper & Row, 1976.

———. *Giving a Good Invitation*. Nashville: Broadman, 1974.

———. *When Heaven Touched Earth: The Awakening of 1858 and Its Effects on Baptists*. Azle, TX: Need of the Time, 1996.

Gaines, Steve. "Professional History." In *Evangelism for a Changing World: Essays in Honor of Roy Fish,* edited by Timothy Beougher and Alvin Reid, 281. Eugene, OR: Wipf & Stock, 1995.

Garrett, James Leo, ed. *The Legacy of Southwestern: Writings That Shaped a Tradition*. North Richland Hills, TX: Smithfield, 2002.

Hadaway, Robin D. *A Survey of World Missions*. Nashville: B&H Academic, 2020.

Head, Eldred Douglas. *Burning Hearts*. Nashville: Broadman, 1947.

———. *Coradoes Abrasados.* Translated by Jabes Torres. Rio de Janiero, Brazil: Casa Publicadora Batista, 1950.

———. *Evangelism in Acts.* Fort Worth: Southwestern Baptist Theological Seminary, 1952.

———. *New Testament Life and Literature as Reflected in the Papyri.* Nashville: Broadman, 1952.

———. *Revivals in the Bible.* Fort Worth: Southwestern Baptist Theological Seminary, 1952.

———. *Why All This Suffering?* Grand Rapids: Zondervan, 1941.

Hudson, Dottie L. *He Still Stands Tall: The Life of Roland Q. Leavell.* Gretna, LA: Dove Inspirational, 2008.

Johnston, Thomas P., ed. *Mobilizing A Great Commission Church for Harvest: Voices and Views from the Southern Baptist Professors of Evangelism Fellowship.* Eugene, OR: Wipf & Stock, 2011.

Kelley, Charles S. *Fuel the Fire: Lessons from the History of Southern Baptist Evangelism.* Nashville: B&H Academic, 2018.

———. *How Did They Do It?: The Story of Southern Baptist Evangelism.* New Orleans: Insight, 1993.

Ledbetter, Gary. *The Southern Baptists of Texas Convention: 20 Years of Reaching Texas and Touching the World.* Grapevine, TX: Southern Baptists of Texas Convention, 2018.

Lefever, Alan J. *Fighting the Good Fight: The Life and Work of Benajah Harvey Carroll.* Austin: Eakin, 1994.

———. "Theological Education." In *Teaching Them: A Sesquicentennial Celebration of Texas Baptist Education,* edited by John W. Storey, 164. Dallas: The Baptist General Convention of Texas, 1996.

Liederbach, Mark, and Alvin L. Reid. *The Convergent Church: Missional Worshippers in an Emerging Culture.* Grand Rapids: Kregel, 2009.

McDonald, Larry Steven, and Matt Queen. *A Passion for the Great Commission: Essays in Honor of Alvin L. Reid.* Greer, SC: Towering Oaks, 2013.

McDow, Malcolm and Alvin L. Reid. *Firefall: How God Has Shaped History through Revivals.* Enumclaw, WA: Pleasant Word, 1997.

Mueller, William A. *A History of Southern Baptist Theological Seminary.* Nashville: Broadman, 1959.

Muncy, W. L. *A History of Evangelism in the United States.* Kansas City, KS: Central Seminary Press, 1945.

Myklebust, Olav Guttorm. *The Study of Missions in Theological Education: An Historical Inquiry into the Place of World Evangelization in Western Protestant Ministerial Training with Particular Reference to Alexander Duff's Chair of Evangelistic Theology.* Oslo: Egede Instituttet, 1955.

Nussbaum, Stan. *A Reader's Guide to Transforming Mission: A Concise, Accessible Companion to David Bosch's Classic Book.* Maryknoll, NY: Orbis, 2005.

Patterson, L. Paige. "Foreword." In *Charts for a Theology of Evangelism,* by Thomas P. Johnston, 1. Nashville: B&H, 2007.

———. "Foreword." In *Urban Impact: Reaching the World through Effective Urban Ministry,* by John L. Thompson. Eugene, OR: Wipf & Stock, 2010.

———. *Hunting the Most Dangerous Game.* Garland, TX: American Tract Society, 2008.

———. "Lifestyle Evangelism." In *Evangelism in the Twenty-First Century: The Critical Issues,* edited by Thom S. Rainer. Wheaton, IL: H. Shaw, 1989.

———. "A Theology of Evangelism." In *The Gospel for the New Millennium: A Collection of Essays,* edited by J. Chris Schofield. Nashville: Broadman & Holman, 2001.

Price, William Craig, ed. *Engage: Tools for Contemporary Evangelism: A Festschrift Presented upon the Retirement of Dr. Charles S. "Chuck" Kelley Jr. in Honor of His Life and Work.* New Orleans: New Orleans Baptist Theological Seminary, 2019.

Queen, Matt. *And You Will Be My Witnesses.* Fort Worth: Seminary Hill Press, 2019.

———. *Everyday Evangelism.* Fort Worth: Seminary Hill Press, 2016.

———. *Mobilize to Evangelize: The Pastor and Effective Congregational Evangelism.* Fort Worth: Seminary Hill Press, 2018.

———. "Satisfied?" Fort Worth: Seminary Hill Press, 2021.

Rainer, Thom S., ed. *Evangelism in the Twenty-First Century: The Critical Issues.* Wheaton, IL: Harold Shaw, 1989.

Ray, Jeff D. *B. H. Carroll.* Nashville: Sunday School Board, 1927.

Reid, Alvin L. *Advance: Gospel-Centered Movements Change the World.* December 29, 2010.

———. *As You Go: Creating A Missional Culture of Gospel-Centered Students.* Colorado Springs: Think, 2013.

———. *Evangelism Handbook: Biblical, Spiritual, Intentional, Missional.* Nashville: Broadman & Holman Academics, 2009.

———. *Introduction to Evangelism.* Nashville: Broadman & Holman, 1998.

———. *It's All Good.* Wake Forest, NC: Inquest Ministries, 2002.

———. *Join the Movement: God Is Calling You to Change the World.* Grand Rapids: Kregel, 2007.

———. *Light the Fire: Raising Up a Generation to Live Radically for Jesus Christ.* Enumclaw, WA: WinePress, 2001.

———. *The Net Mentor Handbook.* Alpharetta, GA: North American Mission Board, Southern Baptist Convention, 2000.

———. *Pursuing God: A 40-Day Guide to Personal Revival.* January 14, 2013.

———. *Radically Unchurched: Who They Are and How to Reach Them.* Grand Rapids: Kregel, 2002.

———. *Raising the Bar: Ministry to Youth in the New Millennium.* Grand Rapids: Kregel, 2004.

———. *Revitalize: Your Church through Gospel Recovery.* Gospel Advance Books. 2013.

———. *Roar: The Deafening Thunder of Spiritual Awakening.* December 29, 2010.

———. *Servanthood Evangelism Manual.* Alpharetta, GA: North American Mission Board, 2000.

———. *Sharing Jesus without Freaking Out: Evangelism The Way You Were Born To Do It.* Nashville: Broadman & Holman Academic, 2017.

———. *Stronger: A Practical Guide to Physical and Spiritual Discipline.* January 14, 2013.

———. *What God Can Do.* Columbia, SC: South Carolina Baptist Convention, 2006.

———. *With: A Guide to Informal Mentoring.* December 29, 2010.

Reid, Alvin L., and Timothy K. Beougher, eds. *Evangelism for a Changing World: Essays in Honor of Roy J. Fish.* Eugene, OR: Wipf & Stock, 2004.

Reid, Alvin L., and Ashley Marivittori Gorman. *Book of Matches.* Colorado Springs: NavPress, 2012.

Scharpff, Paulus. *History of Evangelism: Three Hundred Years of Evangelism in Germany, Great Britain, and the United States of America*. Translated by Helga Bender Henry. Grand Rapids: Eerdmans, 1966.

Spivey, James. "Benajah Harvey Carroll." In *Theologians of the Baptist Tradition*, edited by Timothy George and David S. Dockery, 163–80. Nashville: Broadman & Holman, 2001.

Storey, John W., ed. *Teaching Them: A Sesquicentennial Celebration of Texas Baptist Education*. Dallas: The Baptist General Convention of Texas, 1996.

Walls, Andrew F. "Missiological Education in Historical Perspective." In *Missiological Education for the 21st Century: The Book, the Circle and the Sandals*, edited by J. Dudley Woodberry, Charles Van Engen, and Edgar J. Elliston, 11–22. Maryknoll, NY: Orbis, 1996.

Warneck, Gustav. *Evangelische Missionslehre: Ein Missionstheoretischer Versuch*. Edition Afem Mission Classics 8. Nuremburg: VTR, 2015.

Wills, Gregory A. *Southern Baptist Seminary 1859–2009*. New York: Oxford University Press, 2009.

DISSERTATIONS AND THESES

Benefield, Leroy. "Lee Rutland Scarborough and His Preaching." ThD diss., Southwestern Baptist Theological Seminary, 1970.

Bowman, Mary D. Leavell. "Roland Q. Leavell: A Biography." PhD diss., Louisiana State University and Agricultural and Mechanical College, 1983.

Carson, Glenn Thomas. "Lee Rutland Scarborough: Architect of a New Denominationalism within the Southern Baptist Convention." PhD diss., Southwestern Baptist Theological Seminary, 1992.

Chafin, Kenneth. "The Apologetic Method of Elton Trueblood." ThD diss., Southwestern Baptist Theological Seminary, 1959.

Crisp, Michael Wade. "The Pastoral Theology of B. H. Carroll: An Examination." PhD diss., Southwestern Baptist Theological Seminary, 2015.

Dickard, Daniel C. "A Man between the Times: A Critical Evaluation of Roy J. Fish and His Contributions to the Evangelistic Spirit of Southwestern Baptist Theological Seminary." PhD diss., Southwestern Baptist Theological Seminary, 2017.

Gibson, John Frank. "An Investigation of the Significance of Roland Q. Leavell's Preaching." ThD diss., New Orleans Baptist Theological Seminary, 1993.

Jacobs, Paul David. "The History and Development of the Criswell College, 1971–1990." PhD diss., University of North Texas, 1991.

Hawley, Michael Mark. "A Critical Examination of Lee Rutland Scarborough's Concept of Evangelism." ThD diss., New Orleans Baptist Theological Seminary, 1992.

Head, Eldred Douglas. "The Indian Renaissance." MA thesis, Baylor University, 1927.

———. "Reflections from the Papyri on New Testament Life and Literature." ThD diss., Southwestern Baptist Theological Seminary, 1930.

Kiesling, Brandon D. "An Investigation of Benajah Harvey Carroll's Contribution to Evangelism within the Southern Baptist Convention." PhD diss., Southwestern Baptist Theological Seminary, 2017.

Leavell, David Earl. "A Critical Investigation of Cassius Elijah Autrey's Concepts of Evangelism and an Assessment of His Impact upon the Southern Baptist Program of Evangelism." PhD diss., New Orleans Baptist Theological Seminary, 1992.

Lefever, Alan J. "The Life and Work of Benajah Harvey Carroll." PhD diss., Southwestern Baptist Theological Seminary, 1992.

Lewis, Bobby R. "A Critical Investigation of C. B. Hogue's Concepts of Evangelism and an Assessment of His Impact on Evangelism in the Southern Baptist Convention." PhD diss., Southeastern Baptist Theological Seminary, 2009.

Morrow, Joe Franklin. "The Life and Ministry of Eldred Douglas Head: Leadership in the Midst of Transition." PhD diss., Southwestern Baptist Theological Seminary, 1995.

Queen, Matthew B. "A Theological Assessment of the Gospel Content in Selected Southern Baptist Sources." PhD diss., Southeastern Baptist Theological Seminary, 2009.

Reid, Alvin Lee. "The Impact of the Jesus Movement on Evangelism among Southern Baptists." PhD diss., Southwestern Baptist Theological Seminary, 1991.

Trillet, Timothy R. "The Educational Philosophy of Leighton Paige Patterson." DEd diss., Southeastern Baptist Theological Seminary, 2012.

INTERVIEWS

Autrey, J. Denny, interview with the author. Fort Worth, March 21, 2016. Appendix 1.

Beougher, Timothy, interview with the author. Hurst, TX, May 27, 2020. Appendix 2.

Crawford, Dan R., interview with the author. Hurst, TX, May 15, 2020. Appendix 3.

Davis, Suzanne, email correspondence with the author. Hurst, TX, May 28, 2020. Appendix 5.

Greenway, Adam, interview with the author. Hurst, TX, May 21, 2020. Appendix 6.

Headrick, Richard, interview with the author. Hurst, TX, May 19, 2020. Appendix 7.

Iorg, Jeff, interview with the author. Hurst, TX, May 27, 2020. Appendix 8.

Johnston, Thomas P., interview with the author. Hurst, TX, May 21, 2020. Appendix 9.

Kelley, Charles S., interview with the author. Hurst, TX, May 26, 2020. Appendix 10.

McDow, Malcolm, email correspondence with the author. Hurst, TX, May 19, 2020. Appendix 11.

Nix, Preston, interview with the author. Hurst, TX, May 28, 2020. Appendix 12.

Pate, Edsel D., interview with the author. Hurst, TX, May 18, 2020. Appendix 13.

Patterson, L. Paige, interview with the author. Hurst, TX, May 12, 2020. Appendix 14.

Phillips, Rebekah, interview with the author. Hurst, TX, June 22, 2020. Appendix 15.

Ray, Brent S., email correspondence with the author. May 13, 2020. Appendix 16.

Robinson, George G., email correspondence with the author. May 18, 2020. Appendix 17.

Smith, Sandy L., interview with the author. Hurst, TX, May 28, 2020. Appendix 18.

MINUTES/PROCEEDINGS

Duff, Alexander. *Foreign Missions: Being the Substance of an Address Delivered Before the General Assembly of the Free Church of Scotland on Friday Evening, June 1, 1866.* Edinburgh: Elliot, 1866, 28.

Missouri Baptist Convention. *2011 Annual Reports and Statistics.* Jefferson City, MO: Missouri Baptist Convention, 2011. http://media.mobaptist.org/public/executive-office/annuals/2011.PDF..

Southern Baptist Convention. *Proceedings of the Southern Baptist Convention.* Richmond, VA: H. K. Ellyson, 1845.

Southwestern Baptist Theological Seminary Board of Trustees. Minutes of the Board of Trustees, November 26, 1957. A. Webb Roberts Library, Southwestern Baptist Theological Seminary.

————. Minutes of the Board of Trustees, November 24, 1964. A. Webb Roberts Library, Southwestern Baptist Theological Seminary.

————. Minutes of the Board of Trustees, March 18–19, 1980. A. Webb Roberts Library, Southwestern Baptist Theological Seminary.

————. Minutes of the Board of Trustees, June 11, 1980. A. Webb Roberts Library, Southwestern Baptist Theological Seminary. June 11, 1980.

————. Minutes of the Board of Trustees, October 19–20, 1982. A. Webb Roberts Library, Southwestern Baptist Theological Seminary.

SOUND RECORDINGS

Chafin, Kenneth L. "Donahue Show, June 17, 1985: Paul Pressler and Ken Chafin." Nashville: Southern Baptist Historical Library and Archives, 1988. Videocassette.

www.ingramcontent.com/pod-product-compliance
Lightning Source LLC
Chambersburg PA
CBHW070932150426

42814CB00024B/103